SOVIET FATES AND LOST ALTERNATIVES

SOVIET FATES AND LOST ALTERNATIVES

FROM STALINISM TO THE NEW COLD WAR

STEPHEN F. COHEN

COLUMBIA UNIVERSITY PRESS *New York*

COLUMBIA UNIVERSITY PRESS

PUBLISHERS SINCE 1893

NEW YORK   CHICHESTER, WEST SUSSEX

Library of Congress Cataloging-in-Publication Data
Cohen, Stephen F.
Soviet fates and lost alternatives : from Stalinism to the new Cold War / Stephen F. Cohen.
p.   cm.
Includes bibliographical references and index.
ISBN 978-0-231-14896-2 (cloth : alk. paper)— ISBN 978-0-231-14897-9 (pbk : alk. paper)—
ISBN 978-0-231-52042-3 (e-book)
1. Soviet Union—History—1925–1953.   2. Soviet Union—History—1953–1985.   3. Soviet
Union—History—1985–1991.   4. Soviet Union—Politics and government.   5. Concentration
camp inmates—Soviet Union.   6. Cold War.   7. Gorbachev, Mikhail Sergeevich, 1931– —Political
and social views.   8. Post communism—Russia (Federation)   9. Russia (Federation)—Foreign
relations—United States.   10. United States—Foreign relations—Russia (Federation)   I. Title.

DK266.C587 2009
947.084—dc22

2009000659

FOR NIKA

MAY HER ALTERNATIVES ALWAYS BE GOOD AND HER FATE HAPPY

CONTENTS

INTRODUCTION ALTERNATIVES AND FATES

History is not determined by fate. There is always an alternative.
MIKHAIL GORBACHEV

Most of our history is the lessons of missed opportunities.
YEGOR YAKOVLEV, GORBACHEV-ERA REFORMER

MANY writers, perhaps historians and novelists more than others, find themselves returning again and again to some big theme that captivated them early in life. For me, it has been political alternatives in history, roads taken and not taken, in Russia in particular. Though the chapters of this book treat diverse subjects and were researched and written over many years, several appearing in full or in part in other places, they do not stray far from that theme.[1]

In the beginning, it had nothing to do with Russia. Growing up in a segregated small town in Kentucky, in the 1940s and 1950s, I accepted the world around me, as children do, as perfectly normal. But at the age of fifteen or sixteen, events in my life caused me, as Corinthians instructs, to put away childish things. I began to understand segregation was a terrible injustice and to wonder if there had been an alternative—though I did not yet use the word—in Kentucky's history. After all, I knew my state had produced the Civil War presidents both of the Union and the Confederacy, Lincoln and Jefferson Davis.

A few years later, when I began studying Soviet Russia as an undergraduate at Indiana University, Robert C. Tucker, the professor who became my mentor—and eventually my friend and colleague at Princeton—pressed me to settle on a more specific interest in the country. When I could not, he asked if I had any special historical or political interests apart from Russia. Still not far removed from home, I replied, "Whether or not there had been an alternative to segregation in Kentucky's history." Tucker then sent me on my intellectual way: "Good. The question of alternatives is a very big and understudied issue in Soviet history." So it became, and has remained, for me.

I began with the faction in the Soviet leadership, headed by Nikolai Bukharin, who opposed Stalin and the emergence of Stalinism at the nation's fateful turning point in 1928 and 1929. This led to my biography of Bukharin and, many years later, to the first chapter of this book. Having entered the field during the high point of Nikita Khrushchev's anti-Stalinist reforms, I was then drawn to the alternative for the Soviet future his policies had represented in the 1960s. That interest eventually led me to the subject of my second chapter, the return of Stalin's surviving victims after his death.

Khrushchev's overthrow, in 1964, reaffirmed the belief of many of my colleagues that fundamental reforms in the rigidly authoritarian Soviet system were impossible, partly because they saw no alternative historical experiences or traditions to inspire or sustain them. Seeing a viable anti-Stalinist tradition connecting Bukharin's opposition in the 1920s and Khrushchev's political revivalism thirty years later, I disagreed. During the next two decades, my main project was identifying proreform forces and their ideas inside the murky bureaucratic realm of the ruling Communist Party.[2]

As a result, I was not surprised by the emergence of Mikhail Gorbachev as the Soviet leader in 1985. Historical and political alternatives were at the center of his increasingly radical reforms, from retrieving what he and his supporters believed were lost ideas from the Soviet 1920s to the first multicandidate elections in 1989. (Gorbachev was, as I will explain later on, a kind of heretic, and heretics by nature believe above all in alternatives.) Those historic developments are the focus and context of chapters 3 through 6, especially the two that argue the Soviet Union was reformable and that there had been an alternative to its breakup in 1991.

Even the concluding chapter on contemporary issues derives from "alternativism" and personal experience. Studying the Soviet Union during much of the long Cold War, and living there for prolonged periods, I came to hope, and to think possible, that my country and the other one so large in my life would eventually cease to be adversaries. By 1989, first and foremost because of Gorbachev, though not him alone, that alternative seemed to have been realized. Why it turned out to be another missed opportunity is the subject of chapter 7.

Here I should explain briefly what I mean by historical alternatives. These are not the imaginary or hypothetical constructs of what-if, counterfactual history, though that is a legitimate intellectual exercise, or what some writers dismiss as a "non-existent subjunctive in history." I am interested in alternative possibilities that actually existed at turning points in Soviet and post-Soviet history, ones grounded in realities of the time, represented by leaders, and with enough political support to have had a chance of being realized.[3] We may disagree as to their chances but not that real people fought—and often died—for them.

No what-ifs or other fictions are needed to understand, for example, that the Bukharinist opposition to Stalin's political and economic policies represented a different Soviet road forward, one with widespread support in the Communist Party and in society. Khrushchev's reforms, which were embraced by young people, members of the intelligentsia, and even significant numbers of Party and state officials, had the potential for more far-reaching change in the Soviet system twenty years before it was actually initiated, when some observers thought it was too late. Gorbachev's call for a full-scale Soviet reformation had broad elite and popular support, and although his personal popularity collapsed under the weight of the alternative he pursued, Boris Yeltsin initially claimed to represent the same cause.

One reason this book may not be well received by many of my colleagues is that they never believed there were any real alternatives in the seventy-four-year Soviet experience. During the forty-year Cold War, when the academic field was formed, they saw a "straight-line" history predetermined by one or more ineluctable factors—the ruling Party's organization, its ideology, or Russia's bleak traditions.[4] But history written without defeated alternatives is neither a full account of the past nor a real explanation of what happened. It is only the story of the winners made to seem inevitable. Nonetheless, that view was so orthodox that the few American scholars who challenged it—we were known as "revisionists"—were sometimes accused of having dubious political motives.[5]

Not so coincidentally, something similar, though far worse, befell Soviet historians. For decades, those who wanted to write about historical alternatives to Stalinism, and implicitly to the latter-day system, were prevented from doing so by harsh censorship and even repression. Soviet authorities and unorthodox historians understood the importance of this "deviationism," as such heresy was officially branded. Thus one of the prominent scholars persecuted for believing Bukharin had been right was banished as the "alternativist [Victor] Danilov," as that historian of collectivization defiantly also characterized himself.[6]

Gorbachev's historic reforms and the end of the Soviet Union brought "alternativism" (*alternativnost*), for reasons examined in chapter 6, to the forefront of Russian historical and political thinking. Since 1991, scholars and other intellectuals have been debating whether there were "unrealized alternatives" to the 1917 Revolution, Stalinism, the termination of Khrushchev's initiatives, Gorbachev's approach to reform, and the disappearance of the Soviet Union. Many of them are still searching for "a road that leads to the Temple."[7]

In the United States, however, the "school of inevitability" has regained its dominant position. For reasons also examined in chapter 6, most American scholars, other intellectuals, and media commentators once again treat nearly seventy-five years of Soviet history as having been "closed to real alternatives."[8] As a result, interest in its "losers"— Bukharin, Khrushchev, and Gorbachev, among others—has fallen.

Those names are associated with a related theme of this book—fate, as it is understood in Russia. The words "fate" and "destiny" exist in most languages, but a nation's experiences may instill in them different meaning. For Russians, who believe their history, during which "dozens of generations lived on the edge between life and death," has been especially "accursed," "fate" is not usually the triumphant "destiny," as Americans often say, of a champion athlete. It is an ominous development, "some sinister Beethovean knock . . . at the door," a tragic outcome.[9]

On a personal level, Russians may ask, for instance, about the "fate" of a new friend's parents or grandparents during Stalin's terror, which victimized millions of people, or in World War II, when 27 million Soviet citizens perished. Generations also think and are thought of in terms of their collective "fate." In modern times, they include the military officers of the 1930s made "comrades of a tragic fate" by Stalin's blood purge; the schoolboys who went to the front in 1941, only three of every hundred of whom ever returned; and the generation of the 1960s, known as "the children of Khrushchev," who believed in the late 1980s "history is giving us another chance" to reform the Soviet system.[10]

Above all, Russians associate the "fate" of leaders with alternatives they represented at ramifying junctures in the nation's history. The association sometimes suggests the fatalistic Russian proverb "You can't escape fate," but most often it refers to "fateful choices" of the kind historians have emphasized in historic events elsewhere.[11] And because the roads chosen and not chosen by Russia's leaders have so often been unhappy ones for the nation,[12] they are connected thereafter with the "tragic fate" of those figures—foremost among them in Soviet history, Bukharin, Khrushchev, Gorbachev, and even Lenin. In the pages that follow, the fates of alternatives and leaders therefore remain joined.

In that connection, I should disclose my personal relationships with several people who appear in this book. I was born the year of Bukharin's execution, but decades later developed a friendship with his widow, who figures prominently in the first chapter, and with other Gulag survivors who do so in the second chapter. I have had friendly relations with Gorbachev for more than twenty years; there is even an opinion (though not mine) that my biography of Bukharin once influenced him in a significant way.[13] But still exploring alternatives, I also got to know Gorbachev's main rival in the last Soviet leadership, Yegor Ligachev, the subject of the third chapter. And during the events covered in chapters 6 and 7, I was part of a small group that discussed them with the first President George Bush.

Critics may think these relationships have affected my objectivity. I prefer to think that I gained important insights from them while maintaining my scholarly distance. It is for readers to decide.

WORK on a book about many subjects and so long in the making requires considerable help along the way. My most important intellectual debt is still to Robert C. Tucker, who, in his ninety-first year, remains the pioneering alternativist he has always been. Thirty years of discussions with Russian friends and acquaintances, not all of them mentioned in the book, also enriched my knowledge and understanding of events in many ways. Early on, the John Simon Guggenheim Memorial Foundation twice gave me financial support for a large project I promised to complete long ago. This is the final installment, and again, belatedly, I acknowledge my gratitude.

At various stages, I benefited from the indispensable work of three excellent assistants—Yeugenia Shvets, Andrey Grigoryev, and then Arina Chesnokova. In addition to contributing to my research, they provided the necessary computer-era services my typewriter cannot perform. And most recently, I became indebted to Peter Dimock, my editor at Columbia University Press. Without his wise advice, encouragement, and forbearance, as I missed one deadline after another, this book would still be an unfinished manuscript.

Above all, I am again boundlessly grateful to my wife Katrina vanden Heuvel for all manner of support, help, and guidance. A Russian-speaking and very knowledgeable observer of that country, and my companion of many years in seeking to understand its past and present, she repeatedly took time from her duties as editor and publisher of *The Nation* to correct my memory, understanding, and style. Whatever remains uncorrected is despite her best efforts.

Last but very far from least is our beloved daughter, Nika. It is unusual, as I explained in a previous book, to thank a child for anything other than forgiving an author's absence, but it has been different with Nika. She has been with us during almost every stay in Russia, more than thirty, since her birth in 1991. As she grew and learned the language, her perceptions of what we experienced there challenged and sharpened my own. It is one reason this book is lovingly dedicated to Nika.

S. F. C.
New York City
March 2009

Note on Transliteration

There are various ways of spelling Russian names in English. In the text, I have used the form most familiar or accessible to general readers, not the one used by most scholars. It means, for example, Yegor Yakovlev rather than Egor Iakovlev; Trotsky rather than Trotskii; and Tatyana Zaslavskaya rather than Tatiana Zaslavskaia. In the notes, however, wherever Russian-language sources are cited, I have used the Library of Congress system of transliteration (though without soft or hard signs) so that specialists will more easily recognize and locate them.

SOVIET FATES AND LOST ALTERNATIVES

1 BUKHARIN'S FATE

I wrote the [prison manuscripts] mostly at night, literally wrenching them from my heart. I fervently beg you not to let this work disappear. . . . Don't let this work perish. I repeat and emphasize: *This is completely apart from my personal fate.* Don't let it be lost! . . . *Have pity!* Not on me, *on the work!*

BUKHARIN, PRISON LETTER TO STALIN, 1937

Why is it that [Bukharin's] heresy, so often condemned, so often refuted, so often punished, is so often resurrected? Why does this ghost not keep to his grave, though the stake is driven into his corpse again and again?

BERTRAM D. WOLFE

THE answer to Wolfe's luridly worded but essential question is to be found in the formative history of the former Soviet Union and Communist world more generally: A long and widely held belief that there had been a "Bukharinist alternative" to the horrors of Stalinism and that it could be resurrected for reforming that system after Stalin.

Nikolai Bukharin was only one of the Soviet founders killed by Stalin, but his political fate was special.[1] Barely twenty-nine years old when the Bolsheviks took power, he was the youngest, most genuinely popular, and perhaps most interesting intellectual member of the Communist Party leadership that forged the new Soviet state during the years of revolution and civil war from 1917 to 1921. Lenin, with whom he had a periodically feuding but essentially sonlike relationship, called him the "golden boy of the revolution," the "favorite of the entire Party," and its "biggest theorist." Those special tributes alone were more than enough to doom him in Stalin's terror, which swept away virtually the entire original elite of the Soviet Union.

But it was Bukharin's role in the 1920s that would make him Stalin's most important purge victim in the 1930s. In 1921, after four years of draconian political and economic measures that helped win the civil war but left the economy in ruins and the Party's own constituencies in rebellion, Lenin introduced a fundamental change of course known as the New Economic Policy, or simply NEP. Until Stalin abolished NEP in 1929, it was, to use language popularized later in Soviet history, the first era of Communist liberalization or, as would be said during Mikhail Gorbachev's reforms of the late 1980s, the first perestroika.

Though the NEP 1920s were far from democratic, compared to the decades of despotic terror, bureaucratic tyranny, and deprivation that followed, they were for many citizens a long-remembered "golden era" in Soviet history. Alongside state-owned industries, banks, and transport, private enterprise and market relations were officially encouraged, especially in peasant agriculture, small-scale manufacturing, and retail trade. The Communist Party maintained its repressive political monopoly but permitted much more social, intellectual, and cultural diversity than would ever again be the case until the Gorbachev years. By the mid-1920s, the economy, devastated by years of war and revolution, had largely recovered, civil peace had been restored, and Moscow had become, like Weimar Berlin, a leading cultural capital of Europe.

Lenin created NEP, but after the leader's death in 1924, as his heirs on the ruling Politburo and Central Committee split into factions warring over power and policy, Bukharin became its greatest interpreter and defender. Regretting his own extremist views during the civil war, he now warned repeatedly against the abuses of power inherent in the Party's political monopoly and ideological zealotry—great policy leaps beyond the people's wishes, warfare actions against society, rampant bureaucracy and administrative caprice, economic monopolism, and elite privilege. He advocated instead conciliatory policies to encourage both the private and state sectors to evolve into socialism in mutually beneficial conditions and without further bloodshed. Indeed, in a private letter to the head of the secret police that anticipated democratization under Gorbachev sixty years later, Bukharin wrote: "I think we should move *more rapidly* toward a more 'liberal' form of Soviet rule."[2] He called this philosophy and program "socialist humanism."

Henceforth Bukharin's political fortunes and historical reputation were linked inextricably to NEP. From 1925 to 1928, he and Stalin led the Party's pro-NEP majority against the several left oppositions headed by Leon Trotsky, Grigory Zinoviev, and Lev Kamenev. And when Sta-

2

lin himself turned against NEP at the end of the 1920s, for a draconian kind of rapid industrialization based on forcing the country's 125 million peasants into state-run collective farms, Bukharin's adamant protests put him at the head of the so-called Right Opposition—the last great struggle inside the Soviet Communist Party against its ascendant general secretary.

Even before Stalin's ruthless measures of 1929 through 1933 had left perhaps 10 million peasants dead or enslaved in a vastly swollen Gulag of forced labor camps, Bukharin presciently understood their "monstrously one-sided" intent—and their consequences. Evoking "Lenin's Last Testament," a series of short articles in defense of NEP written by the dying leader in 1922 and 1923, Bukharin protested that socialism could not and must not be achieved through "military-feudal exploitation" of the country's peasant majority. "Stalin's policy is leading to civil war. He will have to drown the revolts in blood." The outcome, he warned, "will be a police state."

Bukharin's prophetic opposition, undertaken on the eve of the Soviet Union's most fateful and ultimately irreversible turning point after 1917, would never be forgotten in Russia or forgiven by Stalin. In late 1929, as catastrophe unfolded across the land, the new Stalinist majority stripped Bukharin of all his leadership positions—member of the Politburo, editor of the Party newspaper, *Pravda*, and head of the Communist International. Once the Party's co-leader and most authoritative ideologist, Bukharin saw his ideas and policies denounced as "anti-Leninist" and "rotten liberalism." He no longer had any real power or influence over political events, though he remained a nominal member of the Party Central Committee and later served as editor of the government newspaper, *Izvestia*, until his arrest on February 27, 1937.

Bukharin was not seen again publicly until March 2, 1938, when the last and most spectacular of the three Moscow show trials opened in a glare of international media attention. (The eleven-day trial made worldwide headlines, though news of Bukharin's execution, on March 15, was overshadowed by Hitler's march into Austria.) By now Stalin had falsely condemned all of Lenin's other co-leaders as covert enemies of their own cause, but none as completely and grotesquely as he would defame the "favorite of the entire Party." Bukharin's defense of NEP, special relationship with Lenin, and lingering personal popularity were the greatest reproach to the official cult of Stalin's infallibility, which had grown in almost direct proportion to the rural holocaust caused by his leadership.

Twenty-one defendants sat in the dock, several of them prominent old Bolsheviks, but for Stalin it was the inquisition and confession of Bukharin that really mattered. The alternative he represented in 1928 and 1929 had to be criminalized and thereby rendered forever anathema. After only the first day, the Stalinist press made clear the trial's purpose and preordained verdict: "Bukharin sits there with his head bowed low, a treacherous, two-faced, whimpering, evil nonentity who has been exposed . . . as leader of a gang of spies, terrorists, and thieves. . . . This filthy little Bukharin." As the pseudojudicial proceedings moved toward their inexorable outcome, Stalin, through his mouthpiece-prosecutor, Andrei Vyshinsky, leveled an exceptional accusation against Bukharin: "The hypocrisy and perfidy of this man exceed the most perfidious and monstrous crimes known to the history of mankind."

For many years to come, Bukharin's trial would be an enthralling and emblematic mystery of twentieth-century politics, the subject of philosophy and fiction: Why had he—indeed, all the illustrious old Bolsheviks in the dock—confessed to preposterously false charges? (Not a few foolish Western observers, it might be remembered, from foreign Communists to the American ambassador in Moscow, actually believed the charges, or said they did.) Perhaps the most popular explanation, elaborated in Arthur Koestler's famous novel *Darkness at Noon*, argued that Bukharin, in his fictionalized counterpart Rubashov, morally bankrupt and sincerely repentant for his past opposition, willingly confessed as a last service to Stalinism.

In fact, Bukharin did not really confess, as was clear even from the edited transcript of the trial published at the time in the heavily censored Soviet press and then in a "stenographic" volume. Forced to participate in the grotesque spectacle, if only in the hope of saving his family, his tactic was to accept personal responsibility for the general indictment dictated by Stalin while denying all its specific charges: "I plead guilty to . . . the sum total of crimes committed by this counterrevolutionary organization, irrespective of whether or not I knew of, or whether or not I took a direct part in, any particular act." Lest anyone fail to understand that the second part of that statement negated the first, Bukharin went on to discredit his whole "confession" (and allude to the torment being inflicted in Stalin's prisons) with a simple aside: "The confession of the accused is a medieval principle of jurisprudence." As for the crucial charges that he had plotted to assassinate Lenin and commit other terrorist acts, overthrow the Soviet government, and betray the country to fascist Germany and Japan, he flatly and repeatedly rejected them: "I do not plead guilty . . . I do not know of this . . . I deny it . . . I categorically deny any complicity."

Indeed, if Bukharin's presence in the dock was a capitulation to Stalin, his conduct there was a last struggle against Stalinism. Taking on his assigned role as representative of a martyred Bolshevik movement, and especially of his own pro-NEP policies of the 1920s, he tried to show— through double-talk, code words, evasion, and digressions—that the criminal accusations were really political falsifications and the doomed Bolsheviks actually the revolution's true leaders, whose non-Stalinist conceptions of socialism were being eradicated. Stalin's bullying prosecutor and judge, panicked by Bukharin's "acrobatics" and refusal to follow the jailhouse script, tried to frighten him from "following definite tactics . . . hiding behind a flood of words . . . making digressions into the sphere of politics," but he persevered day after day. In his final statement he again "confessed" to the indictment but then, according to a foreign correspondent in the courtroom, "proceeded . . . to tear it to bits, while Vyshinsky, powerless to intervene, sat uneasily in his place."

By the 1960s, several Western historians had reexamined the published transcript and concluded that Bukharin's trial, "degrading as it was in many respects, may fairly be called his finest hour."[3] In the Soviet Union, however, it took much longer, including three and a half decades after Stalin's own death in 1953 and five subsequent leaderships, to overturn the court's verdict. After a struggle at high levels—the future maximalist Boris Yeltsin, then a candidate member of the ruling Politburo, initially opposed the move as "too early"—Bukharin was fully exonerated and restored to official honor at Gorbachev's insistence in 1988, a year marking both the fiftieth anniversary of his execution and the centenary of his birth. The subject of popular biographies, novels, and films, his historical reputation continued to grow in public esteem right up to the end of the Soviet Union three years later.[4]

THE Soviet judge who formally reopened Bukharin's case files in 1988 remarked, "He was a fighter to the end, despite the conditions in which he found himself." It has always been possible to imagine those terrible conditions, but only recently have terror-era archives begun to reveal more about what happened to him during the year between his arrest and execution. Even today, however, *more*, not everything, is the correct word. Despite the opening of many former Soviet archives, access to two of the most important ones remains highly restricted and much of their historical material yet to be declassified.

The NKVD archive, which contains most of the records from the "investigation and interrogation" of Bukharin in prison, is still under the control of its post-Soviet successor organization. Special permission is required from that ministry in order to see any of its files, for which no catalogue or other inventory is made available. Even when shown a large quantity of documents, as I was, one cannot be sure they are complete. Probably they are not, but the archive is so vast and its history so long and secretive that not even the staff of Lubyanka, as the secret police headquarters is commonly called, seems to be certain.

Incongruous as it may seem, the Russian Presidential Archive, where significant parts of Stalin's enormous personal archive are still kept, is even more inaccessible. Sometimes called the Kremlin Archive, it passed in 1991 from Gorbachev's control to Boris Yeltsin's and then to Vladimir Putin and Dmitri Medvedev. Some holdings have been transferred to open repositories. But none of its unique remaining materials, not even remote historical ones, can be seen except on instruction of the president, his chief of staff, or a high official acting on their authority. Nor does this zealously guarded citadel of secrets make known a list of its full holdings, though it is known they include the original typed stenograph of Bukharin's trial with handwritten "corrections" by Stalin and his hanging judge, Vasily Ulrikh.[5]

An often unanswered question therefore haunts surviving members of a victim's family and historians even today: Do missing materials confiscated during Stalin's terror still exist? Are they preserved somewhere in those once "top-secret" and still reticent archives, were they bureaucratically mislaid or privately stashed elsewhere, or were they destroyed many years ago?

Russian writers like to quote Mikhail Bulgakov's aphorism, "Manuscripts do not burn," but many did in Stalin's Soviet Union. Some examples are well known and especially lamented. In the bureaucratic language of an official investigation, it was reported that the last prose fiction of Boris Pilnyak, arrested with him in 1937, "has not been preserved." Several unpublished works by Isaac Babel and the great scientist Nikolai Vavilov suffered the same fate. Not even Lenin's letters were safe, a number of important ones evidently having been destroyed along with his old comrades who had received them. But we can never know how many manuscripts, eminent correspondence, government documents, photographs, films, and even paintings perished in the bloody years from 1929 to 1953, when Stalin's regime tried to repress anything that suggested there had been any legitimate alternatives to his leadership and policies.

Some were lost indifferently in the crude haste of millions of arrests, searches, and confiscations; others were frantically discarded by their owners or relatives in fear of such nocturnal visits; but many more were systematically destroyed by the terror regime. From the central Lubyanka Prison in the late 1930s, "a soot-stained chimney . . . sprinkled Moscow with the ash of incinerated manuscripts."[6] Scores of incinerators no doubt were also flaming in provincial Lubyankas throughout Russia and the other Soviet republics. Later, Stalin's political police and its successor, the NKVD and KGB, destroyed masses of paper when Hitler's armies approached in 1941, again when Nikita Khrushchev's revelations threatened the *organy* in the 1950s and early 1960s, and once again, now shredding instead of burning, after the failed putsch against Soviet President Gorbachev in August 1991.

And yet a great many forbidden manuscripts and other materials did survive Stalin's long reign of terror and its aftermath. Some were saved in secret acts of private courage—by relatives and friends of victims who took the great risk of hiding poems, letters, and photographs for decades. But most were actually "preserved forever"—as they were often stamped by the terror apparatus itself—buried in the ever swelling archives ("vaults" seems a more fitting word) of the NKVD and of the chief terrorist, Stalin. There is no fully satisfactory explanation for why the "Boss," as his top henchmen called him among themselves, allowed so much incriminating evidence to be preserved—was it his seminary education or his self-ordained role as "greatest scholar on the planet"?—but for this, if nothing else, the nation could be grateful.

An authentic despot has the personal power to make time for what truly interests him, no matter how petty it may seem. Amid all the political, economic, and social upheavals of the Soviet 1930s, Stalin received and at least scanned an enormous volume of confiscated materials, commonly scrawling on them the instruction "Send to the archive" or, more evocatively, "Let all this 'material' lie deep in the archive."[7] Thus did his personal papers grow year by year and decade by decade into a vast and long-impenetrable repository of forbidden history and culture.

Where, then, are Bukharin's own personal papers, a large and rich collection accumulated during an extraordinary life of revolution, power, and writing? Immediately following his arrest in February 1937, NKVD men hauled away a "mountain of paper" from his Kremlin apartment, the truck "overflowing" with materials, including unpublished manuscripts, photographs, letters from Lenin, and other historical documents.[8] None of it has ever been found.

Consider two subsequent examples. During his year in prison, Bukharin wrote several (evidently revealing) undelivered letters to his wife. One of them, dated January 15, 1938, two months before his trial began, was found fifty-four years later; the others are still missing. When his trial finally got under way, all the proceedings were filmed and sound-recorded on Stalin's orders by NKVD cameramen. Those reels might tell us what actually happened in the courtroom, but they have disappeared. Indeed, it is astonishing that not a single frame of film or photograph showing the faces of the defendants at this most infamous political trial of the twentieth century, an era of unprecedented visual artifacts, has ever been made public.[9]

Nonetheless, archives have now told us more about Bukharin's fate, however grudgingly and fragmentarily, than most historians ever expected to learn. He spent his last year "dangling between life and death" in Stalin's leading factory of false confessions, Lubyanka Prison, fully in the hands of NKVD "investigators" who were under pressing orders to "prepare" him for the trial. Bukharin immediately understood, as he wrote to Stalin from prison, that "they can do with me here anything they want."[10] Except when taken through always dark corridors to an interrogation room, he was confined in a tiny cell harshly lit around the clock by a naked bulb, alone for months but periodically with a cell mate who was actually an informer. Interrogations to extract his testimony for the script being dictated and constantly enhanced by the Kremlin Scenarist usually began late at night and continued into the early morning hours.

For three full months, Bukharin adamantly refused to "confess"—that is, to play his designated role at the trial—despite prospects of physical torture, threats against his family, and shattering face-to-face confrontations with his cherished young protégés of the 1920s, who had been brutally beaten and forced to give lurid testimony against him. Asked to make admissions that "contradict my whole life, my entire being," as he also wrote to Stalin, Bukharin refused "to slander myself out of fear or for other analogous reasons." But on June 1 he capitulated and began inventing "testimony," probably because he learned that the country's top military commanders had now been arrested and was shown their signed statements incriminating him. If those armed and tough men could be taken and broken so quickly—they were brutally tortured—there would be no way out for him. The "other analogous reasons," most fearfully the fate of his family, became inescapable.

For the next nine months Bukharin went along with the Lubyanka inquisitors but haggled stubbornly over the terms of his confession. At first he tried to limit his "crimes" to a history of "theoretical mistakes" and "political opposition," but those concessions were far from what Stalin needed. Finally Bukharin agreed to take on the part of leader of the "counterrevolutionary criminal bloc," but he continued to be vague about specific misdeeds. His tenacious recalcitrance may have been one reason why the trial was postponed at least twice. On several occasions, high-level emissaries from Stalin—notably the NKVD chief, Nikolai Yezhov, and the prosecutor, Vyshinsky—came to deal personally with him. Among other things, they promised he would live if he played the role well. Bukharin desperately wanted to believe them but never really did, and he repeatedly asked to be given poison, "like Socrates," instead of being shot.

Always a fragile personality—"soft" and "artistic," according to people who knew him—Bukharin was already debilitated by months of persecution and a hunger strike undertaken before his arrest. Unlike so many other victims, he seems not to have been physically tortured in prison. But all the other agonies inflicted in Lubyanka—over his family and closest friends, his impending trial, his historical reputation—were enough to leave his "soul shattered and in torment." His "grief and boundless anguish" brought on episodes of "hallucinatory delusions," even an occasional loss of vision, and though he seems to have always revived, his "physical and spiritual strength [were] weakening." (There are hints he may have been given drugs to calm or manipulate him.)

Those rare glimpses of Bukharin's condition in prison are from four letters he sent to Stalin from his cell between April and December 1937. Of all the documents found in archives, they are the most painful to read. On the other hand, they must be interpreted cautiously because different light might be cast on their meaning by several other prison letters he wrote to his captor that have disappeared.[11] Two of the four might be interpreted simply as the pathetic pleadings of a completely broken man. Filled with lachrymose professions of "true devotion" and "enormous love" for his persecutor, along with fantasies of being freed to live under a pseudonym, they assured Stalin, "I acknowledge myself to be entirely yours" and "I would be ready to carry out any of your demands." But the long, densely rambling letters can also be interpreted more complexly, particularly in light of other evidence that Bukharin remained "a fighter to the end," as part of a cruelly inequitable negotiation.

Throughout his imprisonment, Bukharin tried desperately to "bargain" (*vytorgovat*) with Stalin, whom he had known well for many years, but without enraging his now tyrannical suspicions, envies, and personal cult. The Lubyanka prisoner had only one thing to offer: his willingness to satisfy Stalin's profound need for his participation in the macabre trial designed to delegitimate any ideas about a Bukharinist alternative. The Kremlin Inquisitor, on the other hand, had unconstrained power of life and death not only over Bukharin but over his large family, most ominously his twenty-three-year-old wife, Anna Larina, whom Bukharin, at almost forty-six, had married three years earlier; their infant son, Yuri; and Bukharin's thirteen-year-old daughter, Svetlana, by a previous marriage. (Also at Stalin's mercy were Bukharin's elderly father, younger brother, and two previous wives.) In return for going through with the trial, Bukharin wanted assurances of their well-being.

Assurances were given, but falsely. Bukharin went on trial in March 1938 without knowing that his wife and son had been taken from their Moscow apartment nine months earlier, Anna to begin a twenty-year journey through Stalin's prisons, labor camps, and Siberian exile, and Yuri a two-decade odyssey under another family name through foster homes and orphanages. Reunited only in 1956, both survived to be present at Bukharin's 1988 rehabilitation, but not for the reason he had hoped. Many "wives and children of enemies of the people" were summarily shot in the 1930s, but Stalin kept some alive in case they were needed for future trials; spouses made handy coconspirators, and sons and daughters grew into adult defendants. (Svetlana was not arrested until 1949.) The tyrant died, at seventy-three, before he could invent lethal scenarios for all of them.

But Bukharin was also bargaining for something else, second in importance only to his family. It, too, only Stalin could grant. A man for whom politics had always meant writing—his publications numbered in the hundreds[12]—Bukharin wanted permission, exceedingly unusual in that place of debasement, to write in his cell: "I simply would not be able to survive here if not permitted to use paper and pen." Stalin must have interpreted the letter as Bukharin intended, "I would not be able to play my role," and gave the order. Knowing it could be reversed at any moment, the Lubyanka author tried to ensnare his captor in what he was writing. Bukharin's letters carefully apprised Stalin of his projects, even proposing he write a preface for one of them. As weeks turned into months, and tightly handwritten pages into large manuscripts, Bukharin more and more wanted his prison writings to survive him: "*Have pity! Not on me, on the work!*"

Those writings are the most remarkable discovery of an archival investigation into Bukharin's Lubyanka fate. In barely one year, while constantly being interrogated and tormented about his family and the next ordeal that awaited him, this middle-aged intellectual, so often said to have been weak, found the moral and physical stamina to write four books (the equivalent of about 1,400 typewritten pages)—a study of modern politics and culture, a philosophical treatise, a thick volume of thematic poems, and an unfinished novel about his childhood in prerevolutionary Russia.

Exactly how Bukharin managed to write the manuscripts in those circumstances is left to our imagination. The only other person who probably knew was a shadowy thirty-five-year-old Lubyanka officer directly in charge of interrogating and preparing him for the trial, Captain Lazar Kogan; not long after, he, too, was arrested and shot. An educated and soft-mannered man who had begun his NKVD career specializing in intellectual cases, he must have been specially chosen for Bukharin's. Kogan was, of course, a loyal agent of the terror—he was awarded an Order of Lenin in murderous 1937 and on his daughter's ninth birthday that year wished her to "be a worthy daughter of your country and its leader, Comrade Stalin"—but his few surviving traces suggest a complex relationship with his famous victim during their months together in Lubyanka.[13] Hoping to help her husband, Anna Larina was allowed to meet Kogan once and thought she saw "unspeakable remorse in his eyes." Whatever the full truth, he provided his prisoner with writing materials and books, boosted his morale, and watched the manuscripts grow.

Unless more documents are uncovered, perhaps in Kogan's own files, which, in accord with regulations concerning present and former agents, Lubyanka authorities have refused to provide, all we can know with certainty is that Bukharin wrote mostly at night and early morning, sleeping sporadically in the harsh light that blurred his vision, working without a typewriter, sources he needed, or even a reliable supply of paper, using the backs and margins of used sheets when he ran out. We should not be too surprised. It was the same Bukharin who then appeared at the show trial so carefully planned by Stalin and found ways "to tear it to bits."

When Bukharin was taken to be shot, three of his prison manuscripts evidently were still in his cell, including his unfinished memoir-novel, the other having been confiscated months before. All four, along with almost everything else he wrote in Lubyanka, were sent by his jailers, acting on standing orders and their own fearful instincts, to the Kremlin Boss. It is not known whether Stalin read them carefully, but he certainly looked at them. He then buried them deep in his personal archive, the deepest archaeological recess of the Terror Era. They were excavated, at my initiative, fifty-four years later, in 1992.

The role I unexpectedly played in this saga was an outgrowth of my biography of Bukharin, published in the United States in 1973 and eventually in the Soviet Union in 1989, and my close personal relationship with his widow and son from the time we first met surreptitiously in 1975 in pre-glasnost Moscow. While researching that book from afar, I came across vague reports that Bukharin had written some kind of manuscript in prison, as indeed he hinted at the trial, but neither I nor his family, who were still living with a restrictive official stigma, could learn anything more for many years. Only in 1988 did an aide to Gorbachev, who had read and publicly remarked on my book, tell me privately that not one but four such manuscripts existed in closed archives.

On behalf of Anna Larina; her artist son, Yuri Larin; and myself, I began asking for the manuscripts. Gorbachev, although sympathetic to the request, was already locked in a bitter political struggle with Communist Party opponents who resented his revelations about Soviet history and particularly about those kinds of "Party documents." Nonetheless, I still was optimistic in 1991 that he would soon authorize release of the manuscripts. Suddenly, however, with the end of the Soviet Union and his own political office, Gorbachev no longer controlled any of the archives.

In 1992, Anna Larina, now almost eighty and ill with cancer, and I took a different approach. Believing that the Bukharin family was the legal and moral heir to his works, and, according to recently adopted law, had a juridical right in the "new, democratic Russia" to examine all files related to his case, Larina formally named me her proxy and requested that the relevant archives give me full access to the materials. To our surprise, the former NKVD/KGB archive, under the Ministry of Security, responded promptly and more or less positively. My work in that storehouse of historical horrors soon began.

I quickly learned, however, that not even the top archive officials of the new Russian state could authorize access to the Presidential Archive, where the manuscripts and other essential materials were held. It could be done only by someone at the highest levels of the Yeltsin government. Nor was it a good political moment. The end of Communist rule had diminished public interest in all the Soviet founding fathers, and the new government seemed interested only in archival documents that would discredit Gorbachev and enhance its upcoming trial of the Communist Party. The prison writings of a martyred founding father embraced by the last Soviet leader served neither purpose.

Through a mutual Russian friend, I had earlier met a person who now had the power and perhaps the inclination to help, Gennady Burbulis. One of Yeltsin's closest and most influential aides, he had become a high-ranking official in the first post-Soviet government. In July 1992, ironically during the opening session of the government's trial of the Communist Party, I approached him in a corridor and asked his help. Though not a politician with any sympathy for the Soviet founders, Burbulis knew Anna Larina's saga from her best-selling 1988 memoir and was moved by her desire to learn everything about her husband's fate.[14] Within minutes I was in his office while he spoke on the phone to archive administrators, and within a few weeks photocopies of the four manuscripts were in our hands. Another large batch of materials from the Kremlin Archive soon followed, just before its doors again slammed shut.

Thus were Bukharin's widow, son, and daughter, the historian Svetlana Gurvich, able to encounter him anew across an enormous chasm of time and suffering. For Anna Larina, who died in 1996, there was just enough time left, with the help of family and friends, to help prepare her husband's last writings for publication in his homeland.

Two of Bukharin's prison manuscripts, unlike the poems and autobiographical novel, were overtly political and therefore had to be written on a razor's edge between what he desperately wanted to say—to the despot and to posterity—and the desperate plight of his family. Like his later courtroom statements, they must be read on two levels, the outwardly conformist and inwardly polemical, for the non-Stalinist meanings embedded in obligatory Stalinist ritual. Also unlike the poems and novel, the other two manuscripts were very much of their time, the 1930s, a decade already unfolding in the catastrophic ways that would shape the rest of the twentieth century.

Once inside Lubyanka in 1937, Bukharin was given almost no news of the outside world, but by the time of his arrest Hitler and Mussolini were in power, their military ambitions clear, and the Spanish Civil War under way. With those developments on his mind, Bukharin completed the first prison manuscript, *Socialism and Its Culture*, at an astonishing pace, evidently within four weeks of being permitted to write, partly because it was the second half of a larger work begun before his arrest to be called *The Crisis of Capitalist Culture and Socialism*. The first volume, *The Degradation of Culture and Fascism*, was among the papers taken from his apartment and never found, but the nature of the overall project is clear. For Bukharin, "culture" meant modern civilization; fascism was its mortal crisis and socialism its only possible salvation.

Forced to stand trial as the last original Bolshevik, Bukharin was also the last great Soviet antifascist of the 1930s. Alone among Soviet leaders, he had worried about fascism as a new phenomenon and special menace ever since the early 1920s. By the mid-1930s, that worry had grown into profound alarm: not only was Hitlerism in power and ever more virulent, Stalin was speaking publicly of the Nazi Führer as merely another capitalist dictator with whom he could do realpolitik business. (Bukharin no doubt knew of Stalin's secret diplomacy, already under way before 1937, that would lead to the Nazi-Soviet Pact of 1939.) Right up to his arrest, Bukharin used all his remaining personal authority and political positions to urge, in articles and speeches, that the Soviet Union put itself at the head of the antifascist struggle and collective European security. (For this some Western and Russian historians think he represented another alternative, one that might have prevented the enormous Soviet losses in World War II.)

A leading twentieth-century Marxist and Soviet founding father, Bukharin naturally remained loyal, even in Lubyanka, to Marxism and to the Soviet Union. In addition, Stalin's modernizing goals, however brutally pursued, were his as well. But Bukharin knew, as he had made clear before his arrest, that the Stalinist regime, much like Hitler's, was growing into an "omnipotent 'total state' that de-humanizes everything except leaders and 'superleaders.'" *Socialism and Its Culture* tried to overcome that nightmarish paradox. It argued effusively for the "humanist" potential of the Soviet system while pleading with the despot for its humanization, even a "transition to democracy," so that the nation could play its essential antifascist role. Bukharin believed deeply in those historic Soviet missions, even while knowing they were being terribly deformed under Stalin, and a final opportunity to testify on their behalf was another reason he agreed to stand trial.

Though he hoped *Socialism and Its Culture* would reach a world "at the crossroads of history," it was, in effect, a book-length policy memorandum to Stalin. Its urgent importance for Bukharin was clear from letters to Stalin begging him to save the confiscated (and still missing) first volume and publish both quickly, under a pseudonym if necessary, with a preface by the Kremlin leader. (What better way to wed Stalin to Bukharin's policies?) Here, too, Bukharin failed. Seventeen months after the trial, Stalin's pact with Hitler helped unleash world war while leaving Soviet borders virtually defenseless when Nazi armies came in June 1941. Before they were finally driven back into Germany in 1945, at least 27 million Soviet citizens had been killed. If we still honor a handful of political figures elsewhere who understood the dangers of appeasement and fought it, their counterpart in Lubyanka Prison should be added to the list.

By his seventh month in prison, September 1937, Bukharin had largely completed a second manuscript, a collection of poems of "universal scope" entitled *The Transformation of the World*. Though outwardly "chaotic," he explained in his letter to his wife, the collection was based on a "plan." Most of the nearly 200 poems were reflections on previous centuries—particularly their great thinkers, cultural figures, and rebels—and an epic telling of Soviet history from 1917 to the 1930s, culminating in the ongoing "struggle of two worlds," socialist humanism and fascism. In that respect, the second manuscript was an expansive poetic rendition of the first. Whatever the literary quality of the poems—expert Russian opinion is mixed—they are of compelling interest.

Carefully dated with the time of composition, the poems were written during the months when Bukharin was being intensely pressured for the false testimony Stalin demanded. Composed after midnight, when he was returned to his cell from those nocturnal interrogations, they can be read as a chronicle of his emotional state and a quest for spiritual escape. Two sections of the volume, one entitled "Lyrical Intermezzo," are especially moving. Along with autobiographical themes that reappear in the novel, they express his intense love for Anna, longing for their brief life together, and yearning to be free. For any historian of the terror, they are an unexpected view into the soul of a condemned man.

By then Bukharin seems to have understood that he was doomed, which meant the antifascist manifesto would not be published, and to have begun thinking about his posthumous legacy. He had already started another "big" project, *Philosophical Arabesques*, and now considered it the "most important thing" and his most "*mature* work." Even though he lacked most of the books needed for such a wide-ranging treatise (Kogan gave him a few from the prison library and apparently from his own collection), it was full of erudition and remarkably precise references. It, too, was written very quickly, because "much of it was in my head."

This third prison manuscript mattered greatly to Bukharin for at least two reasons. In 1921 he had published a philosophical work, *Historical Materialism*, that immediately became a canon of international communism. Translated into many languages, it established him as a major Marxist thinker and the Party's "biggest theorist." Stalin could not really obliterate that reputation, but serious intellectual and political challenges to Marxism, in addition to the theory and practice of fascism, had arisen since 1921. The still proud and intellectually ambitious Lubyanka inmate wanted to respond to those challenges and complete his long-standing project of bringing nineteenth-century Marxism fully into the twentieth century.

Something else equally personal was on Bukharin's mind. In 1922, while exalting him as the movement's best theorist, Lenin had added a biting caveat, as only a father figure can: Bukharin "has never studied and, I think, never fully understood dialectics." Since dialectical understanding was thought to be at the center of Marxist theorizing, Lenin's paradoxical qualification rankled and lingered. (Most of all, it reflected generational differences between the two men: Lenin's Marxism was imbued with nineteenth-century German philosophy, particularly Hegel, and Bukharin's with early-twentieth-century sociological theory.) Now on the eve of his own death, in a last discourse with his dead leader and revered friend, Bukharin undertook, as "Ilich [Lenin] recommended," a book that would be "*dialectical* from beginning to end."

Whether or not Lenin would have approved, the result was anything but conformist. When *Philosophical Arabesques* was published in post-Communist Russia, an eminent Moscow philosopher noted the "illusions Bukharin shared with many Communists of that time" but emphasized his "secret polemic with Stalinism." The "tragedy of this manuscript," he continued, was in having been kept hidden for so long:

> If the ideas Bukharin developed in this manuscript had been made known even in the *1950s* or *1960s*, they could have led to a fundamentally new Marxist philosophical vision. The kind of philosophy Bukharin outlined here was not the same as the Stalinist version of Marxism, a Marxism crucified. . . . Many themes first raised and discussed by Bukharin were new for Marxist philosophers even in the *1960s!* And the people who kept this manuscript under lock and key . . . are guilty not simply of degrading Marxism, which was transformed into ideological solder, but of a barbaric attitude toward . . . culture, and not only Russian culture.[15]

History often inflicts cruel ironies on its most engaging victims. Bukharin finished his solitary Lubyanka effort to redeem Soviet Marxism just as Stalin's regime was celebrating the twentieth anniversary of the Communist revolution, overnight on November 7–8, 1937. Five nights later, he began his autobiographical novel. The first seven chapters were written by mid-January 1938, when he thought the trial was about to begin and his time had run out. Another postponement, to early March, allowed him to write fifteen more.

Even the twenty-two chapters in this manuscript, which take Nikolai "Kolya" Petrov (Nikolai "Kolya" Bukharin) through childhood to about age fifteen and Russia to the eve of the failed revolution of 1905, a kind of dress rehearsal for 1917, are themselves unfinished. No professional writer, which Bukharin certainly was, would consider any major work complete without revisions, even further drafts. Bukharin had neither time nor paper for such perfections.[16] All his prison manuscripts were written not only at an astonishing pace but with almost no corrections. Misled into believing that they would be given to his family, he expected his elderly father, a great lover of literature, to "polish the poems and the novel." (When the manuscripts were finally retrieved half a century later, a decision was made to publish all of them unedited, if only to honor the circumstances in which he wrote them.)

How It All Began, the title I gave the English-language edition, was written as a novel, but it was virtually a memoir. None of the people were invented or really disguised. In addition to the later world-famous Kolya Petrov-Bukharin, for example, four of the main characters from his childhood became people well known in Moscow political society after 1917: his father, his brother, and two cousins, one a prominent Bolshevik revolutionary and historian, and the other Bukharin's first wife. Elderly friends and members of Bukharin's extended family who were still alive when the novel was obtained in the 1990s were amazed by how exactly he had portrayed those people. (All of them would share his fate under Stalin in one way or another.)

Above all, little Kolya Petrov of the novel was fully recognizable in the legendary Nikolai Bukharin of Soviet history. The Russian Huck Finn ("Kolya's hero") with a classical education, who dismayed his mother and grandmother by already knowing "everything he's not supposed to," grew into the most iconoclastic and intellectual member of the Soviet leadership. The boy who fell in love with painting became the revolutionary who ruefully admitted having had to choose between art and politics. The impish and athletic schoolboy "monkey" was still walking on his hands and springing from trees over courtyard walls in the 1920s and 1930s, now for the amusement of an ailing Lenin and the venerable writer Maxim Gorky. And Kolya's childhood passion for assembling menageries wherever the family migrated through the Russian empire remained with Bukharin everywhere he later lived, from Moscow's Hotel Metropol to the Kremlin, their abandoned denizens still running wild after his execution.

Even the writing of the novel, the only one he ever undertook, can be traced to the literary enthusiasms young Kolya inherited from his underachieving but beloved father. ("He goes out to buy sausage and comes back with a canary.") Though the most surprising of his prison manuscripts, it is consistent with the Soviet leader who wrote extensively about literature and culture, gathered the best writers around the newspapers he edited, *Pravda* and *Izvestia*, and repeatedly did what he could to protect three of Russia's greatest and most endangered poets— Osip Mandelstam, Boris Pasternak, and Nikolai Zabolotsky. Nor was little Kolya's raucous humor uncharacteristic of the zestful man later renowned as a Kremlin caricaturist and punster.[17] He never stopped telling the novel's story of his hapless Latin teacher, a native Czech, who translated the proverb "Life is short; art is long" for his Russian students as "The belly is short, but the thing is long."

We might wonder how Bukharin recalled those distant childhood years in such detail after decades of political upheaval and his own wide-ranging travels and activities. His memories had been refreshed by romance earlier in the 1930s, when he; his brother, Vladimir; their father; and his cousins related their life stories to his new wife Anna. But Bukharin gave an additional explanation in the novel: "Children, like grown-ups, have their superstitions, prejudices, heartfelt dreams, ideals, and unforgettable incidents in life, which are stored in the memory forever and which suddenly, at terrible or tragic moments in life, come swimming into consciousness, surprisingly vivid, in full detail, down to the wrinkles in somebody's face or a spider's web illuminated by the evening sun." Lubyanka Prison, of course, was such a terrible and tragic moment.

How far Bukharin hoped to take his story and Russia's is not entirely clear, but clues strongly suggest that he wanted the novel to encompass or culminate in 1917. In his next to last available prison letter to Stalin, he said it was to be a "big novel," which presumably meant in scope and content and thus including the "Great Revolution." There is also the somewhat enigmatic title Bukharin put on the manuscript, *Vremena*, whose Russian meaning suggests an unending process of time linking the past, present, and future. In the Soviet Marxist imagination, the revolution of 1917 was a kind of nexus between Russia's previous history, ongoing developments, and Communist future.

Why did Bukharin choose to write about the beginning of his life at its very end? Working on a previous prison manuscript, he had assured Stalin that it "calmed me somewhat"; memories of childhood and a loving family may have eased his adult sorrows. But the contents of *How It All Began* hardly suggest that emotional escape from Lubyanka was its primary purpose. For that, he might have written exclusively about his lifelong passions for nature or art, which are secondary themes of the novel. A political man to the end, Bukharin chose autobiography as his last subject for a political reason.

By 1937, entire generations of Russian revolutionaries, Bukharin's in particular, were being massacred in Stalin's terror, their biographies and ideals criminalized in the name of their own once-sacred cause. Though isolated in prison, Bukharin witnessed firsthand the fate of his contemporaries, having been brought face to face with childhood friends who also were being tortured into falsifying his life and their own. For his sake and theirs, he wanted to leave behind a personal testimony of how it had really been—a testament to the idealism that had led them as young students to become Marxist radicals in tsarist Russia—and how, he still hoped, it might be.[18] An unembellished memoir would have been too dangerous and less likely to survive; a novel must have seemed the safest approach and, after the strain of composing three rigorously Aesopian manuscripts, the freest.

As a result, *How It All Began* was the least self-censored of Bukharin's Lubyanka manuscripts, though it, too, was laced with anti-Stalinism. Even under a pseudonym and without its specific family history, the novel could not have been published in the despot's Soviet Union. Multicolored pictures of pre-1917 Russia, sympathetic portrayals of doomed classes, and humanistic characterizations of future Leninists now condemned as "enemies of the people" were already forbidden. And writers were being shot for less literary sedition than Bukharin's fleeting mirror images of Stalin's regime in its considerably paler tsarist predecessor.

No NKVD censor or interrogator would have overlooked, for example, the contemporary parallels with a tsar tightening "all the screws in the terrible system of power"; with a predecessor "officialdom, the chi-novniks [obedient bureaucrats] of all varieties . . . thick-headed, arro-gant, and 'patriotic,' the kind who threw the word *Yid* around contemp-tuously"; or with an old regime that promoted people "who seemed to have been born for police interrogation, provocation, and torture cham-bers" and under which the "best heads are cut off, the flower of the na-tion, as though by a mowing machine."

Certainly no one in Stalin's Russia would have been permitted to say, as does one of Bukharin's characters long before it actually happened, "You have transformed your party into a barracks. . . . You have killed all freedom of criticism among yourselves and you want to expand this barracks to include everything and everyone." And most Soviet read-ers, with their instinct for interpreting what could not be written, would have guessed that the author of such lines was somewhere in a successor to those tsarist prisons where "behind thick walls, interrogations went on, uninterrupted, through the nights."[19]

For some readers, however, the importance and pleasures of *How It All Began*, when it was published, lay not in its polemic with Stalinism but in its intimate portrayal of Russian society and a characteristic family on the eve of a great upheaval. The Russian literary scholar Boris Frez-insky, for example, praised Bukharin's "outstanding writer's memory for all of life's details," his "lush and vivid language," and his "panorama of social, political, and artistic life."[20] The venerable Russian children's writer and poet Valentin Berestov ranked the novel among the "best accounts of childhood in Russian literature." Other readers, including historians, singled out its description of everyday existence in the em-pire's remote provinces, particularly Bessarabia; re-creation of the sights and smells of old Moscow; and portraits of Russia's half-impoverished lower-middle classes, from which so many revolutionaries sprang.

Indeed, *How It All Began* may be the most authoritative firsthand account we have of how and why so many of tsarist Russia's best and brightest young people had already defected from that system on the eve of the twentieth century's most fateful revolution. It is this that Bukha-rin wanted posterity to understand—how they began to identify with the "lower orders of society," to "look at the world from the bottom up instead of from the top down," and why "this world of misery entered [their] soul forever"; how "sedition had crept" into the homes of loyal tsarist parents and why boys privileged to study at elite tsarist-era high schools embraced the "gleaming weapons of Marxism." Bukharin's own story was to stand for all his boyhood contemporaries who soon would be swept into power by a revolution they so wanted and who, twenty years later, would be destroyed in its aftermath.

Bukharin probably knew that the twenty-second chapter, where the manuscript of the novel breaks off, would be his last. Reliving the death of his youngest brother three decades before, he wrote: "The sooner it's all ended, the better." But it was not yet the end of his novelistic alter ego. Immediately after sentencing Bukharin to death, Stalin demanded another humiliating ritual, a formal plea for mercy. Bukharin wrote two, on March 13 and 14, 1938, the first perfunctory but the second an elaborate profession of complete political and psychological repentance: "The former Bukharin has already died; he no longer lives on this earth. . . . Let a new, second Bukharin grow—let him even be called Petrov." Whether or not Stalin already knew the ruse, they were, of course, one and the same Kolya.[21] He was shot the next night.

BUKHARIN's political afterlife has been almost as dramatic as was his actual biography. The struggle over his official historical reputation in the state he had helped create—whether or not he would continue to be an anathematized "enemy of the people"—began soon after Stalin's own death in 1953. During the next three decades, until the end of the Soviet Union itself, Bukharin's status was an important source of conflict between Communist Party anti-Stalinists, who wanted to reform the system of near-total political and economic control inherited from its creator, and neo-Stalinists who did not.[22]

From the mid-1950s to 1964, the de-Stalinizing reforms of the despot's successor, Nikita Khrushchev, repeatedly raised the "Bukharin question" in the Party's leadership councils, as well as among university students who demanded in 1955 and 1956, "Give us Bukharin to read." Behind the scenes, investigators appointed by Khrushchev reported that the infamous Moscow trials of the 1930s, including Bukharin's, had been "falsified." (Khrushchev even circulated among top leaders one of Bukharin's prison letters to Stalin.) Indeed, on a public occasion in 1962, a high Party official unequivocally informed Soviet historians, "Neither Bukharin nor Rykov [Soviet premier in the 1920s and Bukharin's erstwhile ally] was, of course, a spy or a terrorist."[23] Many Communists understandably expected Khrushchev to formally exonerate Bukharin, as his widow and son, now living in Moscow but still under a political cloud, fervently hoped.

Later, in forced retirement, Khrushchev regretted that several considerations had dissuaded him from doing so.[24] The decisive factor was not Bukharin's guilt or innocence, or even Khrushchev's secondary role in his arrest in 1937, but the more ramifying issue of Lenin's NEP and its abolition by Stalin. For Communist conservatives, NEP remained what Stalin had said it was in 1929—a necessarily temporary stage in Soviet development leading inevitably to the traumatic economic upheaval he imposed on the country in the early 1930s. To reinterpret NEP as a historical alternative to that formative turning point would raise grave questions about the foundations of the existing Soviet system, particularly the monopolistic state command economy and the millions of bureaucrats who administered it.

Party reformers had no less compelling reasons for insisting on the heresy that NEP had been a lost and incalculably preferable alternative to Stalinism. Recalling its Leninist pedigree, they emphasized NEP's "mixed" economy of private and state property, market relations and planning, socialist aspirations and capitalist practices, and its commitment to nonviolent, evolutionary development. Those hallmarks of the 1920s, along with the decade's more tolerant political and cultural policies, pointed to the kinds of reforms they sought in the current Soviet system, which they called a "new" or "second edition of NEP."[25]

All thinking about reforming the ailing Soviet economy, an observer noted at the time, "leads to NEP."[26] Both conservatives and reformers understood that the political road back to NEP was blocked by its most important defender, whose fate had been sealed with its destruction. As we will see in the next chapter, more than 700,000 Stalinist victims were exonerated under Khrushchev. But because of growing conservative opposition, which soon led to Khrushchev's overthrow, and his own desire to ameliorate the Stalinist system, not dismantle it, he stopped short of Bukharin. During the long conservative Brezhnev era that followed, Khrushchev's successors rigidly prohibited all such historical reconsiderations. They needed an orthodox Stalinist past to safeguard the system it had produced. In that spirit, they reimposed a full ban on Bukharin, even informing his family that the criminal charges behind his execution "have not been removed."[27]

But just as the post-Stalin Kremlin could no longer monopolize the Communist idea, its official anathema no longer dictated Bukharin's reputation in other ruling Communist parties. As anti-Stalinist ideas spread from Yugoslavia, Poland, Hungary, and Czechoslovakia to China, those reformers were also led back to "lost" antecedents and to their political ancestor, Bukharin. During the short-lived Prague Spring in 1967 and 1968, to take a dramatic example, Czech reformers discovered that his ideas "make themselves heard, so to speak, in the language of the contemporary era."[28] The Soviet invasion of Czechoslovakia ended overt Bukharinism in Eastern Europe, but within a decade it was flourishing in China. Launching their own NEP in the late 1970s, Chinese Communists "began seriously studying Bukharin" and then publishing his writings.[29]

Nor did "this ghost . . . keep to his grave" in the Soviet Union. During the repressive Brezhnev years, economists continued to explore, within the constraints of censored publications, NEP's contemporary possibilities. A Western study of their writings found it "astonishing . . . how many ideas of Bukharin . . . were adopted by current reformers" without mentioning his name. Elsewhere, his name was being mentioned, though privately. In 1977, a seventeen-year-old schoolboy, Sergei Baburin, who grew into a Russian presidential aspirant in the 1990s, sent a letter to Brezhnev demanding Bukharin's rehabilitation. And by 1980, two of Boris Yeltsin's future "radical reformers," Anatoly Chubais and Yegor Gaidar, were secretly discussing NEP and Bukharinist ideas with like-minded economists.[30]

Meanwhile, in the growing number of uncensored Soviet manuscripts circulated by hand, known as samizdat, Bukharin was already heralded as the historical representative of a road not taken in 1928 and 1929. Thus, the leading pro-Soviet Marxist dissident, Roy Medvedev, concluded that if Bukharin had defeated Stalin, "neither collectivization in its Stalinist form nor the terror of the 1930s and 1940s would have occurred."[31] Many anti-Soviet dissidents (and Western academics) insisted that there had never been any Communist alternative to Stalinism, one charitably calling Bukharin the "Don Quixote of Bolshevism." But others agreed with Medvedev, lamenting Bukharin's failed opposition to Stalin's brutal measures against the peasantry as "Russia's greatest tragedy."[32]

Not surprisingly, then, when an unequivocal and determined anti-Stalinist finally became Soviet leader in 1985, one of his first priorities was to fully rehabilitate NEP and "Bukharin in particular."[33] If he did not end the anathema on both, Mikhail Gorbachev could not even begin his mission of dismantling the Stalinist system of all-encompassing controls and replacing it with a substantially marketized and democratized one. To legitimate this "heresy," as it was already being viewed inside his own Communist Party, he needed Bukharin's heretical alternative of the 1920s. As one of Gorbachev's top aides later explained, the decriminalization of Bukharin "opened the floodgates for a reconsideration of our entire ideology."[34]

Bukharin was posthumously rehabilitated, legally and politically, in March 1988, which marked both the centenary of his birth and the fiftieth anniversary of his execution. What followed, in the phrase of two Russian historians, was a "Bukharinist Boom." All the Soviet founders killed by Stalin were soon exonerated, but only Bukharin become the "focus of public attention" and the subject of a "dialogue with the living dead."[35] This new attention included hundreds of mass media tributes, new editions of his writings, three biographies in addition to his widow's best-selling memoirs, a year-long exhibit of his life at the Museum of the Revolution, three feature films, and an array of novels, plays, and poems.

During the three years following his rehabilitation, Bukharin was virtually canonized as Lenin's rightful heir, anti-Stalinist prophet and hero, and forerunner of Gorbachev's perestroika reformation. Most importantly, the rediscovery of Bukharin unleashed tidal waves of truth telling about the Stalinist past, especially the Great Terror, and its millions of victims. For the first (and still only) time, the Kremlin wholeheartedly sponsored a national "repentance" in order to heal the "open wound" and exorcize the "curse hanging over our people" left by Stalin's twenty-five-year rule.[36]

Then suddenly, for reasons to be explored in chapter 5, in the kind of recapitulation of the "tragic fate of NEP" Gorbachev's supporters had feared,[37] the Soviet Union ended—and with it the "Bukharinist Boom." Bukharin's fate now underwent yet another dramatic "turnabout," as his widow Anna Larina, who had lived through the entire Soviet experience, often remarked before her death in 1996 at age eighty-two. The saga of

Bukharin's political status, from Soviet founder and exalted leader in the 1920s to condemned "enemy of the people" and then ancestral icon of Gorbachev's reforms, now seemed to end in irrelevance and indifference. Of what political use or historical interest was a founding father whose state and country no longer existed?

And yet it was soon clear that Bukharin's political afterlife was not over, even in post-Soviet Russia. In some respects, it seemed he might finally be of only scholarly interest, like historical figures in other countries. Academic editions of his prison manuscripts were published in Moscow in the 1990s. The Russian Academy of Sciences, which had expelled him upon his arrest, celebrated the 110th anniversary of his birth. The newspaper *Izvestia*, which he had edited from 1934 to 1937, honored his memory on several occasions. And in 2008, a Moscow university and prestigious publisher announced that Bukharin would be among the authors in a series of classic Russian political and social writings, while another university made plans to reprint his major works.[38]

But by the early twenty-first century, Bukharin's name was again being evoked in a renewed struggle over Russia's past, present, and future. This new chapter in his political afterlife began for two reasons, both related to the post-Soviet 1990s when Russia's first president, Boris Yeltsin, tried to rapidly transform its economy along Western, or "free-market," lines. In doing so, he adopted a "shock-therapy" program that immediately ended Soviet-era price controls and other consumer subsidies and privatized the state's most valuable assets, from natural resources, large industries, and banks to rail and air transport.

The result was the worst economic and social catastrophe ever suffered by a major nation in peacetime. Russia sank into a corrosive economic depression greater than that of the American 1930s. Investment plunged by 80 percent, GDP by almost 50 percent; some two-thirds of Russians were impoverished; the life expectancy of men fell below 59 years; and the population began to decline annually by almost a million people. In 1998, with nothing left to sustain it, despite several large Western loans, the Russian financial system collapsed. State and private banks defaulted on their domestic and foreign obligations, causing still more poverty and widespread misery.

The disaster shattered whatever post-Soviet consensus had existed about the nation's future. A new debate and political struggle began over what kind of economy was needed to save the country from further collapse and foster Russia's general development without its recurring episodes of "modernization through catastrophe," as many viewed the Stalinist 1930s and the Yeltsin 1990s.[39] Most Russian commentators now agreed that the largely privatized, "free-market" model Yeltsin tried to impose had collided with the country's long tradition, before and after 1917, except for the aberrant Stalinist system of 1929 through 1986, of a "mixed economy"—one based on both state and private sectors in a market context over which the government had substantial influence but not control.

Not surprisingly, thus began another rediscovery of NEP as an aborted historical experience whose "lessons" were applicable to present-day Russia. One advocate argued, for example, that having enabled Russia to recover after World War I faster than any other European belligerent, NEP was the "first 'economic miracle' of the twentieth century." Others pointed to China's booming economy as evidence of NEP's contemporary efficacy.[40] Unavoidably, Bukharin, too, was therefore discovered anew. His alternative program and opposition to Stalin's measures in the early 1930s were said to be an enduring reproach to Yeltsin's shock therapists, who had also inflicted devastating policies on the people. "Bukharin . . . gave historical advice to the peasantry (then 80 percent of the population): 'Enrich yourselves!' But the reforms of our liberals condemned 80 percent of the population to impoverishment."[41]

Post-Soviet opponents of any kind of "Bukharinist alternative" were at least as numerous and adamant, but by the early twenty-first century its political significance was again being embraced across Russia's ideological spectrum—sometimes anomalously. The reconstituted Communist Party, having reverted to Stalin as its historical icon, resumed its pre-perestroika vilification of Bukharin, warning its members that "de-Stalinization" always meant "Bukharinization." It now blamed Bukharin for everything from opposing the "Great Stalin" to spawning the hated Khrushchev, Gorbachev, and Yeltsin. Meanwhile, however, the same Communist Party was promising a NEP-like economy in its electoral campaigns.[42]

No less incongruously, anti-Communist guardians of the oligarchic economic system created in the 1990s warned that mounting calls for its abolition threatened to repeat NEP's "tragic fate," thereby confirming the enduring popularity of the pre-Stalinist 1920s. Indeed, Yeltsin's chief shock therapist, Yegor Gaidar, suddenly decided that if Bukharin

had managed to save peasant agriculture from Stalin's assault, the Soviet Union might still exist. And when the oil oligarch Mikhail Khodorkovsky was imprisoned in 2003, his defenders compared his fate (and
prison writings) to Bukharin's. (For the record, President Bill Clinton
compared his own political and legal plight in 1998 to Bukharin's trial.)[43]
More plausibly, when Yeltsin's successor, Vladimir Putin, began reasserting state control over "strategic industries"—called the "commanding
heights" in the 1920s—his representatives implied that he was enacting
a neo-NEP.[44]

Above all, however, Bukharin's afterlife in post-Soviet Russia remains
inseparable from Stalin's. The social pain and perceived "chaos" of the
1990s revived Russia's traditional deference to a "strong-hand" leader. By
the end of the decade, pro-Stalin sentiments were growing both in Russian society and officialdom, and they continued to do so under Putin.
Alarmed by the implications for current policymaking, anti-Stalinists
again called upon Bukharin's "NEP alternative." By arguing anew that it
would have spared the country Stalin's destruction of agriculture, Great
Terror, and unpreparedness when Hitler's armies invaded in 1941, they
hoped to thwart any drift toward a post-Soviet neo-Stalinism.[45]

Russian intellectuals, their humor darkened by their twentieth-
century experiences, often quip, "Our history is unpredictable." As long
as the fight over Russia's present and future continues, so will bitter
political controversies about past roads taken and not taken—and the
Kremlin's attempt to write (or rewrite) that narrative. "Discussions about
lost alternatives," a Moscow historian reminded readers, "have not lost
their relevance today."[46] Until they have, the restless fate of Bukharin's
"ghost" will continue.

2 THE VICTIMS RETURN

GULAG SURVIVORS SINCE STALIN

It can't be covered up. People will come out of prison, return to their native places, tell their relatives and friends and acquaintances what actually happened . . . that those who remained alive had been innocent victims of repression.

NIKITA KHRUSHCHEV

Now those who were arrested will return, and two Russias will be eyeball to eyeball: The one that put people in the camps and the one put there.

ANNA AKHMATOVA

MILLIONS of people perished in Stalin's twenty-year terror along with Bukharin, but other victims survived and began to return to Soviet society after the tyrant's death in 1953. Until recently, relatively little was known about their lives after the Gulag, which is the subject of this chapter. The chapter itself has a long history. My research for it began more than thirty years ago in forbidding circumstances—in Moscow in the still repressive Soviet 1970s and early 1980s, when the entire subject was officially banned. No sensible scholar would have chosen such a project in those prohibitive circumstances, but, as I came to think, the subject chose me.

In 1976, I began living in Moscow for extended periods, usually on a U.S.-Soviet exchange program. By then, Bukharin's widow, Anna Larina, and son, Yuri, had obtained a copy of my Bukharin biography and had welcomed me into their family.[1] Indeed, much of my Moscow social life revolved around their friends and acquaintances, and I soon realized that most of the people I met were also survivors of Stalin's Gulag or children and other relatives of his victims.

Public knowledge of their terrible fate had been proscribed by censorship since shortly after the overthrow of Stalin's successor, Nikita Khrushchev, in 1964, and they had little hope, if any, of ever making it widely known. For that reason, and because Anna Larina assured them of my discretion, they were eager to tell me their stories and even give me unpublished memoirs. Suddenly and unexpectedly, I found myself dwelling in a subterranean history, a kind of living archaeological find, known only fragmentarily in the Soviet Union and almost not at all in the West.[2] Writing that history, it seemed, had fallen to me.

THE book I planned had two purposes. One was a collective biography of Gulag returnees during the years of Khrushchev's reforms from 1953 to 1964, beginning with their liberation and ending with their efforts to rejoin society. The other purpose, reflecting my interest in past and possible future reforms in the Soviet Union, was to explore how the return of millions of "zeks" (the colloquial acronym for prisoners) after Stalin's death had affected policymaking and the system itself under Khrushchev.

Both dimensions were outside the mainstream of Western Soviet studies at that time. Still adhering to the "totalitarianism" model, most studies treated the political system as something apart from both its history and society, largely unaffected by either and thus essentially immutable.[3] The impact of Gulag returnees in the 1950s and 1960s suggested otherwise. Their fates were a central factor in the intensely historicized politics of the period, when controversies over the past, including historical alternatives to Stalinism, became an inescapable aspect of struggles over power and policy at the top. At the same time, the personal needs of so many freed prisoners and their families created both a social constituency for further de-Stalinization and a test of the system's capacity for change. (Before it became commonplace in the field, I was trying to fuse social and political history.)[4]

But where could I obtain the information needed for such an empirical work? Almost no secondary literature existed on the subject; the best Western books about the terror focused on people's victimization, not their subsequent experiences.[5] And in a country of encompassing censorship, closed archives, many still-intimidated victims, and a hostile officialdom, there was, not surprisingly, only one fragmentary Soviet study—the brief account of a few post-Gulag lives at the end of Aleksandr Solzhenitsyn's *The Gulag Archipelago*, which appeared in the West in the 1970s.[6]

This meant I had to rely mainly on primary sources. A number of uncensored Gulag memoirs had been published abroad, but they were of limited value. Most covered years before 1953, were by repatriated foreign prisoners whose later experiences were not typical of Soviet ones, or said little about life after the Gulag.[7] There were, however, two other written sources of information, both of them Soviet and important, though still little used by Western scholars.

One was a considerable body of writings on the "camp theme," including fiction, published under the somewhat relaxed censorship of Khrushchev's "Thaw." The false impression prevalent in the West is that few such texts were printed even at that time in the Soviet Union—in literature, for example, only Solzhenitsyn's *One Day in the Life of Ivan Denisovich*—or that being pro-Soviet, they were unworthy of attention.[8] Many commentaries on Stalin's terror, including memoir accounts by Gulag survivors, appeared in officially sanctioned publications, and not only in the Moscow-based press. Prompted by returnees, I found a wealth of information in intelligentsia journals published in remote Soviet regions where there had been large concentrations of camp inmates and exiles and where many had remained after their release, particularly in Siberia and Kazakhstan.[9]

The other written Soviet source was entirely uncensored—the growing volume of materials circulating in typescript (samizdat) or smuggled abroad for publication (tamizdat). By the 1970s, those expressions of unofficial glasnost—histories, memoirs, contemporary political and social commentaries, documents, fiction, and more—should have been essential reading for most Sovietologists, as they were for me.[10] Indeed, terror-era subjects and returnee authors were a major component of that literature.

Most of all, though, I relied on the firsthand testimonies of Stalin's victims with whom I was in personal contact. In the beginning, I met them through the Bukharin family but very soon also through three other exceptional Muscovites. Two, with whom I developed close personal and professional relations, were dissident historians and themselves sons of victims—Roy Medvedev, whose father had perished in a labor camp; and Anton Antonov-Ovseyenko, who lost both parents to the terror and himself "sat" for almost thirteen years in the Gulag.[11] Admired and trusted by many returnees, Roy and Anton persuaded several of them to help me.

My third enabler, Tatyana Baeva, was a young woman at the center of Moscow's beleaguered human-rights movement, which included a number of survivors of Stalin's twenty-year terror as well as grown children of victims who did not return. Indeed, Tanya's father, Aleksandr Baev, a much-honored, internationally known biochemist and high official in the Soviet Academy of Sciences, had spent seventeen years in Stalinist camps and exile, where she was born.[12] Friendship with Tanya led me to another circle of people whose experiences I needed.

Within two years of periodic visits to Moscow, I was in direct touch with more than twenty returnees or close relatives of other victims, in addition to members of the Bukharin family, whom I interviewed at various lengths.[13] I was not the first person to engage them in oral history—in many instances, Solzhenitsyn, Medvedev, or Antonov-Ovseyenko had been there earlier for their uncensored (or "dissident") books on the Soviet past[14]—but I was, I think, the first foreigner. That circumstance heightened my awareness that by abetting my project they (unlike me) might again be at considerable risk. I was very cautious, which usually meant surreptitious.

I realized, however, that those close encounters were selective cases, most involving elderly people linked to the original Soviet Communist elite and who had lived in Moscow before and after the Gulag. (Contrary to politically motivated myths, the great majority of Stalin's victims, 70 percent or more, were not members of the Communist Party or any Soviet elite.)[15] To reach beyond them, I prepared a lengthy Russian-language questionnaire—also the first on the subject—that friends, acquaintances, and people unknown to me circulated more widely inside the Soviet Union and among survivors who had emigrated.[16] By the early 1980s, it had yielded, through various channels, twenty or so detailed replies. With cases culled from printed and typescript sources, I now had files on nearly sixty individuals. Considering the millions of victims, it was a small sample. But considering recent Western generalizations about the entire Stalin era based on many fewer diaries and other personal materials found in archives, it was substantial.[17]

By then I was running out of time to pursue the project inside the Soviet Union. My Moscow double life—as an official exchange scholar working on an approved subject while increasingly engrossed in a disapproved one—had become known to Soviet authorities, as no doubt had my role in sending banned memoirs and contemporary dissident materials out of the country. My sporadic "tail" became more constant, and a KGB officer at an academic institute bluntly warned me to "stop spending time with people who have grievances against the Soviet government." (Whether he meant Gulag survivors or latter-day dissidents, I didn't ask.)

Inevitably perhaps, that stage of the project ended in 1982, when for the next three years I could no longer obtain a Soviet visa. I turned instead to the large quantity of materials I had already amassed, using some in my publications about past and current political struggles over reform in the Soviet system.[18] I also drafted the original version of this chapter as a summary of the book I intended to write.

That intention was overwhelmed in 1985 and 1986 by the unfolding drama of Mikhail Gorbachev's reforms. The new leader's policies soon represented the attempted Soviet reformation I had long considered possible, and they raised the possibility of access to long-inaccessible documents for a fuller edition of my Bukharin biography. Glasnost filled the Soviet press with new information about Stalin's victims, which I dutifully collected, but my other projects took priority. My swollen returnee files languished in storage until the mid-1990s, when I met the young American scholar Nanci Adler. Impressed by her ongoing work on a similar project, I gave her full access to my materials for her own excellent book, which appeared in 2002.[19]

Even so, Gulag returnees are still a remarkably little known phenomenon, certainly compared to Holocaust survivors.[20] Since the Khrushchev years, returnees have appeared in several Russian and Western novels, including Vasily Grossman's *Forever Flowing*, Vassily Aksyonov's *The Burn*, Andrei Bitov's *Pushkin House*, and Martin Amis's *House of Meetings*; a few memoirs about their post-Gulag lives have been published; and their testimonies have informed a number of more general Western studies.[21] But despite large repositories of relevant manuscripts and published volumes of archive documents, Adler's book remains the only full-scale examination of their experiences, even, inexplicably, in Russia.[22]

An expanded version of my 1983 manuscript, this chapter is an overview of the political and social dimensions of the returnee phenomenon. Incorporating information that has become available since 1983, it takes the story beyond the Khrushchev years and into the post-Soviet era. But enough of the original draft remains to reflect the circumstances in which it originated when many victims (and victimizers) were still alive and, I think, to offset the widespread impression that such research was impossible before Gorbachev's glasnost or the post-Soviet "archive revolution."

As a Russian historian has remarked about writing history during those decades of strict Soviet censorship, "Every era gives rise to its own specific types of sources."[23] Even now, however, I have not named all the sources who, trusting in my pledge of confidentiality, informed my work in the 1970s and early 1980s. Even though most of them are now dead, I remain reticent about several identities, partly because of uncertain developments in post-Soviet Russia or perhaps simply because of promises made and habits ingrained long ago.

RETURNEES from the Gulag were survivors in almost the full sense of victims who had survived the Nazi extermination camps. (Even Soviet newspapers later charged Stalin with "genocide against his own people.")[24] Unlike Hitler's camps, the Gulag's primary purpose was forced labor, but treatment and conditions in Stalin's camps and in the vast associated system of prisons, transport, penal colonies, and "special" places of harsh exile were often murderous. Many of the 12 to 14 million victims swept into that system between the early 1930s and early 1950s died there or were discharged because they were already dying.[25] Most of those liberated in the 1950s had been arrested in the 1940s or later, surviving "only" ten years or less.

Survival was therefore a subject that troubled returnees much as it had tormented Nazi victims.[26] Who had survived, and why? Some zeks endured because of strong bodies and unrelenting wills or the circumstantial good fortune of less arduous work, less brutal climate, or early release into exile. Others did so by becoming informers or collaborating in different ways with camp authorities. Many of the returnees I interviewed did not want to discuss the question or did so without recriminations, but several accused other survivors of perfidious behavior and wanted me to condemn them as well. (I declined to make such judgments, explaining that having never faced such life-and-death choices, I could not be sure how I would have behaved in those circumstances.)

Exactly how many political victims survived to be freed after Stalin's death in March 1953 is uncertain even now. At least 4 to 5 million were still in camps, labor colonies, prisons and exile.[27] To that number must be added, however, the uncounted millions of relatives of "enemies of the people"—or in another formulation of Stalinist repression, "members of families of traitors to the Motherland." (Some renounced their accused kin or managed to hide such relationships, but many would not or could not.) The story of all those collateral victims, whose spouses, parents, or siblings became the inadvertent "culprit of my fate,"[28] as the poet Anna Akhmatova's son characterized her involuntary role in his arrest, remains largely unwritten.

A great many children and other relatives had also been imprisoned or deposited under false names in NKVD-authorized orphanages across the country.[29] Millions more remained nominally free but so stigmatized by their "spoiled biographies" they could not live or work as they desired or obtain essential social benefits. (There were notable exceptions of people, well-known in Russia but not in the West, who nonetheless had honored public careers under Stalin.)[30] They, too, had been "repressed," as the Russian government acknowledged decades later, and they, too, wanted exoneration and full integration into Soviet society. Considering only immediate family members (other relatives were also affected), there could scarcely have been fewer than 10 million survivors of some kind of political victimization by 1953, and possibly considerably more.

Many previous releases had occurred in the Gulag's long history, but the post-Stalin liberation was entirely different—profoundly political, fraught with questions about innocence and culpability, and the source of fearful conflict in the Kremlin. A March 1953 amnesty released 1 million of the approximately 2.7 million camp inmates, most of them said to be ordinary criminals.[31] The freeing of political prisoners, however, unfolded slowly over the next three years, agonizingly for those still in the Gulag.[32] The primary reason was, of course, the new leadership's complicity in Stalin's crimes, particularly that of Lavrenty Beria, Vyacheslav Molotov, Lazar Kaganovich, Kliment Voroshilov, Georgy Malenkov, Anastas Mikoyan, and Khrushchev himself.

During the three years following Stalin's death, his successors, while fighting among themselves over power and policy, relied on bureaucratic procedures to investigate the status of political prisoners, most convicted as "counterrevolutionaries" under the infamous Article 58, and review the mounting flood of appeals. But the victims with the best chance of early release in 1953 and 1954 were those who had personal connections with or were known to Party leaders and other influential Soviet figures. Beneficiaries ranged from relatives of the leaders themselves, a few once prominent Communists whom Stalin had not shot, and surviving Jewish doctors arrested in the tyrant's last terror scenario to famous performers such as the actress Zoya Fyodorova, the Starostin brothers (Spartak soccer players), and the jazzman Eddi Rozner. (Molotov's wife, freed on the day of Stalin's funeral, may have been the first.)[33]

Otherwise, apart from partial amnesties, the procedure was a slow, case-by-case process that usually stretched over months, even years, and often ended in rejection. Of 237,412 appeals formally reviewed by April 1955, barely 4 percent resulted in release.[34] Spurred in part by rebellions in the camps, large crowds of petitioners outside the procurator's building in central Moscow, and thousands of appeals sent to the Party's headquarters and the KGB, the exodus from the Gulag grew. By the end of 1955, 195,353 people were reported to have been released, though only 88,278 from labor camps and colonies, the rest from various kinds of exile.[35] It was a substantial number, but it was growing too slowly to save the lives of many left behind. As Lev Gumilyov wrote despairingly from camp in 1955 to his mother, the great but proscribed poet Akhmatova, "Most likely I'll be rehabilitated posthumously."[36]

Khrushchev's historic assault on Stalin's still cultlike reputation at a closed session of the Twentieth Party Congress in February 1956 was the turning point. The new leader did not tell the full truth, or even mention the Gulag, but by accusing the dead tyrant of "mass repressions" over twenty years, Khrushchev tacitly exonerated millions of falsely condemned victims. His speech was not published in the Soviet Union for thirty-three years, but nor was it ever really "secret." Within a few months, it had been read officially to meetings across the country, making its general contents widely known. A policy of selective releases was no longer tenable. Mass liberation began immediately through special resolutions, accelerated reviews, including of appeals previously rejected, and blanket amnesties.[37]

The most dramatic component of the accelerated release program consisted of ninety-seven special commissions authorized in Moscow and sent directly to many of the Gulag's sixty-five or so largest camps. Each commission was supposed to have three to seven members, including Party and state officials and, to insure "objectivity and justice," one already freed and exonerated veteran Communist, though the latter was often excluded. All the commissions were empowered to review cases on the scene and free prisoners, usually upon a simple denial of guilt. (Zeks called them "unloading parties.") Some, staffed by unsympathetic officials, did not act justly, but many did. Within a few months, they had freed more than 100,000 prisoners, adding significantly to the ever-growing total.[38] By 1959, most of Stalin's surviving political victims had been released from camps, colonies, prisons, and exile.[39]

In the aftermath of Khrushchev's speech, the homeward trek of liberated zeks became a familiar sight on trains and in streets and shops across the Soviet Union. With nothing more than documents authorizing their release and destination, a railway ticket, and a few rubles for food, many looked emaciated and aged and were still in standard Gulag garb.[40] When one arrived at Communist Party headquarters embarrassed by how he was dressed, another former prisoner now working there assured him, "It's nothing. Many people are walking around Moscow today in such clothes."[41]

Not all released prisoners and exiles actually went home. Some arrested in connection with sensitive political cases were banned from Moscow and other capital cities for several years. Not all deported nationalities were permitted to return to their Soviet native homelands. For a great many others, home no longer existed, years of imprisonment having cost them their families, careers, possessions, and sense of belonging.

Hundreds of thousands of freed zeks and exiles—"sensible" ones, according to Solzhenitsyn[42]—remained in the vast regions of the diminished Gulag empire, especially Central Asia and Siberia. They stayed because of new families, salaries offered by state enterprises desperate for their now voluntary labor, a lack of travel documents, psychological attachments to the harsh expanses of their punishment, or because they had nowhere else to go.[43] Long after the Gulag's barbed wire and watch towers had been bulldozed, visitors still stumbled upon terrible traces of that world—camp structures, mass graves, skulls. They also found living traces in the remote former Gulag capitals such as Magadan, Norilsk, and Vorkuta—elderly survivors and a large number of their descendents.[44] Most would fall on new hard times when the post-Soviet state ended essential subsidies to those regions.

But millions of survivors did go home, or tried to. They were people once as diverse as the Soviet Union itself, formerly of all classes, professions, and nationalities. Over the decades, Stalin's terror had victimized virtually every social group, high and low. In the Gulag, however, as the anti-Stalinist poet and editor Aleksandr Tvardovsky, whose own peasant parents had been deported, wrote:

> Fate made everyone equal
> Outside the limits of the law,
> Son of a kulak or Red commander,
> Son of a priest or commissar.
>
> Here classes all were equalized,
> All men were brothers, campmates all,
> Branded as traitors every one.[45]

Now they went their separate ways.

FEW generalizations are possible about the post-Gulag lives of returnees. Some were so broken physically they died soon after release—"from freedom," it was said; others lived into their nineties.[46] (Solzhenitsyn, for example, died in 2008 just before his ninetieth birthday, while Antonov-Ovseyenko was still active in Moscow at eighty-eight.) Some had been so traumatized that they remained fearful, concealed their past, refused to discuss it even with family members, shunned fellow-survivors, and tried to "shed [their] prisoner's skin"; others were "professional zeks," wearing their Gulag experiences as a badge of honor, maintaining life-long friendships with camp comrades, talking and writing because "they could not do otherwise." (A Communist truth teller, when asked menacingly by a Party official if he was in the "Soviet or anti-Soviet camp," defiantly replied, "I am from [the Gulag camp] Kolyma!" And a poet adopted the pen name "Vladimir Zeka.") For such people, as for Solzhenitsyn, "There was never a question of whether to conceal his past or take pride in it."[47] Returnees young enough to aspire to a new or renewed profession usually followed a middle course, confiding in relatives, close friends, and trusted colleagues.[48]

The great majority of survivors slipped back into the anonymity of society, but a significant number went on to eminent Soviet careers. They included several released to fight in World War II—Marshal Konstantin Rokossovsky; General Aleksandr Gorbatov; the father of the Soviet rocket and space program, Sergei Korolev; and an eventual head of the Writers Union, Vladimir Karpov—as well as post-Stalin returnees like Baev, Rozner, Andrei Starostin, the popular actors Georgy Zhzhenov and Pyotr Veliaminov, and many literary figures.[49] Innumerable returnees who lived out their lives privately also achieved a relatively "*kheppi end*," though possibly more did not. Some ended up hopelessly dysfunctional, destitute, and homeless. Even the great writer Varlam Shalamov died in exceptionally lonely circumstances, and the last years of the poet Olga Berggolts were ones of "pain, alcohol, and loneliness."[50]

Nor are political generalizations possible. Many victims blamed the entire Soviet system, a few becoming well-known dissident religious figures such as Anatoly Levitin-Krasnov and Father Dmitri Dudko; others blamed only Stalin and sought restitution of their Communist Party membership as full exoneration; and still others, like my close friend Yevgeny Gnedin, rejoined the Party after their return but later quit in protest.[51]

Political conflicts among survivors were not uncommon. There were disputes among former zeks over Solzhenitsyn's portrayal of camp life in *Ivan Denisovich*, and he developed significant disagreements with the other major Gulag author, Shalamov (who came to dislike Solzhenitsyn), and "ideological" differences with his once close Gulag friend Lev Kopelev. The memoirist Eugenia Ginzburg, who refused to rejoin the Party, despised a Gulag friend because she thought he had reacquired not only his Party card but his prearrest official attitudes.[52] A returnee who rose high in the scientific establishment was angered by his daughter's dissident activities because they "jeopardized what I suffered to achieve," not unlike the reaction of Bukharin's daughter to her half-brother's public protests.[53] Years later, a war of words broke out between rival organizations of former zeks.[54] And while most victims hated Stalin, after the end of the Soviet Union Karpov and Father Dudko praised his historical role.[55]

Collectively, however, the millions of returnees were an important new factor in Soviet life. Their common experiences, needs, and demands generated widespread problems, conflicts, and cultural expressions that required responses from the political-administrative system. Virtually every returnee wanted, for example, a family reunion, medical care, an apartment, a job or pension, financial compensation, and the return of confiscated property. The Soviet government's general response was an unwritten but often spoken social contract: We will meet your needs within limits and leave you in peace, but you must not make political demands or clamor about the past. (When released, many survivors had been warned not to talk about what had happened to them.)

Government agencies could do little for families torn apart by years of mass repression except help returnees locate relatives, and even that was done mainly by friends and other relatives. (Still worse, the KGB continued to lie for several years about the deaths of loved ones.)[56] Children who vanished into orphanages and foster homes were usually found, but some parents were still searching for them decades later.[57] And when children had been young or had not known who their parents were, reunions were frequently difficult and sometimes never fully successful. Even adult returnees often could not reestablish relationships with parents or siblings who had not been arrested. (There was also a cruel coincidence in 1956, the year a soccer star helped his Soviet team win Olympic gold at Melbourne while his brother was returning from the Gulag.)[58]

As for marriages, many were irreparably damaged, even when both the husband and wife had been imprisoned for long periods.[59] When one spouse had remained free (usually the wife), sometimes blaming the victim for the stigma that ensued, the outcomes ranged from joyous to traumatic and tragic. There were countless instances of long marital faithfulness but also many of political renunciation, divorce, and new marriage.[60] Returnees who found no family waiting often quickly remarried, not infrequently to other victims—and many affected children married other children whose parents had been in the camps—while some men sought new lives with much younger women.[61] More women returnees, not surprisingly, remained without spouses, adding to the large number of unmarried women that had resulted from World War II.

Nor did the government do much for Gulag survivors suffering from psychological "post-camp syndrome"—those who lived in constant anxiety, tormented by memories, nightmares, and everyday reminders of their terrible experiences. The Soviet system lacked the will, and its mental health profession did not acknowledge the condition. Quite a few former zeks sought comfort in intimate circles of other victims, who were "like a family," some even expressing "nostalgia" for the survivalist comradeship of the Gulag. How many ever found inner peace is unknown.[62]

The government did, however, meet the basic material needs of most returnees, though many felt the response was not adequate. Despite existing statutes, few survivors were given financial compensation for their years of suffering or their impounded savings accounts, only a flat two months of their prearrest salary; nor, as a rule, were their personal possessions—many of them now in the hands of NKVD-KGB families—returned, though compensation was sometimes granted. (To take a particularly horrific example, Andrei Vyshinsky, the chief prosecutor at Stalin's falsified show trials of the 1930s, took for himself the dacha of one of the defendants he condemned to death.)[63] But most returnees did eventually receive health and dental care (dentures were especially important), living space, work, pensions, and other modest benefits of the Soviet welfare system. A general pension reform of 1956, for example, expanded the definition of time in the workplace to tacitly include years of forced labor.[64]

Recovering those benefits of full citizenship was not automatic or easy. Having been "legally" convicted, returnees needed official exoneration, or "rehabilitation," which amnesty and other release documents usually had not provided. Obtaining the "sacred" certificate of rehabilitation, which was supposed to delete their "dark past" or that of relatives who had perished, involved another case-by-case bureaucratic process.[65]

Here again it was easiest for survivors who had influential help. For elderly Communists, the most active "intervenors" were the few Leninist-era Bolsheviks Stalin had not arrested, notably Grigory Petrovsky, Yelena Stasova, and Vyacheslav Karpinsky. For cultural figures, they were eminent figures such as the writers Ilya Ehrenburg and Konstantin Simonov.[66] Less fortunate returnees were often subjected to grudging, protracted procedures. Nonetheless, between 1954 and Khrushchev's overthrow in 1964, 700,000 to 800,000 of Stalin's victims were rehabilitated, many posthumously.[67] Millions more had to await another Soviet reform leader.

Compared to the twenty years that followed, Khrushchev's leadership favored returnees, but reactions to them in officialdom and society were far from uniform. Some officials were supportive, but many viewed former zeks "with suspicion," rehabilitation as "something rotten," and the rehabilitated as "unclean." Those Party and state officials created obstacles to their return, from liberation to rehabilitation. Even though laws provided for positive actions, frequently bureaucrats refused survivors necessary documents, courts ruled against their claims, state employers rejected their applications, academic directors forbade them to travel abroad, and local Party secretaries punished editors who had "a mania for justice." One official probably spoke for many when he warned a rehabilitated zek, "The mark was removed, but the stain remained."[68]

Society's reaction also varied. Returnees related many instances of welcoming kindness, not only from family and friends but also strangers. The emerging liberal intelligentsia and educated young people viewed them as "something romantic" and gave them "a hero's reception." The justly admired Gnedin, for example, was the subject of a well-known publication, "The Poem's Hero."[69] But many ordinary citizens reacted with suspicion and hostility, mainly, it seems, because of major outbreaks of theft, rape, and murder resulting from the mass amnesty of criminals in 1953 and to decades of Stalinist allegations about "wreckers, traitors and assassins." They saw no difference between released political and criminal prisoners.[70]

One social group had reason to be fearful. Millions of people had been implicated in some way in Stalin's twenty-year terror—from Party and state apparatchiki who implemented his orders and hundreds of thousands, perhaps millions, of NKVD personnel who arrested, tortured, executed, and guarded victims to countless petty informers and eager slanderers spawned by the crimson plague. Millions of other citizens had been implicated indirectly, inheriting the positions, apartments, possessions, and even wives and children of the vanished. Two generations had built lives and careers on the terror's consequences, which killed but also "corrupted the living."[71]

Some Soviet citizens had, of course, resisted complicity in the terror and even tried to help its victims, as did even a few procurators, NKVD interrogators, and camp officials,[72] but by 1956 a profound antagonism was unfolding between two social communities. As Anna Akhmatova, whose son was released that year, foresaw, "Now those who were arrested will return, and two Russias will be eyeball to eyeball: The one that put people in the camps and the one put there." The first, she added, "are now trembling for their names, positions, apartments, dachas. The whole calculation was that no one would return."[73]

Widespread conflicts were inevitable. Most returnees passively accepted the government's assistance, but a significant number wanted more—real compensation, fuller political disclosures, official punishment of the guilty. Some took action, including law suits and later public campaigns identifying secret police agents and informers. Others dreamt of a Monte Cristo–like revenge, though it usually evolved into demands for legal justice.[74] A few survivors concluded that "no one was guilty" because Stalin's terror had deprived people of choice—an outlook that may explain the romance between a leading victim's son and the late dictator's daughter and occasional requests by camp guards that former zeks testify to their humanity. (I witnessed a poignant example in the early 1990s when I brought together Bukharin's widow and the daughter of his Lubyanka interrogator. Anna Larina immediately eased the daughter's anxiety by assuring her, "They both were victims.") But many more returnees insisted that the difference between "victims and hangmen" was absolute and "eternal."[75]

There were many confrontations between them. Some were accidental encounters in public places. One returnee dropped dead upon coming face-to-face with his former tormentor, while another saw "fear of death" in the eyes of his NKVD interrogator. Awkward meetings occurred at professional institutes and clubs, where returning victims unavoidably encountered colleagues they knew had contributed to their arrest, some now in positions of authority. They reacted variously. One spit on his betrayer; another refused to shake the hand of his; yet another pretended not to know.[76]

One other social ramification of the great return should be emphasized. Even in conditions of repressive censorship, experiences of that magnitude and intensity were bound to find cultural expression. The irrepressible percolation of the "camp theme" from the subterrane of Soviet society into unofficial and then sanctioned culture was an important and lasting development of Khrushchev's Thaw. Now more widely studied than when I first observed it in Moscow, Gulag culture emerged across the spectrum from language, music, and literature to paintings and sculptures.

Zeks returning from the "little zone," as they called it, to the "big zone" of society brought with them a jargon common in the Gulag but prohibited in public discourse under Stalin. Some people were offended by its coarseness and seeming romanticizing of the criminal world, but I heard it spoken casually by many Muscovites, especially intellectuals and young people. (It soon became the subject of several dictionaries.)[77] Gulag vernacular also spread widely through songs performed by popular bards, including two sons of victims, Bulat Okudzhava and Yuli Kim. (One musical returnee had an official impact, the saxophonist Rozner being assured by the minister of culture in 1953, "We are rehabilitating the saxophone.")[78]

Visual art, on the other hand, was less portable and thus more easily prohibited, but judging by what I saw and was told, a considerable number of Gulag-related paintings, drawings, and even sculptures were seen in apartments, studios, and, in one instance, on the lawn of a zek who remained in Siberia.[79] Such works, virtually all of them done by returnees, ranged from large oil canvases depicting arrests and life and death in the camps to small graphic drawings of the torture of naked female prisoners. The existence of such art was known in select circles by the 1970s, but its first public showings in the late 1980s were a sensation.[80]

Meanwhile, returnees had begun to put their experiences in prose and poetry. Most of it remained part of the underground or "catacomb" culture until the Gorbachev period, but not all.[81] A small wave of Gulag-related writings made its way into official publications soon after Khrushchev's 1956 speech, well before the "flood" unleashed by his public anti-Stalinist revelations in late 1961, highlighted by Solzhenitsyn's *Ivan Denisovich*. By the mid-1960s, camp literature had grown into a substantial published genre that posed searing questions about the Soviet past and present—about the nation's "dreadful and bloody wound," as even the government newspaper acknowledged.[82]

None of those social developments after 1953 should be understood apart from what was still a harshly repressive political system. To have a larger impact, they required initiatives at the top. Nonetheless, the social and cultural dimensions of the victims' return created pressure "downstairs" for a response "upstairs" (in the imagery of a former Soviet journalist) more radical than Khrushchev's remarks at a closed gathering of the Party elite. When that response came in the early 1960s, this "muffled rumble of subterranean strata" was both a causal and deeply divisive factor in the political struggles that followed.[83]

GULAG returnees played a little-known but significant role in Soviet politics under Khrushchev. Unlike in several East European Communist countries and China, no survivor of political purges returned to the leadership. Stalin had long since killed everyone who might have done so. A number of returnees acquired positions in the ruling Party apparatus, but mostly at lower levels either because of age or because "the stain remained." (Several reported being trusted but, as Arthur Miller could have written, not well trusted.)[84]

Many former zeks did, however, make their way into the nomenklatura class that administered the state bureaucratic system, some even becoming *nachalniki* (bosses). Among them were Marshal Rokossovsky and several generals: Korolev; Baev; Boris Suchkov, who directed the Institute of World Literature; Semyon Kheiman, who held a similar position at the Institute of Economics; and Boris Burkovsky, head of the museum of the iconic revolutionary cruiser *Aurora* docked in Leningrad.[85] I often asked acquaintances in various professions in the 1970s if their *nachalstvo* included anyone who had "sat" under Stalin; almost all answered affirmatively.

But the most important political role belonged to a small group of returnees who unexpectedly appeared near the center of power. All of them—notably Olga Shatunovskaya, Aleksei Snegov, and Valentina Pikina—had been veteran Communist officials before spending many years in Stalin's camps and exile. Freed in 1953 and 1954, they quickly became, thanks to personal connections, part of Khrushchev's extended entourage or that of Mikoyan, his closest ally in the leadership. (Their proximity to the two leaders somewhat eroded lower-level resistance to accommodating returnees.) They were referred to as "Khrushchev's zeks," sometimes admiringly but also derisively.[86]

Khrushchev and Mikoyan clearly trusted those recently released victims more than they did the Stalinist officials who still dominated the Party and state apparatuses. Shatunovskaya and Pikina soon sat on the Party's supreme judiciary body, which oversaw rehabilitation policy; Snegov and Yevsei Shirvindt, another returnee, occupied high positions in the Ministry of the Interior, which administered the Gulag; and Aleksandr Todorsky, a former army officer and zek, was made lieutenant general and deployed in the exoneration of Stalin's military victims.[87]

Snegov and Shatunovskaya, whom an independent Russian philosopher, himself a former zek, called "one of the most remarkable women in the political history of Russia,"[88] were especially influential and active. They "opened the eyes" of Khrushchev and Mikoyan, as their sons later recalled, to the full horrors of Stalin's terror and helped persuade the new Party leader to deliver his historic anti-Stalin speech at the 1956 congress. (In the speech, Khrushchev openly acknowledged Snegov's contribution.) Together Shatunovskaya and Snegov were instrumental in freeing millions of victims, convincing the two leaders to immediately release all the unfortunates in "eternal exile" and to send the "unloading" commissions to the camps. As the fight over de-Stalinization unfolded in ruling circles, according to Khrushchev's son, his father and Mikoyan "needed" Shatunovskaya and Snegov as their "eyes and ears" and also, it seems, for their souls.[89]

All of Stalin's leading heirs had been responsible for thousands of deaths, but only Khrushchev and Mikoyan became repentant Stalinists. (Mikoyan may have been the most committed, though this may have been because of his lesser political and thus less vulnerable position. He personally helped many returnees and even, it seems, pushed for the rehabilitation of Bukharin, a step, as we saw, Khrushchev did not take.)[90] Khrushchev was not the first to adopt de-Stalinizing measures—the police boss Beria set that precedent before his arrest—and he manipulated them in his drive for supreme power.

But that does not explain why Khrushchev made anti-Stalinism such an integral part of his reforms, which eventually affected almost every area of Soviet policymaking; the enormous personal risks he repeatedly took by exposing monstrous official crimes and freeing the survivors; or the immense political capital he expended in, for example, virtually compelling the Party's top leadership to agree to the publication of Solzhenitsyn's *Ivan Denisovich*. It involved a "movement of the heart," as Solzhenitsyn, Medvedev, and other victims concluded, one influenced by "Khrushchev's zeks." How else to explain his astonishing proposal in 1961 to create a memorial to Stalin's victims?[91]

Exposing those crimes brought Khrushchev into recurring conflicts with powerful opponents during his ten years in office, in which his zeks continued to play roles. When he initiated the trials of Beria and several other Stalinist police officials, most from 1953 through 1955, surviving victims appeared as witnesses. When Khrushchev prepared his political bomb for the 1956 congress, he made sure nearly 100 freed zeks would be visible to the 1,500 or so delegates in the hall. When he moved toward a 1957 showdown with leading unrepentant Stalinists—Molotov, Kaganovich, Malenkov, and Voroshilov—Shatunovskaya and Snegov produced evidence of their criminal complicity. When Khrushchev struck publicly at the tenacious Stalin cult by removing the despot's body from the Lenin Mausoleum in 1961, another returnee, Dora Lazurkina, prompted the congressional resolution. And to undermine the myth of Stalin's Gulag as "correctional labor," Khrushchev then arranged for the publication of a former zek's unvarnished portrayal of life in the camps, Solzhenitsyn's *Ivan Denisovich*.[92]

By the 1960s, returnees were contributing to de-Stalinization in another important way. Controversy over the past often inflames politics, but rarely so intensely as in the Soviet 1950s and 1960s (and again in the 1980s). The Stalin era was still "living history" for most Soviet adults, whose understanding of it had been shaped by decades of personal sacrifice and a falsified official history maintained by censorship and continued repression. According to that sanctioned version, Stalin's rule was a succession of great national achievements, from collectivization and industrialization in the 1930s to the nation's victory over Nazi Germany in 1945 and subsequent rise to superpower status. Post-Stalin elites were a product of that era, and for them it legitimized their power and privileges. As a young historian (and victim's son) soon discovered, they were determined to "defend it, defending themselves."[93]

The return of so many victims, even if mute, was irrefutable evidence of a parallel history of equally great crimes. And not all returnees were mute. As Khrushshev foresaw, they told "their relatives and friends and acquaintances what actually happened." For young people in particular, "Their testimonies shed new light on events."[94] Most such returnees were still Soviet loyalists; they contributed to the kind of revisionist history and discussion of historical alternatives needed for a politics of reform. But other repressed traditions were also represented. The old

Menshevik Mikhail Yakubovich and SR Irina Kakhovskaya, for example, wanted justice for their slain comrades. Solzhenitsyn and Father Dudko spoke for older religious and Slavophile values. And Mikhail Baitalsky, a former Trotskyist, had returned to his Jewish origins.

Like Holocaust survivors, many Stalinist victims wrote Gulag memoirs because "This Must Not Happen Again," among them Suren Gazaryan, Ginzburg, Kopelev, Lev Razgon, Gnedin, and Baitalsky.[95] Others became self-made historians. As an official investigator of Stalin's crimes, Shatunovskaya collected documents and interviews that researchers still use today. Snegov's abiding theme, "Stalin Against Lenin," took him into closed archives and on impassioned lecture tours. Todorsky and Aleksandr Milchakov, another Communist survivor, did much the same.[96]

Because their lives lay ahead of them, many children of Stalin's victims, perhaps most of them, later reconciled themselves to the Soviet system and made successful careers in its bureaucracies. There were many examples, but the most high-ranking seems to have been Pyotr Masherov, head of the Soviet Belorussian Communist Party from 1965 to 1980 and a candidate member of the national Politburo, whose father had died in a camp in 1938. In this case, as in others, we are told not to be surprised that the "son of a person illegally repressed by the Soviet authorities (and rehabilitated in 1959) could be a sincere, convinced supporter of that same regime. . . . Such were the times, and the people, forged in the crucible of the 1930s and 1940s."[97]

But other children of victims followed the lead of outspoken returnees. The twin brothers Roy and Zhores Medvedev and Antonov-Ovseyenko wrote histories of Stalin's despotic rule. Yuri Trifonov, Leonid Petrovsky, Yuri Gastev, Pyotr Yakir, and Kamil Ikramov prepared biographies of their martyred fathers. And a group of children of executed generals collected documents "restoring historical truth" for local museums and schools.[98] (Later, in the 1980s, another son of a Stalin-era victim, Arseny Roginsky, would be one of the founders of the Memorial Society, whose mission was to expose those crimes and help the survivors.)

Only a small portion of this historical truth telling could be published in the Soviet Union under and shortly after Khrushchev. But enough became known, along with increasingly explicit literary accounts, to frighten officials throughout the system. It revealed that their power and privileges were also the product of the victimization of millions of their fellow citizens. Not surprisingly, they were "afraid of History."[99]

Victimizers still in high places had the most to lose. Exposing official crimes gave Khrushchev's other policies a moral dimension, rallied popular support for his leadership, and spurred progressive changes. The social needs of the returnees, for example, contributed to welfare and legal reforms of the period.[100] And, of course, the alternative anti-Stalinist ideas and policies that Khrushchev initiated strongly influenced a new generation of Soviet intellectuals and officials, among them Mikhail Gorbachev. But such revelations, which meant victims now "were in fashion," also galvanized powerful opposition. (Kaganovich, with Shatunovskaya in mind, protested that Khrushchev wanted "to let ex-convicts judge us.")[101] Those endangered were not only Stalin's cohorts who had signed his lists condemning thousands of people but also legions of lesser figures with bloodstains on their careers, such as Ivan Serov, the first post-Stalin KGB chief, and Mikhail Suslov, the rising Party ideologist of the Brezhnev era.[102]

Some people who had prospered under Stalin in various fields followed Khrushchev's repentant example,[103] but the great majority of the complicit fought back. Senior members of the leadership, abetted by protégés in the bureaucracies, tried to sabotage his returnee policies and neuter his 1956 speech. Failing that, they collected documents showing Khrushchev's own considerable role in the terror—as, indeed, neo-Stalinists still do today in order to discredit his historical reputation and any Soviet alternative he may have represented—while trying to conceal or minimize their own crimes, as when Molotov, Kaganovich, and Voroshilov formed a commission to investigate episodes in which they had been deeply involved. When all that failed, they moved in 1957 to depose him, nearly succeeding.[104]

Their fear of a "judgment day" was well founded.[105] As conflicts over the past intensified, questions began to emerge about high-level criminal responsibility similar to those formalized at the Nuremberg Trial a decade before. The analogy was hard to ignore. The Soviet Union had been a prosecuting government at Nuremberg. (Indeed, Khrushchev's new prosecutor general, Roman Rudenko, had been the lead Soviet prosecutor.) And with so many Gulag survivors now visible and their experiences increasingly known, the Holocaust-like dimensions of Stalin-era "repressions" were becoming clear.

When Stalin's other successors tried and executed "Beria's gang" from 1953 through 1955, they attempted to obscure any larger implications. The proceedings were closed, Beria was falsely convicted of treason and espionage, and his misdeeds were disassociated from Stalin's remaining heirs. Even then, however, the charge of "crimes against humanity" was made in at least one case. Reactions to Khrushchev's 1956 revelations indicated that such issues were already present just below the surface. Questions were asked at low-level Party meetings (and quickly suppressed) about the entire leadership's responsibility for what had happened.[106]

Nonetheless, Khrushchev soon crossed another Rubicon, though again behind closed doors. At a June 1957 meeting of the Central Committee, he and his supporters staged a kind of trial of Molotov, Kaganovich, and Malenkov.[107] Quoting horrific documents unearthed by Shatunovskaya and others, they accused Molotov and Kaganovich, along with Stalin, of having been responsible for more than 1.5 million arrests in 1937 and 1938 alone and personally sanctioning 38,679 executions during that period, 3,167 on one day. Bloodthirsty orders in their handwriting were read aloud: "Beat, beat, and beat again. . . . Scoundrel, scum . . . only one punishment—death."

A Soviet Nuremberg seemed to be looming. When the accused defended their actions as "mistakes," they were met with shouts, "No, crimes!" A Khrushchev supporter hurled a threat at the three senior Stalinist leaders that must have chilled many other longtime bosses in the hall: "If the people knew that their hands are dripping with innocent blood, they would greet them not with applause but stones." The implication seemed clear, as another Central Committee member "profoundly" objected: "People who headed and led our Party for so many years turn out to be murderers who need to be put in the dock."[108] In the end, however, Molotov, Kaganovich, and Malenkov were only expelled from the leadership and the Central Committee and banished to minor posts far from Moscow.

It was a moment of high drama, but the crimes still greatly exceeded the punishment. After Stalin died, some fifty to one hundred secret police executioners and brutal interrogators were tried and sentenced, between twenty-five and thirty to death and the rest to prison. (Exact numbers still have not been made known.) Another 2,370 are reported to have received administrative sanctions, from loss of their ranks, awards, and Party membership to their pensions.[109] In addition, a dozen or so high-ranking security and political officials committed suicide, among them camp commandants, NKVD generals, and Aleksandr Fadeyev, Stalin's longtime literary commissar, who was shattered by Khrushchev's disclosures, the sudden return of victimized writers, and alcohol.[110]

Khrushchev's zeks regarded those episodes of justice as first steps and implored him to put on trial or otherwise punish many more people. He resisted "a St Bartholomew's Eve massacre," as he put it, no doubt for several reasons. He, too, had signed death lists and had "blood on his own hands," as his admirer Gorbachev later discovered. Khrushchev even admitted in retirement, "My hands are covered with blood up to my elbows." Also, even though Khrushchev was now the top leader, he remained challengeable and without sufficient high-level support. And, as others paraphrased his explanation, "More people would have to be imprisoned than had been rehabilitated and released."[111]

And yet in October 1961, Khrushchev delivered his most ramifying assault on the Stalinist past and its many defenders. At the Twenty-second Party Congress, he and his supporters considerably expanded the revelations and accusations made in 1956 and 1957—and now did so publicly. For the first time, daily newspaper and broadcast reports of the proceedings informed the nation of "monstrous crimes" and the need for "historical justice," along with lurid accounts of mass arrests, torture, and murder carried out under Stalin across the country. (The former zek Solzhenitsyn, whose novels about those events were not yet published, was astonished: "I don't remember reading anything as interesting as the speeches at the XXII Congress in a long time!")[112]

There was more. This time Khrushchev did not limit the indictment to crimes against Communist Party members, as he had done on previous occasions. The resolution removing Stalin's body from the Lenin Mausoleum spoke simply of "mass repressions against honest Soviet people." And for the first time, Khrushchev and his allies publicly accused Molotov, Kaganovich, and Malenkov of "direct personal responsibility" for those "illegal" acts and demanded they be expelled from the Party (as soon happened), which suggested they might then be put on trial. The specter of trials, inflated by references to "numerous documents in our possession" and Khrushchev's call for a "comprehensive study of all such cases arising out of the abuse of power," sent tremors of fear through the thousands who also bore "direct personal responsibility."

The congress was a victory for Khrushchev's zeks, however temporary. They were partly responsible for its radicalized anti-Stalinism. Still more, in preparation for it Khrushchev had established, behind the scenes, the Shvernik Commission, the first "comprehensive study" of dark events of the 1930s, including the assassination of the Leningrad Party chief Sergei Kirov, which ignited the Great Terror, and the trials and executions of Bukharin and other founders of the Soviet state. Returnees, especially Shatunovskaya, were lead investigators for the commission, which concluded that Stalin had plotted those fateful developments in order to launch a mass terror. On the eve of the congress, Shatunovskaya gave Khrushchev a preliminary report based on the "numerous documents" he would cite there. When he read it, she said, "he wept."[113]

Khrushchev's initiatives at the 1961 congress unleashed an unprecedented three-year struggle between the "friends and foes" of de-Stalinization.[114] Relaxed censorship permitted historians to begin criticizing the entire Stalin era, even his long-sacrosanct collectivization of the peasantry and conduct of the war. But the flood of literary depictions of the twenty-year terror had the greatest impact. Read together, they gave a nearly unvarnished picture of what had happened to millions of people and their families. Among the works published, including ones by and about returnees, was, for example, this poem by Lev Ozerov: "The dead speak . . . / From concentration camps. From isolation cells . . . / Life, while it lasted, left its signature / On the prison floor in a trickle of blood."[115]

Similarly emboldened by Khrushchev's example, victims now determinedly pursued other people who had been personally responsible. Two cases became widely known in Moscow. Writers began a campaign to expose the establishment critic Yakov Elsberg as an "informer" complicit in the arrest and death of novelists and poets. And a returnee, Pavel Shabalkin, brought charges against two of the Party's leading philosophers, until recently members of its Central Committee, Mark Mitin and Pavel Yudin, for having contributed to his long imprisonment and for plagiarizing the work of their other victims. The three escaped real punishment, but the threat was enough to inspire "mental breakdowns" among equally guilty power holders.[116]

Nuremberg-like issues now began to appear, guardedly and ellipti-
cally, in the censored press. They were just below the surface in conflicting reviews of Solzhenitsyn and other terror-related literature but were
more open in other publications.[117] In a chapter from his memoirs, to
take an example that entangled even Khrushchev, Ehrenburg admitted
he had "to live with clenched teeth" under Stalin because he knew his
arrested friends were innocent. His confession, or "theory of a conspiracy of silence," brought furious reactions because if the marginalized
writer Ehrenburg had known the truth, so must have the many officials
above him.[118]

Still worse in their view, the early 1960s brought a spate of Soviet
writings about Germany under Hitler. Some of this commentary was,
by inference, clearly about the Soviet system under Stalin. Readers instinctively saw their own recent experiences in descriptions of the Hitler
cult, the Gestapo, Nazi concentrations camps, informers, and the complicity of so many German officeholders. When the powerful American
film *Judgment at Nuremberg* was shown in Moscow in 1963, reactions
were even more pointed.[119] Considering the emerging analogy with Nazi
Germany, increasingly graphic accounts of Stalin's terror, and more insistent calls for justice, it is understandable why "fears of being made to
answer for their crimes" spread throughout Soviet officialdom.[120]

At some point, even the younger men Khrushchev had put on his leadership council decided his initiatives were endangering too many people,
perhaps the system itself. Unlike Suslov, Leonid Brezhnev and others who
would rule for the next twenty years had little or no blood on their hands
but plenty on their feet. Having risen so rapidly under Stalin as their predecessors were being swept away, they had a "complex about the past."[121]
One defected from Khrushchev as early as 1957, when Dmitri Shepilov
objected to putting the senior Stalinists "in the dock." Indeed, most of
Khrushchev's new coleaders disregarded their benefactor's initiative at
the 1961 congress, remaining conspicuously silent about past crimes.

Resistance to his de-Stalinization policies continued to grow after the
congress, as suggested in a 1962 poem by Yevgeny Yevtushenko prominently published in *Pravda* on Khrushchev's instructions. Entitled "The
Heirs of Stalin," it warned of "many" high officials who still "hate this
era of emptied prison camps."[122] Behind the scenes, Khrushchev was
now being defeated or forced to retreat. In 1962, Snegov and Shatunovskaya were driven from their positions, the Shvernik Commission

report went unpublished and was soon buried, and rehabilitations all but ended. More setbacks followed. Despite Khrushchev's support, Solzhenitsyn was denied the Lenin Prize in literature. And in 1964, a major editorial authorized by Khrushchev on "Stalin and His Heirs" was aborted, along with his proposed constitutional changes to prevent a recurrence of past abuses.[123] Meanwhile, the memorial he had proposed to Stalin's victims remained unbuilt.

When the Central Committee overthrew Nikita Khrushchev in October 1964, the formal indictment did not mention the Stalin question. It focused instead on the seventy-year-old Khrushchev's failed economic and foreign policies, ill-considered reorganizations, increasingly erratic behavior, and dismissive attitude toward "collective leadership." Nonetheless, his anti-Stalinist approach to the past and the present was a central factor. This was, after all, the driving force behind his decade-long attempted reformation of the Soviet system, which was now being ended by a sharp conservative shift in official and popular opinion. Solzhenitsyn was almost certainly right in concluding that the opposition in 1963 and early 1964 to deny him the Lenin Prize had been a "rehearsal for the 'putsch' against Nikita."[124]

There were also clearer indications. Suslov, who particularly resented that Khrushchev "had supported all this camp literature," delivered the detailed indictment, while Mikoyan was the only Central Committee member who tried to defend Khrushchev. (During secret discussions before the formal meeting, he was accused of "reviling Stalin to the point of indecency.")[125] Any doubts were removed when the new leaders moved to end anti-Stalinist policies relating to the past and restore some features of Stalinism, including the tyrant's historical reputation. Solzhenitsyn instinctively called Khrushchev's overthrow a "small October revolution," an overstatement but a clear recognition that the prospect of an anti-Stalinist alternative in Soviet politics had been thwarted, as it turned out, for the next twenty years. Certainly, people with special interests understood the meaning of Khrushchev's ouster. While Beria's men in prison rejoiced, Gulag returnees were informed, "The rehabilitated are no longer in fashion."[126]

THE saga of Gulag returnees and Stalin's other victims continued long after Khrushchev. Most generally, their status in the Soviet Union and in post-Soviet Russia was determined by the changing official reputations of Stalin and Khrushchev, and those were shaped by the relative political fortunes of reformers and conservatives, who represented the two viable policy alternatives inside the Party-state establishment.

The Brezhnev years were a long era of Soviet conservatism. To defend the existing order, the new leadership needed a heroic Stalinist past during which the foundations of the system had been created. Accordingly, it ended Khrushchev's revelations and rehabilitations (a "miserly" twenty-four were granted after 1964),[127] excised him from sanctioned history, except as a "subjective voluntarist," and refurbished Stalin's role by ignoring the terror and emphasizing the wartime victory. (In 1970, a flattering bust was placed on his gravesite behind the Lenin Mausoleum.)

Archive documents later revealed how much Khrushchev's successors despised their patron's policies—and his zeks. In 1974, ten years after being nominated for a Lenin Prize, Solzhenitsyn was arrested and deported from the Soviet Union. Privately discussing the decision, Brezhnev's Politburo blamed Khrushchev for "this social riff-raff." Suslov complained, "We still have not eliminated all the consequences that resulted from Khrushchev." Brezhnev, who said Solzhenitsyn had been justly imprisoned under Stalin, had long harbored a resentment: "He was rehabilitated by two people—Shatunovskaya and Snegov." In 1984, the last leader before Gorbachev, Konstantin Chernenko, took another symbolic step, restoring the Party membership of the ninety-three-year-old Molotov, even meeting with him personally. Rejoicing in private, the Politburo again complained bitterly that Khrushchev had exonerated victims "illegally" and permitted "shameful outrages in relation to Stalin."[128]

During those twenty years, while terror-era police officials were given honorable positions and released from prison with good pensions, others deeply involved in the terror reinvented themselves as benevolent public figures. Lev Sheinin, for example, became an honored writer after helping Vyshinsky falsify the Moscow show trials and prepare the judicial murder of the defendants, and former Gulag commandants published sanitized accounts of their camps as exemplary workplaces. Meanwhile, many of the "rehabilitated no longer felt rehabilitated."[129] Most of them led conformist lives and were left in peace, but many agreed with Antonov-Ovseyenko: "It is the duty of every honest person to write the truth about Stalin. A duty to those who died at his hands, to those who survived that dark night, to those who will come after us." (For this and similar statements, the son of a high NKVD official executed under Khrushchev later characterized Antonov-Ovseyenko as a "raging fanatic.")[130]

In the post-Khrushchev 1960s and 1970s, some victims used their semiestablished positions to be partial truth tellers in the censored media, among them the popular novelists Yuri Trifonov and Chingiz Aitmatov, the playwright Mikhail Shatrov, and the poet-singer Bulat Okudzhava, whose fathers had been shot and mothers sent to the Gulag.[131] Many published poets of those years were also former zeks, including Nikolai Zabolotsky, Olga Berggolts, Anatoly Zhigulin, Yaroslav Smelyakov, and Boris Ruchev. (My returnee friends closely perused their lines for oblique references to the Gulag.) Other survivors wrote only "for the drawer," but quite a few eventually let their manuscripts, with themes of "crime and punishment," circulate in samizdat and be published abroad. And some became leading representatives of public dissent, including Solzhenitsyn, Roy Medvedev, and Andrei Sakharov, whose wife's parents had also been victims.[132]

Considering their age and years of abuse, the majority of Gulag returnees probably did not live to witness the great turnabout under Gorbachev. His declared mission of replacing the system inherited from Stalin with a democratized one meant Gorbachev had to expose its entire criminal history. By the late 1980s, a tidal wave of exposés—documented articles, novels, plays, films, television broadcasts—had flooded the Soviet media. Calling for national "repentance," the result was not the "second Nuremberg" some demanded but nonetheless a media trial of Stalinism, with the newly formed Memorial Society, inspired by Khrushchev's unfulfilled proposal, in the forefront.[133]

Surviving victims and victimizers again played leading roles. While the glasnost press went looking for "hangmen on pension" and secret mass graves of the 1930s and 1940s—a search pioneered by Milchakov's son Aleksandr—Stalin's victims were featured at evenings in memory of the "national martyrology," none more famous than Anna Larina, whose memoirs were published in 1988.[134] One such public event, in 1989, was the first to honor Khrushchev, who had been in official disgrace for more than twenty years. Sitting on the dais with returnees I had interviewed in secret ten years earlier, I saw many other former zeks in the overflowing auditorium. Some of them were weeping. Most now knew the dark side of Khrushchev's career—the blood on his own hands, his failure to tell the full truth about the past, his own repressive measures after 1953. But their gratitude, expressed virtually in one voice, remained undiminished: "Khrushchev gave me back my life."[135]

As with his predecessor in reform, legal justice was also an essential component of Gorbachev's policies. Between 1987 and 1990, a million more individuals were officially rehabilitated, and then, by Gorbachev's decree, all of Stalin's remaining victims.[136] Reacting to those and related actions, Gorbachev's enemies occasionally charged that an "ideology of former zeks" underlay his anti-Stalinism. It may have been partially true: several members of his inner leadership were relatives of Stalin's victims, including Gorbachev himself, whose grandfathers had been arrested in the 1930s.[137] (They survived, but his wife's grandfather was shot.)

In the end, however, it was of little material consequence. There were a few happy exceptions. The dacha Vyshinsky had confiscated in 1937, for example, which had passed after his death in 1954 to several other eminent Soviet figures, including Prime Minister Aleksei Kosygin, was finally returned to the rightful owner's elderly daughter. But despite all the attention and promises given to victims by Gorbachev's policies, many survivors remained so destitute that one of their organizations is-sued an "SOS from the Gulag" pleading for private donations. Bankrupt and crumbling by 1991, Gorbachev's government was never able to pro-vide most of the compensation and benefits it had legislated.[138]

The mixed status of Soviet-era victims continued in post-Soviet Rus-sia. Boris Yeltsin, its first president, formally exonerated all citizens po-litically repressed since October 1917, not just those under Stalin, and then included their children, making them eligible for compensation as well.[139] In addition, Yeltsin declared October 30 a national day in memory of the victims and passed a law giving them and relatives ac-cess to their case files in long-secret archives. (Watching elderly people study those terrible, fateful documents in Lubyanka's reading room, as I did while working there on behalf of the Bukharin family, was deeply moving.)

More generally, tales of the terror era became a familiar aspect of post-Soviet popular culture, including its main medium, television. The Memorial Society developed into a nationwide institution that broad-ened the search for mass graves, sponsored monuments at many Gulag sites, and produced major documentary studies of both victims and victimizers. A growing number of Russian provincial cities published their own martyrologies. And in 2004, Antonov-Ovseyenko, nearly ninety, founded in the center of Moscow the first (and still little-known) official Museum of the History of the Gulag, with the backing of the city's mayor.

On the negative side, however, few of the dwindling number of survivors actually received any meaningful compensation for their lost years or property. By 1993, interest in Stalin's terror and its victims had undergone a "catastrophic fall,"[140] and the national memorial proposed by Khrushchev in 1961 and endorsed by Gorbachev while he was in power was still unbuilt. By the early twenty-first century, pro-Stalin attitudes had grown significantly in both official circles and popular opinion, along with the number of burnished reputations of odious NKVD bosses, outspoken Gulag deniers, and attacks on "rehabilitation euphoria." Increasingly it was said, and perhaps believed, that all Gulag zeks had been common criminals because "Stalin did not repress any honest citizens."[141]

Most Western observers attributed favorable post-Soviet attitudes toward Stalin to the increasingly authoritarian rule of Vladimir Putin, the former KGB officer who became Russian president in 2000. In reality, though the phenomenon grew under Putin, most of its elements began in the 1990s, under Yeltsin. Foremost among them was the economic and social pain inflicted by "shock therapy," which was the primary source of the pro-Stalin revival, and the decline of democratic practices after Yeltsin destroyed a popularly elected parliament with tanks and mortgaged the country's future to a new oligarchical elite based on pillaged state property.

Nor was anti-Stalinism suppressed under Putin. Access to relevant archives, though somewhat more limited, continued, at least in those where I worked; thick volumes of previously unknown terror-era documents were published; the number of local Gulag monuments and exhibits grew; the renamed KGB (FSB), carrying on a practice started under Gorbachev, met with and even honored a number of its former victims; films based on popular anti-Stalinist novels, including Solzhenitsyn's *The First Circle* and Anatoly Rybakov's *Children of the Arbat*, were made for and shown on state-controlled television; and an international conference on the Stalinist terror was held in Moscow in December 2008.[142]

Indeed, Putin's own role in this regard was contradictory. On the one hand, he made highly publicized statements supporting a new textbook that gave an almost entirely favorable picture of the Stalinist 1930s as a decade of "mobilization" and "modernization" and of Stalin himself as an indispensable leader to whom there had been no real alternative. On the other hand, one of Putin's first acts as president was to authorize an expanded official investigation of Stalin-era crimes. And two of his last acts as president, in 2007, the seventieth anniversary of the peak of the Great Terror, were to personally present an award to Solzhenitsyn, who still personified the Gulag fate of millions, and to attend a commemoration of Stalin's victims at an infamous NKVD killing field and burial site, the first such appearance ever by a Russian (or Soviet) leader.[143] When Solzhenitsyn died in 2008, the government, now headed by Putin and the new president Dmitri Medvedev, gave him the equivalent of a state funeral and adopted measures to memorialize his life.

The contradiction in Putin's behavior reflected the still profound division in Russia's political elite and society over the Stalinist past. Opinion surveys taken fifty-five years after Stalin died, a half a century after most survivors of his terror had returned, and nearly twenty years after the Soviet Union ended showed that the nation was almost evenly divided between those who thought Stalin had been a "wise leader" and those who thought he was an "inhuman tyrant," with pro-Stalin views no less widespread among young Russians.[144]

Those findings mean that the struggle in Russia's political life (and soul) over the significance of the Stalin era, which is as much about the nation's present and future as about its past, is not over. (In an open letter to Putin and Medvedev in 2008, for example, Gorbachev and other public figures renewed the call for a national monument in memory of Stalin's victims. As before, it aroused both support and determined opposition.)[145] No one can say how or when the struggle will end, but one thing seems certain. No matter how remote and extinguished the heat of the Stalinist past may appear to be, it will make itself felt again in Russian politics, as it did so fatefully in the late 1980s when it inflamed both the friends and foes of Gorbachev's reforms.[146]

This is so for three reasons. First, though most of Stalin's victims are dead, Russia remains a country significantly populated by their descendants, at least 27 percent of the nation according to a 2006 poll, particularly their grandchildren.[147] Second, leadership for a new political reckoning with the past in search of lost alternatives is likely to come from the generation that matured during Gorbachev's glasnost revelations, much as the "children of the Twentieth Party Congress" and Khrushchev's Thaw provided it in the late 1980s. But most crucially, such a reckoning remains on Russia's political agenda because, as events have repeatedly shown, there is no statute of limitations for historical crimes as large as Stalin's. In all these respects, the victims' return is not over.

3 THE TRAGEDY OF SOVIET CONSERVATISM

In the West, they respect people of conservative views.
                    YEGOR LIGACHEV, 1990

We are conservatives, and let us not be ashamed of the word.
                    IVAN POLOZKOV, RUSSIAN COMMUNIST LEADER, 1991

GREAT events, especially unexpected and torrential ones, are not easily understood, even in retrospect. As time passes, they often recede into a historical haze of misconceptions, myths, and, as I will point out more than once in this book, amnesia.

This is certainly true of the fateful Soviet years from 1985 to 1991, when four great transformations—even, it might be argued, revolutions— were begun under the leadership of Mikhail Gorbachev: attempts to transform the authoritarian political system into some kind of democracy, the state command economy into a market-based one, the Moscow-dominated "union" into an authentic federation, and the country's forty-year Cold War with the West into a "strategic partnership." The results included remarkable successes, crushing setbacks, and finally, of course, the end of the Soviet Union, the most consequential event of the second half of the twentieth century.

Not surprisingly, those tumultuous years remain poorly understood. Several of the enduring misconceptions and myths involve one of the most representative figures of the last years of Soviet Union, Yegor Ligachev, the second-ranking politician in the new leadership formed under Gorbachev in 1985. (Even more significant misconceptions about Gorbachev himself are examined in chapter 6.) In most Western accounts since the late 1980s, Ligachev has been portrayed as the archvillain of Soviet reform—the chief "enemy of perestroika," a "diehard conservative," even a reactionary "neo-Stalinist."[1]

Empowered by his position as de facto head of the Communist Party apparatus, Ligachev is said to have opposed and obstructed Gorbachev's political and economic changes for the sake of a dogmatic, orthodox Marxism-Leninism. His intrigues were behind many of the worst deeds in the struggle over perestroika, from protecting corrupt officials and excusing the crimes of the Stalin era to bloodshed in the streets of Tbilisi in April 1989. In short, Ligachev is said to have represented almost everything bad and unrepentant in the Soviet system that collapsed in December 1991.

Some aspects of this standard account have a partial basis in actual events, but most of it continues the long Western practice of imposing gray stereotypes on complex Soviet realities—and now post-Soviet ones. Insisting that he had been made the "fall guy" for Gorbachev's failures and the victim of a "witch hunt" by his enemies, Ligachev took the then almost unprecedented step of publishing candid memoirs—in Russia in 1992 and in the United States in 1993—to refute "blasphemous" accusations that had originated in the Soviet media and spread to the West.[2] Like many American politicians, he may have put too much blame on the press for his misfortunes, but Ligachev's memoirs, along with other evidence, effectively challenged the stereotypical version of his role—and that of other Soviet "conservatives"—in historic events.

Without the full backing of Ligachev and the scores of regional Party bosses he represented, to take a ramifying example, Gorbachev probably could not have come to power in March 1985 against the clear wishes of an aged but entrenched Moscow Party-state oligarchy. Even more crucially, without a coalition for change in which Ligachev played a leading role—about which, more below—Gorbachev would not have been able to initiate any of his liberalizing, and then democratizing, policies of the next three years.

Consider Ligachev's position in three of those early policy disputes. He supported the decision to release a previously banned film, *Repentance*, which reopened public discussion of Stalin's crimes after more than twenty years; the decision to ease the Soviet controls imposed on

Eastern Europe after World War II, which eventually led to the unraveling of the Soviet empire there; and the decision to end the disastrous seven-year Soviet war in Afghanistan, which had obstructed a full rapprochement with the West.[3] And even though Ligachev's policy disagreements with Gorbachev were acute by 1989, along with his feeling of having been betrayed, there is no evidence that he joined any of the intrigues in the apparatus to remove Gorbachev as Communist Party leader. Nor did he participate in, or know about beforehand, the failed armed coup against Gorbachev in August 1991, which so weakened the Soviet leader's central government it could not withstand the centrifugal forces unfolding across the country.

Ligachev's personal qualities are also hard to squeeze into the stereotype. Even political figures loyal to Gorbachev and generally admired in Western accounts characterize Ligachev as being deeply sincere, proudly incorruptible, and habitually straightforward in his political relations.[4] Indeed, such was his reputation in virtually all Soviet political quarters before 1985 and for some time thereafter. Even later, when the leadership was angrily divided, no reliable insider seems to have believed the potentially explosive corruption charges leveled against him in 1989 by two politically motivated and subsequently discredited prosecutors. And while suspicions about Ligachev's behind-the-scenes political role persisted, there is little in the documentary record or personal testimonies to suggest an intriguer, at least not more so than is customary among professional politicians.[5] With the rough-hewn and blunt Ligachev, what friends and foes alike saw seems to have been about what they got.

That was my own impression when I first met him in mid-1990, as he was exiting the political stage, unwillingly and defiantly, at age seventy. A stocky, still strongly built figure of medium height, with thin but impressive white hair atop a ruddy Siberian complexion and riveting blue eyes, Ligachev's emphatic way of speaking and gesturing reminded another American observer of the "hard-knuckle stage presence of James Cagney in old age,"[6] though Spencer Tracy's anachronistic politician in *The Last Hurrah* came to my mind. As I got to know Ligachev and his family better in the 1990s, he always seemed old-fashioned—in his down-home traditional values, political outlook, and courtly manners—and like another familiar American type: the native of the provincial heartland who after many urban years still felt and looked out of place in the big city. Unknowingly, Ligachev once even uttered the Russian version of the

American cliché: "I prefer Siberia, where people tell you what they think to your face. In Moscow they stab you in the back."

Old-fashioned did not, however, mean "dogmatic," though the word was attached to Ligachev like a hereditary title in the radicalized politics of perestroika. In our conversations about history and contemporary politics, he always had strong views but also a willingness, even an eagerness, to consider different opinions. On the few occasions his aides joined us, they seemed more ideologically "dogmatic" than their considerably older boss. In fact, as Ligachev maintains in his memoirs and as the public record indicates, he "rethought many things" about the political and economic system in which he had lived his entire life and risen to the top. Not so many things as Gorbachev and some others rethought but more than we expect from successful politicians well after their middle age.

Even Ligachev's decision to publish revealing memoirs about his years in power was unorthodox in the Soviet context. Like most memoirs of former political leaders everywhere, they were not objective, thoroughly trustworthy, or the whole story. Retired power holders write such books for self-serving purposes, even apart from financial gain: to settle political scores, embellish their biographies, and influence future historians. Several high-level members of Gorbachev's team later wrote their accounts, including the leader himself, but Ligachev's were the first Soviet leadership memoirs to be published inside the country. Until then, they had been precluded by political reticence, repression, Party "discipline," and censorship.[7]

Gorbachev's gradual abolition of all four restraints brought personality into Soviet public politics. A number of purported political memoirs and autobiographies preceded Ligachev's book, but none was comparably revealing about the inner history of perestroika. Andrei Gromyko, the longtime foreign minister and Politburo member, published a thick volume of "memoirs" that maintained his tight-lipped tradition. Gorbachev's foreign minister and Politburo ally, Eduard Shevardnadze, produced a semiautobiographical book that was grandly "not a political memoir." And Boris Yeltsin, briefly a junior member of the Gorbachev leadership, issued in 1990, on the eve of being elected president of the Soviet Russian Republic, a "confessional" autobiography that was surprisingly uninformative and, not surprisingly, more akin to a campaign biography. Again, the "orthodox" Ligachev broke the mold.[8]

None of this means that Ligachev was a political hero, though many Russians who share his view that a hijacking of perestroika led to the collapse of the Soviet system still think of him in that way. Personally, though I liked Ligachev, our outlooks were different, as he noted in his memoirs: "I did not share Cohen's views on the processes taking place in the USSR, and . . . he was not among those who shared my position." But if we persist in the American habit of judging Soviet and post-Soviet leaders by the extent to which they embrace our ideas, try to replicate our system, or otherwise resemble us, we will never understand what has happened in Russia since 1985 or what lies ahead. Ligachev challenges us to understand more by judging less. Or, as another prominent Russian, considerably more Westernized than Ligachev, liked to advise foreigners about the future of his country: "You can't expect people to leap out of their biographies or society out of its history any more than you expect a man to leap out of his skin."[9]

YEGOR Ligachev's biography spanned almost the entire history of the Soviet Union, reflecting many of its contradictions, complexities, and catastrophes. Ten years older than Gorbachev, his personal experiences help explain his more ambivalent attitudes toward the past, which later caused conflicts with other members of the leadership.

Ligachev was born into a Siberian peasant family in November 1920, when Lenin's Communist Party was consolidating its rule during the three-year Russian civil war. As often happened in the 1920s, the family left its village for a city, Novosibirsk, where his father found work in a factory. Unlike Gorbachev and many other leading *perestroishchiki*, Ligachev grew to full manhood and began his career in the Stalin era, when the modern-day Soviet system had been created. Even today, as I emphasized in the preceding chapter, many Russians have profoundly conflicting feelings about the Stalinist 1930s and 1940s, a traumatic epoch of towering achievements and monstrous crimes that are hard to reconcile. Millions of people fell victim to the despot's brutal collectivization of the peasantry and capricious mass terror, but millions of others labored heroically and rose in the campaigns to forge a mighty industrial nation, defeat the Nazi German invaders, and create a superpower.

Both experiences were part of Ligachev's life. Presumably a good student, and even though his father was briefly expelled from the

Communist Party, he was admitted at college age in the late 1930s to a prestigious institute of aviation engineering in Moscow and thus began a not untypical Soviet version of the American Horatio Alger saga. Immediately after graduation, Ligachev returned to Novosibirsk to work in a plant building fighter planes for the Soviet victory in World War II. Among the 27 million or more Soviet citizens who died in that war was Ligachev's older brother, who was killed and buried in Germany.

The war might have been remembered triumphantly, but not so an even darker episode in Ligachev's life. His wife's father, a Soviet army general, had been executed in Stalin's purge of the military high command in 1937 after a typical ten-minute "trial" by a terror tribunal. As Ligachev explained in a memoir chapter on his encounters with Stalin's crimes, he, too, therefore became part of a "family of an enemy of the people." Understandably, he wrote (and spoke) harshly of Stalin and warmly of Nikita Khrushchev, whose rehabilitation policies of the 1950s exonerated Ligachev's father-in-law. On the other hand, not much can be inferred about later political conflicts from that experience since families of other members of the Gorbachev leadership had also been victimized by Stalin's terror.

Little is known about the beginning of Ligachev's political career. Having joined the Communist Party in 1944, he soon left his original profession to become a full-time Party functionary in the local Young Communist League (Komsomol). In a private communication, Ligachev says he was told to do so and had no choice. "Things were simple in those days: Either you agreed or you were expelled from the Party, which meant being fired from the plant." Possibly it happened that way, though Ligachev never seems to have looked back with regret. In his memoirs, he recounts seven unemployed and perilous months in 1949 when he was under Moscow's suspicion of being a Trotskyist "enemy of the people" and had been fired as chief of the Novosibirsk Komsomol organization. But apart from that personal brush with Stalin's terror machine, he moved gradually up the Party's nomenklatura ladder—the far-flung pyramid of appointed officials who oversaw the vast Soviet political and economic system.

After a number of secondary positions in Novosibirsk, Ligachev's political career leaped forward under Khrushchev, whose pioneering reforms, as I noted earlier, inspired a still younger generation of would-be Party officials, most famously Gorbachev. For Ligachev, the turning point was his appointment in 1958 as Party chief of a district where a large Academy of Sciences town was to be built, and in 1959 of the whole Novosibirsk area. Evidently he oversaw the important project admirably and got along well with the freer-minded scientific intellectuals flooding into Academic City, including Abel Aganbegyan, a maverick economist and who eventually became an adviser to Gorbachev. Thirty years later, Aganbegyan recalled Ligachev as having been an innovative, "unorthodox" Party boss and doubted his anti-perestroika reputation.[10] Ligachev's work took him occasionally to Moscow, where he began to meet with top leaders, even Khrushchev. In 1961, he was promoted to the headquarters of the Central Committee apparatus in Moscow, where he served until 1965 as deputy chief of propaganda, and then of Party personnel, for the entire Russian Republic.

Why Ligachev returned to Siberia in 1965 and did not resume a Moscow position for seventeen years is not fully clear. Few Party bureaucrats, or anyone else, would have willingly given up the capital's special powers and privileges for life in the remote provinces. In his memoirs, Ligachev says he requested the transfer because he yearned to work with "real people." Did he feel uneasy with the new Brezhnev leadership that had overthrown Khrushchev and already was staffing Party headquarters with antireformist officials, some of them highly corruptible? Certainly, he was not on a fast track during Brezhnev's long reign.

Ligachev described the seventeen years as head of the Tomsk Regional Party organization as the best of his life but admitted that the appointment was both remote and relatively "insignificant." Thus, while the younger Gorbachev, who held the same position in the Stavropol region, became a full member of the Central Committee in 1971, Ligachev achieved that exalted standing only in 1976. If nothing else, Ligachev's flinty rectitude evidently irritated the Moscow power mafia around Brezhnev, as illustrated by its attempt in the early 1980s to send him into ambassadorial exile and his stubborn refusal to go. (Ligachev told this story several times, probably to contrast his defiance with the compliance of his archrival in the Gorbachev leadership, Aleksandr Yakovlev, who had accepted diplomatic banishment to Canada in 1973.)

On the other hand, Ligachev hardly fell out of the power elite during his years in Tomsk. As Communist Party first secretary for an entire region, he was one of about seventy-five such bosses who directly ruled Soviet Russia, where the great majority of citizens lived. Most Western observers have portrayed provincial Party bosses as having been congenitally conservative tyrants running roughshod over their region's populace and resources. But some scholars have viewed them as increasingly qualified—though never elected—governors or prefects trying to cope with an impossible array of technical problems and everyday responsibilities, from economic production and distribution to educational and cultural life, in an often irrational system.[11] However characterized, they were exceedingly powerful rulers in their provinces, unilaterally capable of benevolent or evil deeds, but frequently at the mercy of higher authorities in Moscow. Nor were all regional Party bosses alike. Among them in the 1970s, for example, were Ligachev, Gorbachev, Shevardnadze, Yeltsin, and a host of others who later enthusiastically supported or opposed the reforms of the late 1980s.

What little we know about Ligachev's role in Tomsk generally corresponds to the sparse account he gives in his memoirs. A teetotaler, self-confident, hard-working, a little self-righteous, and a scandal-free family man, he modernized the region's industry and agriculture, developed new enterprises, preserved Tomsk's historic wooden buildings, patronized the arts, and minded the Party's monopolistic interests wherever necessary. It is easy to understand why Ligachev was proud of his tenure in Tomsk and did not like Gorbachev's post-1985 practice of indiscriminately branding the Brezhnev years an "era of stagnation."

By 1988, Ligachev had become a lightning rod for unleashed resentments against power holders under Brezhnev, even though others in the Gorbachev leadership had been more high-ranking. Rising to defend himself at a nationally televised Party conference, and also to condemn the Brezhnev regime for what it had done to the country, Ligachev made a statement that was widely mocked but no doubt came from the heart:

> In the years of stagnation, I lived and worked in Siberia—a harsh but truly wonderful land. I am often asked what I was doing during that time. I answer with pride: I was building socialism. And there were millions like me. It would be an act of betrayal if I did not mention those with whom I linked my fate and shared joys and sorrow. Many of them have left this life. Not everything turned out as we wanted. . . . But we worked without looking over our shoulders, perhaps because we knew they couldn't send us any farther away than Siberia. We worked in or-

der to give the people a better life, to give the state more, and to protect the interests of the province.[12]

There Ligachev remained until 1983, when Yuri Andropov, Brezhnev's successor as Party general secretary, recalled him to Moscow. Ligachev's admiration for Andropov, who died fifteen months after becoming leader, later bordered on reverential nostalgia. By the end of the 1980s, that sentiment was widespread among Party officials disenchanted with Gorbachev's reforms. Andropov was neither the radical reformer portrayed by some Soviet writers nor the "strongman" Western observers mistook him for when he took office, at sixty-eight and already gravely ill, in November 1982.

Not unlike the conflicted political figures that appear so often in Russian literature, Andropov had been an enthusiastic anti-Stalinist under Khrushchev, but fifteen years as head of the KGB under Brezhnev had deeply implicated him in many "stagnant" policies, from the cover-up of the country's grave economic condition and the repression of dissidents to the 1979 invasion of Afghanistan. So contradictory was Andropov's role—privately he wrote poetry and shunned the rampant corruption around Brezhnev—that even the great Soviet dissenter Andrei Sakharov, one of his victims, later commented sympathetically on this "duality."[13]

Nonetheless, Andropov was the godfather of Gorbachev's original perestroika. Determined to use his brief time in office to address the country's growing problems, Andropov infused political life with expectations of change for the first time since the 1960s, initiated a series of economic "experiments" that promised to be more than half-measures, and behind the scenes encouraged far-reaching reconsiderations of Brezhnev's domestic and foreign policies. Apart from disciplinarian and anti-corruption campaigns directed mainly against the old-guard Brezhnev establishment, few new policies were actually adopted by Andropov. Opposition was great, time short, and his own outlook no doubt deeply ambivalent.

In another respect, however, Andropov mattered greatly. Using the appointment powers of the general secretary, he gathered a team of younger reform-minded officials from various Party and state bureaucracies on behalf of his preferred successor, Mikhail Gorbachev, and put the coalition in position to contend for power. Ligachev, at sixty-three, was one of its oldest but also most important members. They were unable to make Gorbachev leader when Andropov died in February 1984; the septuagenarian old guard, unnerved by prospects of major reforms and retirement, preferred an ailing seventy-two-year-old Brezhnev surrogate, Konstantin Chernenko. But when Chernenko died thirteen months later, Andropov's protégés succeeded, as Ligachev explained in his memoirs more fully than had anyone else.

The Gorbachev leadership that launched the most fateful reforms of the late twentieth century therefore was actually assembled by Andropov. Even the original inner Politburo group—in addition to Gorbachev and Ligachev, it included the new head of the state ministries, Nikolai Ryzhkov, and the KGB chief, Viktor Chebrikov—numbered men of varying political outlooks and loyalties. Later, as Gorbachev began to rely on his more radical Politburo allies, notably Shevardnadze, Yakovlev, and Vadim Medvedev, protests could be heard in the apparatus that he had betrayed Andropov's legacy and that Ligachev was its real representative.[14] Like most political nostalgia, much of this was mythical, but not all of it. Just as the Party elite had always been full of conflicting views and interests, so was the Gorbachev leadership that governed the Soviet Union from 1985 to its breakup in 1991.

CONTRARY to widespread misconceptions in the West, neither the Soviet Communist Party nor its high-level officialdom had ever been politically monolithic. How could they have been in a one-party system with nearly twenty million members by the 1980s, where anyone who wanted to engage in sanctioned politics had to enter the Communist establishment, and in a country with such divisive "living history"? Ideological and policy disputes raged openly in the Party elite from 1917 until Stalin settled those issues by firing squad in the 1930s and frightened the survivors into silence. When terror ended in the 1950s, conflicting policy and ideological views reappeared in the Party-controlled press, sometimes rather candidly but usually in muted and Aesopian ways, depending on the degree of censorship at the time.

In modern times, the fundamental conflict was between Party conservatives and Party reformers.[15] When told this, American conservatives usually reject the idea that they had Soviet Communist counterparts, but it is another example of refusing to understand foreign politics in its own context. Every political society has a status quo and thus conservatives who wish to preserve it, almost always in the name of historical practices and values, and reformers who insist on improving it, arguing that existing practices have become obsolete and national values remain unfulfilled. In the latter-day Soviet Union, the status quo was the system called socialism inherited from Stalin.

In addition to liberating Gulag survivors, Khrushchev's reforms undermined Stalinist dogmas and liberalized the system in important ways, but they did not dismantle its essential institutional nature: the Party-state's monopolistic bureaucratic controls over society, including the vast economy run by Moscow ministries. Nonetheless, his reforms were so divisive that something akin to subterranean crypto-parties formed in the Communist Party, creating a kind of "multiparty-ness," as was later acknowledged, inside the one-party system. Officially concealed and denied in the name of "Party unity," those rival political movements finally burst into the open thirty years later in response to Gorbachev's more radical reforms. In the late 1980s, even the official Communist Party newspaper acknowledged the "secret rivalry that always existed," and wondered: "How many parties are there in our Party?"[16]

At least three intra-Party movements had taken shape by the time Khrushchev was overthrown in 1964: anti-Stalinist reformers who called for a substantial reduction of controls over society, including more political liberalization and some marketization of the state economy; neo-Stalinist reactionaries who charged that Khrushchev's reforms had gravely weakened Party-government controls and orthodoxies and who demanded that they be strengthened, if not fully restored; and Party conservatives who objected to the "excesses" of both Stalin's rule and Khrushchev's reforms and sought mainly to preserve the new post-Stalin status quo by opposing any further significant changes, whether forward or backward. The conservative majority, headed by the authoritarian but mild-mannered Brezhnev, ruled the Soviet Union for the next two decades, with concessions mostly to the neo-Stalinists. The Party's reform movement barely survived, but it eventually came to power with Gorbachev as its leader.

Ligachev's political evolution before 1985 illustrates and helps explain that dramatic turnabout. Several large factors lay behind the reemergence of reform-minded officials in the Communist Party on the eve of Brezhnev's death in 1982—the country's development into a more urban and educated society, the aging and passing of the old guard that had risen to high office under Stalin, the ascent of the Gorbachev generation that had entered politics under Khrushchev, the Soviet elite's greater exposure to the West—but the system's mounting economic problems were the most important. Hypercentralized, bureaucratic management had made the economy increasingly irrational and inefficient, thwarting even minor changes and isolating it from technological developments in capitalist countries. By the late 1970s, economic growth had virtually stopped, while enormous state expenditures for the Cold War military and for the cradle-to-grave welfare provisions of Soviet socialism, including large subsidies for most essential goods and services, continued to grow.

The Brezhnev leadership did nothing about the "pre-crisis," as Gorbachev later termed it, but Ligachev and other regional Party officials could not ignore it. They had long been the political mainstay and beneficiaries of Brezhnev-era conservatism—maliciously called the "golden era of the nomenklatura"—but now had to cope daily with economic decay and a plethora of related social ills. Even provincial Party bosses with no interest in real political reform believed that Brezhnev's status quo policies "had led the country into a dead end."[17] Enlightened bureaucrats (as they were also known in tsarist times) in the Moscow state ministries, represented by Ryzhkov, had reached the same conclusion. Two decades of conservative consensus in the Soviet political elite had ended; longtime conservatives were ready for an "anti-stagnation" coalition with their erstwhile reformist foes. Anti-Stalinist policy advisers and intellectuals were already gathered around Gorbachev, who had earlier put himself at the head of the resurgent reform movement. And there is no reason to doubt Ligachev's memoir account of why and how an influential group of regional Party bosses also backed Gorbachev in March 1985.

That Ligachev and other conservatives turned reformers soon clashed with Gorbachev, and eventually accused him of having betrayed his mandate, is not surprising. They wanted to save the system by improving it, not by reinventing it, as Gorbachev was soon trying to do. But this should not obscure their crucial role in Soviet history. Again, without their participation, there could not have been a reform leadership in the 1980s, or perhaps even later. Like the best conservatives in the history of other countries, they understood that when it was time to change, it was necessary to change. And thus Ligachev and Ryzhkov—Gorbachev's "closest comrades" in the original leadership, according to all of their memoirs—became progressives, moderate reformers, or, as Ligachev liked to say, "realists." That they supported, or tolerated, Gorbachev's increasingly radical policies as long as they did was a tribute to his leadership abilities, but also to their own political qualities. Ligachev may have remained a conservative with old-fashioned Soviet values, but he was hardly a diehard or reactionary one.

In fact, both reformers and conservatives in the Communist Party had "rethought many things" since the 1950s, and again after 1985. Gorbachev's radical reformers evolved far beyond Khrushchev's anti-Stalinist legacy, which called for a return to the more tolerant kind of one-party dictatorship associated with Lenin in the NEP 1920s and for rationalizing the stagnated economy, and then beyond Leninism itself. By the late 1980s, Gorbachev's program called for a mixed economy based on market relations, a multiparty parliamentary democracy based on the rule of law, a real federation of Soviet republics, and "universal human values" instead of Marxist-Leninist ones.[18] Such tenets closely resembled those of European social democratic parties, and not at all those long practiced by the Soviet Communist Party. For some Communist officials like Boris Yeltsin, Gorbachev's "humane democratic socialism" was too little or too late. But for a great many Party functionaries, his heresy, or "ideological AIDS," was far too much.[19] They fought against every plank of Gorbachev's program, clinging to Brezhnev-era fundamentalism or even lurching back to neo-Stalinism.

Ligachev's reaction, like that of a number of other influential antiradicals, was significantly different. As deputy Party leader, and even after losing the post in 1988 but remaining in the leadership, he supported Gorbachev's general reforms while trying to guide them in "healthy" directions and guard against "excesses." Ultraradicals later accused Gorbachev of being a centrist, but that best described the position Ligachev thought he occupied between Gorbachev and the Party's real diehards, as well as its "extremists" on the other side.

Having abandoned many Communist dogmas of the past, Ligachev accepted the need for a significant degree of economic marketization and demonopolization, glasnost, political liberalization, and reforms in the ersatz Union, but always while protesting their "extremes," as he saw them—"anti-Communism" in politics, "slander" in writing history, "capitalism" in economics, "anti-Sovietism" in the republics. Eventually he was willing to relinquish the Communist Party's dictatorship in politics, the state's monopoly in economics, and the central government's dominance over the republics, but not the primacy of those institutions in a reformed Soviet system. To yield any more, he said, "I'd have to cross out my whole life."[20]

In the end, Ligachev became a tragic figure—a moderate reformer in radical times, a progressive conservative when everything sacred fell under attack. He occasionally retreated into fundamentalist postures, but only briefly and not often. In some respects, he shared the tortuous fate of most Communist Party conservatives who until the Gorbachev years had been trapped in a pseudo-revolutionary ideology. Despite their authentic conservatism—a deep reverence for the past, abiding attachment to the present, and instinctive anxiety about change—they could not even acknowledge their real political identity: officially, "conservatives" were all those anti-Soviet forces in the West.

Liberated by Gorbachev's political reforms and the advent of "pluralism," the conservatives finally came out of the closet to protest the radicalization of perestroika. In 1990, younger, tougher-minded conservatives formed their own, predominantly anti-Gorbachev Russian Communist Party. Its leader, Ivan Polozkov, responded candidly to Communist reformers "who call us conservatives, investing that word with exclusively negative meaning. But the real content of conservatism, if we take its scholarly definition, is the preservation and maintenance of the basic foundations of state and social life. . . . In this sense, we are conservatives, and let us not be ashamed of the word."[21]

As was clear from Ligachev's memoirs, he remained, if not ashamed, a little ambivalent about the word. For him, the "real conservatives" were now forces in the country that wanted to abolish the Soviet socialist system for a capitalist one, and to destroy the Union on behalf of nationalist separation. But ultimately he counted himself among the proponents of "healthy conservatism"—the "true supporters of perestroika who were trying to prevent it from falling into the pernicious trap of radicalism." The new generation of Communist conservatives, however, had little use for Ligachev by the early 1990s. In their eyes, he had supported Gorbachev too much and for too long, was insufficiently militant, and perhaps too old. When Ligachev rose to commit another unorthodox act by running for election as deputy Party leader against Gorbachev's hand-chosen candidate at the national congress in July 1990—the first ranking Communist to act so boldly in sixty years—they gave him a rousing ovation and then voted against him.[22]

THE Soviet Communist Party Congress that retired Ligachev turned out to be its last. In the aftermath of the failed coup in August 1991, the Party was banned by Russian President Yeltsin and, after his release from house arrest, by Soviet President Gorbachev; it largely disintegrated, before reemerging as a post-Soviet party. Four months later, a Yeltsin-led group of former Communist officials, now acting as presidents of Soviet republics, declared their respective independence and dissolved the Union. For Gorbachev, it was the end of his six-year struggle to carry out a full-scale Soviet reformation, and of his power, indeed, his country. For Ligachev, it was the collapse of everything he held "most sacred."

Russian political culture has always been leader-dominated, so it is not surprising that in his memoirs Ligachev puts much of the blame on Gorbachev. If he often does so more indirectly and gingerly than we might expect, surely it is because he stood alongside Gorbachev, sharing "full responsibility," as he ruefully acknowledges, for much of the time. Indeed, his relationship—perhaps obsession—with Gorbachev is a central theme of his memoirs, whose original Russian title was *The Gorbachev Enigma*, an odd choice for a book about his own life. (For the second Russian edition he changed the title to *A Warning*.)[23] As Ligachev tells the story of perestroika, and thus the last chapter in Soviet history, the country came to ruin partly, even largely, because of his own inability to win the "battle for Gorbachev" against ever-destructive forces around the leader.

According to his account, the golden years of perestroika—and in his relations with Gorbachev—were from 1985 to 1987, or perhaps to early 1988. It is easy to understand why Ligachev always eulogized this period. He was at the height of his power and contentment as the number-two Party leader, and Gorbachev was still in the initial stage of his emergence as a radical reform leader. The new leadership removed a large number of corrupt and "diehard" antireformist officials; began to end the decades-long cover-up of both historical crimes and contemporary problems by reducing media censorship; introduced limited innovations to "accelerate" the state economy; took consequential steps in foreign policy to defuse the Cold War, including Gorbachev's meetings with President Ronald Reagan of the United States; and cajoled the Party's Central Committee into endorsing several more ambitious aspects of Gorbachev's domestic program. Apart from a disastrous antialcohol campaign, and a lack of glasnost during the first days of the Chernobyl nuclear disaster in 1986, those years were for Ligachev a model of moderate, gradual reform.

Even though Gorbachev's own radical intentions were evident earlier, the first unmistakable harbinger of fundamental change did not come until the Nineteenth Communist Party Conference in mid-1988, whose proceedings were televised nationally. The conference had great ramifications for two reasons. First, the public spectacle of the Communist ruling elite deeply divided over policy and ideology, for the first time since the 1920s, quickly incited—or inadvertently legitimized—more boundless kinds of "pluralism" in society. For example, a direct confrontation between Ligachev and Yeltsin, still a ranking Party official, was electrifying.[24] Second, after a major struggle, and with considerable guile, Gorbachev manipulated the delegates into voting for the "democratization" of the Soviet system. Most Party functionaries no doubt thought the resolution would be merely ceremonial, as others had been in the past, but that was not the case.

Some readers will recall the dramatic events that followed. In March 1989, Gorbachev's democratizing policies produced the country's first relatively free, multicandidate national elections since 1917, and its first real parliament ever. (Some of the 2,250 deputies were given uncontested seats, including Ligachev, Gorbachev, and ninety-eight other representatives of the Communist Party establishment, but this concession did not inhibit the proceedings.) Sitting as a constitutional congress, the legislature later elected Gorbachev president of the Soviet Union, thereby partially freeing him from constraints imposed by the Party Central Committee, which had made him its general secretary in 1985. In 1990, parliamentary elections took place in Russia and other republics that further changed the Soviet political landscape. A multiparty system began to emerge, along with political leaders unbeholden to the Communist Party nomenklatura.

The election of a national parliament and the creation of Gorbachev's executive presidency in 1989 and 1990 were turning points in Soviet history. They broke the Communist Party's seven-decade monopoly on political life and thus fundamentally eroded the Leninist political system. Much that now ensued, and was so greatly lamented by Ligachev, was aftermath. The democratization process greatly outran Gorbachev's economic reforms while generating popular protests against growing consumer shortages, rising inflation, and longstanding elite privileges. Even more destabilizing, the political change allowed nationalist discontent in several of the fifteen republics to develop into anti-Soviet movements for independence, first and most assertively in the Baltics. By 1990, powerful counterreform forces had regrouped and begun to strike back, finding many allies among unnerved Andropov-style reformers in the state, Party, and security bureaucracies. Their self-appointed leaders, most of them members of Gorbachev's own government, staged the abortive coup in August 1991 that promised "national salvation" and "order" but triggered the disintegration of everything they had sent the tanks to save.

In his memoirs, Ligachev insists that his own serious concerns about the direction of Gorbachev's reforms surfaced only in the fall of 1987, when he clashed with Aleksandr Yakovlev over the media's "slanderous" portrayal of Soviet history. It was an important confrontation that sharpened divisions in the Gorbachev leadership. Opinions about the Stalinist past were inherently related to opinions about the degree of reform needed in the existing Stalinist system; Ligachev wanted a "balanced" approach to both questions. And though Yakovlev was not the éminence grise behind Gorbachev's stunning radicalization, as Ligachev (and others) have presented him, he had been Gorbachev's confidant for several years and now was a member of the top Party leadership, the Politburo. It is also true that Yakovlev had considerable influence among liberal Communist intellectuals and journalists, many of whom he appointed to important editorial positions.

But this was not the first serious conflict inside the Gorbachev leadership; earlier ones, about which Ligachev's memoirs are silent or highly elliptical, were equally portentous. At the first Party Congress held under Gorbachev, in February 1986, for example, Ligachev strongly protested attacks on the Party apparatus's power and privileges; only Gorbachev could have stood behind such attacks at the time. That issue continued to fester and contributed to the infamous Yeltsin affair in October 1987, when Gorbachev, in effect taking Ligachev's side in a bitter controversy, moved to expel Yeltsin from the leadership. Ligachev portrays himself as a relatively minor participant in this prolonged and ramifying affair; his only regret is having recommended Yeltsin for a leadership position in the first place. Similarly, though Ligachev criticizes at length a "fateful" economic decision made in late 1987, he is silent about earlier disputes over proposals to marketize sections of the Soviet economy. That controversy probably delayed such decisions and thus made them harder to implement.

Above all, Ligachev's memoirs are silent about behind-the-scenes struggles over political reform beginning in mid-1986, or perhaps even earlier, and leading up to a watershed meeting of the Central Committee in January 1987. It was there that Gorbachev first persuaded the recalcitrant assembly of Communist oligarchs to adopt at least a faint version of his calls for the democratization of the Soviet system and of the Communist Party itself. The latter proposal, if actually carried out, would have destroyed Ligachev's base of power in the central Party Secretariat, which oversaw all high-level political appointments, as Gorbachev did by other means only in September 1988. Nor is it clear where Ligachev stood on a related and highly symbolic issue: the decision made in December 1986 to free Andrei Sakharov from seven years of internal exile, which was a major step toward legitimizing liberal democratic dissent, past and present.

In short, most of the great disputes that later disenchanted Ligachev and plunged the Communist Party into its fateful schism were latent in the Gorbachev leadership from the beginning and divided its members almost as soon as they began to exercise power. Ligachev's memory of his original relationship with the number-one leader therefore needs revision. It was a political alliance, with all the need for bargaining and potential for conflict inherent in such arrangements everywhere, not a perfect marriage that fell apart because of the envious competitors, unwise decisions, and inexplicable behavior recounted in Ligachev's memoirs.

Several factors eventually estranged Ligachev and Gorbachev, but the crucial one was historic. Gorbachev remained devoted to the "socialist idea," but for whatever reasons, at some moment in his own biography he crossed the Rubicon from Communist Party liberalizer to authentic democratizer. His personal transformation is not widely understood or appreciated in the United States even today, but there is considerable evidence to support it, as a few Western scholars have shown.[25] Hence

Gorbachev's dramatic evolution after 1985, which Ligachev attributed to the baneful influence of others, from proponent of "socialist pluralism" to proponent simply of "pluralism," from advocate of "socialist democracy" to advocate of "democracy," from defender of the Communist Party's "leading role" to defender of the need for a multiparty system.

Both Gorbachev and Ligachev had spent their entire political lives rising through a ruling Communist Party apparatus created under Lenin, transformed into a vast, caste-like system by Stalin, and largely preserved by Khrushchev and Brezhnev. Gorbachev—like his closest Politburo colleagues, Yakovlev, Shevardnadze, and Vadim Medvedev— somehow broke with that world and its characteristic ideology. Like the great majority of Party officials, Ligachev, for all his notable evolution in other respects, did not, at least until after 1991, when it no longer mattered.

Ligachev was partly right, therefore, about a Gorbachev "enigma": How did he evolve from provincial Soviet Party apparatchik into a seminal leader of Russian and twentieth-century democracy? Though many books have been written about Gorbachev, he still awaits his real biographers. Like all students of modern Soviet history, they will be indebted to Ligachev's memoirs for valuable information and firsthand insights. Few of them, however, are likely to accept his interpretations of major political developments or his answer to the large "mystery of Gorbachev."

Some of Ligachev's explanations of Gorbachev's behavior, while not implausible, were contradictory and lacked context. He was right, for example, that Gorbachev often was captive rather than master of events. But was this primarily because of the "personal qualities" of an indecisive and evasive leader, or was it another factor discussed by Ligachev, which he and others called "the Khrushchev syndrome"—Gorbachev's fear of being deposed behind closed doors by the Central Committee, as was his reformist predecessor? On the one hand, Ligachev always insisted that Gorbachev had no reason to fear such a fate because provincial Party bosses, who formed the most powerful bloc on the Central Committee, "supported Gorbachev and only him." In fact, by 1989 many of them feared and loathed Gorbachev and wanted to be rid of him. On the other hand, Ligachev's memoirs retrospectively and inadvertently confirmed Gorbachev's anxiety about a vengeful Party apparatus by pointing out that the leader did not try to oust him from the leadership until 1990 because the Central Committee "would not have supported it."

Above all, Ligachev could never explain why Gorbachev ultimately remained "loyal to the radicals," by which he means the democrats. When told that Gorbachev "wants to go down in history as a clean man, whom no one can accuse of dictatorship," Ligachev did not understand the last Soviet leader's resolve to break with centuries of Russian and Soviet leadership practices. Instead, he believed that a rudderless, impressionable Gorbachev had been captured and remade politically by Yakovlev and his band of "pseudo-democrats." Yakovlev and many other people did influence Gorbachev's thinking over the years, but no leader determined enough to initiate and sustain a radical reformation in such dangerously hostile circumstances, as Gorbachev did from 1988 to 1991, could have been as weak-willed, indecisive, or susceptible to far lesser figures as Ligachev's memoirs suggested.

Indeed, they also suggested a Ligachev "enigma," as even one of his most admiring aides later acknowledged.[26] Readers may wonder why such a purposeful, self-confident man, who, by his own admission, had "much influence" in the Party's power structure, did not oppose Gorbachev's policies more forcefully or, when disillusionment set in after 1987, try to remove him as leader. Even the latter course might have been possible in the Party's Central Committee before the 1989 national elections, which gave Gorbachev a new power base in the parliament and presidency and millions of aroused citizens a stake in the political process. Why instead did Ligachev acquiesce to policies he did not like? In only two substantive instances was he even accused of playing an aggressively anti-Gorbachev role—the Andreyeva affair of March 1988, when an anti-perestroika manifesto mysteriously appeared in a leading Party newspaper, and the Soviet army's attack on street demonstrators in Tbilisi in April 1989. (Ligachev denied having instigated either, and the evidence in both cases remains inconclusive.)[27]

Indeed, Ligachev intended his memoirs to be in part an apologia for having borne "full responsibility" for Gorbachev's policies and for his own "unprincipled" passivity. At most, Ligachev began to function as unproclaimed leader of a loyal Communist opposition at the 1988 Party conference, but his loyalty—or old-fashioned adherence to the idea of "Party unity"—still seemed to exceed his opposition. He wrote long (sometimes prophetic) letters of protest to Gorbachev and the Central

Committee but appears never to have acted on them. Under previous leaders, such behavior would have been risky, but no longer, as Ligachev later acknowledged in a revealing lament: "Under Stalin, you would have lost your head for a letter like that. Under Khrushchev, you would have been fired. Under Brezhnev, you would be made an ambassador to Africa. And under Gorbachev, you were simply ignored." In the end, when Gorbachev finally moved to retire him, Ligachev's most defiant protest was to try to become his deputy again—this time by election.

Ligachev's memoirs did provide some clues as to why he had been unwilling or unable to break decisively with Gorbachev. In his role as the Party's number-two leader and overseer of its nationwide apparatus, Ligachev represented the powers and resentments of regional officials, though probably not so fully as Western writers have thought. By 1987, some of their resentments were directed at him for having fired, on behalf of Andropov and then Gorbachev, a large number of their colleagues. And others who remained in place could not have been happy with Ligachev's contempt for the "former style of the ruling Party apparatchik," who "groveled before the strong and lorded it over the weak." Still more, by 1988 and certainly after the March 1989 elections, many provincial bosses could hardly forgive his complicity in political reforms that were already destroying their traditional power and privileges. No wonder they began looking for a younger, less tainted, more reliable representative.

As for Ligachev, his policy stance between Gorbachev's radical reforms and the Party's reactionary wing put him in an inherently ambivalent position. Unlike the majority of Party functionaries, in 1985 he had "cast his fate" with the small group of leaders who began perestroika, and even when Gorbachev's version grew too radical for his taste, Ligachev had no wish to turn the clock back to 1985, only to 1987. Despite his angry charges that Gorbachev and Yakovlev let democratization and nationalist movements run out of control, there's no evidence he was ready to use the kind of force necessary by then to restore "discipline and order."

To these larger political factors that bound Ligachev to Gorbachev should probably be added the lack of any personal animus in relations between the two men, at least at the time, as well as any indication that Ligachev ever saw himself as an alternative leader. (Yeltsin's attitude toward Gorbachev and the top leadership position, a matter that I treat in chapter 5, was entirely different.) Whatever the full explanation, when push finally came to shove, Ligachev was not among the coup plotters against Gorbachev in August 1991, though several of his comrades from the Party apparatus were. Amid wild rumors that he and Gorbachev (and even Yeltsin) had actually staged the failed putsch in order to enhance their eroding power, Ligachev again cast his lot with the embattled leader: "I know one thing for sure. Two people from the Party knew nothing about the plans . . . Gorbachev and Ligachev."[28]

EVEN after the Soviet Union ended, Ligachev did not retire from politics, not even as he approached his eighty-ninth birthday in 2009. Until 1999, he was "on pension" but also on permanent call as the most respected senior statesman of the former Soviet Communist Party, now reconstituted as a successful Russian electoral party headed by Gennady Zyuganov. In 1999, two years after the death of his beloved and long-ailing wife Zinaida, Ligachev returned to "big politics" by winning direct election to the Duma, as the post-Soviet parliament was renamed, as the Party's candidate in his adopted Tomsk.[29] (Many deputies were selected indirectly by their party's proportion of the national vote.) He did not run in the next election, in 2003, but remained a member of the Party's Central Committee and deputy head of a union of Communist parties of the former Soviet republics.

Like two other Russians who appear in this book in the ninth decade of their lives, Solzhenitsyn and Antonov-Ovseyenko, Ligachev never changed his political views, though his were different, of course, from those of the former zeks. Throughout his post-Soviet years, he continued to insist that the Soviet breakup and the "restoration of capitalism" in Russia constituted a "tragedy" for ordinary people. And while acknowledging that Putin's leadership was better than the "catastrophe" of Yeltsin's presidency in the 1990s, Ligachev never stopped insisting that the "progress" achieved in the Soviet era in economics, science, education, health care, and other social benefits could be regained only by returning to some kind of socialism.[30]

That constancy of conviction, while so many other former Soviet officials were reinventing themselves, earned Ligachev considerable respect in many quarters, not just in his own party. For that reason, a longtime aide concluded that Ligachev's "political fate . . . can be called both tragic and happy." It was "tragic since everything to which he had given his life as a politician is now totally destroyed." It was "happy" because despite all the disappointments and personal attacks he had endured, "he did not break internally and change, renounce his Communist faith, or become a turncoat and traitor."[31]

When asked on his eightieth birthday about no longer participating in "big politics," Ligachev replied: "I can walk freely wherever I want. I ride public transportation without any anxiety. I have nothing to fear. In the streets, many people recognize and speak to me, but no one has ever given me a hostile look or said a bad word. For me, this is fully reward enough for the life I have lived." He added, "But let 'them' [now in the Kremlin] try to go out to the people without their bodyguards."[32]

Nonetheless, Ligachev's conservative views may seem to have become a relic of a bygone age, irrelevant in an era when the Soviet Union had been broken into fifteen independent states and the Communist Party driven from the Kremlin. But it would be a mistake to think that the Soviet system over seven decades, or Sovietism, was nothing more than the Moscow state and its ruling Party. It was also a political civilization with defining features, including collectivist economic attitudes, popular concepts of social justice, authoritarian rulership, and bureaucratic practices that had deep roots in Russia's pre-Communist history. If Soviet Communism had simply been imposed on Russia, as many Western and Russian commentators maintained after 1991 and Ligachev always denied, the nation should have quickly escaped its twentieth-century past. That, of course, did not happen.

This does not mean that Russia has not changed since 1991 and will not change still more in the years ahead. Important Soviet and older traditions persist within both society and the political elite, but the nation, even with its devastating setbacks "in transition," is already considerably more Westernized, economically and politically, even more democratized, than it was when Gorbachev and Ligachev came to power in March 1985. Since that turning point, Ligachev has been proved right about one essential issue: Russia can borrow from the West but it cannot transplant an American or other Western-style system into its native soil, as was attempted so disastrously in the post-Soviet 1990s.

In that regard, Ligachev's "healthy conservatism" should not be dismissed. After all, as he remarked plaintively, no doubt thinking of his own reputation, "In the West, they respect people with conservative views."[33] In Russia past and present, however, moderate conservatives of all stripes have usually fared badly, marginalized or driven to reactionary positions by the nation's traumatic history and recurring polarized politics. If every society needs conservatives, as Ligachev came to believe, the tragedies Russia experienced in the twentieth century are probably not over.

More disputed is the core tenet of Ligachev's conservatism—his conviction that the Soviet system should and could have been reformed, not discarded. It rested on his belief that the alternative program of change represented first by Andropov and then himself and abandoned by Gorbachev, one much like the successful Chinese Communist model of market economics and authoritarian politics, would have resulted in a reformed and viable Soviet Union. The issue may now seem to be merely historical, but in post-Soviet Russia its political heat, like that of the Stalinist past, has not been extinguished.

4 WAS THE SOVIET SYSTEM REFORMABLE?

There are no unreformable social systems; otherwise there would not be any
progress in history.

MIKHAIL GORBACHEV

OF all Russia's "accursed" twentieth-century questions, one will continue to torment the nation more than any other in the twenty-first century: Why did the Soviet Union, or "Great Russia," as its former citizens sometimes call it, perish? Russian scholars, politicians, and public
opinion have been bitterly divided over the question ever since that state
disappeared in December 1991, but most Western commentators think
they know the answer: The Soviet system was not reformable and thus
was doomed by its inherent, irremediable defects.

Considering the historic prodemocratic and promarket changes that
took place under Mikhail Gorbachev from 1985 to 1991, all of them far
exceeding the mere liberalization thought possible by even the most
"optimistic" Western Sovietologists, was the system really unreformable? Certainly there was no such consensus at the time. Virtually to the
end, Western governments, including the United States, thought and indeed hoped that a reformed Soviet Union might result from Gorbachev's
leadership. (The primary issue here is not, however, his role as a reform
leader but the system's capacity for fundamental change.) And while
scholarly "pessimists" maintained, as most Sovietologists always had,

that the system could not be reformed and that Gorbachev would there-fore fail, many studies conducted during the perestroika years took it for granted that "systematic change was possible in the Soviet context." An American economist soon to be the top Soviet expert at the White House of the first President George Bush was even more emphatic: "Is Soviet socialism reformable? Yes, it is reformable, and it is already being reformed."[1]

WHY, then, have so many specialists of different generations and schol-arly persuasions, with few exceptions, maintained since 1991 that the "USSR could not be reformed," that it was "fundamentally, structur-ally unreformable," indeed, that Soviet reform was a "contradiction in terms, like fried snowballs," and therefore that Gorbachev merely "failed to reform the unreformable"? Still more, why do they insist, as though to preclude any reconsideration, that this towering historical question "has been answered"?[2]

Understanding their reasoning is not always easy because the "in-trinsic irreformability of Communism" is one of the worst formulated axioms in the literature. In some cases, it is mere tautology, as with the French Sovietologist who could "not see the Soviet system reforming it-self into something really different without ceasing to be the Soviet sys-tem," or the *New York Times* columnist who insisted that "fundamental changes . . . would make it totally un-Soviet."[3] Apart from that kind of pseudoanalysis, four somewhat different reasons are usually given by different specialists for the assertion that the system could not be reformed.

One is that an "original sin" in the history of the Soviet Union—its aberrant founding ideology, the illegitimate way it came into being, or the crimes it then committed—made it forever an "absolute evil" with-out redemptive, alternative possibilities of development and thus "too fatally flawed to be reformed." Through seven decades of Soviet history, according to this view, nothing essential ever changed or could change; the system never produced any real reformers or reforms just, as with Gorbachev's perestroika, the "illusion of reformability." The Soviet evil could end only with the system's total destruction into "economic and social rubble," a "victim of its own illegitimacy . . . its own murder-ousness." Despite pretenses of scholarly objectivity, this is essentially a theological kind of argument, and like most sacred ideological beliefs, it crams history into Manichean interpretations and stubbornly rejects all evidence and logical arguments that do not fit.[4]

This view can be challenged, however, on its own terms. Most world theologies offer no such certitude about the role, duration, or resolution of evil and allow more room for alternatives and human choice than we find in this rigidly deterministic sermon on the Soviet experience. Moreover, if original sin forever disqualifies a political or economic system from redemption, how did slave-holding America eventually become a leading example of democracy?

Can it be plausibly or morally argued that an original Soviet evil was greater, more formative, or more at odds with the state's professed values than was slavery in the United States, that "accursed thing," which John Adams called "an evil of colossal magnitude" and which a contemporary American historian and a modern-day U.S. president rank as "one of history's greatest crimes"? Eight to twelve million souls were held in absolute bondage over two hundred years, while perhaps another twelve million died in transit from Africa. And, we are told, "slaves represented more capital than any other asset in the nation, with the exception of land." Nations and systems, it seems, can change. And in fact, the leading American crusader against the Soviet "evil empire," President Ronald Reagan, decided that it had ceased to be malevolent after only three years of Gorbachev's reforms.[5]

A second and more commonly held view is that the end of the Soviet Union was proof of its unreformability—on the assumption, evidently, that death is always caused by incurable disease. It is Sovietology's longstanding habit of reading, or rereading, history backward in light of a known outcome: "With hindsight, of course, it is now clear that Gorbachev's historical mission was not to succeed, but to fail." According to another veteran specialist, "After the implosion of the Soviet Union, the outcome now appears to have been inevitable all along." Even worldly scholars and journalists, it seems, need to believe that epochal events are predetermined by some inexorable logic.[6] But such assertions are an abdication of real analysis and explanation. For outcomes to seem inevitable, historical complexities, alternatives, contingencies, and other possible results have to be minimized, rescripted, or expunged from the story.

Even apart from the anomaly that the Soviet breakup, as Tocqueville remarked of the French revolution, may have been the least foreseen "inevitable" major event in modern times, the "fallacy of retrospective determinism," or "hindsight bias," can also be exposed on its own terms.[7] Many of its practitioners emphasize Gorbachev's "mistakes" while proffering their own prescriptive policies, thereby implying that Soviet reform would have succeeded had he acted differently or had it been led by someone else. Such criticisms of Gorbachev are contradictory. Some specialists say he should have reformed faster, others slower; some say he should have been more democratic, others more authoritarian. But all these coulda-woulda-shoulda analyses tacitly concede the existence of alternatives and thus implicitly raise what-if or counterfactual questions that undermine their own conclusions about an unreformable Soviet system and its inevitable collapse.

Consider a few counterfactual questions about alternatives and contingencies, a form of analysis well-established in other fields of historical interpretation but rarely undertaken seriously in Sovietology.[8] Most writers agree that Gorbachev's fast-track democratization policies made his leadership vulnerable to growing economic hardships and nationalist unrest; that his failure to stand in a popular election for the Soviet presidency in 1990—like another first president, George Washington, he was elected by a congress—later deprived him of legitimacy, especially in 1990 and 1991 when confronted by Yeltsin's electoral rise to the presidency of the Russian Republic; and that the combination of Yeltsin's anti-Kremlin politics and the August 1991 putsch did much to doom Gorbachev's efforts to hold the Soviet Union together.

But what if Gorbachev had tried to introduce market reforms before or without democratization, in some version of the Chinese model that many Russian reformers still think would have been the best approach, or if the 1986 Chernobyl nuclear accident and 1988 Armenian earthquake had not devastated the federal budget, or if world prices for Soviet oil had not fallen sharply or had risen as sharply as they did during Vladimir Putin's presidency? Even later, popularly elected or not, what if Gorbachev had used force early, as he could have easily done, to discourage secessionist activities in one or two republics? And what if he had sent Yeltsin into remote ambassadorial exile after the future oppositionist's ouster from the leadership in 1987 or denied him access to state-controlled television in 1990 and 1991, as Yeltsin later denied his Communist rival, Gennady Zyuganov, during the 1996 Russian presidential campaign?

Alternately, would Yeltsin ever have challenged the Union govern-ment if he had become president of the Soviet Union instead of its Rus-sian Republic, as was conceivable in 1990 and as he considered doing after the failed coup in August 1991? And when he and two other So-viet leaders did stealthily abolish the Union in December 1991, what if the Soviet military or other security forces had moved against them, as Yeltsin worried they might? As for the fateful putsch attempt in August, would it have taken place if Gorbachev had removed those ringleaders from their high-level positions when they first conspired against him a few months earlier? Indeed, if the United States and other G-7 nations had committed large-scale financial assistance to Gorbachev's reforms in mid-1991, as he requested, would any Soviet opponent have dared to move against him?

Those are only some of the legitimate questions disregarded by yet an-other standard explanation of why the Soviet system purportedly could not change: "The system simply would not accept reform." Derived from the old totalitarian model, which portrayed the system as immu-table, the argument that the Soviet Union was structurally unreformable comes in several versions but evidently rests on two basic assumptions: first, the monolithic Communist ruling class, or bureaucratic nomen-klatura, would never permit any changes that actually threatened its monopolistic hold on power and would therefore "oppose all types of reform"; and second because "the political system had been constructed along totalitarian lines . . . its institutions could not be retooled to serve pluralist goals."[9]

But these, too, turned out to be false assumptions. All of Gorbachev's major domestic reforms during the decisive period from 1985 to 1990 were introduced, discussed, and ratified in the highest Communist no-menklatura assemblies—the Politburo, Central Committee, a national Party conference, and two Party congresses. Those bodies even voted to abolish the practice underlying their own bureaucratic domination, ap-pointment to all-important political offices, in favor of elections. And in the process of enacting these "pluralist" reforms, those institutions be-came deeply divided, factionalized, and thus themselves pluralist, as did the constitutional bedrock of the system, the legislative councils called soviets.

That remarkable development brings us to the argument most favored by writers who insist that the Soviet Union could not be reformed: the system was "mutually exclusive with democracy" and therefore could only die from it.[10] Even if true, however, this would not mean that the system was completely unreformable but that it was un-democratizable, which is also questionable. The argument assumes that once Gorbachev permitted relatively free speech, political activity, and elections, as he did by 1989, mass anti-Soviet sentiments—long suppressed and usually attributed to an insurgent "civil society"—were bound to "delegitimize" and sweep away the system in favor of a radically non-Soviet one.

Not surprisingly, this explanation of both the unreformability and the end of the Soviet Union was seized upon by Yeltsin and his allies in late 1991 when they were jettisoning Gorbachev's gradualist perestroika and dismantling the Union. In the writings of many Western scholars and other commentators, particularly American ones, it has since become an axiom that the last years of the Soviet Union brought forth "an accelerating revolution from below," a "genuinely popular revolution," a "popular democratic revolution." In this telling, ordinary citizens rejected socialism, "like a mass internal defection," and "mounted the greatest bloodless revolution in history to remove that Soviet regime."[11]

In reality, no anti-Soviet revolution from below ever took place, certainly not in Russia itself, which is the focus of most of these assertions. In 1989 through 1991, popular support for democratization and marketization was growing, as were protests against Communist Party rule, corrupt elites, bureaucratic abuses, and economic shortages. But the evidence, particularly public opinion surveys, clearly showed that large majorities of Soviet citizens, ranging up to 80 percent and even more on some issues, continued to oppose free-market capitalism and to support fundamental economic-social features of the Soviet system— among them, public ownership of large-scale economic assets, a state-regulated market, guaranteed employment, controlled consumer prices and other standard-of-living subsidies, and free education and health care. Or as a nonpartisan Russian historian of the period has concluded, the "overwhelming majority of the population shared the idea of the 'socialist choice.'" (It was still the preference of the majority twenty years later.)[12]

Evidence of public support for the multinational Soviet state itself is even clearer and more precise. In a March 1991 referendum held in Russia and eight other republics, which included 93 percent of the entire Soviet population, 76.4 percent of the large turnout voted to preserve the Union—only nine months before it was abolished. The validity of that democratic voting result as an expression of public opinion in Russia, where the popular anti-Soviet revolution is alleged to have been centered, is confirmed by two developments. Even Yeltsin rose to electoral power in the Russian Republic on the widespread aspiration for a reformed Soviet system, not its overthrow. And after 1991, public regret over the Union's abolition remained high, between 65 and 80 percent of those surveyed, in the early twenty-first century before beginning to decline.[13]

Nor is it true that a mass anti-Soviet "August Revolution" in 1991 thwarted the attempted coup by hard-line officials seeking to restore order throughout the country a few months after the referendum. Contrary to this equally widespread myth, there was no "national resistance" to the putsch. As heroic and determined as they were, barely 1 percent of Soviet citizens actively opposed the three-day tank occupation even in pro-Yeltsin Moscow, and considerably fewer resisted in provincial cities, the countryside, and outside the Russian Republic. The other 99 percent, according to an authoritative observer, "were feverishly buying up macaroni and pretending that nothing was going on" or, as the British ambassador reported, waiting "to see which way the cat would jump." Whatever the exact percentages, even opponents of the coup knew "how few people" had come out to oppose it.[14] (There was, for example, little if any response to Yeltsin's call for a general strike against the putsch.)

We are left, then, without any theoretical or conceptual reason to think that the Soviet system was unreformable and thus, as is so often said, "doomed" from the beginning of Gorbachev's reforms. Indeed, if the question is formulated properly, without the customary ideological slant, and examined empirically in light of the changes actually introduced under Gorbachev, particularly in the years 1985 through 1990, before crises destabilized the country, we might reasonably conclude that it turned out to be remarkably reformable. But in order to ask the question correctly, we need exact rather than cavalier understandings both of reform and of the Soviet system.

The universal meaning of reform is not merely change but change that betters people's lives, usually by expanding their political freedom, economic freedom, or both. Nor is it revolution or total transformation of an existing order but normally piecemeal, gradualist improvements within a system's broad historical, institutional, cultural dimensions.

Insisting that "real reform" must be rapid and complete, as does so much commentary on the Soviet system, would disqualify, for example, historic but incremental expansions of voting, civil, and welfare rights over decades in Great Britain and the United States, including the New Deal of the American 1930s. It should also be remembered that reform has not always or necessarily meant democratization and marketization, though that has increasingly been the case in modern times.

In those plain terms, it is not true historically that the Soviet system was unreformable—that it had experienced only "failed attempts at reform." NEP greatly expanded the economic and, to a lesser degree, political freedom of most citizens in the 1920s, and Khrushchev's policies also benefited them in several important and lasting ways in the 1950s and 1960s. Most Western specialists evidently believe those were the limits of possible Soviet reform, arguing that even Gorbachev's professed democratic socialism was incompatible with the system's more legitimizing, antidemocratic historical icons—the October Revolution and Lenin.

But this assumption too lacks comparative perspective. French and American generations later reimagined their national revolutions to accommodate latter-day values. Why could not Lenin and other Soviet founders, who had professed democracy while suppressing it, eventually be viewed and forgiven by a democratic nation as products of their times, which were shaped by the unprecedented violence of World War I, much as American founding fathers—among them Washington, Jefferson, and Madison—were forgiven their slaves? (The United States had slave-owning presidents for almost fifty years and proslavery ones for even longer; slave labor was used to build the nation's Capitol and the White House; and many textbooks still obscured or portrayed slavery as a benign institution nearly a hundred years after its abolition.)[15] In fact, such reconsiderations of October and Lenin were well under way by the late 1980s as part of the larger process of public "repentance" inspired by Gorbachev's reforms.

Arbitrary definitions of "the Soviet system" must also be set aside. Equating it with "Communism" is the most widespread, as in the ubiquitous axiom "Communism was unreformable." In this usage, Communism is a nonobservable and meaningless analytical notion.[16] No Soviet leaders ever said it existed in their country or anywhere else, only socialism, and the last Soviet leader, Gorbachev, doubted even that. "Communist" was merely the name given to the official ideology, ruling Party, and professed goal; and its meaning depended on the current leadership and varied so greatly over the years that it could mean almost anything. Thus, by 1990, Gorbachev decided it meant "to be consistently democratic and put universal values above everything else." Western observers may not understand the difference between the abstraction "Communism" and the fullness of the actual Soviet system, or Sovietism, but the Soviet (and later Russian) people made it clear that about this at least they agreed with Gorbachev: "Communism is not the Soviet Union."[17]

Instead, the Soviet system, like any other, has to be defined and evaluated not as an abstraction or ideological artifact but in terms of its functioning components, particularly its basic institutions and practices. Six of these had always been emphasized in Western Sovietological literature: the official and obligatory ideology; the especially authoritarian nature of the ruling Communist Party; the Party's dictatorship over everything related to politics, buttressed by the political police; the nationwide pyramid of pseudodemocratic soviets; the state's monopolistic control of the economy and all substantive property; and the multinational federation, or Union, of republics that was really a unitary state dominated by Moscow.

To ask if the Soviet system was reformable means asking if any or all of those basic components could be reformed. Contrary to the view that the system was an indivisible "monolith" or that the Communist Party was its only essential element, it makes no sense to assume that if any components were transformed, supplemented by new ones, or eliminated, the result would no longer be the Soviet system.[18] Such reasoning is not applied to reform in other systems, and there are no grounds for it in Soviet history. The system's original foundations, the soviets of 1917, were popularly elected, multiparty institutions, only later becoming something else. There was no monopolistic control of the economy or absence of a market until the 1930s. And when the Stalinist mass terror, which had been a fundamental feature for twenty-five years, ended in the 1950s, no one doubted that the system was still Soviet.

By 1990, Soviet conceptions of legitimate reforms within the system varied considerably, but many Gorbachev and Yeltsin supporters had come to believe they should and could include multiparty democracy, a marketized economy with both state and private property, and an authentic federation of republics.[19] Those contemporary beliefs and the country's political history suggest that for a reformed system still to have been Soviet, or to be regarded as such, four general elements had to be preserved in some form: a national (though not necessarily well-defined or unanimous) socialist idea that continued to memorialize antecedents in 1917 and the original Leninist movement, which had called itself social democratic until 1918; the network of soviets as the institutional continuity with 1917 and constitutional source of political sovereignty; a "mixed" economy with enough social entitlements to be called socialist, however much it might resemble a Western-style welfare state; and a union of Russia with at least several of the Soviet republics, whose number had grown over the years from four to fifteen.

WITH those well-defined and unbiased understandings of the question of the Soviet system's reformability, we can now ask which, if any, basic components of the old system were actually reformed under Gorbachev. There can hardly be any doubt about the official ideology, which in the minds of many members of the elite underwent a significant "evolution." By 1990, decades of Stalinist and then Leninist punitive dogmas had been largely replaced by Western-style social democratic and other "universal" tenets that differed little from liberal-democratic ones. What had been heresy for generations now became official Soviet ideology, ratified by the newly elected Congress of People's Deputies and even by an at least semiconverted Communist Party congress.[20] Still more, the government's ideology was no longer obligatory, even in once thoroughly proscribed realms such as education and official Communist publications. "Pluralism" of thought, including religious belief, was the new official watchword and growing reality.[21]

Nor was this a superficial or inconsequential reform. Western specialists had always stressed the role of ideology in the Soviet system, many even arguing that it was the most important factor. That was an exaggeration, but ideology did matter. Just as Gorbachev's radical "New Thinking" about international affairs paved the way for his reformation in Soviet foreign policy in the late 1980s, disestablishing old ideological strictures about Soviet socialism was imperative for carrying out far-reaching reforms at home.[22]

The next and larger reform was dismantling the Communist Party monopoly on politics, particularly on public discourse, the selection of

office holders, and policymaking. The magnitude of this change was already so great by 1990 as a result of Gorbachev's policies virtually ending censorship, permitting freedom of political organization, promoting increasingly free elections, and creating an authentic parliament that
some Western scholars called it a "revolution" within the system.[23] Party
dictatorship and the primacy of Communist officials at every level, established during the Leninist era seventy years before, had always been
(with the arguable exception of the Stalin terror years) the bedrock of
Soviet politics. In the "command-administrative system" inherited by
Gorbachev, the nationwide Party apparatus was commander in chief
and overriding administrator. In only five years, a fundamental change
had therefore taken place: The Soviet political system had ceased to be
Leninist or, as some writers would say, Communist.[24]

That generalization requires qualification. In a country so vast and
culturally diverse, political reforms legislated in Moscow were bound
to have disparate results, from fast-paced democratization in Russia's
capital cities and the Western Baltic republics to less substantial changes
in the Central Asian party dictatorships. In addition, the Communist
Party's exit from power, even where democratization had progressed,
was still far from complete. With millions of members, units in almost
every institution and workplace, longstanding controls over military
and other security forces, large financial resources, and the deference
exacted from citizens for decades, the Party remained the most formidable political organization in the country. And though political prisoners had been released, human rights were rapidly being established,
and security forces were exposed to growing public scrutiny, the KGB
remained intact and under uncertain control.

Nonetheless, the redistribution of the Communist Party's long-held
powers—to the reconstituted parliament, to the new presidency, and
now to the popularly elected soviets in the regions and republics—was
already far along. Gorbachev did not exaggerate when he told its congress
in 1990, "The Communist Party's monopoly on power and government
has come to an end." The demonopolization process abruptly termi-
nated another longtime feature of the Soviet system—pseudodemocratic
politics. A broad and clamorous political spectrum, exercising almost
complete freedom of speech, emerged from decades of subterranean
banishment. Organized opposition, scores of would-be parties, mass
demonstrations, strikes, and uncensored publications, repressed for

nearly seventy years, were rapidly developing across the country and be-ing legalized by the reformist legislature. Gorbachev was also close to the truth when he remarked with pride that the Soviet Union had sud-denly become the "most politicized society in the world."[25]

Russia had been intensely politicized before, fatefully so in 1917, but never under the auspices of an established regime or in the cause of con-stitutional government. Indeed, constitutionalism and legal procedures were the watchwords of Gorbachev's political reformation. The country had a long history of laws and even constitutions, before and after 1917, but almost never any real constitutional order or lawful constraints on power, which had traditionally been concentrated in a supreme leader-ship and exercised through bureaucratic edicts. (An estimated one mil-lion ministerial decrees were still in force in 1988.)[26]

Therein lay the unprecedented nature of Gorbachev's political re-forms. The entire Soviet transition from a dictatorship to a fledgling re-public based on a separation of the Communist Party's former powers and a "socialist system of checks and balances" was carried out through existing and amended constitutional procedures. The legal culture and political habits necessary for rule-of-law government could not be en-gendered so quickly, but it was a remarkable beginning. By September 1990, for example, the nascent constitutional court had struck down one of Gorbachev's first presidential decrees, and he complied with the ruling.[27]

Considering those achievements, why is it so often said that even Gorbachev's political reforms failed? The answer usually given is that the Communist Party of the Soviet Union, or CPSU as the pivot of the old system was called, turned out to be unreformable. The inadequacy of this generalization is twofold. First, it equates the entire Soviet system with the CPSU in ways that assume the former could not exist without the latter. And second, it treats the Party as a single, undifferentiated organization.

As a result of its long and complex history, the CPSU had grown by the 1980s into a vast realm inhabited by four related but significantly different entities: the notorious but relatively small apparat that dictato-rially controlled the rest of the Party and, though to a decreasing extent, the bureaucratic state itself;[28] the apparat-appointed but much larger and more diverse nomenklatura class that held all important positions in the Soviet system; 19 to 20 million rank-and-file members, many of whom had joined for reasons of conformity and career; and, lurking in the shadows, as I explained in the preceding chapter, at least two crypto-political parties—reformist and conservative—that had been developing in the "monolithic" one-party system since the 1950s. Not surprisingly, these components of the CPSU reacted to Gorbachev's reforms in different ways.

Whether or not the Party apparatus—traditionally some 1,800 functionaries at its Moscow headquarters and several hundred thousand at other echelons of the system—was reformable hardly mattered because by 1990 it had been largely disfranchised by Gorbachev's policies. (In this connection, the growing opposition of Ligachev, the Party apparat's chief representative, was particularly indicative.) The Moscow nerve center of apparat operations, the Secretariat, had been all but dismantled, its Party committees in state economic ministries withdrawn or marginalized, and the authority of their counterparts at lower government levels assumed by elected soviets. The process lagged in the provinces, but the dethronement of the CPSU apparatus was formalized when powers exercised for decades by its Central Committee and Politburo were ceremoniously transferred to the new Soviet parliament and presidency. The apparat's control even over its own Party had been substantially diminished, and in 1990 its head, the general secretary, previously selected in secret by the Communist oligarchy, was elected for the first time by a national Party congress.[29]

Gorbachev may have continued to fear "this mangy, rabid dog," but the CPSU apparatus turned out to be something of a bureaucratic paper tiger. Confronted by his electoral reforms, it fell into a "state of psychological shock" and "complete confusion."[30] As its role in the system shrank and its organizations disintegrated, apparat representatives stepped up their anti-Gorbachev activities, but to little effect. Muscular antireform forces were now effectively based elsewhere—in the state economic ministries, military, KGB, and even parliament. How little the Communist Party apparatus still mattered was dramatized in August 1991. A majority of its central and regional officials evidently supported the coup against Gorbachev, but, contrary to many Western accounts, the Party apparatus did not organize or probably even know about it beforehand.[31] (Nor did the apparatus have the power or will to resist the dissolution and banning of the Party after the coup failed, when it was easily dispersed.)

Unlike the Communist apparat that created it, large segments of the nomenklatura class survived the Soviet Union. That alone invalidates any simple generalization about its adaptability. Broadly understood, the millions of nomenklatura appointees throughout the system included many of the nation's administrative, economic, cultural, and other professional elites, and thus significant parts of its middle class. As is the case elsewhere, this large stratum of Soviet society, though nominally composed solely of Communist Party members and indiscriminately vilified in Western accounts, was divided internally by privilege, occupation, education, generation, geographic location, and political attitudes.[32]

It therefore makes no sense to characterize the Party-state nomenklatura as unreformable. Even its high-level officials reacted to Gorbachev's reforms in conflicting ways and went in different directions.[33] By 1990, they could be found almost everywhere along the emerging political spectrum, from left to right. Many were in the forefront of opposition to perestroika. But virtually all the leading Soviet and post-Soviet reformers of the 1980s and 1990s also came from the nomenklatura class, foremost among them Mikhail Gorbachev, Boris Yeltsin, and their ranking supporters. And after 1991, large segments of the old Soviet nomenklatura reemerged as mainstays of post-Communist Russia's political, administrative, and property-owning elites, some of them in the ranks of what would now be called "radical reform."[34] Indeed, one of its younger members, Vladimir Putin, would become Russia's first president in the twenty-first century.

Still less is it correct to characterize the Communist Party's almost 20 million rank-and-file members as unreformable. Most of them differed little in actual power, privilege, or political attitudes from other ordinary Soviet citizens, and they behaved in similarly diverse ways during the Gorbachev years. By early 1991, approximately 2 million had left the Party, mostly because membership was no longer worth the time or dues required. Among those who stayed, there was a "silent majority," but many supported Gorbachev's policies, as they had done from the beginning, and waged a grassroots struggle against the apparat.[35] Many others became a social base for anti-perestroika movements forming inside and outside the Party.

The real question about the Communist Party's reformability, given Gorbachev's democratization policies, was whether a competitive elec-

WAS THE SOVIET SYSTEM REFORMABLE?

toral parliamentary Party could emerge from it as part of a reformed Soviet system. What we loosely call "the Party" had actually been different things during its eighty-year history—an underground movement in tsarist Russia, a successful vote-getting organization in revolutionary 1917, a dictatorship but with factions openly struggling over policy and power in the NEP 1920s, a decimated and terrorized officialdom in the Stalinist 1930s, a militarized instrument of war against the German invader in the 1940s, a resurgent institution of oligarchical rule in the post-Stalin 1950s and 1960s, and by the 1980s an integral part of the bureaucratic statist system.[36]

After all of those transformations, Gorbachev now wanted the Party, or a significant segment of it, to undergo yet another metamorphosis by becoming a "normal political organization" capable of winning elections "strictly within the framework of a democratic process."[37] Pursuing that goal involved ramifications he may not have fully foreseen but eventually came to accept. It meant politicizing, or repoliticizing, the Soviet Communist Party, as Gorbachev began to do when he called for its own democratization in 1987, which meant permitting its several embryonic parties to emerge, develop, and possibly go their separate ways. It meant ending the fiction of "monolithic unity" and risking an "era of schism."[38] Though cut short by the events of late 1991, the process unfolded inexorably and quickly.

By early 1988, the schism in the Party was already so far along that it erupted in unprecedented polemics between the Central Committee's two most authoritative newspapers. Defending fundamentalist, including neo-Stalinist, "principles," *Sovetskaya Rossiya* published a long, defiant protest against Gorbachev's perestroika; *Pravda* replied with an equally adamant defense of anti-Stalinist and democratic reform.[39] At the national Party conference two months later, delegates spoke publicly in strongly opposing voices for the first time since the 1920s. Central Committee meetings were now a "battlefield between reformers and conservatives." In March 1989, Communists ran against Communists across the country for seats in the Congress of People's Deputies. Though 87 percent of the winners were members of the same Party, their political views were so unlike that Gorbachev announced they were no longer bound by a Party line.[40]

By 1990, the growing schism had taken territorial and organizational forms, as parties began tumbling out of the CPSU like Russian nestling dolls. The three Baltic Communist parties left the Union Party to try to compete in their native and increasingly nationalistic republics. At the center, apparat and other nomenklatura conservatives compelled Gorbachev to allow the formation of a Communist Party of the Russian Republic, initially headed by Ivan Polozkov, nominally within the CPSU but under the conservatives' control. Formally embracing more than 60 percent of all Soviet Communists, it, too, almost immediately split when reformers formed a rival organization, the Democratic Party of Communists of Russia.[41]

All sides now understood that the "CPSU is 'pregnant' with multiparty-ness" and that its political spectrum ranged "from anarchists to monarchists."[42] No one knew how many parties might spring from its womb—Gorbachev thought in 1991 there were "two, three, or four" just among the 412 Central Committee members[43]—but only the two largest mattered: the pro-reform or radical perestroika wing of the CPSU led by Gorbachev and now all but social democratic; and the amalgam of conservative and neo-Stalinist forces that opposed fundamental changes in the name of traditional Communist beliefs and practices.

A formal "dividing up" and "parting of the ways" was already being widely discussed in 1990, but neither side was ready.[44] Conservatives still lacked a compelling national leader and feared the ascending Yeltsin, who quit the CPSU in mid-1990, almost (though not quite) as much as they hated Gorbachev. Several Gorbachev advisers urged him to lead his followers out of the CPSU or drive out his opponents and thereby create an avowedly social democratic movement, but he still feared losing the national apparatus, with its ties to the security forces, to his enemies, perhaps even his presidency to opponents in the Congress, and, like any politician, was reluctant to split his own party. Only in the summer of 1991 were both sides ready for a formal "divorce." It was to take place at a special national congress later that year but became another casualty of the attempted coup in August.[45]

Splitting the enormous Communist Party into its polarized wings, as Gorbachev's close associate Aleksandr Yakovlev had proposed privately in 1985 and still believed in, would have been the surest and quickest way to create a real multiparty system in the Soviet Union, and indeed one more authentic and substantial than existed in post-Soviet Russia in the early twenty-first century.[46] In a "civilized divorce" that involved voting on opposing principles, framed by Gorbachev's social-democratic program, both sides would have walked away with a sizable proportion of the CPSU's membership, local organizations, printing presses, and other assets. Both would have immediately been the largest and only nation-wide Soviet parties, far overshadowing the dozen of "pygmy parties," as they were called, that were to dot the political landscape for years to come, some of them barely larger than the Moscow apartments in which they were conceived. (Based on a secret survey, Gorbachev believed that at least 5 to 7 million party members would remain with him in a new or recast party.)[47]

Nor is there any reason to doubt that both wings of the CPSU would have been formidable vote-getting parties in ongoing local, regional, and eventually national elections. Although a majority of Soviet citizens now held the existing Communist Party responsible for past and present ills, both divorcees could have escaped some of the onus by blaming the other, as they were already doing. Both would have had consider-able electoral advantages of organization, experienced activists, media, campaign funds, and even voter deference. In surveys done in 1990, 56 percent of Soviet citizens distrusted the CPSU. But 81 percent dis-trusted all the other parties on the scene, and 34 percent still preferred the Communist Party over any other.[48] Given the growing polarization in the country, both offshoots of the old Communist Party would have been in a position to expand their electorate.

Constituencies for a social democratic party led by Gorbachev in-cluded those millions of Soviet citizens who now wanted political liber-ties but also a mixed or regulated market economy that preserved wel-fare and other elements of the old state system. In all likelihood, it would have been strongest among professional and other middle classes, skilled workers, pro-Western intellectuals, and generally people who remained socialists but not Communists.[49] As Soviet and Russian electoral results showed in the late 1980s and 1990s, as well as those in Eastern Europe, the kind of democratic Communists and former Communists who would have been the core of a social democratic party were fully capable of organizing campaigns and winning elections.

In this case, analytical hindsight can tell us something important about real possibilities. Gorbachev's failure to carve out of the CPSU what in effect would have been a presidential party may have been his biggest political mistake.[50] If he had done so at the already deeply polar-ized (and essentially multiparty) Twenty-eighth Communist Party Congress in July 1990, to take a beckoning moment, he would not have been isolated politically when crises swept the country later in 1990 and 1991, and his personal popularity fell precipitously. In particular, if he had seized the initiative by taking such a bold step, which would have redefined and realigned the Soviet political landscape, many of his original supporters, perhaps even Yeltsin, might not have deserted him.[51]

Gorbachev's orthodox Communist opponents, contrary to most Western accounts, also had plenty of potential as a Soviet electoral party. As proponents of "healthy conservatism," they had an expanding base of support in the millions of officials, factory workers, collective farmers, anti-Western intellectuals, and other traditionalists aggrieved by Gorbachev's political and economic reforms.[52] As change eroded the social guarantees and other certainties of the old order, the number of "newly discontented," which had been steadily growing since 1985, was bound to increase. Conservative Communists had another growing appeal. The militant statist, or "patriotic," nationalism that had characterized their "Communism" since the Stalin era was becoming a powerful ideological force in the country, especially in Russia.[53] (Indeed, both anti-Gorbachev Communists and the now anti-Communist Yeltsin were already seizing on it.)

Nor should it be thought that the antireform wing of the Soviet Communist Party was incapable of adapting to democratic politics. After their shocked petulance over the defeat of a few dozen apparat candidates in the March 1989 elections, conservative Communists began to identify and organize their own constituents.[54] By 1990, they were a large electoral and parliamentary party in the Soviet Russian Republic. Whatever their private ambitions, they behaved in a generally constitutional manner, even after Yeltsin won executive power in the republic and Communists suddenly became an opposition party for the first time in Soviet history.

The electoral potential of the Gorbachev wing of the CPSU, which dispersed after the end of the Soviet Union, can only be surmised, but his conservative enemies soon demonstrated their own capabilities. In opposition, as a Russian observer remarked several years later, they "got a second wind." In 1993, they reemerged as the Communist Party of the Russian Federation and quickly became the largest and most successful electoral party in post-Soviet Russia. By 1996, it governed many regions and cities, had more deputies by far than any other party in the national parliament, and officially won 40 percent of the vote (some analysts thought even more) in Zyuganov's losing presidential campaign against Yeltsin, who still had not been able to form a mass party.[55] Indeed, until 2003, it won more votes in each parliamentary election than it had in the preceding one. In short, if the reformability of the old Soviet Communist Party is to be judged by its electoral capacities, both of its wings were reformable.

Two major components of the Soviet system still need to be reconsidered—the statist economy and the Union. On close examination, no real case can be found in the specialized literature that the Soviet economy was unreformable. There is a near consensus that Gorbachev's economic reforms "failed miserably," but even if this is true, it speaks to his leadership and policies, not the economic system itself.[56] As noted earlier, many Western specialists not only assumed that the economy could be reformed but proffered their own prescriptions for reforming it.[57] Assertions that the Soviet economy had been unreformable were yet another afterthought inspired by Russian politicians (and their Western patrons) who later decided to launch an all-out, "shock-therapy" assault on the old system.

Once again we must ask what is meant by "reform." In the Soviet case, if it meant the advent of a fully privatized, entirely free-market capitalism, the economy was, of course, not reformable; it could only have been replaced in its entirety. By 1991, some self-appointed Western advisers were already urging that outcome and never forgave Gorbachev for disregarding them.[58] But few Soviet politicians or policy intellectuals, including radical reformers at that time, advocated such an economic system. Overwhelmingly, they shared Gorbachev's often and by 1990 emphatically stated goal of a "mixed economy" with a "regulated" but "modern full-blooded market" that would give "economic freedom" to people and "equal rights" to all forms of property ownership and still be called socialist.[59] Most of the disagreements among Soviet reformers, and with Gorbachev, continued to be over the methods and pace of the change.

Gorbachev's proposed mixed economy has been the subject of much Western derision, and Yeltsin's retort that the Soviet leader "wanted to combine things that cannot be combined"—or as a Western historian put it, "like mating a rabbit with a donkey"—found much applause.[60] But this, too, is unjustified. All modern capitalist economies have been mixed and regulated to various degrees, the combination of private and state ownership, market and nonmarket regulation, changing repeatedly over time—the U.S. government's response to the 2008 and 2009 financial crisis being only a recent example. None of them have chosen actually to practice the fully "free market" their ideologues often preach. Moreover, it should again be emphasized, economies with large state and private sectors had been the tsarist and Soviet Russian tradition, except during the years since the end of NEP in 1929.

Introducing "capitalist" elements into a reformed Soviet system was more difficult politically and economically than had been adding "socialist" elements to, for instance, American capitalism in the 1930s. But there was no inherent reason why nonstate, market elements could not have been added to the Soviet economy—private manufacturing firms, banks, service industries, shops, and farms alongside state and collective ones—and encouraged to compete and grow. Something similar had been done under far greater political constraints in Communist Eastern Europe and China. It would have required adhering to Gorbachev's principle of gradualism and refusal to impose a way of life on people, even a reformed life. The reasons it did not happen in Soviet or post-Soviet Russia were primarily political, not economic, as were the causes of the country's growing economic crisis in 1990 and 1991, a subject examined in the next chapter.

We must also ask if Gorbachev's economic policies really "failed miserably" because this suggests that the Soviet economy did not respond to his reform initiatives. As often as not, this, too, is an afterthought in scholarly and media commentary. Even as late as 1990, when Gorbachev's policies were already generating an ominous combination of growing budget deficits, inflation, consumer shortages, and falling production, a number of Western economists nonetheless thought he was moving in the right direction. One wrote, for example, that the "sequencing of the economic reforms is sensible: Gorbachev has a fine strategic sense."[61] In this case, however, we are interested in larger and more long-term questions.

If economic reform is a "transition" composed of necessary stages, Gorbachev had launched the entire process by 1990 in four essential respects. He had pushed through almost all the legislation needed for a comprehensive economic reformation.[62] He had converted large segments of the Soviet elite to market thinking to the extent that even the most neo-Stalinist candidate in the 1991 Russian presidential election conceded, "Today, only a crazy person can deny the need for market relations." Indeed, by discrediting longstanding ideological dogmas, legalizing private enterprises and property, and thus market relations, and personally lauding "lively and fair competition" for "each form of property,"[63] Gorbachev had largely freed the economy from the clutches of the proscriptive Communist Party apparatus. And as a direct result of these changes, the actual marketization, privatization, and commercialization of the Soviet economy were under way.

These developments require special attention because later they would usually be attributed to Yeltsin and post-Soviet Russia. By 1990, the private businesses called cooperatives already numbered about 200,000, employed almost 5 million people, and accounted for 5 to 6 percent of GNP. For better or worse, state property was already in effect being privatized by nomenklatura officials and others. Commercial banks were springing up in many cities, and the first stock exchanges had appeared. New entrepreneurial and financial elites, including a soon-to-be formed "Young Millionaires Club," were rapidly developing along with these market institutions. By mid-1991, an American correspondent was filing a series of reports on "Soviet capitalism."[64] Western commentators may dismiss Gorbachev's policies as failed half-measures, but many post-Soviet Russian economists knew better: "It was during his years in power that all the basic forms of economic activity in modern Russia were born."[65] The larger point is that they were born within the Soviet economy and thus were evidence of its reformability.

Finally, there is the question of the largest and most essential component of the old Soviet system—the Union or multinational state itself. Gorbachev was slow to recognize that Moscow's hold on the fifteen republics was vulnerable to his political and economic policies, but by 1990 he knew that the fate of the Union would decide the outcome of all his reforms and "my own fate."[66] During his final two years in office, he became a Lincolnesque figure determined to "preserve the Union"—in his case, however, not by force but by negotiating a transformation of the discredited "super-centralized unitary state" into an authentic, voluntary federation. When the Soviet Union ended in December 1991 and all of the republics became separate and independent states, so ended the evolutionary reformation Gorbachev called perestroika.[67]

Was the Union reformable, as Gorbachev and many Russian politicians and intellectuals insisted before and after 1991? Two biases afflict

Western writing on this enormous "question of all questions."[68] The anti-Sovietism of most Western accounts, particularly American ones, inclines them to believe, with however much "hindsight bias," that the Soviet Union was a doomed state. The other bias, probably unwitting, is again the language or formulation of the question. It is almost always said, perhaps in a tacit analogy with the end of the tsarist state in 1917, that the Union "collapsed" or "imploded," words that imply inherently terminal causes and thus seem to rule out the possibility of a reformed Soviet state. But if we ask instead how and why the Union was "abolished," "destroyed," "dissolved," "disbanded," or simply "ended," the formulation leaves open the possibility that contingencies or subjective factors may have been the primary cause and therefore that a different outcome was possible.[69]

The standard Western thesis that the Union was unreformable is based largely on a ramifying misconception. It assumes that the nationwide Communist Party apparatus, with its vertical organizational discipline imposing authority from above and compliance from below, "alone held the federal union together." Therefore, once the dictatorial Party was disfranchised by Gorbachev's reforms, there were no other integrative factors to offset centrifugal forces and the "disintegration of the Soviet Union was a foregone conclusion." In short, "No party, no Union."[70]

The role of the Party should not be minimized, but other factors also bound the Union together, including other Soviet institutions. In significant respects, the Moscow state economic ministries, with their branches throughout the country, had become as important as Party organizations.[71] And the integrative role of the all-Union military, with its own kind of discipline and assimilation, should not be underestimated. The state economy itself was even more important. Over many decades, the economies of the fifteen republics had become virtually one, sharing and depending upon the same natural resources, energy grids and pipelines, transportation, suppliers, producers, consumers, and subsidies. The result, as was commonly acknowledged, was a "single Soviet economic space."

Nor should compelling human elements of integration be discounted. Official formulas boasting of a "Soviet people" and "Soviet nation" were overstated, but they were not, reliable sources assure us, merely an "ideological artifact."[72] Though the Soviet Union was composed of scores of different ethnic groups, there were many millions of mixed families and some 75 million citizens, nearly a third of the population, lived outside their ethnic territories, including 25 million Russians. Shared historical experiences were also a unifying factor, such as the terrible losses and ultimate victory in World War II, or "Great Patriotic War," as was the language of the Moscow center. More than 60 percent of non-Russians spoke Russian fluently, and most of the others had assimilated some of Russia's language and culture though the all-Union educational system and media.[73]

Given the right reform policies and other circumstances, these multiple integrative elements, along with a history of living with Russia and one another for centuries before and since 1917, were enough to hold most of the Soviet republics together without the Communist Party dictatorship. Indeed, a decade after the end of the Soviet Communist state, an American historian traveling through its former territories still found "Sovietness at almost every turn."[74] If nothing else, tens of millions of Soviet citizens had much to lose in the event of a breakup of the Union. That understanding no doubt helps explain the result of the March 1991 referendum, which was, an American specialist confirmed, an "overwhelming vote for the Union."[75]

It is also true that the voluntary Soviet federation proposed by Gorbachev would have meant fewer than the fourteen non-Russian republics. He hoped otherwise but acknowledged the prospect by enacting a new Law on Secession in April 1990. The tiny Baltic republics of Lithuania, Latvia, and Estonia, annexed by Stalin's Red Army in 1940, were almost certain to choose renewed independence, and Western Moldova reunion with Romania (though it changed its mind after 1991).[76] One or two of the three small Transcaucasian republics also might have seceded depending on whether the bitter enemies Armenia and Azerbaijan sought Russia's protection against the other and whether Georgia decided it needed Moscow's help in preserving its own multiethnic state. (Its decision eventually contributed to the Georgian-Russian war in August 2008.)

Even so, all of these small nationalities were on the Soviet periphery, and the remaining eight to ten republics constituted more than 90 percent of the old Union's territory, population, and resources. They were more than enough to form and sustain a new Soviet Union. Even fewer grouped around Russia would have been adequate. Indeed, according to a non-Russian leader who participated in the abolition of the Soviet state a few months later, a new Union could "consist of four republics." (Presumably he meant Russia, Belorussia, Ukraine, and Kazakhstan with its large number of ethnic Russians, as indeed Solzhenitsyn and others had already proposed.)[77]

Popular opinion may have been overwhelmingly pro-Union, but after early 1990, when regional parliamentary elections devolved considerable power from the Moscow center, it was the leaders and elites of the republics who would decide their future. There is strong evidence that a majority of them also wanted to preserve the Union, at least until late 1991. This preference was clearly expressed in negotiations for a new Union Treaty that Gorbachev began directly with the willing leaders of nine Soviet republics—Russia, Ukraine, Belorussia, the five Central Asian republics, and Azerbaijan—in April 1991, a crisis-ridden time somewhat beyond the period analyzed here but therefore all the more significant.

The negotiations, known as the Novo-Ogarevo process, resulted in an agreement to form a new "Union of Soviet Sovereign Republics." Scheduled to be signed formally on August 20, 1991, the treaty was initialed by all nine republic leaders, including the three who would abolish the Soviet Union only a few months later—Yeltsin of Russia, Leonid Kravchuk of Ukraine, and Stanislav Shushkevich of Belorussia.[78] Gorbachev had to cede more power than he wanted to the republics, but the treaty preserved an all-Union state, elected presidency and parliament, military, and economy. It was so finalized that even disputes over seating at the signing ceremony and the order of signatures—Yeltsin insisted that his appear near the top, not alphabetically—which were to be followed by a new constitution and elections, had been resolved and special paper for the text and souvenir stamps agreed upon.[79]

The familiar argument that Novo-Ogarevo's failure to save the Soviet Union proved its unreformability therefore makes no sense. Those negotiations were successful, and, like Gorbachev's other reforms, they developed within the Soviet system, legitimized by the popular mandate of the March referendum and conducted by the established multinational leaderships of most of the country. Instead, the Novo-Ogarevo process should be seen as the kind of elite consensus, or "pact-making," that many political scientists say is necessary for the successful democratic reformation of a political system.[80] That is how even a leading pro-Yeltsin democrat anticipated the signing of the new treaty—as a "historic event" that could be "as long-lived as the American Declaration of Independence, and serve as the same reliable political and legal basis of the renovated Union."[81]

In other words, the treaty did not fail because the Union was unreformable but because a small group of high-level Moscow officials staged an armed coup on August 19 to stop its successful reform. (Nor was the coup inevitable, but that is another story.)[82] Though the putsch quickly collapsed, primarily because its leaders lacked the resolve to use the military force they had amassed in Moscow, its fallout dealt a heavy blow to the Novo-Ogarevo process. It profoundly weakened Gorbachev and his central government, emboldened the political ambitions of Yeltsin and Kravchuk, and made other republic leaders wary of Moscow's unpredictable behavior. According to most Western accounts, it eliminated any remaining possibility of saving the Union.

In fact, not even the failed but calamitous August coup extinguished the political impulse to preserve the Union or expectations by leading Soviet reformers that it would still be saved. In September, some 1,900 deputies from twelve Soviet republics resumed their participation in sessions of the Union Congress. In October, an agreement on a new economic union was signed. And as late as November 1991, Yeltsin assured the public, "The Union will live!"[83] Seven republics, including Russia, continued to negotiate with Soviet President Gorbachev—a majority, not counting the now independent Baltic states—and, on November 25, they seemed to agree on yet another treaty. It was more confederal than federative but still provided for a Union state, presidency, parliament, economy, and military.[84] Two weeks later, it, too, was aborted by a coup, this one carried out by Yeltsin, Kravchuk, and Shushkevich, fewer conspirators but men with greater resolve.

We must conclude, then, that just as there are no conceptual reasons for believing the Soviet system was unreformable, nor are there any empirical ones. As the historical developments reconsidered here show, by 1991 most of the system was in a process of far-reaching democratic and market reformation. The Soviet Union under Gorbachev was, of course, not yet fully reformed, but it was in full "transition," a term usually reserved for the post-Soviet period. All that remains of the unreformability axiom is the insistence that because Gorbachev's reforms were avowedly pro-Soviet and prosocialist, they were merely a "fantasy" or "chimera."[85] This is, of course, ideological bias, not historical analysis.

WHY, contrary to the assertions of so many specialists for so many years, did the Soviet system turn out to be remarkably reformable? Was it really some kind of "political miracle," as an American historian later wrote?[86] Important elements of a full explanation include the enduring power of anti-Stalinist ideas dating back to the 1920s and even to 1917; the legacies of Khrushchev's policies, among them the birth of a proto-reform party inside the Communist Party; the Soviet elite's increasing exposure to the West and thus awareness of alternative ways of life (both socialist and capitalist); profound changes in society that were eroding Party-state controls and de-Stalinizing the system from below; growing social and economic problems that further promoted proreform senti-ments in the high nomenklatura; and, not to be minimized, Gorbachev's exceptional leadership. But there was an equally crucial factor.

Most Western specialists had long believed that the Soviet system's basic institutions were too "totalitarian" or otherwise rigged to be fun-damentally reformed. In fact, the system had been constructed all along in a dualistic way that made it potentially reformable, even, so to speak, reform-ready. Formally, it had most of the institutions of a represen-tative democracy—a constitution that included provisions for civil liberties, a legislature, elections, a judiciary, a federation. But inside or alongside each of those components were "counterweights" that nulli-fied their democratic content, most importantly the Communist Party's political monopoly, single-candidate ballots, censorship, and police re-pression.[87] To begin a process of democratic reform, all that was needed was a will and a way to remove the counterweights.

Gorbachev and his closest aides understood the duality, which he characterized as "democratic principles in words and authoritarianism in reality." To democratize the system, he later observed, "it wasn't neces-sary to invent anything new," only, as an adviser remarked, to transform the democratic components of the Soviet Union "from decoration into reality." This was true of almost all of Gorbachev's reforms, though the most ramifying example was, as he emphasized, the "transfer of power from the hands of the Communist Party, which had monopolized it, into the hands of those to whom it should have belonged according to the Constitution—to the soviets through free elections."[88] Not only did its dualistic institutions make the Soviet system highly reformable, but without them the peaceful democratization and other transformations of the Gorbachev years probably would not have been possible, and certainly would not have been as rapid or historic.

5 THE FATE OF THE SOVIET UNION

WHY DID IT END?

[It is] the question of all questions.

LEON ONIKOV, VETERAN COMMUNIST OFFICIAL

MOST explanations of the end of the Soviet Union in December 1991 assume in one way or another that it had been unreformable. But if that was not the case, why did the vast state long known as the world's "second superpower," one that had survived and even grown stronger from repeated turmoil, trauma, and internal changes during its seventy-four-year existence, abruptly disappear? For the answer, or to search for an answer, we must first recall the context in which that historic event occurred.

By mid-1990, in the sixth year of Gorbachev's reforms, the Soviet Union was being destabilized by growing crises and disorder on almost every front—economic, social, and political. During the next year and a half, the government's budget deficit and foreign debt soared, as did inflation caused by relaxed controls over wages and the money supply, while the state's financial resources—gravely depleted by the plunge in world prices for Soviet oil since 1985—declined to virtually nothing. By 1991, production had begun to fall, and a growing number of basic consumer goods all but disappeared from state shops. The economic hardships—rationing was introduced in several regions for some essential goods—shattered any remaining social consensus about Gorbachev's perestroika. Many Soviet citizens now wanted the reforms ended, even reversed; an influential minority called for more far-reaching and rapid economic marketization and privatization; and still others, in an older Russian tradition, were "waiting for a Messiah,"[1] a role soon ascribed to Boris Yeltsin.

The political crisis was the most serious, threatening to destabilize the Soviet state from bottom to top. Gorbachev's democratization measures had created public space for all manner of long repressed discontents and newly aroused demands. By 1991, this space was being amply filled by, elections across this most vast country; nationalist demands for more sovereignty in many republics, including outright secession in the Baltics Western Ukraine, and parts of the Caucasus, and even ethnic pogroms; mass political strikes by miners in the coal fields of Russia and Ukraine; and a nationwide "rally mania" featuring large anti-Communist (and, often overlooked, pro-Communist) demonstrations in the streets of Moscow and other cities.[2]

Meanwhile, parliamentary elections in the Soviet Russian Republic in 1990 produced a movement of self-described "radical reformers" rallying around the maverick former Politburo candidate Yeltsin. Virtually all of the prominent new "radical democrats," as they also called themselves, had begun as Communist Party members and fervent Gorbachev supporters. In the summer of 1990, following Yeltsin's lead, a growing number of them began deserting the Party, repudiating both its present-day role and historical record all the way back through Stalin to Lenin himself.

Gorbachev's personal leadership was also in deep crisis. In the second half of 1990, his public popularity, which had remained remarkably high for five years, fell precipitously while Yeltsin's soared.[3] His authority was further diminished in June 1991, when Yeltsin was elected president of the Russian Republic by popular vote; Gorbachev's presidency of the Soviet Union, bestowed by a vote of its Congress the pervious year, now seemed substantially less legitimate. The same was true of his once liberator-like standing with the proreform intelligentsia, which had been perhaps his most important constituency. No longer united around him or by his conception of a socialist reformation, some of its best-known figures, his own "foremen of glasnost and perestroika," defected to Yeltsin.

More ominously in those uncertain conditions between dismantled dictatorship and democracy, support for Gorbachev in the Party-state elite plummeted. By the fall of 1990, his original perestroika coalition with moderate nomenklatura reformers, which had enabled him to enact such great changes since 1985, had completely collapsed. For its most influential members, notably Ligachev and Ryzhkov, Gorbachev's policies had finally become not just too radical but destructive acts bringing the country "to ruin." Even his close allies could no longer support him, as his chief military adviser explained: "Gorbachev is dear to me, but the Fatherland is dearer!"[4] Neither Ligachev nor Ryzhkov yet directly opposed him, but nor did they any longer stand between him and the growing bureaucratic wrath directed at his leadership.

Having discovered the uses of glasnost for themselves, leaders of every powerful Soviet institution were now openly aligned against Gorbachev—the Party apparatus, state economic ministries, the military, the KGB, and even his own Congress. They charged that his reforms had "destroyed the Communist Party, shattered the Union, lost Eastern Europe, liquidated Marxism-Leninism . . . dealt a blow to the entire army, devastated consumer shops, fostered crime," and more. The depth of their opposition was reflected in the emotionally charged accusation that he had put "our Fatherland in a danger even more threatening than in 1941," the year of the Nazi invasion. At first privately but then increasingly in public forums, they threatened to remove him if he did not quickly "restore order." Rumors of an anti-Gorbachev coup were now rife.[5]

They were not empty threats. Anti-Gorbachev attitudes were rabid among military and other security officials, "men with guns," as one of his advisers reminded observers.[6] They particularly despised his foreign policies, which by 1991 included major disarmament concessions to the United States, the withdrawal of Soviet troops from Eastern and Central Europe, the reunification of Germany on Western terms, and support for the American war against Saddam Hussein's invasion of Kuwait. Gorbachev insisted that these unprecedented steps were necessary for ending the Cold War and the arms race with the United States, bringing the Soviet Union into a reunited Europe, and thus enhancing the country's security. His enemies saw them as a "Soviet Munich," the "betrayal of everything our wartime generation achieved," a "catastrophe equal in its consequences to defeat in a third world war," and, of course, as "criminal."[7]

Beleaguered by reactionary threats on one side and demands for more radical changes on the other, as well as over three-fourths of the public calling for "firm order in the country," Gorbachev made a desperate political shift in late 1990 and early 1991 that has been widely misunderstood.[8] Known as his "turn to the Right," he distanced himself publicly from several of his most prominent proreform associates and reconstituted his government in a way that seemed to put it "in the hands of hardline opponents of reform," creating the impression he had become, "in a profound sense, conservative," even "head of a revived authoritarianism."[9] Many onetime followers bitterly accused him of abandoning perestroika, and his close ally and foreign minister, Eduard Shevardnadze, resigned.

In fact, Gorbachev, who had promised only a few months earlier to "radicalize" his political and economic policies and still proclaimed himself to be "a democrat who is inclined toward radical views," was trying to save his reforms by forging a new coalition with different high-level officials who he thought, not unreasonably, were moderates in the circumstances of 1990 and 1991. He called his revised stance "centrism" and defended it against what he understood to be growing "extremism" on both sides of his leadership.[10] During these few months, Gorbachev did adopt a number of tougher measures in the name of "order and stability." But he assured sympathizers that they were a "tactical maneuver," promising that his reforms were "eternal values" and he would never "turn back." Nor did he actually reverse any of his prodemocracy changes and, indeed, even pushed forward with the unprecedented national vote on the Union. As one of his "radical" critics remarked at the time, "That Gorbachev has suddenly turned into a rightist . . . is absurd." Two scholars later agreed, concluding that Gorbachev "did not suggest turning back but simply going ahead more cautiously."[11]

However interpreted, the maneuver was a political disaster and short-lived. In those highly polarized circumstances, there was no stable center. Torn between his cherished role as the father of a Soviet democratic reformation and his perceived need to stabilize the country, as well as his leadership position, Gorbachev fluctuated between Yeltsin's radicals and his own government, while his new ministers, who did not trust

him, intrigued against him. And when he gathered Yeltsin and other republic leaders at his residence at Novo Ogarevo, in April 1991, to negotiate a radically decentralized Union, his appointees set into motion the
fateful August coup.

As serious as those crises were, they do not explain the end of the Soviet Union. They resulted primarily from the abolition of "command"
elements in the prereform political and economic administrative system
before new democratic and market processes could fully function. Given
time, the further development of new institutions and anticrisis measures proposed by Gorbachev and other leaders were feasible solutions.
Indeed, the Soviet system had survived much worse kinds of destabilization, including those caused by collectivization and famine in 1929
through 1933 and the German invasion in the early 1940s. Moreover, the
crises of 1990 and 1991 were often exaggerated by contemporary commentators, whose accounts strongly influenced later studies. They came
to overstate the problems partly for partisan reasons, partly because it
had become "fashionable to speak and write about crisis," but mainly
because such political and economic disorders, while not uncommon
elsewhere, were unprecedented in the Soviet Union and therefore had
an extraordinary psychological effect.[12]

Even so, few, if any, informed observers at the time saw the crises as
the death knell of the Soviet system. Most interpreted them instead as a
general "crisis of recuperation"—as symptoms, even positive signs, of
the country's ongoing transformation or "transition."[13] In this respect,
they agreed with Gorbachev: "The logic and values of stability . . . do not
coincide with the logic and values of reformationist breakthroughs." Or
as he expressed this philosophy of high-wire reform elsewhere, "stability
would mean the end of perestroika" and therefore "there is no reason to
fear chaos."[14] The world's leading intelligence services evidently agreed.
Reporting to their governments in 1991, none foresaw the end of the Soviet Union, only of the form in which it had previously existed.[15]

How, then, is that historic outcome to be explained? The importance of
the question can hardly be overstated. For many Russians, probably most
of them, the end of the Soviet Union naturally remains the "question of
the century," to which "no one has given the people a straight answer."
It is a question that arouses passions like those of "religious fanatics" and

becomes "harder to understand as the years pass."[16] But the disappearance of that enormous, epochal nation-state, and why this happened, is
also a vital part of our own history. More than any other modern event,
it has shaped the world in which we have lived since 1991. (Why, then,
would a prominent Western scholar think that explaining the Soviet
breakup is "a can of worms . . . perhaps best left unopened"?)[17]

Most of the answers given in the large specialized literature are, like
many interpretations of Soviet history, riddled with fallacies, myths,
ideological bias, and conceits of hindsight. A senior scholar assures us,
to take an example similar to one quoted in the preceding chapter, that
"in retrospect," the end of the Soviet Union "is easily understood and
not at all surprising," even though he did not foresee it and does not really explain it.[18] Readers may be surprised to learn, however, that despite
many emphatic assertions in the literature, there is no consensus what-
soever as to what factors actually explain the end of the Soviet Union.

There are, instead, as many as ten different explanations.[19] Some of
them, like generalizations about the purported unreformability of the
Soviet system, are too poorly formulated to be useful. These include,
for example, assertions that the system "really collapsed of its own
weight" or "simply imploded and collapsed of itself." Others, as a Russian scholar noted, are "extraordinarily impressionistic and superficial,"
little more than a "collection of banalities" and "stereotypes." And still
others, though serious and substantial, emphasize so many different,
even contradictory explanatory factors as to add up to no coherent explanation at all.[20]

Putting those unhelpful accounts aside, and combining several related factors frequently cited in the specialized literature, six different
but widely propounded explanations require attention:

- The end of the Soviet Union was "inevitable" because it was
  "doomed" by some irremediable genetic or inherent defect
- The system fell victim to a popular anti-Soviet revolution from
  below, a democratic one in Russia, nationalist revolts in the
  other ethnic republics, or both
- The Soviet system was undermined by an unworkable economy
  that resulted in economic collapse
- The gradualist reformation (perestroika) attempted by Gorbachev unleashed and succumbed to a Russian tradition of

ideological and political maximalism, or extremism, as had happened before in the nation's history, which destroyed the foundations of the system
- The disappearance of the Soviet Union was a classic example of the crucial role of leaders in history, in this case first Gorbachev and then Yeltsin
- The Soviet breakup was an "elite-driven" event, which means the explanation is to be found in the behavior of the nomenklatura, or segments of it, in the late 1980s and early 1990s

To begin with inevitability, the argument that the Soviet Union was inescapably doomed is, as Russian intellectuals often point out, a simplistic kind of historical determinism not unlike the crude Marxism once taught in Soviet schools.[21] It is also a quintessential example of post facto predetermination. Consider these revealing statements about Western scholarly opinion by three of its leading representatives. In 1990, according to the first, the end of the Soviet Union "seemed absolutely unthinkable." But in 1998, the second reported, "Nobody really expresses any surprise that the Soviet Union collapsed." And in 2002, according to the third, the "prevailing view" was that "the breakup was inevitable."[22] Was it conceptual revelation, hindsight bias, or political fashion that led expert opinion from unthinkable to inevitable?

As for the fatal defect said to have doomed the Soviet Union, three are variously cited. Each relies, of course, on the axiom that the system was unreformable. One, which I already rejected as both theological and disproved by the historical experiences of other nations, including America, is a fatal original Soviet sin or inherent evil. The second is the "effects of socialism," which is construed to be an unnatural ideology that killed the system. This, again, is mostly an expression of intense ideological dislike, and therefore little more needs to be said about it.[23] The third inherent feature of the system purported to have been the doomsday factor is less simplistic: the Soviet Union was an "empire," and all "multinational empires are doomed." (For the sake of this discussion, I leave aside the report that four leading Western historians of empire could "agree on only one thing: that none of them know what an empire is.")[24]

There are several serious problems with this widespread explanation. First, its proponents frequently confuse or conflate the end of the

Soviet Union itself in 1991 with the fall of the Soviet empire in Eastern Europe two years earlier, which is a different matter. (This is not to say there was no spillover effect from the developments in Eastern Europe, though its importance can be debated.)[25] Second, this, too, is almost entirely a retrospective analysis. Many Western scholars later decided the "Soviet Union was clearly an empire," but before 1991, few of them actually treated that multinational state as an empire.[26] Third, it too has a strong ideological flavor, "empire" being a pejorative characterization of the Soviet Union. As a result, this explanation lost some of its analytical integrity (and ideological satisfaction) after September 11, 2001, when a broad spectrum of U.S. policy opinion decided that there was, or should be, an American empire—and not an evil or doomed one, but even, some argue, a "benevolent empire."[27]

The main question, however, is whether the Soviet Union was an empire at home and, even if so, whether that is an adequate explanation of its disappearance. Writers often assert that the "USSR fell apart because it was an empire." But three leading Western authorities on the subject conclude that its end was not inevitable; another resists classifying it as an empire; and yet another denies it was an empire, as do a large number of post-Soviet Russian scholars and democratic thinkers.[28] Indeed, even proponents of the explanation concede that the Soviet Union was a "peculiar kind of empire" and "differed . . . in several important ways" from traditional ones.[29] For all the political repression over the years, there was not, for example, a pattern of economic exploitation of the other republics by the Russian center. Instead, the backward ones were considerably modernized under the Soviet system, arguably to the economic detriment of Russia.[30]

Nor did the Soviet Union end like most traditional empires, including its presumed tsarist predecessor, which disintegrated under the pressures of war and political opposition on their colonial peripheries. In the Soviet case, there was no war, and seven republics were still negotiating a new Union with Moscow at the end. Among them were the five Central Asian republics, presumably the most "colonized" but that least of all wanted to abandon the Union. Instead, the Soviet Union was broken up first and foremost by its own "imperial" center, Moscow, now controlled by Yeltsin. In short, whatever imperial aspects the Soviet state may have had, they were not enough to mean, as most authoritative studies conclude, that "it was necessarily doomed to disintegration."[31]

The equally widespread idea that a revolutionary "vast movement from below" destroyed the Soviet Union is no more persuasive.
There are two versions of these "populist interpretations" and "political myths," as a Russian expert on the subject labels them.[32] By now,
the first requires no special attention. As I showed in chapter 4, there
was no popular anti-Soviet revolution in Russia itself. Nor does the evidence support a related argument that the Soviet system succumbed to
a "legitimacy crisis"—essentially a "delegitimization" of its socialist ideology primarily as a result of Gorbachev's glasnost ideas and historical
revelations.[33] Russians may have valued their new political liberties and
turned against the Communist Party, but the "overwhelming majority"
remained pro-Soviet and prosocialist.

The second version of "revolution from below" locates it primarily
outside Russia, in the other Soviet ethnic republics. In this dramatic and
sweeping explanation, sometimes coupled with the empire thesis, the
Union was overthrown by the "peoples . . . of all those republics," a "rebellion of the [Soviet] nations," and a "remarkable nationalist mobilization" resulting in "multiple waves of nationalist revolt." In a word, it was
the "popular will . . . that the Soviet Union should die."[34]

This explanation is at odds with the essential facts, not the least being the 76 percent pro-Union vote in the referendum held only nine
months before the breakup. It is also contradicted by the submissive
behavior of most of the Soviet republic leaders, from Central Asia and
Transcaucasia to Ukraine, in August 1991. When they thought the military coup in Moscow might succeed and forcibly reimpose the center's
control throughout the country, they were either compliant or silent.[35]
For these and other reasons, a number of Western and Russian analysts
give a different account of the end of the Soviet Union. There was "only
limited mobilization of the masses"; it "was not broken up by crowds of
people who came into the streets under nationalist slogans"; and, as a
group of (non-Communist) Russian experts concluded five years later,
the Union's breakup occurred "against the will of its peoples."[36]

The ramifying mistake made by proponents of the nationalist
revolution-from-below explanation is interpreting all or most of the
thousands of ethnic protests during the Gorbachev years as demands for
secession and full independence.[37] In reality, the great majority of them
sought redress of various grievances within the framework of the Union,
were "not a struggle against the USSR" but against other ethnic groups,

and became separatist only after the end of the Soviet state—or, several Russian observers point out, were "decoration" for the self-interested politics of regional elites,[38] an important subject to which I will return.

The mistake is compounded by failing to understand the confusion that developed, and remains, over the words "sovereignty" and "independence." Even according to the pre-Gorbachev Soviet constitution, every Union republic was "sovereign." In early 1990, he urged the newly elected republic congresses to reaffirm their sovereignty as preparation for negotiating a new Union Treaty.[39] All but one did so without any of them, outside the Baltics, construing it to mean independence from the Union. Even the fateful sovereignty resolution adopted by the Russian Republic at its congress in June 1990, despite later claims, "actually had nothing to do with independence." That is why 907 of 929 deputies voted for it, including the adamantly pro-Union Communist delegates.[40] And it is why the agreement reached by Gorbachev and republic leaders at Novo Ogarevo in mid-1991, including the Russian leader, could call for a new "Union of Soviet Sovereign Republics."

And yet, construing "sovereignty" to mean full independence did play a critical role in the end of the Soviet Union. This is partly because of the ambiguous meaning of the word, which was used differently in various Soviet languages, but mainly because it suited the political ambitions of several republic leaders and elites, particularly Russia's Yeltsin and Ukraine's Leonid Kravchuk. By late 1991, the words "sovereignty" and "independence" figured prominently in political struggles under way across the country, but not even longtime students of Soviet media could be sure what exactly was meant by either.

That helps explain the incongruous result of the December 1991 referendum in Ukraine, which is usually cited as conclusive evidence of a popular nationalist revolution. In this instance, 90 percent of the turnout voted for "independence" even though nine months before, in the March referendum, 70 percent of Ukrainians (and 80 percent in a supplementary ballot) had voted for the Union. Ukraine, along with Russia, Belarus, and Western Kazakhstan, were the Slavic core of the Soviet Union. And when Yeltsin, Kravchuk, and, following their lead, the leader of tiny Belarus abolished it a few days later, they used the December referendum as justification.

But did so many Ukrainians, linked to Russia for centuries and scarcely distinguishable from their fellow Slavs, really vote to leave the

Union? In Ukraine, there was already "considerable confusion" over the words "sovereignty" and "independence," which were being used almost interchangeably and manipulated by the former Communist elite, turned nationalist and headed by Kravchuk.[41] Protesting Kravchuk's use of the referendum vote, Gorbachev could tell him "with some justice," as an American scholar notes, that other republics had declared independence without it meaning an "obligatory exit from the Union." Moreover, as another American scholar argues based on polling data, the wording of the referendum was ambiguous, simply asking voters if they favored "the independence of Ukraine"; had it said this meant leaving the Union, the outcome probably would have been significantly different.[42] (A decade later, 60 percent of Ukrainians favored some kind of union with Russia and only 46.5 percent said they would have voted for a referendum on independence.)[43]

Whatever the result, Ukraine, like most of the other republics, did not experience a popular secessionist revolution. There and elsewhere, the growth of anti-Union sentiment was "more at the level of elite politics than of mass public opinion," and "separatism came . . . from above."[44] Looking back on the events of 1990 and 1991, a Russian specialist concluded that there had been an "almost complete absence of any serious separatist attitudes in the Soviet republics except the Baltics and Georgia." A leading British scholar, warning that "hindsight can mislead," agreed: "Only in the Baltic (and perhaps Transcaucasia) did the local national question take the form of a demand for immediate independence."[45]

The third common explanation of the end of the Soviet Union argues the entire system was "nonviable" because of a "fundamentally unworkable" economy that finally resulted in "utter and complete collapse." (In some of these accounts, President Reagan's military buildup of the early 1980s is incorrectly credited with having precipitated or accelerated the economic collapse.) As evidence, it emphasizes the economic crisis of 1990 and 1991, which is said to have left the country on the brink of catastrophe, even "teetering on the edge of famine."[46] An explanation propounded with equal certainty by anti-Marxists and some Marxists, though by very few economists, it also contains strong ideological elements: some of its proponents portray the "doomed" Soviet economy as perversely socialist, others as fatally nonsocialist.[47] It also draws on self-serving assertions by Yeltsin's "radical reformers." Their "shock therapy" having brought even greater misfortunes to Russia in the 1990s, they insisted that the "collapse of the Soviet economy" had left them with no choice.[48]

This explanation is no more convincing than the other two. Long-established economies do not suddenly "collapse" or destroy nation-states. It did not happen, for example, earlier in Soviet history, despite periods of greater economic disorder and misery; during the corrosive American Great Depression of the 1930s; or later in Russia when the post-Soviet economy plunged into considerably worse crises.[49] Moreover, what was in crisis in 1990 and 1991 was not actually the Soviet economy, which still recorded growth from 1985 to 1989, but an already post-Soviet or transitional one.[50] By 1990, Gorbachev's reforms and other developments had removed or weakened the elements of Party-state command and control that had defined the Soviet economy and made it workable in important ways for decades.

Nor was the economic crisis, however severe, truly a "collapse." (An American economist later concluded, using new information, that "the Soviet economy was a lot sturdier than it appears in hindsight.") Citizens continued to work and be paid, and the overall economy, even in mounting disarray, continued to function, occasionally even showing some signs of recovery.[51] Industrial production began to fall sharply in 1990, but the agricultural output that year was one of the highest in decades. Indeed, citizens were earning more disposable income than ever before, which contributed to the crisis: "Too many rubles," as the saying went, were "chasing too few goods," as many essential items, including foodstuffs, disappeared from state shops.

Those widespread shortages helped foster the myth of a total economic breakdown, but the problem was primarily one of distribution. Anticipating a major upsurge in state-controlled prices, both consumers and suppliers were hoarding goods, the former at home in fear of higher costs, the latter in warehouses in hope of greater profits.[52] (Thus, goods would soon suddenly reappear on store shelves in abundance, far from all of them imports, after January 1992, when Yeltsin's policies decontrolled prices and vaporized the value of rubles.) And even that crisis of supply has been exaggerated. Although Soviet citizens had endured periodic shortages for decades, overwrought predictions of impending catastrophe, including a nationwide famine, became part of the general "hysteria" of 1990 and 1991 and passed into now standard accounts.

(Panicky buying of household basics in response to rumors of shortages, thereby creating them, was and remains a Russian tradition. In 2006, for example, it happened in pursuit of salt, when it was correctly diagnosed as a "psychological" phenomenon having "nothing to do with the actual economy.")[53]

Bare shelves in state stores, to take the starkest example, did not mean mass hunger. In the countryside, people grew much of their own food, as they always had, but even many urban dwellers were not greatly dependent on official shops. In addition to resorting to more costly but readily accessible nonstate markets and cultivating their own food gardens, almost all employed Soviet citizens and students traditionally received their main meal at midday in workplace and school cafeterias, where employees could also buy take-home supplies. That long-standing system continued to operate in 1990 and 1991, though no doubt with declining quantity and nutrition. In any event, as was later pointed out, the "sausage thesis" hardly explains the end of a Soviet state that had endured more severe food shortages before.[54]

But no matter how serious the crisis may have been, its primary cause was not economic. As many Western and Russian economists agree, "The USSR was killed . . . by politics, not economics."[55] From the late 1980s to 1991, one political decision and development after another steadily dismantled or undermined the old Soviet economic system without leaving time for another to develop in its place. As a direct result, the economic crisis unfolded while the longstanding problem of implementing new policies inherent in the Soviet bureaucratic system became even worse. (By mid-1990, Gorbachev, despite his new presidential powers on paper, was unable to have any major economic initiative actually carried out. "The boldest reform decisions," a top aide complained, "are left hanging in the air.")[56]

Political factors that destabilized the economy began with Gorbachev's adoption of democratizing and other decentralizing reforms, which soon diminished the Party-state's controls on enterprises, resources, wages, the money supply, and eventually property. They were followed by the "parade of sovereignty," which many regions and republics increasingly interpreted to mean economic autonomy over their own resources and products; by spontaneous "privatization" with little concern for production; and by a series of premature official announcements of forthcoming price increases, first by Gorbachev's ministers and then by

Yeltsin's, that triggered the hoarding of goods. Even aspects of Gorbach- ev's foreign policy had a negative effect on the economy, the use of so much railway capacity to remove military equipment from East Europe further disrupting food distribution. In response to growing shortages, regional officials—among them, it seems, some of Gorbachev's enemies, who engaged in sabotage—began withholding their products from the national market, crippling it still more.[57]

Here, too, the August 1991 coup, by further weakening Gorbachev's central government, made everything worse, from hoarding to the dis- memberment of the Union economy. By late autumn, Yeltsin was not only refusing to pay his Russian Republic's taxes to the Union budget but in Russia's name systematically stripping the Union of its economic and financial assets.[58] "Economics," as Gorbachev lamented, had be- come the "hostage of politics."[59] And as politics grew increasingly radi- cal and extreme, so did the economic crisis.

The political radicalism afflicting the country in 1990 and 1991, es- pecially in the capital cities Moscow and Leningrad, is the focus of the fourth explanation of the Soviet breakup. Believing that Russian history is "cyclical,"[60] it argues that Gorbachev's perestroika collapsed for much the same reason as had all previous attempts to modernize the nation through a gradualist or evolutionary reformation—as a result of impas- sioned and ultimately destructive extremism.

In this "tragic" view of Russia's long tradition of failed reforms and lost opportunities, "with its terrible grimaces and cruel irony," the out- come was always a reactionary backlash, revolution, or both.[61] Thus, the liberalizing reforms of Aleksandr II in the 1860s led to his assassination by radicals, harsh crackdowns by successor tsars, and the revolutionary upheaval of 1905; the modernizing land policies begun by Prime Min- ister Pyotr Stolypin in 1907 ended in his assassination and eventually the collapse of tsarist rule in the revolution of February 1917; the centrist, prodemocracy government emerging from that historic event was swept away by the Bolshevik coup of October; Lenin's evolutionary NEP of the 1920s perished in Stalin's revolution from above; and even Khrushchev's limited de-Stalinizing reforms of 1956 through 1964 resulted in his over- throw and twenty years of reactionary "stagnation."[62]

The agent of destructive radicalism in the tsarist era is said to have been the extremist wing of the Russian intelligentsia—educated, oppo- sitionist, often guilt-ridden people of some privilege who emerged in the second half of the nineteenth century. Usually described as politically immoderate, impatient, and nihilistic, the radical intelligentsia repeatedly sought to destroy Russia's existing order for the sake of a new one inspired by Western ideas, most fatefully Marxist socialism.[63] This nihilistic tradition, according to the explanation, reasserted itself under Gorbachev, as longtime Communist Party intellectuals, now enamored with free-market capitalism and calling themselves radical democrats, undermined his evolutionary perestroika with an onslaught of impatient criticism and increasingly anti-Soviet demands.

This interpretation of the end of the Soviet Union appears only occasionally and fragmentarily in Western studies—possibly because most of them sympathize with that anti-Soviet "extremism"—but it is widespread in Russia, where the primary role of the intelligentsia is seen as an "immutable law of all Russian revolutions."[64] A leading Russian historian is unequivocal: "There is no doubt that the intelligentsia was the main force in shattering the Soviet order." Another scholar agrees that it was those "political opponents of Gorbachev and his cautious, evolutionary course" who "suffocated perestroika and destroyed the Soviet Union." Other Russian writers are even more prosecutorial. One asks the "sacred question, 'Who is to blame?'" and answers emphatically, "the intelligentsia."[65]

Unlike several other explanations of the Soviet breakup, this one is not an afterthought. From 1988 to 1991, moderate Soviet intellectuals, anxiously pointing to the "notorious" precedents, warned "ultraradicals" against an "inverted Bolshevism" that would again "raze everything to the ground." They feared that traditional intelligentsia "impatience and extremism," the new "spell of maximalism," would lead to "more historical upheavals" and again abort the "evolutionary possibilities of our civilization."[66] So great was the fear that tradition would doom the ongoing Soviet reformation that its supporters, from self-described "moderate democrats" to the Gorbachev leadership itself, began worrying publicly about the most ominous analogy: "Our perestroika [might] suffer the tragic fate of NEP."[67]

The intelligentsia tradition clearly did play a significant role during the last years of the Soviet Union. The "revolution of ideas" sometimes attributed to "the people" was actually limited primarily to a radicalized segment of the intelligentsia. It was apparent in the behavior of the many middle-aged Communists who turned so quickly and completely against their own long-professed ideology (including the anti-Stalinist ideas that had spawned perestroika) and, in a "peculiar Oedipus complex," against the Soviet leader who had just liberated them. (In turn, Gorbachev resented the "betrayal of the intelligentsia, to which I gave everything," though he almost never said so publicly.) As with their tsarist-era predecessors, such radicalism often seemed to be "personal repentance" for the "shameful fact" of their prior lives of privilege— this time as conformist Party intellectuals.[68] Not surprisingly, it included another characteristic aspect of the tradition—enthusiasm for a new maximalist "fairy-tale," a revolutionary leap, in only "500 days," to a fully privatized, marketized economy. (Even though the International Monetary Fund and other Western financial institutions also initially opposed the plan, when Gorbachev rejected this first draft of shock therapy in 1990 as unworkable, fraught with social pain, and likely to break up the Union, the radical intelligentsia's impatience with him only grew.)[69]

Like their forerunners, from nineteenth-century underground revolutionaries to Lenin himself, perestroika-era *intelligentsy* became passionately active in politics. (A fellow intellectual was "horrified by . . . the 'revolutionary throng' made up of PhDs and academics.")[70] Having been entrusted with an important part of the mass media by Gorbachev for purposes of his glasnost policies, they used them increasingly to polarize the political atmosphere. Meanwhile, by 1990, they were in the forefront of the most radical movements of the period and abandoning Gorbachev for a maximalist hero—one declared, "The smartest people take Yeltsin's side"—which some of them would later deeply regret.[71] By November, and again following official violence in the Baltics in January 1991, for which they held Gorbachev responsible, even "foremen of glasnost" whom he had promoted and protected since 1985 were demanding his resignation.[72]

In the end, however, the radical intelligentsia did not cause the breakup of the Soviet Union. It did much to focus popular discontents on Gorbachev's leadership and to bolster Yeltsin's, but it had no effective power apart from those commanding figures. However great their public prominence and loud their voices, radical intellectuals had almost no standing with rank-and-file Russians, who mostly disliked them. Nor did they represent the entire intelligentsia even in Moscow or Leningrad, and still less in the provinces, where they were scarcely present. As was true during most of Russian history, the intelligentsia was a secondary actor.

WE come, then, to the role of leaders—Gorbachev, Yeltsin, or both—in the fateful drama of 1985 through 1991. Understood in its context, this "subjective" factor was the primary cause of the end of the Soviet Union or what some Russians call its "imposed dissolution."[73] Many Western specialists (though few Russian ones) strongly disagree. Like most modern-day interpreters of history, but also for their own Sovietological reasons, they dislike explanations of great events that point to the behavior of individuals, even powerful ones. They prefer equally great causes—in this case, "objective processes" determined by those large, defining elements of the Soviet system said to have "doomed" it.[74]

But the "decisive role of the subjective factor" in the Soviet breakup, to quote a Russian scholar, is clear from a simple counterfactual exercise: Remove the two leading protagonists, particularly Gorbachev, and it becomes almost impossible to imagine the events that led from 1985 to 1991 but easy to imagine, as a senior American scholar argued, the Soviet Union having "continued to muddle through without overt instability. That is the only possible conclusion."[75] The great majority of Russian writers on the question agree with that conclusion, as do most of the Russian citizens periodically surveyed and at least a few Western authors. They too "do not see the kind of powerful objective economic, social, and political causes capable of destroying such a strong and large state."[76]

Even among proponents of the leadership explanation, however, there are substantial disagreements. Disputes (especially in Russia) about the nature of that leadership—whether it was well intentioned or malign, wise or bungling, worthy or unworthy of admiration, and whether its results were intended or unintended—are important but not my main interest here. More to the point is which leader was primarily responsible for the disappearance of the Soviet state. Some Western and Russian "subjectivists" point to Gorbachev, others to Yeltsin, and a few to both leaders.

At first historical glance, it would seem to have been Yeltsin. On December 8, 1991, at a secluded hunting resort for top officials in the Belovezh Forest near Minsk, the capital of Soviet Belorussia, he met secretly with two junior republic leaders to sign an agreement abolishing the Soviet Union. But the absent Gorbachev's contribution to that fateful outcome was larger and more essential, even though he desperately tried to prevent it. Without the political changes Gorbachev had introduced during the preceding six years, neither Yeltsin nor any of the other factors said to have caused the Soviet breakup would have played a significant role, certainly not in the foreseeable future.

It was, after all, Gorbachev's democratization policies that freed the intelligentsia to speak openly about the "sins" of the past and present, permitted popular discontents to be aired and organized, enabled nationalist sentiments to grow into defiant movements, and contributed to the economic crisis by loosening central controls. As for Yeltsin, he was the biggest individual beneficiary of Gorbachev's prodemocracy reforms, being elected to the first Soviet Congress in 1989, the first Russian parliament in 1990, and Russia's first popularly chosen presidency in 1991. No matter what part any of those developments may have had in ending the Soviet Union, Gorbachev's leadership was therefore the "critical precipitating factor"—so much so that another American scholar reasonably concludes: "Without Gorbachev there would still be the Soviet Union."[77]

Judgments about the consequences of Gorbachev's leadership vary enormously in both Russia and the West. They range from the view that he "led [Russia] out of bondage" and, as the "liberator of such a country," was the "only great Russian reformer whose reform succeeded"; to the verdict that his "mind-boggling political ineptitude" made him "one of the greatest examples of failed leadership in history"; to darker indictments of Gorbachev (and Yeltsin) as knowing or unknowing agents of a U.S. conspiracy to destroy the Soviet Union.[78] (Widespread Russian conspiracy theories are the counterpart of American triumphalist assertions that a U.S. president or secret agency "ended Communism." Neither has any merit, and both are therefore excluded from this consideration.)[79]

But whatever the judgment of informed commentators, none of them doubt that in 1985 Gorbachev was the only person in the ruling Communist Party leadership, even in the expanding political class, willing and able to begin such reforms and during the next few years radicalize them in the face of growing opposition. It is why several American and Russian scholars argue that Gorbachev was an exceedingly rare figure in history—an "event-making" leader or, as one characterizes his equally singular role in ending the Cold War, a "historically fateful personality."[80]

As a direct result of Gorbachev's influence on events, Yeltsin, a little-known provincial Party boss until the new Soviet leader promoted him to Moscow, also became a fateful personality. ("Had there been no Gorbachev," a man in a position to know assures us, "there would have been no Yeltsin.")[81] By 1991, as president of Russia, the Union's only truly indispensable republic, leader of the growing legion of "radical reformers," and for now the people's "messiah," Yeltsin held the fate of his former patron's crisis-ridden, evolutionary reformation in his hands, most directly the future of the Union. Until the failed August coup, he alternated between opposing and supporting Gorbachev. But immediately after that event, Yeltsin began, in a kind of unfolding coup of his own, to diminish his already weakened rival by systematically dismantling the institutions of the Union center and arrogating to his Russian Republic virtually all of the political powers and economic assets of Gorbachev's Union government.[82]

Abolishing what remained of Gorbachev's presidency—his state and country—was the final step. Formally, three men signed away the Soviet Union in the Belovezh Forest, but in effect it was one. Without Yeltsin, as a former republic leader later explained, "there would not have been a Belovezh document."[83] Of the other two, the head of Soviet Belorussia (soon to be Belarus), faithful to its tradition as Moscow's "little Slav brother," deferentially followed the Russian leader. And though Ukraine's Kravchuk was now bent on "independence," he, too, had been influenced by Yeltsin, perhaps even his secret collaborator for several months.[84]

Echoing Yeltsin's justification of Belovezh—he insisted it had been "inevitable"[85]—most Western authors have concluded that by December 1991 the Union alternative no longer existed. But clearly it did—in the form of Gorbachev's ongoing negotiations with republic leaders and in polls showing continuing public support for the Union, as Yeltsin himself had acknowledged only a month before and one of his top advisers at Belovezh later confirmed.[86] Moreover, a Yeltsin-backed Union of the remaining seven or eight republics, considering its size and resources, might have persuaded others to return, including Ukraine. The real problem was different. Yeltsin had already decided, even while negotiating with Gorbachev, that the Union alternative no longer suited him.[87]

What drove these two leaders toward the destruction of a twentieth-century superpower, a development almost no one foresaw even a few months before? Obviously, both were men of extraordinary political will but, it is clear, of different kinds: Gorbachev's was a will to reform, Yeltsin's a will to power. The distinction can be made without prejudging either man; the consequences of Gorbachev's pursuit of reform may be applauded or condemned, as may his rival's pursuit of power. But there can be no doubt about their mutual role in the events that led from the seemingly indestructible Soviet state of 1985 to its disappearance barely six years later.

Gorbachev's remarkable will to reform the Soviet system he inherited—and, inseparably related in his mind, the international order based on the long U.S.-Soviet Cold War—is often obscured by the misperception that he was a half-hearted reformer who moved too slowly. In reality, as I explained earlier, a passionate, unrelenting commitment to the reformation he called perestroika was the defining feature of Gorbachev's leadership, and many knowledgeable observers thought it caused him to introduce changes too quickly. With that almost evangelical reformism in mind, a onetime critic dubbed Gorbachev the "Apostle Mikhail," pointing out that he had used power "not for the sake of power" but out of "concern for the fate of the reconstruction of life he had begun." Nor did most observers doubt that "all the titanic changes for the better" by 1990 were due to the "political will of Gorbachev."[88]

Only that overriding will to reform can explain the fateful steps Gorbachev took—and did not take. It explains his launching of heretical changes, trampling over totems and taboos even though he lacked any such mandate within his own perestroika coalition, and his radicalization of those policies even while confronted by increasingly menacing opposition. It explains why he could tell an aide early on, "No one knows how far I will go," as indeed he did, crossing one political Rubicon after another while abandoning both the Communist Party dictatorship at home and the Soviet empire abroad, and never turning back.[89]

No less remarkably, Gorbachev's will to reform explains two elements of his leadership that were, and remain, unprecedented in Russian political history. One was his systematic dispersal—literally, giving away—of the immense personal power he had inherited as general secretary. Had he not done so in pursuit of a democratic reformation, as he often said truthfully and without regret, "I could have operated just like they . . . ruled before me, like Brezhnev . . . like an emperor," adding for emphasis: "Is there another case in history of a person receiving power and giving it away himself?"[90] As a result, he became more and more powerless.

The other unique feature of Gorbachev's rule was his "deep aversion to the use of force." How often he actually resorted to armed force is disputed—many Russians still resent that he did not use it more often and effectively—but considering the country's violent past and the turbulent changes during his years in power, he left with remarkably little or, arguably, "no blood on his hands."[91] This, too, is explained by his commitment to an unprecedented kind of Russian reformation—a modernizing "revolution without shots." Gorbachev largely adhered to his "credo of reform," or "principled non-violence," insisting that "for me they are not merely words but a firm conviction, a vitally important idea," to the end. It was, a Russian scholar emphasizes, "his victory over centuries-long Russian, and later Soviet, traditions." For the sake of his reform mission, another pointed out, Gorbachev "was ready to give up everything—his crown, state, and allies."[92]

If Gorbachev's will to reform was sometimes in doubt, Yeltsin's will to power was not. The distinction was recognized even by one of Gorbachev's critics: "He fights for programs and ideas while his opponents fight for power." (Gorbachev said the difference between them was that "Tsar Boris," as he derisively called him, "worships power.")[93] From the moment Yeltsin appeared on the Soviet national scene, he was perceived as a man who believed he was "destined to rule." He had, wrote a British correspondent, "a huge thirst for power and a shrewd nose for finding it." A Russian journalist and early admirer later characterized him as a "power alcoholic, addicted to power." Yeltsin himself did not entirely disagree: "To be 'first' probably has always been part of my nature." Nor did one of his former press secretaries: "Power is his ideology."[94]

That was not, of course, the sole aspect of Yeltsin's political personality. He thought of himself as the heroic "father of an independent, democratic Russia," as did his many admirers.[95] But his relentless pursuit of power—compounded by a "pathological, destructive, all-consuming hatred of Gorbachev"[96]—ultimately determined his political positions. At various times, Yeltsin was for and against every disputed issue of the period—perestroika, the Communist Party, shock therapy and a free market, the emerging parliamentary system, nomenklatura

Communists, the Union—and for "neither a capitalist nor a socialist" Russia. Even his touted support for Baltic independence was thought to be "a way of asserting himself against Gorbachev." Indeed, most of his increasingly radical positions seem to have been adopted "not as ends in themselves but primarily to advance his personal political objectives." This pursuit of power led Yeltsin, the American ambassador observed. "to tell people what they wanted to hear, and he did so with abandon," or as a Russian academic quipped: "For the sake of power, he can become whomever you want, even a Muslim."[97]

The ultimate expression of Yeltsin's will to power was the historic coup d'etat at Belovezh that overthrew what was still, despite its crises and defections, a nuclear superpower with some 280 million citizens. Yeltsin and his collaborators always denied Belovezh was a coup, insisting that after the aborted August putsch the "Soviet Union had in fact already ceased to exist, and it was necessary to declare this de jure," though their real concern may have been that the "cunning Gorbachev" was making a political comeback and his pro-Union position gaining new support.[98] But if it was necessary to formally end the Soviet Union, Yeltsin could have stated the case openly and turned to the leaders or legislatures of all the remaining republics or even to the people in a referendum, as Gorbachev had done nine months before and was now calling for again.[99]

Instead, Yeltsin acted illegally, in complete disregard for a longstanding constitution, in (as he admitted) "super-secrecy," and—a telltale sign of a coup—in some fear of being arrested. (As precautionary measures, the heavily guarded Belovezh conspirators met near the Polish border and the first person they informed, to assure him that he would still be the top military commander, was the head of the now former Soviet armed forces.) The result, as a broad spectrum of independent observers, including the British ambassador, concluded, was a coup—or, considering the failed putsch against Gorbachev in August, a "second coup." It was, a Yeltsin supporter widely admired in the West later acknowledged, "neither legitimate nor democratic."[100]

Yeltsin took that fateful step, as many Russian and Western authors also agree, primarily to be completely rid of Gorbachev.[101] To be "first," the presidency of a republic of the Soviet Union, even the most important one, was far from enough; he needed the seat and symbol of supreme power, Gorbachev's Kremlin. No other anti-Gorbachev, proreform leader in Russia had that kind of will to rule. Nor did anyone on the other side of the political barricade. The August plotters amassed overwhelming military force in the center of Moscow, but did not use it or even arrest Yeltsin or any of his allies. Various reasons were given, but they all came down to one—"a fatal lack of will."[102]

Thus did the opposing but symbiotic wills of two extraordinary figures—extraordinary also in that they appeared at the same historical moment and the fate of each would have been different without the other—lead to the end of the Soviet Union. Readers may still resist attributing such an epochal development to two individuals, but it was in keeping with Russia's long tradition of leader-dominated politics. Two eminent students of that tradition, a Russian and an American, understood the roles Gorbachev and Yeltsin had played. The first expressed it in a Russian historical analogy: "Gorbachev was our February revolution, and Yeltsin our October." The American expressed it in a Western idiom: "The Gorbachev-Yeltsin rivalry seemed to contain all the elements of a Shakespearean tragedy."[103]

That is the essential explanation of the end of the Soviet Union, which means, of course, the outcome was not inevitable. But is it a sufficient explanation? It remains to be asked why Yeltsin, who had no armed forces or even a political party, was able, almost on his own, to abolish an enormous, seventy-four-year-old state, even in its weakened condition, without any significant resistance by ordinary citizens, the parliament, or other important groups, at least in Soviet Russia itself.

Three factors seem to explain why there was no popular resistance to Yeltsin's extraordinary step at Belovezh, despite widespread support for the Soviet Union during and after 1991. The passivity of the Russian people during fateful political struggles among the nation's leaders, whether out of deference, indifference, hope, or fear, was another strong tradition. December 1991 was not the first time "the people kept silent," in an often-quoted expression from Pushkin's *Boris Godunov*, about a sixteenth-century breakup of the Moscow state.[104] The second factor was contemporary. Public opinion had turned so sharply against Gorbachev by 1991 that many Russians undoubtedly saw Belovezh not as the end of the Soviet state but as the welcomed end of its unpopular president.[105]

The third factor was closely related and almost certainly the most important. At Belovezh, Yeltsin and his co-abolitionists announced that the Soviet Union was immediately being replaced by a Commonwealth of Independent States that would keep most of the former republics, peoples, armed forces, and economies together. On paper, it strongly resembled the "soft" union recently proposed by both Gorbachev and Yeltsin. As such, a Russian historian points out, Belovezh "was presented not as the liquidation but as the transformation of the previously existing state," which was the view of 66 percent of Russians surveyed at the time.[106] Whether the Commonwealth was an authentic aspiration on the part of Yeltsin and Kravchuk or a ruse that "deceived their own people," they immediately led Russia and Ukraine away from any such unity. (Reports of heavy drinking, even drunkenness that night, especially on the part of Yeltsin, may explain why one of the three signatories later felt confused or "deceived" by what had happened there.)[107]

Why the Soviet Russian parliament, or Supreme Soviet, ratified the Belovezh agreements almost unanimously after barely an hour of mostly perfunctory discussion—188 deputies voted in favor, 6 against, and 7 abstained—is less obvious.[108] Popularly chosen in 1990 by an electorate that also voted for the Union in the March 1991 referendum, it was the same parliament which only two years later, in October 1993, defied Yeltsin to the point of an armed showdown. For some of Russia's independent democrats, the ratification vote would "forever remain the indelible shame and guilt of the Russian parliament." And for Gorbachev, who sent a desperate pro-Union plea to the deputies, nothing could ever fully explain their "lunacy."[109]

Above all, this would involve explaining why the large bloc of Communist delegates, most of whom had supported the attempted August coup to "save the Union," "rubber-stamped" Yeltsin's abolition of the Soviet Union or did not even attend the fateful session on December 12. (Nearly a third of the membership of the parliament was conspicuously absent.) Some of the Communists were motivated, not surprisingly, by hatred of Gorbachev, one exulting before casting his vote, "Thank God, with this the Gorbachev era is ended."[110] And like the general electorate, many of them believed, or hoped, that in voting at the same session for the new Commonwealth, they were actually ratifying a "renewal, a rebirth of the Union," as Yeltsin seemed to suggest in his remarks to the assembly and several observers later testified.[111]

But a darker, more compelling consideration also motivated Communist and possibly other pro-Union deputies—a "fear of repression."

(Even Yeltsin's vice president, head of a democratic Communist Party, was opposed to the Union's abolition but remained silent.) Since the failed coup in August, for which the Communist Party had been menacingly blamed and banned, anti-Communism had been the political watchword of the new Yeltsin regime, inspiring a kind of "witch-hunt." Since their Party had repressed so many people in the past, "disoriented and crushed" Communists feared their turn had now come. And just as millions had bent to the will of their predecessors, they now bowed, under the weight of "a genetic fear inherited from previous eras," to Yeltsin's.[112] With scarcely a word of protest, Communist delegates voted to end the state that embodied their ideas, history, and current ambitions, as they would be loudly reminded seven years later when they tried, in a different Russian parliament, to impeach him for that "crime."

Not even those factors fully explain, however, the seeming indifference of more important Soviet elites, the high-level bureaucratic nomenklatura, to Yeltsin's abolition of the state that had created and rewarded them with power, status, and privilege. The compliance of the armed elites, the KGB and military, is perhaps the most easily understood. Having been drawn into the disastrous coup attempt against Gorbachev three months earlier, they were demoralized and fearful of becoming entangled in yet another conflict between the country's political leaders. In addition, the military had long since soured on Gorbachev, and, even more, only Yeltsin now could guarantee generals and other commanders their salaries, benefits, and promotions.[113]

The acquiescence of Soviet economic and administrative elites, who, observers agree, "still remained firmly in control of the formidable state machine,"[114] was more complex. It brings us to the last explanation of the end of the Soviet Union to be considered here: by the early 1990s, a small but strategically located segment of the nomenklatura was zealously "privatizing" the great wealth shaken loose from the Soviet state by Gorbachev's economic reforms. They were "transforming power into property," as most accounts agree, and thus potentially into even greater power. They therefore had little if any self-interest in defending a state whose assets they were stripping.

DIFFERENT interpretations of the crucial question of "nomenklatura privatization" appear in the many Russian writings and in the considerably fewer Western studies that present this explanation of the Soviet breakup. Some see it as the outcome of a long historical process during which the appointed nomenklatura strove to become an independent ruling class owning the enormous state property it only administered and could not legally profit from or bequeath to its families; others view the frenzied privatizing as a spontaneous, opportunistic reaction to the undoing of the nomenklatura's dominant position by Gorbachev's political reforms, and to economic developments in East Europe, a "golden parachute" to a new system.[115] Some depict it as the natural (in Soviet circumstances) emergence of a Russian capitalist class, others as "criminal" looting of the nation.[116]

Whatever its origins and nature, the development was exceptionally important. When Gorbachev became leader in 1985, the vast Soviet economy was almost entirely state-owned, at least 90 percent of it under the control of Moscow ministries and their nationwide nomenklatura. As Gorbachev's promarket policies increasingly liberalized property rights in the late 1980s, high-level officials, particularly the managerial elite and others with direct access to state (and Party) assets, began to find ways—legal, semilegal, and illegal—to make themselves, their associates, and even their relatives owners or primary shareholders of that property.[117]

By 1991, the process had spread from Moscow to the republics and localities, and from modest confiscations to oil and other natural resources, major manufacturing enterprises, banks, export-import and trade networks, and real estate. Typically, ministers privatized and commercialized their industries, financial executives their capital, factory directors their plants, the Party's officials its enormous holdings, and even high-ranking military officers their assets.[118] (An undetermined number of these transactions also involved "criminal" elements from what until recently had been the black-market or "shadow" economy.) Formal privatization came later in the 1990s, in post-Soviet Russia under Yeltsin, but by late 1991 "spontaneous" property seizures, as they were called, had already consumed multi-billion-dollar components of the Soviet economy and were growing into a "true bacchanalia of redistribution."[119]

Compelling political ambitions were an integral part of the nomenklatura's "grab-it-ization," as it also became known, particularly at high levels in the fifteen Soviet republics. By the late 1980s, republic leaders, following Gorbachev's own example in Moscow and mindful of the fate of their East European comrades, were shifting their power base from the slumping Communist Party to new parliaments and presidencies on their own territories. (The ethnic nature of Soviet federalism and the official nurturing of native elites had long made such a centrifugal shift possible.)[120]

Soviet elites knew instinctively, in part no doubt because of their Marxist upbringing, that power without the authority and resources of the Party apparatus could best be secured by property. With less than 10 percent of the Soviet economy under direct control of the republics, their leaderships began claiming "sovereignty" over the Union's assets located within their borders. By 1990, almost every dispute between Gorbachev's government and the republics included the ongoing struggle over "redistribution of property and power,"[121] and even more so as he tried to negotiate a new Union treaty.

That development was the primary force behind many of the nationalist and secessionist movements that swept across the Soviet Union in 1990 and 1991. Those movements are often attributed to "the people" and characterized as a "revolution from below," but the majority were actually "extremely elite-dominated" by "nomenklatura nationalists."[122] Certainly, there is no mistaking their leaders, longtime Party bosses who quickly reinvented themselves as declared nationalists of their respective republics, from Yeltsin in Russia and Kravchuk in Ukraine to Communist chieftains in Central Asia and Azerbaijan, where one now insisted he had long been a "secret Muslim" and "genuine anti-Communist."[123]

In that new guise, republic elites played a crucial role during the last years of the Soviet Union—one much larger that that of "the people," except perhaps in the Baltics and parts of the Caucasus—but it should not be misunderstood. Their drive for property-based power eventually determined the lines along which the Union was dissolved, each of the fifteen republics becoming an independent state. And their zealous privatizing of state assets sometimes made it seem that the Soviet breakup was an act of "self-dissolution," "self-destruction," or "suicide."[124]

But authors who focus on spontaneous privatizing are wrong in concluding that the Soviet breakup was "elite-driven" and the nomenklatura was the "catalyst."[125] Again, by 1991, that primary role belonged to Yeltsin. The related argument that the institution of ethnically based republics doomed the system is unconvincing because institutions behave largely as their elites choose.[126] And little in the history or contemporary behavior of most Soviet republic elites suggests defiance of Moscow to the point of secession. In the 1980s, they complied even as Gorbachev's prodemocracy policies undermined their power, and they did so again in August 1991 when Moscow putschists threatened to reimpose control over their republics. Indeed, several "sovereign" republic heads telephoned the coup leaders in the Kremlin to negotiate their place in the "new order."[127] They went their independent ways only when Yeltsin, in Moscow, paved the way.

In short, though the property-seeking nomenklatura was the main beneficiary of the Soviet breakup,[128] it was not the primary causal factor, even at the center of its bureaucratic power in Russia. It was, however, the crucial enabling factor. It may be true that "no force would have brought down the Soviet Union if the Russian elite had not wanted this."[129] But in this regard, the nomenklatura was mostly indifferent. Its attention fixed on untold wealth, it simply "kept silent," as Gorbachev bitterly remarked, while Yeltsin, the real "catalyst,"[130] abolished the Soviet state.

Why property-grabbing Soviet elites, who now favored some kind of capitalism over any kind of socialism and about whom it was said "property is more important than ideology," preferred Yeltsin to Gorbachev is easy to understand. Their antipathy to the Soviet leader began during his democratic reforms, when " 'nomenklatura' became a curse word,"[131] but by 1991 they had a more important reason—the devoutly socialist nature of Gorbachev's perestroika reformation. Adamant in the face of new political fashions and rampant greed, his goal remained a social-democratic Soviet Union based on "mixed" state and private economics and a "regulated" market to preserve the social benefits of the old system.

That "socialist idea" underlay Gorbachev's opposition to the rapid wholesale privatization called for by the 500-Day Plan and other shock-therapy proposals. He was prepared "to go boldly" toward "destatization," but "on the condition . . . that property created by whole generations does not fall into the hands of thieves" and end with "someone standing over us." As people around him often emphasized, "Perestroika was not created to convert power into property." Warning against a Soviet "Klondike," he wanted a privatization that was gradual, partial, guided by "high legal and political standards," and "in the interests of the working people."[132] Western writers mock Gorbachev's belief in such a "socialism with a human face," but Soviet elites knew he was determined and therefore was a major obstacle to their ongoing property seizures.[133]

Yeltsin, on the other hand, was sending them a different message. He had emerged as a popular politician by opposing nomenklatura privileges, but in mid-1990, and even more upon becoming president of the Russian Republic a year later, he began appealing to disaffected Soviet elites in his campaign against Gorbachev.[134] Yeltsin's "radical reform" positions were interpreted by the mass electorate as populism but by the nomenklatura as an endorsement, even an incitement, of their freelance privatizing, or "eagerness to seize," as a well-known reformer viewed it. That was the case, for example, with his demonstrative support for the "free-market" 500-Day-Plan and his astonishing exhortation to regional elites: "Take as much sovereignty as you can swallow."[135]

If any doubt remained as to what Yeltsin meant by "sovereignty," it was removed by his confiscation of the Union's vast economic assets on his Russian republic's territory, from natural resources to banks, during the second half of 1991. Elites throughout the Soviet Union, observers recalled, "watched Yeltsin's behavior" and "imitated" it. (Some of their representatives, including his collaborator at Belovezh, Kravchuk, he simply bribed with property.)[136] By the time Yeltsin went to Belovezh in December to abolish the Union, soon-to-be-post-Soviet elites knew he was the leader who would ratify their privatized holdings. They knew, as a Yeltsin aide understood at the time, "who would play first fiddle in this historic divvying up. That was the main thing."[137]

6 GORBACHEV'S LOST LEGACIES

Do I think I realized my goals, and in this respect am I happy? There's no simple answer to this question. . . . In general, I do not know of any happy reformers.

History will show who was right and who was wrong.
MIKHAIL GORBACHEV, 1993/2000

IN conventional political terms, Gorbachev failed, and did so catastrophically: the "democratic reformation" he tried to enact in the Soviet Union ended in the breakup of his state and country. But that is not the full story of his six and a half years as leader, during which Gorbachev had two unprecedented achievements. He led Russia (then Soviet Russia) closer to real democracy than it had ever been in its centuries-long history.[1] And, with the partners he found in American presidents Ronald Reagan and the first George Bush, he came closer to ending the decades-long Cold War than had anyone before him.

Nor is it reasonable to think that Gorbachev should have completed those undertakings. Few transformational leaders, even "event-making" and "historically fateful" ones, are able to see their missions to completion. This is especially true of leaders of great reformations, whose nature and duration generate more opposition and problems than their initiators (unless they are a Stalin) have power or time to overcome. Franklin Roosevelt's New Deal, to take a familiar example, a perestroika of American capitalism, continued to unfold and undergo setbacks long after his death. Most such leaders can only open political doors, leave behind alternative paths that did not exist before, and hope, as Gorbachev often did publicly, that what they began would be "irreversible."[2]

Historic opportunities to modernize Russia gradually and consensually and to end the Cold War were Gorbachev's legacies. That they were missed, or squandered, was the fault of elites and leaders who followed him, both in Moscow and Washington. Indeed, those possibilities were soon misrepresented and then half-forgotten. Despite the democratic breakthroughs under Gorbachev examined earlier, the role of "father of Russian democracy" was soon reassigned to his successor, Boris Yeltsin. Along with the Washington political establishment, leading American journalists now informed readers that it was Yeltsin who began "Russia's transition from totalitarianism," who "set Russia on a course toward democracy," and under whom its "first flickerings of democratic nationhood" occurred.[3] Remarkably, many academic specialists concurred: "Democracy emerged in Russia after the collapse of Soviet Communism in 1991."[4] In effect, Gorbachev's model of evolutionary democratization was deleted from history and thus from politics.

How is this historical amnesia to be explained? In post-Soviet Russia, the primary cause was political expediency. Fearing a backlash at home against their role in the Soviet breakup and worried about Gorbachev's continuing popularity abroad, Yeltsin and his inner circle insisted that the new Russian president was the "undoubted father of Russian democracy" and Gorbachev merely a half-hearted reformer who tried to "save Communism."[5] Early on, even a few Russian supporters of Yeltsin understood that this was both untrue and dangerous for the country's future. Recalling Gorbachev's role as "liberator," one wrote: "Miracles do not happen. People who are not capable of appreciating a great man cannot successfully lead a state."[6]

In the West, and particularly in the United States, a more ideological politics inspired the revised history. Gorbachev's historic reforms, along with Washington's previous hope that they would succeed, were quickly obscured as the Soviet breakup and purported U.S. victory in the Cold War became defining moments in a new American triumphalist narrative. The entire history of the "defeated" Soviet enemy was now presented in the press as "Russia's seven decades as a rigid and ruthless police state," a "wound inflicted on a nation . . . over most of a century," an experience "every bit as evil as we had thought—indeed more so." Reagan's condemnation of the Soviet Union as an "evil empire," which he had happily rejected because of Gorbachev's reforms only three years before, was reinstated. An influential columnist even declared that a "fascist Russia" would have been a "much better thing."[7]

American scholars, some of them also inspired by "triumphalist belief," reacted similarly. With few exceptions, they reverted to old Sovietological axioms that the system had always been unreformable and its fate predetermined. The view that there had been promising "roads not taken" in its history was again dismissed as an "improbable idea" based on "dubious assumptions." Gorbachev's "evolutionary middle path . . . was a chimera," just as NEP had been, an attempt "to reform the unreformable," and the Soviet Union therefore died from a "lack of alternatives." Accordingly, most scholars no longer asked, even in light of the calamities that followed, if a reforming Soviet Union might have been the best hope for the post-Communist future of Russia or any of the other former republics.[8] On the contrary, they insisted that everything Soviet "must be discarded" by "razing the entire edifice of political and economic relations," an exhortation that translated into American cheerleading for Yeltsin's extremist measures after 1991.[9]

The revised history of the Soviet Union also required a revised memory of its last leader. Once seen as the Soviet Union's "No. 1 radical" and acclaimed for his "boldness," Gorbachev was now dismissed as having been "irresolute and unproductive," as well as insufficiently "radical."[10] The leader who said of himself while in power, "everything new in philosophy begins as heresy and in politics as the opinion of a minority," and whose own Communist fundamentalists were "against me, hate me" because his policies were "heresy," was recast as a man with "no deep convictions," even as an "orthodox Communist."[11] That persistent ideological response to Gorbachev's belief in a "socialism with a human face" also promoted the assertion that Yeltsin had "introduced markets and democracy to Russia."[12]

The notion that Gorbachev's pro-democracy measures and other reforms had been insufficiently radical misunderstands a fateful difference between his approach and Yeltsin's. From Peter the Great to Stalin, the dominant leadership method of transforming Russia had been a "revolution from above" that imposed wrenching changes on society through state coercion. Looking back, many reform-minded Russians rejected those methods as "modernization through catastrophe" because of their extraordinary human and material costs and because they kept the Russian people as subjects of the state rather than freeing them to become democratic citizens. Yeltsin's "shock-therapy" measures of the early 1990s, though his purpose was different, continued that baneful tradition.[13]

Gorbachev emphatically rejected the tradition. From the beginning, he was determined to "ensure that for the first time in its centuries-long history our country would go through a turning point without bloodshed." Perestroika, he vowed, was a "historic chance to modernize the country through reforms, that is by peaceful means"—a process "revolutionary in content but evolutionary in methods and form." Once initiated from above, it meant putting the "cause of perestroika in the hands of the people," not the state, through "democratization of all spheres of Soviet life." Readers already know the price Gorbachev paid for choosing a "democratic reformation"—itself a kind of leadership heresy—as an alternative to Russia's history of imposed transformations.[14]

As political and social calamities unfolded under Yeltsin in the post-Soviet 1990s, Russian scholars and other intellectuals, unlike their American counterparts, began to rethink the consequences of the Soviet breakup. A growing number concluded that some form of Gorbachev's perestroika, or "non-catastrophic evolution," even without him, had been a chance to democratize and marketize Russia in ways less traumatic and costly, and thus more fruitful, than those adopted by Yeltsin. Russia's historians (and politicians) will debate the issue for many years to come, but the fate of the country's democratization suggests why some of them already believe that Gorbachev's approach was a "lost alternative."[15]

Consider briefly the "trajectory," as specialists say,[16] of four essential components of any democracy as they developed in Russia before and after the end of the Soviet Union in December 1991:

• Without a significant number of independent media, other elements of democracy, from fair elections and constraints on power to the administration of justice, cannot exist. In 1985 and 1986, Gorbachev introduced "glasnost," his necessary initial reform, which meant a gradual diminishing of official censorship. By 1990 and 1991, the process had given rise to a plethora of independent publications and, more importantly at the time, to substantially uncensored state-owned national television, radio, and newspapers. The latter development was attributable to Gorbachev's committed leadership, continued government funding of national media, and the absence of other forces that might seize those opinion-shaping instruments for their own purposes.

A reverse process began after Yeltsin's victory in the failed August 1991 coup and his abolition of the Soviet Union in December. In both instances, he closed several opposition newspapers while reasserting Kremlin censorship over television. These were temporary measures, but more lasting control of the post-Soviet national media followed Yeltsin's armed destruction of the Russian parliament in 1993 and his "privatization" decrees, which made a small group of men, known as "oligarchs," owners of the nation's most valuable assets, including the media.

The 1996 presidential election, which Yeltsin was at risk of losing to the Communist Party candidate, marked the end of truly free and independent nationwide media in post-Soviet Russia. Though some pluralism and independent journalism remained, mainly because of internecine warfare among the media's oligarchic owners and a residual effect of Gorbachev's glasnost, they steadily declined. As a leading independent editor during both the Gorbachev and post-Soviet years later emphasized: "In 1996, the Russian authorities . . . and the largest business groups . . . jointly used the mass media, above all television, for the purpose of manipulating voter behavior, and with real success. Since that time, neither the authorities nor the oligarchs have let this weapon out of their hands."[17]

Other Russian journalists later compared their experiences during the Gorbachev years favorably to what followed under Yeltsin and Putin, but here is the judgment of a knowledgeable American head of an international monitoring organization, written in 2005: "During glasnost, courageous journalism pried open closed doors to history, sparked vigorous debates on multiparty democracy, and encouraged Soviet citizens to speak freely. . . . But in today's Russia, courageous journalists are endangered. . . . Reporting on basic public issues is increasingly restricted, and the public is kept in the dark about corruption, crime, and human rights abuses."[18]

•Russian elections naturally took the same "trajectory." The first ever national multicandidate balloting in Soviet history, for a Congress of People's Deputies, took place in March 1989. Though half of the deputies were chosen by institutions rather than popular vote, it was a historic breakthrough in Gorbachev's democratization campaign and was soon followed by more important ones. Voting for a counterpart legislature of the Soviet Russian Republic in early 1990 remains the freest and fairest parliamentary election ever held in Russia.[19] The same is true of the 1991 electoral campaign for the new presidency of that Soviet republic, in which a defiant Yeltsin defeated the Kremlin's candidate by a wide margin.

No further Russian parliamentary or presidential elections occurred until after the end of the Soviet Union, and when they did, each, while maintaining an innocuous degree of competition, was less free and fair than its predecessors. By 1996, Yeltsin's backers had developed enough "political technologies" for the "managed democracy" later associated with Vladimir Putin—overwhelming use of funds, control of the mass media, restrictions on independent candidates and parties, and falsified returns—to assure that effective power remained with whoever already ruled Russia. Even the referendum results said to have ratified Yeltsin's new constitution in 1993, unlike Gorbachev's 1991 referendum on the Union, were almost certainly falsified.[20]

Most telling, Yeltsin's election as Soviet Russian president in 1991 was the first and the last time executive power was allowed to pass from the Kremlin to an opposition candidate. In 2000, Yeltsin transferred power to Putin by means of a "managed" election, and Putin made Dmitri Medvedev his successor as president in a similar way in 2008. Even an American specialist unsympathetic to Gorbachev's reforms concluded that "Gorbachev-era elections were less fixed and fraudulent than most post-Soviet parliamentary and presidential elections in Russia have been." A Russian commentator was more succinct: "The peak of electoral democracy in our country came toward the end of perestroika."[21]

•But no Gorbachev-era democratic achievement was more important, or decline more fateful, than the popularly elected Soviet legislatures he promoted in 1989 and 1990. Democracy is possible without an independent executive branch but not without a sovereign parliament or its equivalent, the one truly indispensable institution of representative government. From tsars to heads of the Soviet Communist Party, Russian authoritarianism had featured overwhelming executive power and nonexistent or doomed representative assemblies, from the Dumas of the late tsarist period to the popularity elected soviets and Constituent Assembly of 1917 and 1918.

In that context, the Soviet Congress elected in 1989 and its Russian Republic counterpart in 1990 — each chose a smaller Supreme Soviet to continue as a sitting parliament—were the most historic result of Gorbachev's prodemocracy policies. The first functioned as an increasingly independent constitutional convention, enacting legislation for the further democratization of the Soviet Union by separating the powers previously monopolized by tsars and commissars alike, while also empowering investigative commissions and emerging as a source of opposition to Gorbachev. The second did the same in the Russian Republic, most importantly by amending its constitution to institute an elected presidency for Yeltsin. Nonetheless, Gorbachev was so committed to real legislatures as an essential component of democratization that he agreed only reluctantly to his own executive presidency in 1990, worrying it might diminish their independence, and he then endured, however unhappily, their mounting criticism of his leadership.[22]

Twenty years later, Russia's post-Soviet Parliament, renamed the Duma, had become a near replica of its weak and compliant tsarist-era predecessors, and the presidency a nearly all-powerful institution. Two turning points marked this fateful development. The first was in late 1991, when the Soviet Congress was permitted to play almost no role during the last months of the Soviet Union and then none at all in its dissolution. The second came in late 1993, when Yeltsin forcibly abolished the 1990 Russian Parliament and enacted a superpresidential constitution. Thereafter, each successive parliament, like each election, was less independent and influential, eventually becoming, in the eyes of its critics, a "decorative" or "imitation" legislature, like post-Soviet democracy itself.

• Finally, viable democracies require governing elites whose ranks are open, at least periodically, to representatives of other parties, nonofficial institutions, and civil society. Until the onset of perestroika, the self-appointed Soviet nomenklatura monopolized political power and even participation in politics. Breaking that monopoly by allowing the rise of new political actors from different backgrounds and professions— an academic economist and a law professor were elected the mayors of Moscow and Leningrad/St. Petersburg—was another democratic breakthrough of the Gorbachev years. By 1990, such people made up a significant minority in the Soviet Congress and a majority in the Soviet Russian Parliament.

After 1991, that development was also reversed. The post-Soviet ruling elite soon grew into a narrow group largely composed of the leader's personal entourage, financial oligarchs and their representatives, state bureaucrats, and people from military and security institutions. The growing number of military and security officers at the highest levels of government, for example, is usually attributed to Putin, a former KGB colonel, but it began soon after the Soviet breakup. Before 1992, under Gorbachev, they accounted for 4 percent of the ruling elite; this more than tripled to 17 percent under Yeltsin and then climbed to some 50 percent under Putin.[23]

Civil society fared accordingly. Contrary to civil-society "promoters," it always exists, even in authoritarian systems, whether in the form of parties, trade unions, other nongovernmental organizations, or simply the everyday interactive activities of citizens. But in post-Soviet Russia, by the late 1990s, most of its political representatives had lapsed back into pre-perestroika passivity, sporadic actions, or impotence. The turnabout was caused by several factors, including exhaustion, disillusion, the state's reoccupation of political space, and the decimation of once large and professionalized Soviet middle classes, usually said to be a prerequisite of stable democracy, by Yeltsin's shock-therapy measures of the early 1990s. On the eve of the twentieth anniversary of perestroika, Gorbachev's partner in democratization, Aleksandr Yakovlev, spoke "a blasphemous thought: Never in the history of Russia has there been such a deep divide between the ruling elite and the people."[24] It was a considerable exaggeration, but an expression of the fate of what Gorbachev and he had begun.

In short, these four indicators document the downward trajectory of Russian democratization after the end of the Soviet Union. Other political developments were in the same direction. Constitutionalism and rule of law were the guidelines of Gorbachev's reforms. They did not always prevail but stand in sharp contrast to Yeltsin's methods, which destroyed an entire existing constitutional order in 1993, from its parliament and fledging Constitutional Court to reanimated councils of local government. Yeltsin then ruled primarily by decree during the rest of the 1990s, issuing 2,300 in one year alone. There was also the rise and fall of official respect for human rights, always a sensitive indicator of the degree of democracy. On this subject we have a Western study published in 2004: "Human rights violations have increased dramatically in Russia since the collapse of the Soviet Union."[25]

The conclusion seems clear: Soviet democratization, however dictatorial the system's preceding history, was Russia's missed democratic opportunity, an evolutionary road not taken. In the context of American triumphalism and its political correctness, it is a heretical conclusion, but not in post-Soviet Russia. Even early Yeltsin supporters and Gorbachev critics later reconsidered the choices they had made in 1990 and 1991. Looking back, one concluded, "Gorbachev . . . gave us political freedoms, without costs or bloodshed—freedoms of the press, speech, assembly, and a multiparty system." Another pointed out, "How we used these freedoms is already our problem and responsibility, not his." And a third, who had lent his political support to Yeltsin's abolition of the Soviet Union, wondered aloud "how the country would have developed" had it continued to exist.[26]

TWENTY years after the Soviet state ended, most Western observers agreed that a far-reaching process of "de-democratization" was under way in Russia. Explaining when and why it began again revealed fundamental differences between the thinking of Western specialists, particularly American ones, and Russians themselves.

Unlike Americans, a majority of Russians, as readers already know, regretted the end of the Soviet Union not because they pined for "Communism" but because they lost a familiar state and a secure way of life. Even an imprisoned post-Soviet oligarch, like so many of his fellow citizens, saw the event as a "tragedy," a view that produced the adage: "Those who do not regret the breakup of the USSR have no heart."[27] If only for that reason, Russian intellectuals and political figures were less constrained by ideology and politics than were Americans in examining the origins of de-democratization. A growing number joined Gorbachev partisans in believing that the end of perestroika, which had been abolished along with the Soviet Union, had been a "lost chance" for democracy and a "tragic mistake."[28]

Most American commentators insisted on a different explanation and continue to do so. Having deleted Gorbachev's reforms from the Soviet Union's "evil" history and attributed democratization to Yeltsin, they blamed Putin for having "taken Russia in the opposite direction."

Political, media, and academic commentators who had been vocal cheerleaders for "Yeltsin-era democracy" initiated the explanation, but it became conventional wisdom: "The democratizing Russia that Putin inherited" fell victim to his "anti-democratic agenda" and "blueprint for dictatorship."[29] Only a few American specialists disagreed, faulting Yeltsin rather than his successor for beginning the "rollback of democratic reforms."[30]

Wary perhaps of doubting "one of the great moments in history,"[31] even fewer have asked if the "rollback" began earlier, with the Soviet breakup itself. The failure of journalists and policymakers to consider the possibility may be understandable. But not even established scholars who later regretted their "optimism" about Yeltsin's leadership have rethought the end of the Soviet Union.[32] They should do so because the *way* its breakup occurred—in circumstances about which standard Western accounts are largely silent or mythical—clearly boded ill for Russia's future. (One myth is the "peaceful" and "bloodless" nature of the dissolution.[33] In reality, ethnic strife soon broke out in Central Asia and the Caucasus, killing or brutally displacing hundreds of thousands of citizens, a post-Soviet fallout still ongoing in the 2008 war in Georgia.)

Most generally, there were ominous parallels between the Soviet breakup and the collapse of tsarism in 1917. In both cases, the way the old order ended resulted in a near total destruction of Russian statehood that plunged the country into prolonged chaos, conflict, and misery. Russians call what ensued "*Smuta*," a term full of dread derived from previous historical experiences and not expressed in the usual translation, "Time of Troubles." (In this respect, the end of the Soviet Union may have had less to do with the specific nature of that system than with recurring breakdowns of the state in Russian history.)

The consequences of 1991 and 1917, despite important differences, were similar. Once again, hopes for evolutionary progress toward democracy, prosperity, and social justice were crushed; a small group of radicals imposed extreme measures on the nation; zealous struggles over property and territory tore apart the foundations of a vast multiethnic state, this time a nuclear one; and the victors destroyed longstanding economic and other essential structures to build entirely anew, "as though we had no past."[34] Once again, elites acted in the name of an ideology and a better future but left society bitterly divided over yet another "accursed question"—why it had happened.[35] And again the people paid the price, including catastrophic declines in life expectancy.

All of those recapitulations unfolded, amid mutual (and lasting) charges of betrayal, during the three months from August to December 1991 when the "dismantling of Union statehood" actually occurred. (Gorbachev felt betrayed by the August coup plotters and by Yeltsin, Yeltsin by his Belovezh partner Kravchuk, and millions of Russians by the Belovezh dissolution of the Soviet Union, leading a foreign correspondent to label post-Soviet Russia "the country of the broken word.")[36] The period began and ended with the coups in Moscow and Belovezh and culminated in a revolution from above against the reforming Soviet system led by its own elites, analogous to, again allowing for important dissimilarities, Stalin's abolition of NEP Russia in 1929. Looking back, Russians of different views would conclude it was during these months that political extremism and unfettered greed cost them a chance for democratic and economic progress.[37] Few thought it happened a decade later under Putin.

Certainly, it is hard to imagine a political act more extreme than abolishing a state of 280 million citizens, one laden with countless nuclear and other weapons of mass destruction. And yet, Yeltsin did it, as even his sympathizers acknowledged, precipitously and in a way that was "neither legitimate nor democratic."[38] A profound departure from Gorbachev's commitment to gradualism, social consensus, and constitutionalism, this was a return to the country's "neo-Bolshevik" and earlier traditions of imposed change, as many Russian, and even a few Western, writers have characterized it.[39] The ramifications were bound to endanger the democratization achieved during the preceding six years of perestroika.

Yeltsin and his appointees promised, for example, that their extreme measures were "extraordinary" ones, but, as had happened before in Russia, most recently under Stalin from 1929 through 1933, they grew into a system of rule.[40] (The next such measure, already being planned, was "shock therapy.") Those initial steps had a further political logic. Having ended the Soviet state in a way that lacked legal or popular legitimacy, the Yeltsin ruling group soon became fearful of real democracy. In particular, a freely elected independent parliament and the possibility of relinquishing power in any manner raised the specter of "going on trial and to prison."[41]

The economic consequences of Belovezh were no less portentous. Liquidating the Union without any preparatory stages shattered a highly integrated economy. In addition to abetting the destruction of a vast state, it was a major cause of the collapse of production across the former Soviet territories, which fell by nearly half in the 1990s. That in turn contributed to mass poverty and its attendant social pathologies, from declining longevity to massive corruption, which remained the "main fact" of Russian life even in the early twenty-first century.[42]

The economic motivation behind elite support for Yeltsin in 1991, which I examined in chapter 5, was even more malignant. As a onetime Yeltsin supporter wrote thirteen years later, "Almost everything that happened in Russia after 1991 was determined to a significant extent by the divvying-up of the property of the former USSR."[43] Here, too, there were foreboding historical precedents. Twice before in twentieth-century Russia, the nation's fundamental property had been confiscated—the landlord's vast estates and the bourgeoisie's industrial and other large assets in the revolution of 1917 and 1918, and then the land of 25 million peasant farmers in Stalin's collectivization drive in 1929 through 1933. The aftereffects of both episodes plagued the country for many years to come.[44]

Soviet elites took much of the state's enormous wealth, which for decades had been defined in law and ideology as the "property of all the people," with no more regard for fair procedures or public opinion than there had been in 1917 and 1918. Indeed, an anti-Communist Russian intellectual thought that the "Bolshevik expropriation of private property looks simply like the height of piety against the background of the insane injustice of our absurd privatization."[45] To maintain their dominant position and enrich themselves, Soviet elites wanted the most valuable state property distributed from above, without the participation of legislatures or any other representatives of society. They achieved that goal first by themselves, through "spontaneous privatization" on the eve of the Soviet dissolution, and then, after 1991, through decrees issued by Yeltsin. As a result, privatization was haunted from the beginning by a " 'dual illegitimacy'—in the eyes of the law . . . and in the eyes of the population."[46]

The political and economic consequences should have been easy to foresee. Fearful for their dubiously acquired assets and even for their lives and families (many were sent abroad to live), the property holders, who formed the core of the first post-Soviet ruling elite, were as determined as Yeltsin to limit or reverse the parliamentary electoral de-mocracy and media freedoms instituted by Gorbachev. In their place, they strove to create a kind of praetorian political system devoted to and corrupted by their wealth.

The role played in post-Soviet "de-democratization" by the "divvying-up of the property of the former USSR," which was still under way during the financial crisis of 2008 and 2009, is rarely noted in Western accounts. Its full history lies outside the framework of this book, but several milestones should be emphasized. "Privatization" of billions of dollars worth of state assets was a central issue in the struggle between Yeltsin and the parliament in 1993 and its destruction by tank fire in Oc-tober. It was also a motive for the superpresidential constitution im-posed on the country in December of that year, as well as the coalition between the Kremlin and the new oligarchs to keep Yeltsin in power by rigging the 1996 presidential election.

The endangered well-being and security of that Kremlin-oligarchical "Family," as it became known, then inspired the "democratic transi-tion" of power from Yeltsin to Putin in 1999 and 2000. With demands for social justice, criminal accountability, and impeachment growing in the country and in the new parliament, and Yeltsin in failing political and physical health, the oligarchs desperately needed a new protector in the Kremlin. (In late 1999, 90 percent of Russians surveyed did not trust Yeltsin and 53 percent wanted him put on trial.) The plan was to appoint his successor as prime minister, who would, according to the constitution, become acting president upon Yeltsin's retirement until a new "election" was held.

Several candidates were rehearsed for the position before the forty-seven-year-old Putin, a career KGB officer and head of its successor agency, the FSB, was chosen. Though he later became a leader unlike the oligarchs had intended, the reason behind Putin's selection was clear: as FSB chief, he had already demonstrated he was "willing to help" a previous patron escape criminal indictment. And, indeed, his first act upon becoming president was to grant Yeltsin, as agreed beforehand, lifetime immunity from prosecution. For the first time in Russia's cen-turies of police repression, thus did a career secret policemen become its supreme leader.[47] (Yuri Andropov headed the KGB before becoming Soviet general secretary in 1982, but it had not been his original or pri-mary profession.)

The economic consequences of the "divvying-up" were no less profound. Uncertain how long they could actually retain their immense property, the new oligarchs were initially more interested in stripping assets than investing in them. Capital flight soon far exceeded investment in the economy, which fell by 80 percent in the 1990s. This was a major cause of a depression worse than the West's in the 1930s, with the GDP plummeting by half and real wages (when they were paid at all) by even more, and some 75 percent of Russians plunged into poverty. As a result, post-Soviet Russia lost many of its hard-gained twentieth-century achievements, becoming the first nation ever to undergo actual demodernization in peacetime.[48]

Not surprisingly, as the new elite and its top bureaucrats were increasingly perceived as a rapacious "off-shore aristocracy," popular hatred of them spread and grew more intense. In a 2005 survey, Russians rated them well below their Soviet-era counterparts in their concern for the nation's welfare, their patriotism, and their morals. Having unfolded under the banner of "democratic reform," all of these developments further discredited democracy, now termed "shit-ocracy," in public opinion.[49] Twenty years after it began, the political and economic consequences of the "divvying-up of the property of the former USSR"—and the conviction that "property without power isn't worth anything"[50]—remain both the primary cause of Russia's de-democratization and the primary obstacle to reversing it.

Considering all these ominous circumstances, why did so many Western commentators, from politicians and journalists to scholars, hail the breakup of the Soviet Union as a "breakthrough" to democracy and free-market capitalism and persist in these misconceptions?[51] Where Russia was concerned, their reaction was again based on anti-Communist ideology, hopeful myths, and amnesia, not historical or contemporary realities. Alluding to that myopia on the part of people who had long sought the destruction of the Soviet state and then "exulted" in it, a Moscow philosopher remarked bitterly, "They were aiming at Communism but hitting Russia."[52]

Among the most ideological myths surrounding the end of the Soviet Union was that it "collapsed at the hands of its own people" and brought to power in Russia "Yeltsin and the democrats"—even "moral leaders"—who represented "the people."[53] As I pointed out in the preceding chapter, no popular revolution, national election, or referendum mandated or sanctioned the breakup, and so there is no empirical evidence for this supposition. Indeed, everything strongly suggests a different interpretation.

Even the most event-making leaders need supporters in order to carry out historic acts. Yeltsin abolished the Soviet Union in December 1991 with the backing of a self-interested alliance. All of its groups called themselves "democrats" and "reformers," but the two most important ones were unlikely allies: the nomenklatura elites who were pursuing the "smell of property like a beast after prey," in the revealing metaphor of Yeltsin's own chief minister, and wanted property much more than any kind of democracy or free-market competition—many had opposed Gorbachev's reforms—and the impatient, avowedly prodemocracy wing of the intelligentsia.[54] Traditional enemies in the prereform Soviet system, they colluded in 1991 largely because the intelligentsia's radical economic ideas seemed to justify nomenklatura privatization.

But the most influential pro-Yeltsin intellectuals, who would play leading roles in his post-Soviet government, were neither coincidental fellow travelers nor real democrats, foremost among them Yegor Gaidar, Anatoly Chubais, and their "team" of shock therapists. Since the late 1980s, Chubais and others had insisted that market economics and large private property would have to be imposed on a recalcitrant Russian society by an "iron-hand" regime. This "great leap," as they extolled it, would entail "tough and unpopular" policies resulting in "mass dissatisfaction" and thus would necessitate "anti-democratic measures."[55] Like the property-seeking elites, they saw the new legislatures elected in Russia under Gorbachev, still called soviets, as a major obstacle. "Liberal admirers of Pinochet," the general who had brutally imposed economic change on Chile in the 1970s and 1980s, they said of Yeltsin, now their leader, "Let him be a dictator!"[56]

Little else could have been worse for Russia's nascent democracy in 1992 than a Kremlin belief in the need for a Pinochet-like leader to implement market reforms, a role Gorbachev had refused to play, and a team of "reform" intellectuals to encourage it. From there it was only a step back to Russia's authoritarian traditions and on to the overthrow of an elected parliament, privatization by decree, a Kremlin-appointed financial oligarchy, and corruption of the media and elections. A Russian law professor later summarized what happened: "The so-called democratic movement ceased to exist at the end of 1991. . . . Some of its members took part in the divvying up of property and primitive accumulation of capital; others hired themselves out to the new property owners and served their interests politically."[57]

Certainly Chubais and his "democratic reformers" were there at each stage, planning and justifying the undoing of democratization, including the transition to Putin, while still yearning for a Russian Pinochet.[58] They became much more (or less) than intellectuals, serving as ministers in Yeltsin's government, notably Chubais himself, Gaidar, Alfred Kokh, Boris Nemtsov, and a dozen or so others. (Their service and deeds, it should be emphasized, also had the enthusiastic support of American policymakers, media opinion makers, and academic specialists.)[59]

Underlying the Pinochet syndrome among Yeltsin's intellectual supporters was a profoundly antidemocratic contempt for the Russian people (*narod*). When election returns went against the "liberals," they questioned the "psychological health of voters"; declared, "Russia! You've lost your mind!"; and concluded that "the people are the main problem with our democracy." And when their policies ended in economic disaster, they pointed to the "rot in the national gene pool" and again blamed "the people," who "deserved their miserable fate."[60] When the Soviet Union ended, however, Russia's future was not in the hands of the people, who had responded admirably to Gorbachev's democratic reforms, but in those of the elites now in power.

Political and economic alternatives still existed in Russia after 1991. Other fateful struggles and decisions lay ahead. And none of the factors contributing to the end of the Soviet Union were inexorable or deterministic. But even if genuine democratic and market aspirations were among them, so were cravings for power, political coups, elite avarice, extremist ideas, widespread perceptions of illegitimacy, and anger over the "greatest betrayal of the twentieth century."[61] All of these factors continued to play a role after 1991, but it should already have been clear which would prevail—as should have been the fate of the democratic alternative Gorbachev bequeathed to Russia.

ON the occasion of Gorbachev's seventieth birthday in 2001, a Soviet-era intellectual who had deserted him in 1990 and 1991 reevaluated his leadership. After acknowledging that Russia's democratization was his achievement, she added another: "Gorbachev ended the 'Cold War', and that fact in itself makes him one of the heroes of the twentieth century."[62] Though Gorbachev himself always credited the "key role" played by his "partners" Ronald Reagan and George H. W. Bush, few nonpartisan historians of that process, or participants in it, deny he was the main "hero."[63]

Here, too, however, his legacy may have been lost. In August 2008, almost exactly twenty years after Gorbachev delivered a historic United Nations speech disavowing the Soviet ideological premise of the Cold War, Washington and Moscow were fighting a proxy hot war in the former Soviet republic of Georgia. Surrogate U.S.-Soviet military conflicts had been a regular feature of the Cold War, in the Third World and elsewhere, but this was a more direct confrontation by half. Washington was represented by Georgia's military forces, which it had amply funded for several years, but Moscow's own troops fought (and won) the war. Whatever the view from America, many Russians, Georgians, and South Ossetians, on whose territory it began, "perceived the conflict as a proxy battle between two global powers—Russia and the United States."[64]

The war caught most Western governments and observers "totally by surprise" primarily because they had failed to understand that a new (or renewed) cold war had been developing long before the U.S.-Russian conflict in the Caucasus.[65] In particular, American officials and specialists, almost without exception, had repeatedly denied that a new cold war was even possible. Some dismissed the possibility adamantly (in reply to a small number of critics, myself included, who warned of the mounting danger), presumably because they had formulated, implemented, or defended policies contributing to it. Secretary of State Condoleezza Rice, for example, announced officially that "talk about a new Cold War is hyperbolic nonsense." And a *Washington Post* columnist denounced the "notion" as "the most dangerous misjudgment of all."[66]

Personal motives aside, most commentators apparently misunderstood the nature of cold war, assuming that the one following World War II was the only model. The essential meaning of cold war is a relationship between states in which exacerbating conflicts and confrontation are dominant in more areas than not and usually, though not always, short of military fighting. To take two disparate examples, the fifteen-year U.S. nonrecognition of Soviet Russia, from 1918 to 1933, was a kind of cold war, but without an arms race or other direct dangers to either side. The Sino-Soviet cold war, from the 1960s to the 1980s, on the other hand, witnessed occasional military skirmishes along a long border. Cold-war relationships vary in form, causes, and content, the last U.S.-Soviet one being exceedingly dangerous because it included a nuclear arms race.

Other misconceptions underlay the assumption that a U.S.-Russian cold war was impossible after the end of the Soviet Union. Unlike before, it was widely argued, post-1991 conflicts between Washington and Moscow were not the product of different economic and political systems, were not ideological or global, and, in any event, post-Soviet Russia was too weak to wage another cold war.[67] (The "friendship" between President George W. Bush and President Putin was often cited as further evidence, even though Richard Nixon and Leonid Brezhnev had professed the same personal relationship thirty years before.)

All of these assertions, which are still widespread in the United States, are misinformed. Russia's "capitalism" is fundamentally unlike America's, economically and politically. Exaggeration of ideology's actual importance in the previous Cold War aside, ideological conflict, or a "values gap," between U.S. "democracy promotion" and Russia's "sovereign democracy"—"autocratic nationalism," even "fascism," as new American cold warriors label it—has been growing for several years, along with the number and prominence of ideologues on both sides. And this gap, we are told, "is greater today than at any time since Communism's collapse." Indeed, one of the Americans assures us, "Ideology matters again."[68] Nor did the Cold War after World War II begin globally, but in Eastern Europe, as did the new one, which is rapidly spreading. As for Russia's inability to fight it, that assumption was shattered by the 2008 war in Georgia in less than a week.[69]

The tenacious fallacy of deniers of a new cold war is illustrated by their own accounts of the U.S.-Russian relationship, the "worst in a generation," as it evolved during the first decade of the twenty-first century. Though couched in euphemisms, worsening relations could hardly be mistaken for anything other than a new cold war. Consider the following passages from a front-page *New York Times* "news analysis," under the heading "No Cold War, But Big Chill," published a week after the war in Georgia broke out:

"The cold war is over," President Bush declared Friday, but a new era of enmity between the United States and Russia has emerged nevertheless. . . . As much as Mr. Bush has argued that the old characterizations of the cold war are no longer germane, he drew a new line . . . between countries free and not free, and bluntly put Russia on the other side of it. . . . Tensions are manifest already, and both sides have done their part to inflame them. . . . The United Nations Security Council has reverted to a cold-war-like stalemate. . . . The Russian offensive—the first outside its territory since the collapse of the Soviet Union in 1991—has crystallized a realignment already taking place in Central and Eastern Europe. . . . The administration dropped its opposition to sending Patriot missiles, which would defend the Polish site [for U.S. missile defense]. . . . A senior Russian general promptly gave credence to Poland's worst fears by saying Friday that the country had just made itself a target of Russia's nuclear arsenal. . . . It may seem outdated to speak of blocs in Europe, but they are emerging just as clearly, if less ideologically, as those that existed on either side of the Iron Curtain. . . . In fact, the alienation between the United States and Russia has rarely, if ever, been deeper.[70]

If so, what happened to the "end of the Cold War?" The next chapter proposes an answer, but this one must end where it began, by emphasizing yet another instance of historical amnesia and revisionism. In this case, it involves the crucial question: How and when did the Cold War end?

When Gorbachev came to power in 1985, he was already determined to pursue not merely another relaxation of East-West tensions but an abolition of the forty-year Cold War.[71] He was committed to doing so for three reasons: He believed that its most dangerous element, the U.S.-Soviet nuclear arms race, threatened human existence. He wanted the Soviet Union to become an integral part of the West, of a "Common European Home," in which he included the United States. And without substantially reducing both the international tensions and economic costs of the Cold War, Gorbachev had little hope of mobilizing the political support and resources at home necessary for his perestroika reformation.

Gorbachev's anti–Cold War mission was informed by what he and his aides called "New Thinking." Also decried as heresy by Communist Party fundamentalists, it brought about a "conceptual revolution" in

Soviet foreign policy.[72] Those ideas, together with Gorbachev's remarkable leadership abilities and the essential participation of a U.S. president who also feared the potential consequences of nuclear weapons, Ronald Reagan, quickly transformed East-West relations.

In 1986, barely a year after Gorbachev's rise to power, the two leaders agreed in principle that all nuclear weapons should be abolished, an impossible goal but a vital pursuit. In 1987, they signed a treaty eliminating for the first time an entire category of those weapons, in effect putting the long arms race in reverse gear. In 1988, while joining Gorbachev in other important disarmament initiatives, Reagan absolved the Soviet "evil empire," saying of America's new partner, "That was another time, another era." And when he left office in January 1989, Reagan explained why there was a new era: "The Cold War is over."[73]

Even if true, it had to be affirmed by Gorbachev and by Reagan's successor, the first President Bush. They did so emphatically in November and December 1989, first when Gorbachev refused to respond with military force, as his predecessors had done in similar situations, to the fall of the Berlin Wall and the disintegration of the Soviet empire in Eastern Europe; and then together at a Malta summit meeting, which they agreed marked the onset of a "brand new era in U.S.-Soviet relations."[74] Other formal ratifications soon followed, but ultimate evidence of a post–Cold War era, however brief, was provided in 1990 by two instances of unprecedented U.S.-Soviet cooperation: an agreement on German reunification and Moscow's support for the U.S.-led war to drive Saddam Hussein's Iraqi army, a Soviet client, out of Kuwait.

Three elements of this history were crucial. First, even allowing for the "key" roles of Reagan and Bush, the Cold War would have continued unabated, possibly grown worse, had it not been for Gorbachev's initiatives. Second, objective historians and participants disagree about exactly when the Cold War ended, but they agree it occurred sometime between 1988 and 1990—that is, eighteen months to three years before the end of the Soviet Union in December 1991.[75] And third, the termination of the Cold War was negotiated in a way, as Bush initially confirmed, "so there were no losers, only winners" or, as future Secretary of State Rice wrote, with "no winners and no losers."[76]

On the American side, however, those historical realities were soon rewritten. Immediately after December 1991, the end of the Cold War was conflated with and attributed to the end of the Soviet Union, and both were recast for a new American triumphalist narrative. Bush himself wrote the first draft, declaring in his January 1992 state-of-the-union address, "America won the Cold War. . . . The Cold War didn't end—it was won." He repeated the claim, which was noted and bitterly rejected by Gorbachev's admirers in Moscow, throughout his campaign for re-election that year.[77]

George F. Kennan, the iconic (but usually disregarded) authority on U.S.-Soviet relations, later dismissed the claim of a U.S. victory as "intrinsically silly" and "simply childish,"[78] but virtually all American politicians and the mainstream media followed Bush's lead, as they continue to do today. So have leading scholars who should know better, two even claiming that Boris Yeltsin, who became president of the Soviet Russian Republic only in June 1991, well after the turning-point events of 1988 through 1990, had been the "catalyst for the Cold War's end."[79]

The result was a "new history" written, in the words of a critic, "as seen from America, as experienced in America, and told in a way most agreeable to many Americans"—a "fairytale," another wrote, "with a happy ending."[80] When future historians search for the beginning of the new cold war, they may find it at the moment when Americans rewrote the end of the preceding one by deleting Gorbachev's legacy.

7 WHO LOST THE POST-SOVIET PEACE?

> The Owl of Minerva spreads its wings only with the falling of dusk.
>
> HEGEL

IN the early 1990s, the U.S. government undertook a far-reaching crusade to transform post-Soviet Russia into "the kind of Russia we want."
Amply funded by Washington and private institutions, the missionary
campaign mobilized many Americans who claimed to have the necessary expertise—economists and other academics, investors, think-tank
specialists, and journalists—to prevent the new state from taking "a
strange, ambivalent path of its own confused devising."[1] When the crusade, with its legions of onsite "advisers," contributed instead to economic ruin, creeping authoritarianism, and surging anti-Americanism,
the media and other observers asked, "Who lost Russia?"

In one respect, the question, reminiscent of political accusations regarding China in the 1940s, was a false one. Russia, it now was rightly
said, even by lapsed missionaries, "had never been ours to lose." Accepting the tutelage of a foreign power and its ill-conceived advice had
been the Kremlin's own choice. But in a different and crucial respect,
Russia had been America's to lose—as a strategic partner in the post–
Cold War relationship initiated from 1988 through 1991 by Mikhail Gorbachev, Ronald Reagan, and the first President Bush.

The question of who lost that historic opportunity is almost never asked in the United States.[2] One reason is the deficient memory described in the preceding chapter. As U.S.-Russian relations worsened in the first decade of this century, leading American officials, newspapers, and scholars issued amnesiac assurances that the relationship was nonetheless "far better" and the "foundation for a genuine partnership . . . far stronger" than in 1991.[3] Evidently, the opportunity U.S. and Soviet leaders created in the years from 1988 through 1991 had already been forgotten.

A more dangerous factor, however, also contributed to the missed opportunity: a widespread American belief in the 1990s, particularly in Washington, that post-Soviet Russia, shorn of its superpower status, was "virtually irrelevant" and that the United States could therefore pursue its vital interests in "a world without Russia."[4] That folly has diminished, but it persists in the belief that a new cold war is impossible or would not matter because "the Russian phoenix won't rise again."[5] In reality, Russia remains more important to America's national security than any other country, both as the Soviet Union did and in a new, even graver way.

Despite its diminished status after the Soviet breakup, Russia alone still possesses weapons that can destroy the Unites States, a military complex nearly America's equal in exporting arms, and the world's largest oil and natural gas reserves, along with a disproportionate share of the planet's other natural raw materials, from iron ore, nickel, and timber to diamonds and gold. With its highly educated and creative people, Russia also remains the world's biggest territorial country, pivotally situated in both the West and the East, at the crossroads of colliding civilizations, with strategic capabilities from Europe, Latin America, Iran, and other Middle East nations to Afghanistan, China, North Korea, and India. All of this means that no vital American national security interest is attainable without Russia's full cooperation, from preventing nuclear proliferation and international terrorism to guaranteeing regional stability and reliable flows of energy and other essential resources. More generally, a "world without Russia" would be globalization, on which the well-being of today's nations is said to depend, without a large part of the globe.

But Russia is vital to American security also because it represents an unprecedented danger that did not exist during the forty-year Cold

War. As a result of the Soviet breakup in 1991, a state bearing every nuclear and other device of mass destruction virtually collapsed. During the 1990s, Russia's essential infrastructures—political, economic, and social—disintegrated. Moscow's hold on its vast territories was weakened by separatism, official corruption, and mafia-like crime. The worst peacetime depression in modern history brought economic losses more than twice those suffered by the nation in World War II. Most Russians were impoverished, death rates soared, and the population shrank. In August 1998, the financial system imploded. No one in authority anywhere had ever foreseen that one of the twentieth century's two superpowers would plunge, along with its arsenals of mass destruction, into such catastrophic circumstances.

Ten years later, on the eve of the 2008 international financial crisis, Russia seemed to have recovered. Its economy had grown annually by 6 to 8 percent, doubling the GDP, and its gold and foreign-currency reserves were nearly $600 billion, the world's third largest. Its stock-market index had increased by 83 percent in a single year, and Moscow was booming with gentrified construction, frenzied consumption of Western luxury goods, five-star hotels, and fifty-six large casinos. Some of the new wealth had spread to the provinces and to the middle and lower classes, whose incomes were rising. But those advances, loudly touted by the Russian government and Western investment-fund promoters, were largely caused by unusually high prices for the country's oil and stood out mainly in comparison with the wasteland of 1998.

More fundamental realities indicated that Russia was still in an unprecedented condition of peacetime demodernization and depopulation. Investment in basic infrastructures remained barely a third of the 1990 level. The government claimed that less than 20 percent of its citizens now lived in poverty, but the actual figure was probably closer to 50 percent and included 60 to 75 percent of families with two or more children, pensioners, and rural dwellers, as well as large segments of the educated and professional classes, among them teachers, doctors, and military officers. The gap between rich and poor, according to Russian experts, had become "explosive."

Most indicative, and tragic, Russia continues to suffer wartime death and birth rates. Already with seven million fewer people than in 1992, its population is still declining by 700,000 or more each year. Deaths exceed births by three to two; male life expectancy is barely fifty-nine years; and, at the other end of the life cycle, 2 to 3 million children are homeless. The country's health, a Western authority reports, "is a disaster," with old and new diseases, from tuberculosis to HIV infections, growing into epidemics. Nationalists may exaggerate in charging that "the Motherland is Dying," but even the founding head of Moscow's most pro-Western university warned in 2006 that Russia remained in "extremely deep crisis."[6] And the financial crisis in 2008 and 2009 made everything even worse.

To the extent that Russia is a modern European country, the political system atop this bleak post-Soviet landscape is an anomaly. In 2009, its stability still rested heavily, if not entirely, on the personal popularity and authority of one man, Vladimir Putin, who admitted in 2006 that the state was "not yet stable."[7] While Putin's favorable rating in opinion surveys reached an extraordinary 70 to 75 percent and he had managed to generate similar figures for his nominal successor as president, Dmitri Medvedev, the country's actual political institutions and other would-be leaders had almost no popular support.

This was even more the case of the country's top business and administrative elites. Having continued to "divvy up" the state assets they privatized in the 1990s and having again been favored by the state with enormous bailouts in 2008 and 2009, they were still widely despised by ordinary Russians, probably a majority of them. Lacking popular legitimacy, their possession of that immense property therefore remained a time bomb embedded in the political and economic system. (New oligarchs created by Putin's Kremlin have even fewer recognized property rights.) This lurking danger was another reason knowledgeable observers worried that a sudden development—a sharp fall in world oil prices (as happened in 2008), a repetition of the kind of ethnic violence or large-scale terrorism that had already occurred in post-Soviet Russia several times, or Putin's disappearance—might plunge the nation into an even more wrenching crisis. Indeed, an eminent Western scholar asked "whether Russia is stable enough to hold together."[8]

As long as catastrophic possibilities exist in that nation, so do the unprecedented threats to U.S. and international security. Experts differ as to which danger is the gravest—the proliferation of Russia's enormous stockpiles of nuclear, chemical, and biological materials, all of which are sought by terrorist organizations; poorly maintained nuclear reactors on land and on decommissioned submarines; an impaired early-warning system controlling nuclear missiles on hair-trigger alert; or a repetition of the first-ever civil war in a shattered superpower, the terror-ridden Chechen conflict. But no one should doubt that together they constitute a much greater constant threat than any the United States faced during the Soviet era. If nothing else, the widespread assumption that the danger of a nuclear apocalypse ended with the Soviet state is a myth.

Nor is a catastrophe involving weapons of mass destruction the only possible danger. Even fewer petrodollars may buy Russia longer-term stability, but this will possibly be on the basis of the growing authoritarianism and xenophobic nationalism witnessed in recent years not far from the center of power. Those ominous factors derive primarily not from Russia's lost superpower status (or Putin's KGB background), as the American media regularly assert, but from so many lost and damaged lives at home since 1991. Sometimes called the "Weimar scenario," this outcome is unlikely to be truly fascist, but it could lead to a Russia that both possesses weapons of mass destruction and large proportions of the world's energy resources and is headed by men much less accommodating than Putin and Medvedev and even more hostile to the West than was its Soviet predecessor.

And yet, despite all these ways that Russia can singularly endanger or enhance America's security, by 2009 Washington's relations with Moscow were, it was generally agreed, "the worst in a generation." U.S. and Russian warships were again probing the other nation's perceived zone of security; military officials talked in tones from the "darkest days of the cold war"; the foreign departments expelled the other's diplomats as they had during that era; and the legislatures issued threatening statements. No less indicative, enemy images of the other resurfaced in popular culture and journalism, as in a book subtitled *Spies, Murder, and the Dark Heart of the New Russia.* Even Winston Churchill's Cold War aphorism was revived to warn a well-intended West against a menacing Russia as "a riddle, wrapped in a mystery, inside an enigma."[9]

What happened to the opportunity created from 1988 through 1991 for a post–Cold War relationship? In the United States, the overwhelmingly consensual answer is that Putin's Russia destroyed it. According to this explanation, Presidents Bill Clinton and Boris Yeltsin seized the opportunity in the 1990s, before Russia "changed from a relatively friendly democracy into a belligerent police state," to develop a U.S.-Russian strategic partnership, even friendship. After 2000, it was "betrayed" by Putin's "autocracy" at home and "crude neo-imperialism" abroad, which included "militarily threatening [Russia's] neighbors," "America bashing," and other "serial misbehavior."[10]

Blaming the Kremlin for the lost post–Cold War opportunity is orthodoxy among U.S. policymakers, mainstream editorialists, and most influential academics. Some point to resurgent tsarist or Soviet traditions (that is, to the nature of Russia),[11] some to Putin, but all of them to Moscow alone, emphasizing with Secretary of State Condoleezza Rice, "It is simply not valid: to blame Russia's behavior on the United States."[12] Reiterating the consensus, a *New York Times* writer rejoiced, "People of all political persuasions now seem to get it about Russia." And, indeed, even a critic of U.S. policy ended an article, "Of course, Russia has been largely to blame."[13]

If this explanation is true, there would seem to be nothing Washington can do to prevent an even worse relationship with Moscow. But it is not true, or at least far from fully true. The new cold war and the squandering of the post-Soviet peace began not in Moscow but in Washington.

AFTER President George H. W. Bush's reelection defeat, formulating a long-term policy toward post-Soviet Russia fell to Bill Clinton, who became president in January 1993. The general approach adopted by the Clinton administration—its underlying assumptions, purposes, and implementation—has been Washington's policy ever since, through both terms of the second President George Bush. It was still in place when President Barack Obama took office in January 2009. Given Russia's singular potential for both essential cooperation and unprecedented dangers, the Clinton administration inherited a historic responsibility for, as pundits say, getting Russia policy right. It failed disastrously, though officials involved in those decisions have continued to defend them.[14]

It does not require a degree in international relations to understand that the first principle of policy toward post-Communist Russia should have been to heed the Hippocratic injunction: Do no harm! Do nothing to undermine its fragile stability, nothing to dissuade the Kremlin from giving first priority to repairing the nation's crumbling infrastructures, nothing to cause it to rely more heavily on its stockpiles of superpower weapons instead of reducing them, nothing to make Moscow less than fully cooperative with the West in those and other vital pursuits. Everything else in that shattered country was of far less consequence.

Instead, beginning in the early 1990s, Washington simultaneously conducted, under Democrats and Republicans, two fundamentally different policies toward post-Soviet Russia—one decorative and outwardly reassuring, the other real and exceedingly reckless. The decorative policy, which was generally taken at face value in the United States, professed to have replaced America's previous Cold War intentions with a generous relationship of "strategic partnership and friendship." The public image of this approach featured happy-talk meetings between the American and Russian presidents, first "Bill and Boris" (Clinton and Yeltsin), then "George and Vladimir" (Putin).

The real U.S. policy was different—a relentless, winner-take-all exploitation of Russia's post-1991 weakness. Accompanied by broken American promises, condescending lectures, and demands for unilateral concessions, it was, and remains, disregarding official rhetoric, even more aggressive and uncompromising than was Washington's approach to Soviet Communist Russia. It is important to specify the defining elements of this actual policy as they unfolded—with fulsome support in both major American political parties, influential media, and liberal and conservative think tanks—since the early 1990s, if only because they are firmly lodged in Moscow's memory:

• A growing military encirclement of Russia, on and near its borders, by U.S. and NATO bases, which by August 2008 were already ensconced or being planned in at least half the fourteen other former Soviet republics, from the Baltics and Ukraine to Georgia, Azerbaijan, and the new states of Central Asia. The result is a reemerging iron curtain and the remilitarization of American-Russian relations, developments only belatedly noted, and almost always misexplained, in the United States. In the aftermath of the 2008 Georgian War, for example, a U.S. senator angrily declared, "We're not going to let Russia, so soon after the Iron Curtain fell, to again draw a dividing line across Europe." A *New York Times* editorial added that such a "redivision of Europe" could "not be tolerated."[15] But it was the eastward expansion of the NATO military alliance, beginning in the 1990s, that imposed "new dividing lines in Europe," certainly in the eyes of Russia's political leaders, and threatened their country with "being pushed" behind a new "iron curtain."[16]

• A tacit (and closely related) U.S. denial that Russia has any legitimate security concerns outside its own territory, even in ethnically akin or contiguous former Soviet republics such as Ukraine, Belarus, and Georgia. Perhaps aware the denial is preposterous, U.S. officials occasionally concede that "even authoritarian regimes have legitimate security interests," invariably followed, however, by "but" and the unmistakable implication that it is for Washington to decide what those "interests" might be.[17] How else to explain, to take a bellwether example, the thinking of Richard Holbrooke, perennial Democratic would-be secretary of state and a "special envoy" under Obama? While roundly condemning the Kremlin for promoting a pro-Moscow government in neighboring Ukraine, where Russia has centuries of shared linguistic, marital, religious, economic, and security ties, Holbrooke declared that faraway Slav nation part of "our core zone of security."[18]

• Even more, a presumption that Russia does not have full sovereignty within its own borders, as expressed by constant U.S. interventions in Moscow's internal affairs since 1992. The ultimate expression of that missionary presumption was, of course, the American crusade of the 1990s, which featured Washington's efforts to dictate the Kremlin's domestic and foreign policies, along with swarms of onsite "advisers" determined to direct Russia's "transition" from Communism. The grand crusade ended, or at least diminished, but endless U.S. sermons from afar continued, often couched in threats, on how Russia should and should not organize its political and economic systems, and so did active American support for Russian anti-Kremlin groups, some associated with hated Yeltsin-era oligarchs in exile.

By 2006, that interventionary impulse had grown even into suggestions that Putin be overthrown by the kind of U.S.-backed "color revolutions" carried out since 2003 in Georgia, Ukraine, and Kyrgyzstan. Thus, while mainstream editorial pages increasingly called the Russian president "thug," "fascist," and "Saddam Hussein," one of the Carnegie Endowment's several Washington crusaders assured policymakers of "Putin's weakness" and vulnerability to "regime change."[19] (Do proponents of "democratic regime change" in Russia ever consider that it might mean destabilizing a nuclear state?) In that same vein, the more staid Council of Foreign Relations suggested that Washington reserve for itself the right to reject Russia's future elections and its leaders as "illegitimate."[20]

•Underpinning these components of the real U.S. policy have been familiar Cold War double standards condemning Moscow for doing what Washington does—such as seeking allies and military bases in former Soviet republics, using its assets (oil and gas in Russia's case) as aid to friendly governments, regulating foreign money in its political life, and recognizing secessionist territories after using force to abet them.

More specifically, when NATO expanded to Russia's front and back doorsteps, gobbling up former Soviet-bloc members and republics, it was "fighting terrorism" and "protecting new states"; when Moscow protested, it was engaging in "Cold-War thinking." When Washington meddled in the electoral politics of Georgia and Ukraine, it was "promoting democracy"; when the Kremlin did so, it was "neo-imperialism." When American bombers attacked Serbia on behalf of Kosovo, it was "defending human rights"; when Russian forces crossed into Georgia on behalf of South Ossetia and Abkhazia, it was "an affront to civilized standards and completely unacceptable."[21] And not to forget the historical background: When in the 1990s the U.S.-supported Yeltsin overthrew Russia's elected parliament and constitutional order by force, gave its national wealth and television networks to Kremlin insiders, imposed a constitution without real constraints on executive power, and began to rig elections, it was "democratic reform."[22] When Putin continued that process, it was "authoritarianism."

•Finally, the United States has been attempting, by exploiting Russia's weakness, to acquire the nuclear superiority it could not achieve during the Soviet era. That is the essential meaning of two major steps taken by the Bush administration in 2002 and another in 2007 and 2008, all of them against Moscow's strong wishes. One was the administration's unilateral withdrawal from the 1972 Anti-Ballistic Missile Treaty, freeing itself to try to create a system capable of destroying incoming missiles and thereby the capacity to launch a nuclear first strike without fear of retaliation. The second was pressuring the Kremlin to sign an ultimately empty nuclear weapons reduction agreement requiring no actual destruction of weapons and indeed allowing development of new ones; providing for no verification; and permitting unilateral withdrawal before the specified reductions were required. The third step was the decision to install missile defense components near Russia's western flank, in Poland and the Czech Republic. Though Washington continues to insist the system has no implications for Russia's security, independent U.S. specialists confirm the Kremlin's concern that it could undermine Moscow's ability to respond to a U.S. nuclear attack.[23]

The history of these extraordinarily anti-Russian policies contradicts two American official and media axioms: that the "chill" in U.S.-Russian relations was caused by Putin's behavior at home and abroad after 2000 and that the Cold War ended with the Soviet Union. The first axiom is false, the second only half true: the Cold War ended in Moscow, but not in Washington.

Even at the time, it was far from certain that it would end in Washington. Declarations alone could not terminate decades of warfare attitudes. While President Bush was agreeing to end the Cold War from 1989 through 1991, a number of his top advisers, like many members of the U.S. political elite and media, were strongly resisting. (I witnessed that rift firsthand on the eve of the 1989 Malta summit, when I was asked to debate a pro–Cold War professor, in front of Bush and his clearly divided foreign-policy team, on the possibility of an unprecedented U.S.-Soviet strategic partnership. Many of the top-level officials present clearly shared my opponent's views, though the president did not.) Further evidence came with the Soviet breakup in December 1991. As I pointed out in chapter 6, U.S. officials, led by Bush himself, and the media immediately presented the purported "end of the Cold War" not as the mutual Soviet-American decision it had been but as a great American victory and Russian defeat.

That (now standard) triumphalist assertion was the primary reason the Cold War quickly revived—not in Moscow a decade later under Putin but in Washington in the early 1990s. It led the Clinton administration to make two fatefully unwise decisions. The most fundamental was to treat post-Communist Russia not as a strategic partner but as a defeated nation, analogous to Germany and Japan after World War II, which was expected to replicate America's domestic practices and bow to U.S. international interests. The approach was pursued, of course, behind the decorative facade of the Clinton-Yeltsin "partnership and friendship" and adorned with constant tributes to the Russian president's "heroic deeds" as the "father of Russian democracy."[24] (Why Yeltsin's Kremlin was the first ever to submit to foreign tutelage, causing him to be perceived at home as "a puppet of the West," is a different, and complex, story.)[25]

But the real policy was clear from the aggressive winner-take-all advantages pursued by the Clinton administration and from remarks made later by its top officials. In his memoirs, for example, Strobe Talbott, Clinton's "Russia hand," recalls the president worrying how long they could "keep telling Ol' Boris, 'Okay, now here's what you've got to do next—here's some more shit for your face.'" And Talbott recalls how, as he and Clinton knew it would, "Yeltsin's bluster in public had almost always given way to submissiveness in private." Similarly, the administration's top envoy admitted that bombing Serbia to separate Kosovo from Belgrade against Moscow's protests, which had humiliated the Kremlin at home and elsewhere, had been possible because "the Russians were still flat on their backs."[26]

From that triumphalism came the still-ongoing intrusions into Moscow's internal affairs and the abiding notion that Russia has few, if any, autonomous rights at home or abroad. Indeed, most of the follies of the next Bush administration began in the Clinton White House, including the pursuit of Caspian oil though military and political interventions in the Caucasus and Central Asia rather than cooperation with Moscow. Throughout the Clinton years, as two policy intellectuals close to the administration later recalled, there remained the presumption that "the USSR had lost the cold war," though "the defeat of the enemy was not as complete in 1991 as in 1945."[27]

Clinton's other fateful decision was to break the first Bush administration's promise to Soviet Russia in 1990 and 1991, in return for Moscow's agreeing to a reunited Germany as a NATO member, never to move that Western military alliance "one inch to the east." Clinton instead began its expansion to Russia's borders.[28] From that profound act of bad faith, followed by other broken strategic promises, came the dangerously provocative military encirclement of Russia and Moscow's evergrowing belief that it had been "constantly deceived," as Putin charged, by the United States. Thus, while U.S. officials, journalists, and even academics continued to insist that "the Cold War has indeed vanished" and that concerns about a new one are "hyperbolic nonsense" and "silly," Russians across the political spectrum believed that in Washington "the Cold War did not end" and, still more, that "the U.S. is imposing a new Cold War on Russia."[29]

Developments during the incoming Bush administration only heightened the perception of U.S. aggression. By Bush's second term, Washington and the U.S. political establishment generally seemed to have declared an "anti-Russian fatwa," as a former Reagan appointee termed it.[30] Among its highlights were a fresh torrent of official and media denunciations of Moscow's domestic and foreign policies, another expansion of NATO taking in still more of Russia's neighbors, and calls by virtually all of the 2008 Democratic and Republican presidential candidates for "very harsh" measures against Putin's Kremlin. The Pentagon even revived discredited rumors that Russian intelligence had given Saddam Hussein information endangering U.S. troops in Iraq. And Secretary of State Rice, violating diplomatic protocol, echoed the regime-changers by urging Russians, "if necessary, to change their government."[31]

For its part, the White House finally ended the fictitious relationship. It deleted from its 2006 National Security Strategy the long-professed U.S.-Russian partnership, backtracked on agreements to help Moscow join the World Trade Organization, and adopted sanctions against Belarus, the Slav former republic most culturally akin to Russia and with whom the Kremlin was negotiating a new union state. For emphasis, in May 2006 it dispatched Vice President Dick Cheney to an anti-Russian conference in former Soviet Lithuania, now a NATO member, to denounce the Kremlin and make clear it was no longer "a strategic partner and a trusted friend," thereby ending fifteen years of official pretense.[32]

More astonishing was the "task force report" on Russia by the influential Council on Foreign Relations, cochaired by a Democratic presidential aspirant, issued in March 2006.[33] The "nonpartisan" council's reputed moderation and balance were nowhere in evidence. An unrelenting exercise in double standards, the report blamed all the "disappointments" in U.S.-Russian relations solely on "Russia's wrong direction" under Putin—from meddling in the former Soviet republics and backing Iran to conflicts over NATO, energy politics, and the "rollback of Russian democracy."

Strongly implying that President Bush had been too soft on Putin, the council report flatly rejected partnership with Moscow as "not a realistic prospect." It called instead for "selective cooperation" and "selective opposition," depending on which suited U.S. interests, and, in effect, Soviet-era containment. It concluded by urging more Western intervention in Moscow's political affairs. An article in the council's influential journal, *Foreign Affairs*, menacingly added that the United States was quickly "attaining nuclear primacy" and the ability "to destroy the long-range nuclear arsenals of Russia or China with a first strike."[34]

EVERY consequence of this bipartisan American cold war against post-Communist Russia undermined the historic opportunity for an essential partnership and exacerbated the lethal dangers inherent in the breakup of the Soviet state. The crusade to transform Russia during the 1990s, with its "shock" economic measures and resulting antidemocratic politics, further destabilized the country, fostering an oligarchic system that plundered the state's wealth, deprived basic infrastructures of investment, impoverished the people, and nurtured dangerous forms of official and mafia-like corruption.

In the process, Yeltsin's U.S.-backed measures discredited Western-style reform and generated mass anti-Americanism where there had been almost none, not even during the Cold War 1970s and early 1980s when I lived in Moscow. Indeed, America's friends in Russia have diminished since the early 1990s in almost direct proportion to America's growing need for Russia's cooperation. By 2008, Washington's policies had instilled "negative attitudes" toward the United States in two-thirds of Russians surveyed and eviscerated the once-influential pro-American faction in Kremlin and electoral politics, whose parties in effect no longer existed.[35]

Military encirclement, the Bush administration's striving for nuclear supremacy, and recurring U.S. intrusions into Russian politics had even worse consequences. They provoked the Kremlin into suspending its participation in arms agreements, undertaking its own conventional and nuclear buildup—which relied more rather than less on compromised mechanisms of control and maintenance—and continuing to invest inadequate sums, further reduced by the consequences of the Georgian War and the deepening financial crisis in 2009, in the country's decaying economic base and human resources.

These same American policies also caused Moscow to cooperate less rather than more in existing U.S.-funded programs to reduce the multiple risks represented by Russia's materials of mass destruction and to prevent accidental nuclear war. More generally, and not unrelated, they inspired a new Kremlin ideology of "emphasizing our sovereignty" that is increasingly nationalistic, intolerant of foreign-funded NGOs as "fifth columns," and reliant on anti-Western views of the "patriotic" Russian intelligentsia and the Orthodox Church. (In particular, the new doctrine of "sovereign democracy" was a direct response to the U.S. "democracy-promotion" crusade.)[36]

Moscow's reactions abroad were also the opposite of what Washington policymakers should want. Interpreting U.S.-backed "color revolutions" in Ukraine and Georgia as a quest for military outposts on Russia's borders and along pipelines flowing with Caspian oil, the Kremlin opposed prodemocracy movements in former Soviet republics more than ever and supported the most authoritarian regimes in the region, from Belarus to Uzbekistan. Meanwhile, Moscow began forming a political, economic, and military "strategic partnership" with China and lending support to Iran and other anti-American governments in the Middle East. In addition, it threatened to install its own retaliatory system near Poland to counter U.S. missile-defense sites in that country and began considering the reintroduction of surface-to-air missiles in Belarus, which also borders NATO.

And all of that may be only the beginning of a new dark era. If American policy and Russia's predictable countermeasures continue to develop into a full-scale cold war, several new factors could make it even more dangerous than was its predecessor. These post-Soviet factors contributed to the deterioration of relations between Washington and Moscow in the 1990s and have continued to do so ever since.

Above all, the growing presence of NATO and American bases and U.S.-backed governments in the former Soviet republics moved the "front lines" of the conflict, in the alarmed words of a Moscow newspaper, from the epicenter of the previous Cold War in Germany to Russia's "near abroad."[37] As a "hostile ring tightens around the Motherland," Russians of different political persuasions begin to see a growing mortal threat. Putin's political aide Vladislav Surkov, for example, expressed alarm over the "enemy . . . at the gates," and even the Soviet-era dissident Aleksandr Solzhenitsyn warned of a "complete encirclement of Russia and then the loss of its sovereignty."[38] The risks of direct U.S.-Russian military conflict therefore became greater than ever, as the 2008 proxy war in Georgia showed.[39]

Making the geopolitical factor worse were radically different American and Russian self-perceptions. By the mid-1960s, the U.S.-Soviet

Cold War had acquired a significant degree of stability because the two superpowers, perceiving a stalemate, began to settle for "parity" and to develop détente as a way of managing the dangers. Since 1991, however, the United States, now the self-proclaimed "only superpower," or "indispensable nation" as the Clinton administration boasted, has had a far more expansive view of its international entitlements and possibilities. Moscow, on the other hand, has felt weaker and less secure than it did before 1991. That asymmetry, along with conflicting understandings of how the Cold War ended, has made the new cold-war relationship between the two still fully armed nuclear states less predictable, again as the Georgian War demonstrated.

Another new factor in the deteriorating relationship has come from feelings of betrayal on both sides. Though they choose not to recall it, American officials, journalists, and academic specialists effusively welcomed Putin in 2000 as Yeltsin's rightful heir—as a man with a "commitment to building a strong democracy" and to continuing "Russia's turn to the West."[40] Having misunderstood both Yeltsin and his successor, they felt deceived by Putin's subsequent policies.

Thus, Americans who had once been pro-Kremlin "democracy promoters," to take an important example, now saw Putin as "surly, preening, and occasionally vulgar" and turned into implacable cold warriors.[41] Two characteristic *Washington Post* commentaries said it all: the second President Bush had a "well-intentioned Russia policy," but "a Russian autocrat . . . betrayed the American's faith." Another added, "We have been played for fools," while a *New York Times* columnist complained bitterly that the West had been "suckered by Mr. Putin. He is not a sober version of Boris Yeltsin."[42]

Meanwhile, Putin's Kremlin was reacting to a decade of U.S. tutelage and broken promises (as well as Yeltsin's boozy compliance), as the new leader made clear as early as 2002: "The era of Russian geo-political concessions [is] coming to an end."[43] Disregarded, Putin gave an unusually candid explanation of Moscow's newly independent foreign policy at a high-level international forum in Munich in 2007. His speech was a landmark in the "sovereignization" of Kremlin thinking and policy.

Asking his Western audience "not to be angry with me," Putin stated "what I really think about" Washington's "one master, one sovereign" approach to Russia and U.S. moves "to impose new dividing lines and walls on us." He ended on a conciliatory but unapologetic note: "We are open to cooperation." In response, he was widely accused of declaring a "Second Cold War." In the eyes of the Russian leadership, however, nothing changed, and in November 2008, Putin's successor, Medvedev, repeated the general contents of his predecessor's Munich speech, while adding the threat to target U.S. missile defense sites in Poland and the Czech Republic.[44]

Still worse, if a *second* Cold War had begun, it lacked the substantive negotiations and cooperation of détente that restrained the previous one. Behind the facade of "candid discussions," according to well-informed Russians in 2008, "real dialogue does not exist."[45] This was alarmingly true in regard to nuclear weapons. The Bush administration's jettisoning of the ABM treaty and real reductions, its decision to try to build an antimissile shield with sites near Russia, and its talk of preemptive war and first nuclear strikes had all but abolished the U.S.-Soviet agreements that kept the nuclear peace for nearly fifty years.[46] In short, as nuclear dangers grew and a new arms race developed, efforts to curtail or even discuss them ended.

Finally, by the early 1990s, anti–Cold War forces that had played an important political role in the United States in the 1970s and 1980s, had ceased to exist.[47] Cold War lobbies, old and new, therefore operated virtually unopposed, some of them funded by anti-Kremlin oligarchs in exile. Support for the new U.S. cold-war policies was fully bipartisan, from Clinton to Bush, Secretary of State Madeleine Albright to her successor Condoleezza Rice, the presidential candidate Barack Obama in 2008 to his Republican opponent John McCain. There was scarcely more opposition at lower levels. Once robust pro-détente public groups, particularly anti-arms-race movements, had been largely demobilized by official, media, and academic myths that "the Cold War is over" and with it lethal dangers in Russia.

Also absent (or silent) were the kinds of American academic specialists and other intellectuals who had protested Cold War excesses. Meanwhile, a legion of new intellectual cold warriors emerged, particularly in Washington's liberal and conservative think tanks. Congressional and media favorites, their anti-Kremlin zeal also went largely unchallenged. There were notable exceptions—also bipartisan, from Reaganites who resented the squandering of what they regarded as their hero's greatest achievement to contributors to *The Nation* magazine—but "anathematizing Russia," as an alarmed Gorbachev lamented, had become a chilling kind of political correctness.[48]

Those new factors have been enough to make another cold war exceedingly dangerous, but they were made even worse by the "pluralist" American mainstream press. In the 1970s and 1980s, editorial pages (and television broadcasts) provided an important forum for debate by regularly featuring opposing views on U.S.-Soviet relations. After the end of the Soviet Union, however, they increasingly favored one opinion to the exclusion of others. In the 1990s, the outlook of pro-Yeltsin crusaders was favored, so much so that the situation reminded a senior American historian of the "fellow-traveling of the 1930s" though the "ideological positions are reversed." After 2000, in a political turnabout, equally impassioned Kremlin bashers were given a near monopoly on interpreting relations between Washington and Moscow and developments inside Russia.[49]

By 2004, the reporting, "news analysis," and editorial-page commentaries of the most influential U.S. newspapers had filled with the Manichean perspectives of the Cold War era—along with accusations that the Kremlin, sometimes Putin personally, was responsible for the deaths of Russian oppositionists, from crusading journalists in Moscow to a KGB defector in London, even though the charges were politically illogical and the evidence nonexistent. Putin's Kremlin was, leading papers told readers, if not the headquarters of "a fascist Russia," then run by "thugs masquerading as a government."[50] Not surprisingly, when the Putin-Medvedev leadership reacted with force to Georgia's military assault on South Ossetia in August 2008, it was widely compared with Soviet invasions of Eastern European countries and even Hitler's annexations of the late 1930s.

Readers who lived through the U.S.-Soviet Cold War might have thought someone had hit a replay button. A *Wall Street Journal* editor declared it "time we start thinking of Vladimir Putin's Russia as an enemy of the United States"; a *Washington Post* columnist announced "2004 as the year when a new iron curtain descended across Europe"; and outside contributors to the *Post* demanded a policy of "rolling back the corrupting influence of Russian power in regions beyond its borders." Once again, readers would have had to search for even a suggestion that anyone was responsible for these ominous echoes other than the Kremlin, which, a *New York Times* reporter explained, had "dusted off cold war vocabulary."[51]

The *Post*'s incessant demonizing of Putin put it in the forefront of the new American cold war, but the *Times*, the *Journal* (the two other newspapers regarded as authoritative by the U.S. political class), and other media were not far behind. Less staid dailies followed their coverage to its logical conclusion, reporting a new "contest between two contrasting cultures. To the east: state control over the political, legal, and economic system . . . dominated by Slavophile nationalism and nostalgia for the Soviet era. To the west: an open society, with democracy, the rule of law, and free market capitalism. It is a contest from which only one side can emerge the victor, a duel to the death—perhaps literally."[52]

In international relations, as President Reagan liked to point out, "it takes two to tango." For several years, however, Putin's policy toward the United States was primarily "reactive" and his preference "not to return to the Cold War era" the main reason relations did not worsen more quickly.[53] "Someone is still fighting the cold war," a British academic wrote in 2006, "but it isn't Russia."[54] In Moscow, however, a struggle was already underway over how Russia should respond to the new U.S. "aggression."

Misled by the decline of democracy and repeating a common misperception of policymaking in the Soviet system, even usually informed American commentators assumed that "In Russia, there's no real politics. All the politics takes place in the brain of Vladimir Putin."[55] In reality, factional disputes over Kremlin decisions never ended in high political circles, those over foreign policy being the most intense. In that political realm, where he was viewed as the "most pro-Western leader," Putin was soon being accused of continuing Gorbachev-Yeltsin "policies of national capitulation" and of "appeasing" Washington to the point of "betraying the interests of the Motherland."[56]

At issue was the future of Russia. The overriding priority of Putin and his allies, including Medvedev, was the modernization of the country's disintegrating economic and social foundations, a long-term project requiring cooperation with the West. For the "hawks," as they were again called,[57] that foreign policy was "naive," an "illusion," because "hatred of Russia" in the West, where "Russia has no friends," had not begun or ended with the Cold War. It was a permanent "geo-political jihad" against Russia now spearheaded by the U.S.-led NATO expansion.[58]

Cooperating with the West, in particular the United States, which was "ready to resort to any kind of deceit, any lie, in relations with us," therefore "would be criminal, like calling for cooperation with Hitler after World War II was declared."[59] Instead, proponents of a "more hardline" (*bolee zhestkogo*) policy, whose supporters numbered high-level military and security officers as well as influential ultranationalist ideologues, saw Russia's security and future in its own vast Eurasian space and further East, where it would find real "strategic partners." For them, the nation's natural resources and military-industrial complex were enough for economic development and a "fortress" against the West's encroaching military power.[60]

By 2006, even centrists in the dispute had become "very critical of Russia's foreign policy." They, too, had concluded that the forty-year Cold War had not been an "aberration" and that "the idea of becoming a strategic partner of the Unites States has failed," as hard-liners said it would. They also began calling on Putin to "stop being much too accommodating and compliant." The main cause of their turnabout was, of course, U.S. policy, as a result of which "we have surrendered everything" but "without gaining anything for Russia."[61] As happened decades before, a symbiotic axis had formed between American and Russian cold warriors.[62]

As a result, the Kremlin was now ready, if necessary, to wage another cold war regardless of the costs and unprecedented dangers it might entail. That was the emphatic message sent by the Putin-Medvedev leadership's military response in Georgia in August 2008 and its declared readiness to target U.S. missiles in Eastern Europe with its own. Knowledgeable Russian observers believed that by then Putin and Medvedev were at grave risk of appearing "defeatist" and therefore no longer had a choice. Whatever the case, as Medvedev explained, "We have made our choice."[63]

THE new cold war began in Washington, and the first steps to end it will also have to be taken there. Almost twenty years of U.S. policy have left the Kremlin and Russia's larger political class "tired of playing the dupe. Russia has made so many advances to the West. . . . It is now America's turn to persuade Moscow of its good intentions, not the other way around." Nor will the Kremlin settle any longer for "illusions of partnership" or accept blame for the new cold war and arms race it now sees unfolding. "It is not our fault," Putin declared in 2008, "we did not start it."[64]

It is a mistake to think these opinions are held only by Russia's increasingly nationalistic elites. Pro-American policy intellectuals, who based their hopes (and careers) on a U.S.-Russian partnership, now share the Kremlin's "eye-for-an-eye" determination: "What is allowed for [the United States] will be allowed for Russia."[65] At the same time, their despair, and whom they blame, is also unmistakable: "The foundations of U.S. policy toward Russia must be revised."[66]

For U.S. policy to actually change, the bipartisan fallacies that have underlain it since the early 1990s will have to be acknowledged and rejected. All of them sprang from unbridled triumphalism. It was Washington's decision to treat post-Soviet Russia as a vanquished nation that squandered the historic opportunity for an essential partnership in world affairs—the legacy of Gorbachev, Reagan, and George H. W. Bush—and established the premise that Moscow's "direction" at home and abroad should be determined by the U.S. government. Applied to a country with Russia's size, cultural traditions, and long history as a great power—and whose political class did not think it had been vanquished in the Cold War[67]—the premise was inherently self-defeating and in time certain to provoke a resentful backlash.

That folly produced two others. One assumed that the United States had the right, wisdom, and power to remake post-Communist Russia in its own image. A conceit as large as its disregard for Russia's traditions and contemporary realities, it led to the counterproductive crusade of the 1990s, whose missionary attitudes persist. Crusaders still long for the Yeltsin years when "Russian authorities granted Western governments huge opportunities to intervene in the sovereign affairs of Russia." One proposes a new crusade to correct Russia's memory of its Stalinist past; another, direct U.S. support for a secessionist movement in Russian Tatarstan; while the *Washington Post* continues to insist the White House "champion" the Kremlin's opponents at home.[68] Putin's response was not surprising: "Why do you believe that you have the right to interfere in our affairs?"[69]

The other triumphalist assumption was that Russia should be "a junior partner of the United States" in foreign policy, "see the world the way we do," and not expect to "be treated as an equal."[70] This, too, has persisted, as expressed in recurring complaints that Putin has "deeply disappointed" by not being a "loyal ally to America" or "doing much for the U.S. national interest," and by his general "unhelpfulness in foreign affairs."[71] Behind these complaints was, of course, the corollary presumption that Russia should have no interests abroad except those determined by Washington.

The policy outgrowth of this American thinking practically guaranteed the onset of a new cold war. The most consequential position has been Washington's demand, in effect, that Moscow vacate its traditional spheres of political, military, and energy security in former Soviet republics so the Unites States and NATO can occupy them. (The Kremlin has even been expected, it seems, to subsidize the defection of those new states by continuing to supply them with energy at discounted rates.) With this, Washington has been telling Russia that it not only has no Monroe Doctrine–like rights in its own backyard but no legitimate security rights at all.

No less remarkable has been the U.S. reaction to Moscow's growing alarm over NATO's expansion to Russia's former Soviet-bloc allies in Eastern Europe and the former Soviet republics on its borders. The Russian protests have invariably been dismissed as "gratuitously hostile," "laughable," or "bizarre and paranoid."[72] But what would be Washington's reaction, the Kremlin might wonder, if Russian bases multiplied on U.S. borders with Canada and Mexico along with devices in Cuba and Venezuela that might neutralize America's defense against that threat? Would Washington be satisfied with Moscow's assurances, to reverse the names of the countries, "This is not an encirclement of America. This is not a . . . strategy going against American interests?"[73]

The Kremlin hardly needs such a counterfactual exercise in order to be alarmed. Declarations on leading U.S. editorial pages have been enough. One in the *Wall Street Journal*, for example, explained NATO expansion as "a strategy that will permanently guarantee Western overall interests in the [former Soviet] South Caucasus and Central Asia. Such interests include: direct access to energy resources . . . and forward bases for allied operations." A *Washington Post* columnist spelled out the larger mission: "The West wants to finish the job begun with the fall of the Berlin Wall and continue its march to the east." Meanwhile, a former Clinton official warned in another paper, "Washington will hold the Kremlin accountable for the ominous security threats that are developing between NATO's eastern border and Russia."[74]

Nor was this kind of aggressive American triumphalism merely a fleeting reaction to the end of the Soviet Union in 1991. A decade later, the tragedy of September 11 gave Washington a second chance for a real partnership with Russia. At a meeting on June 16, 2001, President Bush famously sensed in Putin's "soul" a partner for America. And so it seemed to most commentators after September 11, when Putin's Kremlin did more than any NATO government to assist the U.S. war effort against the Taliban regime in Afghanistan, and to save American lives, by giving it valuable intelligence, a Moscow-trained Afghan combat force, and unhindered access to crucial air bases in former Soviet Central Asia.[75]

The Kremlin understandably believed that in return Washington would at last give it the equitable relationship it had expected in the early 1990s. Instead, it got U.S. withdrawal from the ABM treaty; Washington's claim to permanent bases in Central Asia (as well as Georgia) and independent access to Caspian oil and gas; the invasion of Iraq, which the Putin leadership strongly opposed; a second round of NATO expansion taking in several former Soviet republics and bloc members; and a growing indictment of Moscow's domestic and foreign conduct. Not even September 11 was enough to end Washington's winner-take-all principles. Americans may have forgotten their government's indifference to Putin's strategic wartime aid, but Russians have not. Many still remember it as another "illusory" hope for partnership with the United States, or as President Medvedev recalled in 2008, another "missed . . . historic chance."[76]

Why have Democratic and Republican administrations alike believed they could act in such relentlessly anti-Russian ways without endangering U.S. national security? The answer is another fallacy—the belief that Russia, diminished and weakened by its loss of the Soviet Union, had no alternative to either bending to America's will or being "a weak, isolated power."[77] Even apart from the continued presence of Soviet-era weapons in Russia, this was a grave misconception. Because of its extraordinary material and human attributes, Russia, as its intellectuals say, has always been "destined to be a great power." This was still true of the enfeebled, crisis-ridden Russia of the 1990s. The only question was what kind of political state would rise from its knees. The answer, as should have been obvious at the time, depended significantly on how Russia was treated during its agony, particularly by the United States.[78] (Russia's backlash against its treatment in the 1990s was associated with Putin, but it would have come regardless of him.)

Even before 2000, when world energy prices began to refill its coffers, the Kremlin had alternatives to the humiliating role scripted by Washington. Above all, Russia could forge strategic alliances with eager anti-U.S. and non-NATO governments in the East and elsewhere, becoming an arsenal of conventional weapons and nuclear knowledge for states from China and India to Iran and Venezuela, as the "Kremlin hawks" were urging. (To illustrate that possibility, Medvedev's first trips abroad after becoming president in 2008 were to Kazakhstan and China.) Indeed, a prominent Russian analyst thought his country had already "left the Western orbit" in 2006, though it had not yet actually done so. When President Obama took office in 2009, Putin and Medvedev were still proposing "a partnership," though for how long was uncertain.[79]

Still more, even a diminished Russia can fight, perhaps win, a cold war on its new front lines across the vast former Soviet territories.[80] Along with considerable military capabilities, it has the advantages of geographic proximity, essential markets, energy pipelines, and corporate ownership, as well as kinship, language, and common experiences. These give Moscow an array of soft and hard power to use, if it chooses, against neighboring states considering a new patron in faraway Washington, as it demonstrated in Georgia. The Kremlin's advantages are even greater in Ukraine, Washington's next preferred candidate for NATO membership. That country's economy is heavily dependent on Russia for energy—a fact of life underscored in January 2009 when the Kremlin halted gas supplies in response to Kiev's failure to pay for them in full—and many of its citizens for employment. Politically, Moscow has widespread support in Ukraine's large ethnic Russian provinces and could encourage separatist movements there even more consequentially than it did in Georgia.

There are other problems for Washington in former Soviet republics. In the U.S.-Russian struggle in Central Asia over Caspian oil and gas, even apart from the "gas OPEC" Moscow formed with fifteen other exporting states in December 2008, Washington, as a triumphalist theorist acknowledged, "is at a severe disadvantage."[81] The United States has already lost its military base in Uzbekistan and may eventually lose the only remaining one it has in the region, in Kyrgyzstan. The new pipeline it backed to bypass Russia runs through Georgia, whose security and stability now depend considerably on Moscow. Washington's friend in oil-rich Azerbaijan is an anachronistic dynastic ruler whose pro-American commitments were shaken by the Kremlin's show of force in Georgia. And Kazakhstan, whose enormous energy reserves have made it a particular U.S. target, has its own large Russian population and has moved back toward Moscow.

Nor is the Kremlin powerless in direct dealings with the West. It can mount more than enough warheads and related devices to defeat any missile shield and illusion of "nuclear primacy." It can shut U.S. businesses out of multi-billion-dollar deals in Russia and, as it has reminded the European Union, which gets 25 percent of its gas from Russia, in time "redirect supplies" to hungry markets in the East.[82] And Moscow could deploy its resources, international connections, and UN Security Council veto against vital U.S. interests, among them energy, nuclear proliferation, Iran, Afghanistan, and possibly even withdrawal from Iraq. More generally, as one of Washington's best-informed specialists warned, "Russia does not yet have the power or the inclination to lead a global anti-American coalition. But it can help to shape the evolution of the international system in ways that would damage the United States. . . . [It] could tip the balance in unpredictable and destructive ways."[83]

Contrary to exaggerated American accusations, the Kremlin had not, as of early 2009, resorted to such measures in any significant way, though the previous year's military action in Georgia and then January's gas embargo against Ukraine, and the attendant disruption of Europe's supplies, left no doubt about its resolve. If Washington continues to abase and encroach upon Russia, its leadership is unlikely to see any "sovereign" reason why it should not retaliate. Certainly nothing Moscow has gotten from the United States since 1992—and it has gotten nothing of substance except ill-advised loans in the 1990s that burdened the country with debt—"compensates for," even a Western security specialist has pointed out, " the geopolitical harm the United States is doing to Russia."[84]

None of these looming dangers have dissuaded American crusaders, however, from insisting that they are worth the risk in order to democratize Russia. Readers may instinctively sympathize with that goal, and, having observed firsthand the struggle for democracy in both Soviet and

post-Soviet Russia for more than thirty years, I hope to live to see it ac-
complished. But the tenacious idea that the United States can directly
promote that country's democratization is also based on dangerous
fallacies.

To begin with "strategic" ones, the common assertion that a non-
democratic Russia can never be an essential or reliable U.S. ally because
its interests will differ ignores the Soviet-American cooperation that
maintained the nuclear peace and provided other safeguards in perilous
circumstances for four decades, as well as Washington's alliances with
various authoritarian regimes over the years. It also disregards Palmer-
ston's axiom that nations have "no eternal allies," only "perpetual" interests, which rightly assumes that not even partners always have identi-
cal interests.

Consider one crucial example that has both united and divided Moscow and Washington in recent years. No less than the White House, the
Kremlin does not want to be faced with a nuclear-armed Iran, but its
interests in that country are inescapably more complex. As a Eurasian
nation with some 20 million Muslim citizens of its own and with Iran
one of its few neighbors that is not a candidate for NATO membership,
Russia cannot risk being drawn into what it fears is America's emerging "holy alliance" against the Islamic world, whether in Iran, Iraq, or
anywhere else.[85] Its predicament is not unique. "You can't have a foreign
policy that goes against your geography," as a former Soviet republic
tried to explain to its new suitor in Washington.[86]

Nor is disregarding Russia's imperative interests the worst strategic
folly of democracy promoters. Since 2000, their frustration over the
country's "de-democratization" and their hatred of Putin, whom they
blame, has grown, as I noted earlier, into calls for "regime change" in
that already fragile nation. They seem indifferent to what it might actually mean—if not political chaos, even civil war, certainly not a "regime" of their anointed Russian "democrats," who lack any meaningful
popular support in the country, but of forces much more repressive,
nationalistic, and uncompromising than those represented by Putin. As
for Russia's vast stockpiles of devices of mass destruction in such destabilized circumstances, one of the "democrats" assured an American
supporter: "When this regime collapses, be aware that we are here."[87]
Neither seemed concerned by the consequences of "collapse" for those
stockpiles.

There is another profound fallacy of "democracy promotion" in Russia: it is inherently counterproductive, intrusive U.S. actions having only discredited the cause since 1992.[88] Praising the despised Yeltsin and his shock-therapy "democrats" while condemning the popular Putin further associated democracy with Russia's social pain and humiliations of the 1990s. Ostracizing Belarus's leader while demonstratively embracing dictators in Caspian Sea states related democracy to America's need for oil.[89] Linking "democratic revolutions" in Georgia and Ukraine to NATO membership equated them with U.S. military expansionism. Focusing on the victimization of billionaire Mikhail Khodorkovsky but never on grassroots protests against Russia's poverty and other social injustices, together with Washington's role in the Yeltsin-era "privatization" schemes and other misdeeds of the 1990s, suggested that democracy is only for oligarchs.[90]

Still worse, American crusaders, by insisting on their indispensable role, are suggesting (wrongly) that Russians are incapable of democracy on their own, a "kind of racism" in the view of a former British ambassador to Moscow.[91] Journalists, embittered by the failure of projects they backed in the 1990s, have gone further. Some express doubt "whether even today Russia can be considered a civilized country," while others flatly inform readers, "Russia is not a normal country." Features previously attributed to Communism, from "brutish instincts" and "murder and mayhem" to "autocratic" politics, are now said to be "embedded in Russia's DNA."[92]

Such demeaning commentaries, reported in the Moscow media, have reinforced dark Russian suspicions of American intentions. Many ranking and ordinary citizens now believe that Washington's real purpose since the end of the Soviet Union has been to seize control of their country's energy resources and nuclear weapons and use encircling NATO satellite states to "de-sovereignize" Russia, turning it into a "vassal of the West." Indeed, U.S. policy has fostered the belief that the long American Cold War was never really aimed at Soviet Communism but at Russia and that a new cold war would also be so motivated.[93]

Dispelling these perceptions of Russia is a necessary step toward ending the new cold war before it is too late. It means, of course, abandoning the triumphalist fallacies that inspired them, including the conceit that the U.S. "victory" in the Cold War meant "the total exhaustion of viable systematic alternatives to the American way" and "settled fundamental issues once and for all" in Washington's favor. Two U.S. policies have been especially responsible, as even Secretary of State Condoleezza Rice tacitly acknowledged.[94] One is expressed in missionary intrusions into Russia's internal affairs, the other in flagrant double standards regarding its national security. Defenders of those policies often insist "there is no alternative," but there is, and it is not the "declinism" they allege.[95]

The alternative to the triumphalist conceit that Moscow's "direction" at home should be determined in Washington was adumbrated by George Kennan, the esteemed diplomat and scholar, forty years before the Soviet Union ended. In 1951, anticipating the waning of Communist rule, he warned:

> Let us not hover nervously over the people who come after, applying litmus paper daily to their political complexions to find out whether they answer to our concept of "democratic." Give them time; let them be Russians; let them work out their internal problems in their own manner. . . . The ways by which peoples advance toward dignity and enlightenment in government are things that constitute the deepest and most intimate processes of national life. There is nothing less understandable to foreigners, nothing in which foreign interference can do less good.[96]

The ineluctable lesson of the Cold War, of both its duration and its end, is that Russia can "advance toward dignity and enlightenment in government" only when its relations with the outside world, particularly the United States, are improving, not worsening. In increasingly cold-war circumstances, its ruling circles, where such initiatives must be taken and opposition overcome, will never risk "letting go." That is why Gorbachev' s anti–Cold War and prodemocracy policies were inseparable. Twenty-five years later, support for democratic reform, though considerably diminished, still exists among Russia's people and even its elites.[97] If Washington really wants to "promote democracy," it must have a Russia policy that gives it a chance, not the one pursued since the early 1990s. America must also have, a Moscow democrat adds, a "moral authority" that it now lacks.[98]

Alternatives to "double standards in the policy of the United States," as the Kremlin now views them,[99] may be more contentious, but they have to begin with a recognition of Russia's legitimate security concerns about threats in regions along its own borders. In 2008, the Putin-Medvedev leadership made clear, in words and in deeds in Georgia, that it would no longer bow to the prospect of Western military bases in Moscow's "sphere of strategic interests."[100] The Kremlin's new resolve was immediately denounced by the Bush administration as "archaic" and "paranoid," but a Moscow admirer of U.S. history replied, "Every great nation has its own Monroe Doctrine. Do the Americans really think that they are entitled to one and the Russians are not?"[101]

In this regard, NATO expansion was for Russia the "original sin."[102] As the military alliance continued "its march to the east," taking in former Soviet-bloc countries and republics along the way, it finally convinced Moscow that U.S. policy was not "strategic partnership" but a quest for domination. The Kremlin no longer believed, as the Yeltsin leadership may have, repeated Western assurances that NATO's move eastward was "not directed at Russia." For that, too, it had only to read counterassurances by leading American commentators that the West's Cold War military force would not "lose its original purpose: to contain the Russian bear" and "guarantee overall Western interests."[103]

In the end, the expansion of NATO confirmed Kennan's foreboding that it would be "the most fateful error of the entire post–Cold War era."[104] It massively violated an essential principle on which Gorbachev and Reagan had agreed: Russian and American national security would either be mutual, in actions and perceptions, or it would not exist for either because one side's military buildup or threatening move invariably provokes the other to do the same. Putin's reaction was therefore to be expected: "The emergence of a powerful military bloc at our borders will be seen as a direct threat to Russia's security."[105]

As a result, NATO's expansion, contrary to assurances by its American promoters, has undermined everyone's security. When it became convinced that Washington was seeking "military-strategic superiority," the Kremlin was compelled "to act in response."[106] Meanwhile, NATO membership, or simply the promise of it, discouraged small states on Russia's borders, from the Baltics to Georgia, from negotiating disputes with their giant neighbor. Certain the United States and NATO would protect them, they were satisfied instead to let the problems fester and grow, even to "poke the Russian bear." The Kremlin may have overreacted, but it had resolved to no longer "permit the red lines of its national strategic interests to be crossed, especially in surrounding regions."[107] The U.S.-Russian proxy war in Georgia was the result.

The situation will grow even worse if Washington continues its campaign to bring Ukraine into NATO. Its state having originated in Kiev, Moscow thinks of Ukraine as "the cradle of Russia."[108] Nor is this unilateral or merely sentiment. Of all the former Soviet republics, Russia and a large part of Ukraine, along with Belarus, are the most intricately and intimately related—by geography, history, language, religion, marriage, economics, energy pipelines, and security. In Moscow's view, Ukraine entering NATO would be "hammering the final nail into the coffin of Russia as an independent great power."[109] (This is, of course, one motive behind the U.S. campaign to incorporate Ukraine into the Western military alliance.)

"No Russian leader can remain in power," according to a Moscow specialist admired in Washington, "if he 'loses' Ukraine to the United states as a member of NATO."[110] And yet American cold warriors seem determined to make this happen, declaring Ukraine a "strategic country," part of "our core zone of security," and "the great prize."[111] If they succeed, the Kremlin has publicly warned that the West's "relations with Russia will be spoiled once and for all" and "the price will be high." Privately, it is said that it would be seen as a "declaration of war."[112] If so, nuclear-armed Russia and America would be closer to self-inflicted catastrophe than ever before.

Zealous NATO expansionists insist the United States cannot "surrender" Ukraine back to Moscow as a "satellite nation," but here, too, there is an alternative. It is nonaligned status for both Ukraine and Georgia along the lines that enabled Finland to be neutral, peaceful, and prosperous after World War II.[113] This would mean Russia accepting the full political independence of those nations, including the results of their elections, in return for a promise of no further NATO member states and no NATO or U.S. military bases at all on its borders, including in the three Baltic nations already in the alliance. Whether the compromise is done informally or by treaty matters less than the benefits to all parties. A "red" front line in U.S.-Russian relations would be rolled back along with the new cold war itself. And the politics and economics of Georgia and Ukraine could turn to the real needs of their long-suffering peoples.

The alternative to this solution might well be a geopolitical splintering of Ukraine into two countries, one aligned with Russia, the other with the West. (Some two-thirds of its citizens surveyed have repeatedly opposed NATO membership, with less than 20 percent in favor.) Such a development would reinstitutionalize the Cold War division of Europe in even more unpredictable ways. Adjacent to Russia, it would represent a constant threat of new U.S.-Russian proxy wars more dangerous than the one in Georgia.

That possibility was foreshadowed by a little-known event in late May and early June 2006, at a port in Ukraine's ethnic Russian region of Crimea. A U.S. naval ship suddenly appeared, and a contingent of marines went ashore to prepare for a NATO-Ukraine military exercise. Angry crowds of local citizens blockaded the port and confronted the marines, shouting "No to NATO in Ukraine!" An eyewitness account conveyed their mood: "American soldiers . . . Do you want a new Vietnam here? You will get it, and your mothers will cry!" Meanwhile, "Loudspeakers blasted a throaty rendition of 'Holy War,' the song that sent Russian soldiers off to battle during World War II."[114]

PRESIDENT Barack Obama took office twenty years from the day outgoing President Ronald Reagan declared, in January 1989, "The Cold War is over."[115] In the interim, not only was that historic opportunity squandered, but relations between the United States and post-Soviet Russia fell to an all-time low and were growing worse. As a result, so was America's national security, which remained more dependent on its former superpower adversary than on any other country.

Above all else, Russia's stability and thus control over its innumerable devices of mass destruction, including safeguards against accidental nuclear launches, remained far from adequate. Despite billions of dollars of oil revenue, the nation was still an "infrastructural nightmare" and a "fragile state," as even U.S. hardliners acknowledged, though without any apparent concern about that unprecedented danger.[116] By 2009, the global financial crisis and plunge in world oil prices had shattered illusions that Russia's economy was an "island of stability" based on "a dynamic stable society." Mounting corporate debt, bankruptcies, unemployment numbers, poverty rates, unpaid wages, and signs of social unrest, along with the state's rapidly diminishing financial reserves, seemed to remind even Putin of "the shocks of 1991 and 1998."[117]

There were also bleaker perspectives. An experienced American observer thought the new Russian system had become "even more rickety than its tsarist and Soviet predecessors" and "could fold every bit as easily as they did." Two years before the 2008 crisis, Russian sociologists were already reporting "unpredictably explosive situations" in the country.[118] And some historians warned that the "dual power" of Putin and Medvedev was inherently destabilizing, as such arrangements had repeatedly been in the country's history. Those prognoses were exaggerated, but they echoed warnings by top Clinton officials in the late 1990s that the destabilization of nuclear Russia would put America "at greater risk than it [has] ever been."[119] This was still true a decade later.

The disintegration of U.S.-Russian cooperation, essential to virtually every important American concern from nuclear proliferation and international terrorism to the war in Afghanistan and other regional crises, was almost as alarming. By early 2009, "real dialogue [did] not exist" because, according to Russia's foreign minister, there had actually been "more mutual trust and respect during . . . the Cold War." (A well-informed Russian reported that there was now even more mistrust in Moscow than in Washington.)[120] In the aftermath of the Georgian proxy war, both sides demanded that the other make a fateful choice. The Bush administration insisted that "Russia faces a decision: to be a fully integrated and responsible partner" or "an isolated and antagonistic nation." The Kremlin replied that U.S. leaders had to finally decide "what kind of relations they want with Moscow."[121]

Still worse, with "missile madness" spurring a new arms race and "hawks" ascending in Washington and Moscow,[122] each side threatened to violate the other's "red lines." In November 2008, Russian warships appeared in the Caribbean and the Panama Canal, and President Medvedev, in Venezuela and Cuba. The Bush administration took a more extreme step. It called for accelerated NATO membership for Georgia and Ukraine, even though neither qualified by the alliance's criteria; most U.S. allies were opposed; a real war with Russia had just been averted in Georgia; and Ukraine's leadership may have colluded with Tbilisi in provoking that event. Alarmed by the brinkmanship, a respected Moscow analyst could no longer "rule out military conflict in the post-Soviet space between NATO and Russia"—or that Moscow might "be obliged to have recourse to nuclear weapons."[123]

Clearly, Washington urgently needed a fundamentally new approach to Russia, but officials and other commentators did not think so—not even with the United States bogged down in wars in Iraq and Afghanistan and crippled by economic crisis. Their response to increasingly dangerous relations with Moscow made Hegel's bleak axiom "The Owl of Minerva spreads its wings only with the falling of dusk" seem naively optimistic. The great German philosopher believed that although we are unable to comprehend historic developments until they unfold, we do then understand them.[124]

In this case, however, there was no American understanding. In late 2008, a European foreign minister warned that the continent was "already in a new cold war," and another respected Moscow analyst proclaimed that U.S.-Russian relations were "in some respects even worse." But wielders of influence in Washington still insisted, "No serious observer thinks we face a new Cold War."[125] Myopia was leading to more reckless American proposals. Several suggested that another "implosion" of the Russian nuclear state would be a positive development or at least, according to Secretary of State Rice, its "infrastructural nightmare" cause only for "calm." Another advocated building an even more provocative missile-defense facility—this one in the former Soviet republic of Lithuania. Yet another urged bringing Finland, a longstanding model of successful neutrality, into NATO.[126]

Not even American public figures and publications reputed to be the most thoughtful on foreign policy seemed capable of rethinking Russia. An admired former congressman was as triumphalist as his colleagues, predicating U.S. policy on "the health of Russian democracy."[127] The most influential newspaper, the *New York Times*, still excluding alternative views, continued to feature misleading articles indicting Putin for everything from the "new cold war" and fighting in Georgia to neo-Stalinism in Russia.[128] (The most important policy journal, *Foreign Affairs*, was scarcely different, while the *Washington Post*'s editorial pages continued to read like a bygone *Pravda* on the Potomac.) Broadcasts by the major television networks were no less one-sided in their coverage. Exasperated, two leading academic authorities on U.S.-Russian relations finally expressed their "concern that the American public is simply not hearing the other side."[129]

The inability of the political elite to reconsider its two-decade policy toward post-Soviet Russia, which had been a disaster from the outset, was not out of character. Its limited capacity for introspection, independent thinking, and civic courage was also expressed in its acquiescence in the disastrous Iraq War. (A few prominent figures did profess to rethink Russia policy, but most of them again blamed Moscow alone for bad relations or proposed no fundamental changes in the U.S. approach.)[130] A British resident in Washington was astonished that so few members of the political and media elites openly opposed Russia policy, though some did so privately. He attributed their conformism to being "intimidated" by the prevailing consensus and to careerism, adding: "This is the way that most of the Washington think-tank world works."[131]

The role of intimidation should not be underestimated. In another characteristic sign of a new American cold war, the few outspoken critics of Washington's policy have been the target of defamatory attacks, even in purportedly liberal publications, for "once again taking the Russian side." Among the charges familiar from the previous Cold War are "appeasement" and "willful blindness," "cheerleaders of Russian President Putin" and "Putin apologists," and "freedom-hater."[132] Even Henry Kissinger was labeled "naive" for suggesting that the Kremlin was motivated primarily by its "quest for a reliable strategic partner" in Washington.[133]

The actual alternative to Washington's twenty-year failed policy is nothing like what the new cold warriors allege. It begins with America's real national security priorities, which remain twofold: a stable Russia relying less, not more, on its nuclear weapons; and, as a *Boston Globe* columnist reminded readers, "an unprecedented strategic partnership between Moscow and Washington."[134] Those priorities should have excluded any number of U.S. follies, such as Clinton's myopic notion that "Yeltsin drunk is better than most of the alternatives sober" as the custodian of a nuclear state[135] and Bush's reckless promotion of tail-wagging-the-dog client states on its borders. (Even after the U.S.-Russian proxy war in August 2008, both Washington and Tbilisi continued to act recklessly toward Moscow. The Bush administration threatened to rearm Georgia and signed bilateral security agreements with both Tblisi and Kiev, while Georgia's president staged events, including a purported Russian attempt to assassinate himself and the president of Poland, designed to further embroil the United States in his conflicts with the Kremlin.)

With a clear understanding that America's road to national security runs through Moscow, the overriding goal now is to replace the new cold war, before it is too late, with, as one U.S. official understood, "a virtuous cycle of cooperation."[136] It cannot be the "selective cooperation" espoused by proponents of the failed triumphalist policy, according to which Washington expects Moscow's assistance on behalf of America's vital interests while denying that Russia has any comparable ones.[137] It will be either a fully reciprocal partnership or none at all. Achieving the "virtuous " kind requires at least four fundamental changes in American thinking.

First, triumphalism must be replaced, in words and in deeds, as the underlying principle of U.S. policy by the original premise that ended the Cold War in the years from 1988 through 1991—that there were no losers but instead a historic chance for the two great powers, both with legitimate security interests abroad and full sovereignty at home, to escape the perils and heavy costs of their forty-year confrontation. This also means recognizing that there are no longer any "superpowers." Post-Soviet Russia does not claim to be one, and if America really was a superpower today it would not have been so easily attacked on September 11, so unable to gain military victory in either Iraq or Afghanistan, so burdened with economic crisis and debt, or so lacking in the "soft" power of goodwill in the world.[138]

Second, the "Blame Russia First syndrome," which is both unfair and a source of constant antagonism, has to end.[139] No U.S. leader can go as far as I have in this book in holding Washington primarily responsible for the new cold war. But an acknowledgment that a mutual opportunity was missed and that both sides bear responsibility would be enough for a new beginning. It would, for example, assuage an abiding Russian grievance against the United States. "We do not want to aggravate the situation," President Medvedev tried to explain, "but we want to be respected."[140]

The third fundamental change follows from the previous two and is the most crucial. NATO expansion toward Russia, which has failed on all counts, must stop. It has served only to undermine the security of all parties involved; generate a militarized U.S.-Russian relationship where there should be a diplomatic one; bring the two nations closer to war than ever before; and all but exclude the possibility of further nuclear arms reductions. By encircling Russia with military bases, along with facilities that have the potential to deprive Moscow of its hard-achieved defense capabilities, NATO's encroachment has also caused even pro-Western Russians to feel "our fate is not in our hands."[141] A nation fearing for its future will never wager on a partner that threatens it.

Finally, a new policy is not possible until the White House and Congress tell the American people the truth about our relationship with post-Soviet Russia. It was never a strategic partnership, only the pretence of one in Washington and the cause of bitter disappointment and mistrust in Moscow. Whether U.S. leaders call the actual relationship a new cold war, as I have, or simply "the worst in a generation" matters less than candidly acknowledging its unprecedented dangers. Two other common practices are also misleading. America does not need meaningless claims about a "friend" in the Kremlin; it needs a real partner there. And constant assurances that the Soviet Union no longer exists, while post-Soviet failures and perils mount, as the Bush administration made a habit of, is no substitute for a national security policy. (It is instead an ideological kind of decision making that repeatedly makes its leading officials seem profoundly uninformed about Russia and surprised by Moscow's actions.)[142]

Not long ago, these fundamental principles were considered mainstream, little more than common sense. Now they are regarded as heresy by an American political establishment that abandoned them. A defender of Reagan's anti–Cold War initiatives has warned that critics seeking to change Washington's subsequent approach to Russia "will have to enter the fray with light hearts and thick skins and the courage of their convictions."[143] Considering the attacks they have experienced and the powerful forces with deeply vested interests in the wrong-headed policy, from officials, editorialists, and academic specialists to military-defense firms profiting from NATO's enlargement, critics will also need a determined leader.

As I finish this book, in early 2009, the best and possibly last hope is the new American president, Barack Obama. Grassroots movements can play a role, but Russia policy has always been decided by the White House, for better and worse, from Roosevelt and Truman to Nixon,

Reagan, Clinton, and Bush. President Obama—young, with few ties to the failed policies, elected with a mandate for reform at home incompatible with the economic and political costs of the new cold war, and having emphasized Moscow's weapons of mass destruction as the "greatest threat" to America's security and the need to "reset U.S.-Russia relations" and "initiate a new era of American diplomacy"[144]—would seem the ideal agent of a new thinking about Russia.

But the prospects for this urgently needed alternative may not be good. Obama's own party expressed its rare dissent from Bush's Russia policy by accusing him of having "been too soft on Vladimir Putin," having "given Putin a blank check," even of having thereby "lost Russia."[145] The Democrats' alternative was a more cold-war approach. During his presidential campaign, Obama differed only slightly on Washington's relations with Moscow from his orthodox Democratic and Republican rivals, and his main Russia adviser was a Yeltsin-era missionary crusader and now neo-cold warrior.[146]

In this regard, the foreign-policy team Obama assembled as president seemed no better. His vice president, Joseph Biden, was a longtime zealous proponent of the triumphalist policy, including NATO expansion and the U.S. projects in Georgia and Ukraine, and of "direct confrontation" with the Kremlin. Accepting his nomination, Biden rededicated himself to those pursuits.[147] Obama's secretary of state, Hillary Rodham Clinton, was the spouse of the president who originated that general policy and staffed her department with people who had implemented it. Robert Gates, Obama's secretary of defense, had a longer governmental involvement in the failed policy than anyone else in Washington. The new national security adviser, General James L. Jones, was a former NATO commander and an enthusiastic advocate of its expansion. Even Obama's chief economic adviser, Lawrence Summers, had been an architect of the Clinton administration's shock-therapy crusade in Russia in the 1990s.

None of those people had ever publicly expressed any rethinking of their triumphalism or doubts about its failures and increasingly dangerous consequences. None openly rejected U.S. hardliners' clamorous warnings to Obama that Moscow was trying to "intimidate" and "test" him and that any "kowtowing" or "capitulation" on his part would only whet the Kremlin's "imperialist" appetite. Among those appointees, or anywhere around Obama, there appeared to be no heretical thinkers on Russia, and certainly none of the critics who had warned against the bipartisan policy from the beginning.[148]

Hope may die last, but historical memory must also persist. Twenty-five years earlier, at another exceedingly dangerous juncture in relations between the White House and the Kremlin, a leader emerged from the Soviet Communist Party system, a much more dogmatic, rigid, and menacing battleground than Washington, espousing what he called "New Thinking." With only a few other heretics at his side, and at considerable risk to his position and even his life, Mikhail Gorbachev followed those ideas and their vision to the end of the forty-year Cold War.

A quarter of a century later, Kremlin leaders of a different generation are still clinging to hope for "a partnership between the U.S. and Russia," despite growing opposition in their own political establishment.[149] This time, however, the United States and its new president will have to take the initiative. Is American democracy any less capable of such an alternative than was the Soviet Communist system?

EPILOGUE FOR THE PAPERBACK EDITION

Alternatives are returning.

GLEB PAVLOVSKY, 2010

In Moscow and in Washington, people have been known to lose opportunities . . . We have to hope that this time we won't lose the opportunity.

MEMBER OF THE RUSSIAN PARLIAMENT, 2010

ANYONE who writes with the purpose of changing established thinking about fateful turning points in political history, as I have done in this book, must be patient. Orthodoxies never yield quickly to facts or logic. This is even more the case with American thinking about the former Soviet Union—and, it turns out, about post-Soviet Russia. As Will Rogers aptly quipped many years ago, "No matter what you say about it, it's true."

It is too soon, therefore, to know the impact of *Soviet Fates and Lost Alternatives*, which first appeared in hardcover only in mid-2009. Several reviewers have welcomed my reconsideration of missed opportunities in Soviet and post-Soviet history and in U.S.-Russian relations, but others, one observer concluded, have shunned the book because of its "realistic, but scarcely diplomatic, indictment of a . . . broad swath of academics, journalists, and intellectuals."[1] If so, we should not be surprised. "You can't expect people," as a Moscow columnist I quoted earlier remarked, "to jump out of their biographies."[2]

I did not intend this book, with the exception of chapter 7, to be an "indictment," but a revisionist endeavor of this kind always risks offending political correctness. To give a recent example, a distinguished historian was accused of "nostalgia" for the Soviet Union and of yearning for "a restoration of the old repressive norms" because he focused on Soviet-era intellectuals who believed in reforming the system, not abolishing it.[3] Considering that such derisive attitudes are still widespread among reviewers and other commentators, a full rethinking of roads that might have been taken during and after the Soviet experience may require a new generation of Americans unaffected by the legacies of the Cold War.

Certainly, nothing has changed in American (or, more generally, Western) mainstream thinking to diminish the purpose of this book. Except for a very few writers, all of the views contested in the preceding pages are still presented as axiomatic. To reiterate them briefly:

- There were no viable alternatives for the better in Soviet history—not those represented by Bukharin, Khrushchev, Gorbachev, or any other leader treated in the book—only predetermined outcomes.
- The Soviet Union was not merely unreformable; "even incremental reform was too much for the system to bear."
- The end of the Soviet Union was "a deliverance of biblical proportions" resulting in "a golden age of the most profound peace and prosperity."
- "How America won the cold war" is an essential leadership lesson for all subsequent American presidents.
- It was Putin, not the U.S.-backed Yeltsin, who "began dismantling Russian democracy."
- The "U.S.-Russian relationship soured" after 1991 largely because of policies made in Moscow, not in Washington.[4]

All of these false, or at least questionable, axioms have become mythic aspects of a post-1991 American narrative. And myths are even harder to dispel than historical orthodoxies.

In Russia, on the other hand, despite continuing elements of state censorship, there is no longer an orthodox position, no "general line" or "single viewpoint," regarding any of the historical or political developments examined in *Soviet Fates and Lost Alternatives*. (Four of the chapters have been published in translation in Moscow.)[5] Each of those fateful turning points and their outcomes continues to be the subject of conflicting views and intense debate. Twenty years later, the end of the Soviet Union—whether it was predetermined or avoidable, whether or not it was "legitimate"—remains the most fiercely disputed issue,[6] but not the only one that is still politically consequential.

Various reasons explain why there is so little historical closure in Russia today. One is that two leaders reexamined in this book remain active in political life. Gorbachev, who turned eighty in 2011, and Ligachev, ninety in 2010, continue to defend the conflicting "missed opportunities" they represented, as do their supporters. Even Bukharin, more than seventy years after his execution, hovers over contemporary discussions of Russia's present and future, his NEP alternative still cited as a market system suited to the country's long tradition of mixed state and private economies. As for Stalin, both his admirers and harshest critics say he is "more alive than ever."[7]

But the primary reason remote events are "living history" in Russia is that roads taken in the past have so often led to catastrophic destinations. As a young journalist wrote in 2010, "All of Russia's suffering has roots in its history, although we cannot agree on which period is most to blame." (Fifty years before, Mikoyan, Khrushchev's anti-Stalinist ally, put it more colloquially: "History can drive you crazy.")[8] These disputes over when, what, and whom to blame range over several centuries but concentrate, of course, on the nearly one hundred years from the 1917 revolution to the present, thereby perpetuating all of the interpretive questions raised in *Soviet Fates and Lost Alternatives.*

Indeed, by 2011, the book's overarching theme was again central to Russian politics. With the country at yet another crossroads, one side in the struggle defended the nation's historical "culture of non-alternatives" as consistent with its traditions while another rejected "history without alternatives" and hoped that "alternatives are returning." (That these opposing perspectives were formulated by a political intellectual close to the Kremlin, Gleb Pavlovsky, indicated the high-level nature of the recurring conflict.)[9] Leading to the new crossroads was a divisive issue that had afflicted the nation repeatedly before and after 1917—the belief that Russia was in urgent need of "modernization."

The revived imperative is understandable. As I emphasized in chapter 7, Russia's basic infrastructures have perilously disintegrated because of the precipitous fall in investment since the 1980s, the economic depression of the 1990s, a decade of unprecedented demodernization, and the state's budgetary overreliance on energy exports. Not only alarmists now warn that Russia has already lost decades of the modernity it achieved at great costs during its Soviet twentieth century and is in danger of losing essential elements of its future as a great nation—the development of its people, technical and scientific progress, economic competitiveness, military power, and even its oil and natural gas sectors. Few in the political class disagree that "Russia again faces its age-old problem: Modernize or be crushed."[10]

Apart from agreeing that the country must develop a diversified economy less dependent on natural resources, there is, however, no consensus, only fundamental disagreement, about the meaning of "modernization" and "the sacramental question—how to do this."[11] Proposals range from implanting technical innovations in the existing order, such as a Russian Silicon Valley, to transforming the entire post-Soviet political and economic system. By 2011, the dispute dominated domestic- and even foreign-policy discussions and had spread to the highest levels, with Prime Minister Putin, still the preeminent leader, and President Medvedev, his protégé, taking noticeably different positions. But the underlying divide remains as it has been throughout the nation's long history of modernizing controversies and campaigns, and as I spelled out in chapter 6 in contrasting Gorbachev's gradualist perestroika to Yeltsin's shock therapy.

Once again, one side in the struggle over "the alternatives of modernization" insists that Russia's dire condition, the recalcitrance of its bureaucrats and people, and mounting dangers abroad mean that the state, armed with power "to eliminate all obstacles," must impose the transformation on society. And once again, the opposing side warns against another "modernization through catastrophe" that will result in more dictatorship and political "slaves," arguing instead for a "democratic" or "soft" modernization promoted by the state but carried out "from below" by free citizens. The Kremlin might follow a centrist course for several years, but eventually, as has happened in the past, it is likely to choose one or the other. The alternatives therefore again pose "fateful choices."[12]

For Russia's dwindling prodemocracy forces, the new modernization debate has had one unexpected benefit: it has reopened discussion of the country's aborted democratization. Some commentators, referring to Gorbachev's reforms, call this approach "Perestroika II."[13] But despite high-level proponents, a fledgling (though weak and conformist) middle class, and opinion surveys indicating that many Russians still want free elections and uncensored media, there is little that favors a democratic outcome. Nor are the reasons for this primarily the nation's authoritarian traditions or Putin's KGB background, as is usually said.

The main obstacles to "democratic modernization," or any other resumption of democratization, lie elsewhere. One is the fate of the first perestroika. Though I argue otherwise in chapters 4–6, most officials and ordinary citizens believe that Gorbachev's democratizing reforms were directly responsible for the "collapse" of the Soviet state and thus the ensuing chaos, economic looting, and social misery of the 1990s.[14] That perspective, inspired by the two breakdowns of Russian statehood in the twentieth century, in 1917 and 1991, has revived an older belief, stretching back to tsarist times, that Russia is too big geographically and too diverse ethnically to be governed democratically.

In this fearfully conservative and widespread view, the country's stability and security depend on a concentration of executive power in the capital, the "vertical of authority," as Putin's administration termed it. Such an outlook rules out, of course, the kind of empowered legislature and real federalism that Gorbachev tried to create. Even Medvedev, sometimes identified with a democratic alternative at the top, declared that "parliamentary democracy here in Russia . . . would be a disaster."[15] Considering the nation's history of overweening executive power based in the Kremlin, tsarist and Communist, it is impossible to imagine any kind of democratic system without those representative institutions.

Readers may be surprised, remembering the enormous crimes and millions of victims described in chapter 2, that Russia's statist modernizers boast of having Stalin on their side. Their economists draw an analogy between the crisis of post-Soviet Russia, which has almost exhausted the infrastructure and other capital inherited from the Soviet Union in 1991, and the crisis of the new Soviet state in the late 1920s, which had reached the limits of the tsarist economic heritage. Looking back, they argue that just as Bukharin's gradualist NEP alternative was not the "way out" then, the "optimal program" for Russian modernization today "should consist of a kind of neo-Stalinism."[16]

Indeed, the modernization imperative has both revived discussion of democracy and made the antithetical Stalinist experience, sometimes referred to as "modernization without Westernization," seem more relevant. Appealing not only to distant history but to widespread popular beliefs that the post-Soviet state abandoned the people—to oligarchs, impoverishment, crime, and corruption—authoritarian modernizers trumpet the Stalinist state's "salvation of the country" in the 1930s and 1940s in order to maintain, "We can be saved only by civilized Stalinism," even by "Stalinist modernization."[17]

The result has been a third nationwide controversy over the Stalinist past, after those under Khrushchev and Gorbachev. It, too, has exacerbated already deep policy divisions in the political class. For example, while pro-Stalin historians with patrons in high circles seem to "justify any number of victims and crimes for the sake of rebuilding the country," President Medvedev endorsed a campaign, led by Gorbachev and others, to build a national memorial to Stalin's victims. Medvedev went on to reject the reemerging idea that modernization "can be achieved at the price of human grief and loss."[18] Neither elite nor rank-and-file neo-Stalinists actually want a return to terroristic despotism, but even "civilized Stalinism" would destroy any remaining prospects for democracy.

There is, however, an even larger barrier to both democratization and modernization—the immense state property "privatized" in the 1990s. Though examined in chapters 5 and 6, that obstacle needs to be reemphasized because it continues to be ignored in most Western commentary, as are the opinions of informed Russian thinkers. Those scholars and other intellectuals tell us, as readers will recall, "Almost everything that happened in Russia after 1991 was determined to a significant extent by the divvying up of the property of the former USSR," which is still haunted by a " 'dual illegitimacy'—in the eyes of the law . . . and in the eyes of the population."[19]

That "historic divvying up" by the Soviet high-level nomenklatura and its collaborators continues to thwart Russian democracy and modernity in two critical ways. Knowing the traditional social-justice beliefs of the people, of whom 80 percent or more have no savings, and fearing popular retribution, the small financial elite—or oligarchs—who still control much of that enormous wealth and exercise considerable political influence, remain determined to prevent free elections and representative institutions. Meanwhile, their profits from natural resources and other vital assets, much of it transferred to off-shore havens, is needed to rebuild the country's infrastructures. For Russia's oligarchs, fundamental change is an existential threat.

Nor is the political obstacle merely the business elite. An entire oligarchical system, based on the merger of privatized property and privatized state policy making, emerged during the Yeltsin 1990s. Shaped by mass and prolonged redistribution of existing property, asset stripping, capital flight abroad, and fearful uncertainty about the duration of the new wealth-seizing possibilities, it grew into a demodernizing system antithetical to economic development. As Gorbachev, who had pursued a differing kind of economic change, complained, the system "divided up more than was produced, built, or developed."[20] During the following decade, Putin made significant alterations in the system, separating Yeltsin-era oligarchs from Kremlin power, and a few from their property, while creating new oligarchs of his own, but he did not change its underlying nature.

A characteristic and poorly interpreted feature of the system is Russia's endemic corruption, both official and private, and the violence accompanying it. The shadowy, illicit procedures and contract murders that fostered the birth of the oligarchy spread with the new system. As a result, corruption also now deprives Russia of billions of dollars and the efficiency needed for modernization. Meanwhile, most of the frequent assassinations of journalists and related crimes, usually attributed to the Kremlin, are actually commissioned by corrupt "businessmen" and officials against reporters and other investigators who have gotten too close to their commercial secrets.

It is widely believed in Russia today, virtually across the ideological spectrum, that the existing political system is incapable of modernization.[21] Major policy change in Russia has almost always originated among reform-minded people in the ruling class, as happened under Khrushchev and Gorbachev, but today's elites have little interest in any kind of transformation. Even if a Kremlin leader initiates change, as many observers think President Medvedev was attempting, implementing such initiatives through the "vertical of authority," which sometimes thwarted even Putin's decrees, would be exceedingly difficult. They would be vulnerable, in Russia's long bureaucratic tradition, to fierce resistance and outright sabotage.

Still more, the post-Soviet state bureaucracy, now larger than its predecessor, has been widely infected by the malignancies of "divvying up." At every level of the "vertical," from Moscow to the vast provinces, "commercial partners" and "friends of oligarchs" (*oligofrendy*) have proliferated, forming a "caste of immune officials." Hundreds of thousands of bureaucrats have grown accustomed to multiplying their salaries by lucrative bribes and other "percentages" on transactions and enterprises requiring official permits, as well as the still ongoing redistribution of assets. Their way of life, whether grand or modest, depends on the existing system. (Thus, while surveyed Russians continue to rate today's bureaucrats significantly below their Soviet counterparts in honesty, efficiency, and "patriotism," a third of young people aspire to such a position because of the monetary possibilities.)[22]

Here, too, proposals for "exiting the oligarchical system" range from liberal to authoritarian. Some call for a onetime supertax on privatized property designed both to supplement the government's modernizing funds and to legitimize the "divvying up" in the eyes of the law and the people. Others propose rigorous antimonopoly, promarket measures. Still others, in an older Russian tradition, demand expropriation and punishment of oligarchs, corrupt officials, and their political enablers.[23] With moderate anti-corruption campaigns having failed or never been implemented, the enormous discrepancies between rich and poor still growing, terrorists striking repeatedly even in Moscow, and indignant nationalist moods spreading in officialdom and breaking out in political assassinations and in street violence, demands for harsh approaches have become more clamorous. Increasingly desperate, even Russia's self-professed democrats seem able to hope only that "progressive" oligarchs and their representatives will lead the modernization effort.[24]

Whatever the outcome of this fateful struggle, and whatever the alternatives lost since 1991, Russia's present and future scarcely resemble those once imagined by Western commentators. As I pointed out in preceding chapters, those expectations, especially American ones, were shaped by ideological assumptions, not Russian realities. The same has been true of assumptions about post-Soviet Russia's role abroad.

THE concluding chapter of *Soviet Fates and Lost Alternatives*, "Who Lost the Post-Soviet Peace?," has been the most controversial. I anticipated this reaction because the chapter recounts the only historic opportunity discussed in the book that was missed because of decisions taken in Washington, initially by the Clinton administration in the 1990s, not in Moscow. A few reviewers applauded my analysis, comparing it favorably with George Kennan's validated criticism of U.S. policy, but most thought it "goes too far" in blaming Washington and found it "an exaggeration" and "less compelling" than other chapters.[25]

The best way to evaluate my treatment of U.S.-Russian relations during the Clinton and Bush administrations is to extend it to developments since I completed the book in January 2009, the month President Obama took office. As I wrote then, his call for a "reset" in relations with Moscow suggested an awareness that a necessary partnership with post-Soviet Russia had been missed and might still be retrieved. Moreover, the real meaning of Obama's "reset" was, of course, detente.[26] And since detente had always meant replacing Cold War conflicts with cooperation, the president's initiative also suggested an understanding that he had inherited something akin to a new cold war, as I argued in chapter 7.

The long, episodic history of detente, or previous resets, which began in 1933 when President Roosevelt established diplomatic relations with Soviet Russia after fifteen years of nonrecognition, may tell us something important about Obama's reset. Each episode was opposed by powerful ideological, elite, and institutional forces in Washington and Moscow; each required strong leadership to sustain the process of cooperation; and each, after a period of success, dissipated or collapsed in a resurgence of Cold War–like conflicts, as did even the historic detente initiated by Gorbachev and Reagan that promised to abolish cold wars altogether.

When the Soviet Union ended, it was widely assumed that the cycle of unabated cold war temporarily moderated by detente was over because there would be few, if any, serious conflicts with a noncommunist Russia. The cessation of profound ideological differences and worldwide superpower competition did create a historic opportunity for a more fully cooperative, less conflictual American-Russian relationship, even a strategic partnership. But as I made clear in chapter 7, much depended on the nature of U.S. policy, which failed disastrously in the 1990s. Unless the lessons of that period were heeded, Obama's detente would almost certainly share the fate of its predecessors.

In 2009 and 2010, many commentators believed that the reset, a term also adopted by the Kremlin, was "remarkably successful" and had already achieved a "new partnership" and led to a "new era in relations."[27] Discourse between Washington and Moscow became more conciliatory. Both Obama and President Medvedev, who met frequently, declared the revamped relationship a success, citing their personal friendship as evidence. There were also tangible signs. Moscow began cooperating on two top U.S. priorities: the war in Afghanistan and curbing Iran's nuclear-weapons aspirations. In addition, in 2010, a treaty named New START was negotiated that would reduce U.S. and Russian long-range nuclear arsenals by almost a third.

Nonetheless, at the beginning of 2011, Obama's reset remained limited and inherently unstable. This was caused in part by political circumstances over which he had little control. Opposition in both capitals was fierce and unrelenting. Drawing on a traditional Russophobia that attributes sinister motives to every Moscow initiative, in this case from arms control to Iran, Afghanistan, and Europe, American cold warriors assailed Obama's reset as "capitulation" and "betrayal," a "retreat," a "dangerous bargain," and a policy of "seeing no evil." One even likened it to the 1939 Nazi-Soviet Pact.[28] Without a countervailing pro-Russia lobby or a significant U.S.-Russian economic relationship to buffer the reset, it was highly vulnerable to such attacks.

In Moscow, equally harsh attacks were leveled against Obama's designated partner, Medvedev. According to a leading Russian nationalist, "The West stands behind Medvedev. The president relies on ultraliberals . . . who speak for a pro-American, traitorous policy oriented on surrendering positions and helping the Americans maintain a monopolar world. . . . No one stands behind Medvedev except enemies of Russia." More ominously, a prominent general also accused Medvedev of "treason."[29] A number of Russia's "democratic" oppositionists were also adamantly against Obama's reset, denouncing it as "facilitating the autocracy's self-preservation" and as "another Munich. . . . A full, absolute, and unconditional surrender to the regime." Nor did Russian public opinion favor the new policy. In 2009, a majority surveyed stated a "positive dislike of the West in general, and particularly of America."[30]

Still worse, both Obama and Medvedev were relatively weak leaders. Obama's authority at home was diminished by his declining popularity and by Democratic Patty losses in the 2010 congressional elections. (By then, he had already yielded to demands for a "reset of the reset," restoring democracy promotion to his agenda and embracing the Georgian leader, Mikheil Saakashvili, who had brought America and Russia close to war in August 2008.)[31] Medvedev's own authority remained limited by Putin's preeminence and the possibility he might reclaim the Russian presidency in 2012. Increasingly perceived as a possible one-term president, neither Obama nor Medvedev was able or willing to aggressively defend their reset or even prevent apparent attempts to disrupt it by members of their own administrations.[32]

Obama's decision to base his Russia policy on the presumed "liberal" Medvedev, with the intention of promoting his political fortunes over Putin's, further limited support for the reset in Moscow. (Along with the U.S. media, Obama and his advisers continued to denigrate Putin as an "outdated" cold warrior, even a man who "doesn't have a soul.")[33] The political wager on Medvedev, which became part of the media narrative of the reset in both countries, repeated the longstanding White House practice of mistaking a personal friend in the Kremlin—"my friend Dmitri," as Obama soon called Medvedev—for broad support in the Russian policy class. It also revived Moscow's resentment of American interference in its internal affairs since the 1990s.[34]

These political failings of the reset may have been transitory, but a number of underlying fallacies of Obama's Russia policy were fundamental and, it seemed, still congenital in Washington. All of them were in the spirit of the American winner-take-all triumphalism of the 1990s, which, as I showed in chapter 7, had destroyed the possibility of a strategic partnership with post-Soviet Russia and led instead to the renewed cold war Obama inherited.

One was the enduring conceit of "selective cooperation": seeking Moscow's support for America's vital interests while disregarding Russia's. After having been tried and seen to fail repeatedly since 1991 by Presidents Clinton and Bush, it was, wrote a Moscow specialist, "a case of déjà vu." (Even an implacable Russian opponent of the Kremlin pointed out that in relations with President Bush, Putin had "constantly backed down.") Nonetheless, the Obama White House sought more one-way concessions as the basis of the reset: "We're going to see if there are ways we can have Russia cooperate on those things that we define as our national interests, but we don't want to trade with them."[35]

Obama did gain Kremlin cooperation on Afghanistan and Iran without yielding on the two U.S. policies most resented by Moscow—locating missile defense sites close to Russia and expanding NATO in the same direction—but at a high and lasting political cost. The disparity further undermined Medvedev's position as well as general support for the reset in Moscow, where it now bore his "brand," to the extent that Putin, who usually left the U.S. relationship to his protégé, remarked publicly, "So, where is this reset?"[36]

Indeed, missile defense was a time bomb embedded in the New START treaty and thus in the reset itself. During negotiations, Moscow believed the Obama administration had agreed to respect Russian objections to putting antimissile sites in Eastern Europe, an understanding reflected in the treaty's preamble. But in December 2010, Obama, seeking ratification from the U.S. Senate, personally promised that the agreement "places no limitations on the development or deployment of our missile defense programs," which he pledged to pursue fully "regardless of Russian actions." In its resolution of ratification, the Senate went further, spelling out this intention in detail. Remembering previous violated agreements, Moscow reacted with such suspicion that Medvedev felt the need to personally vouch for Obama as a president who "keeps his word."[37]

More generally, the unresolved conflict over missile defense exemplified the futility of "selective cooperation." Medvedev's earlier announcement, in November 2010, that Russia might participate in a NATO version of the project was heralded as another success of the reset. But both he and Putin quickly emphasized that "Russia will participate only on an absolutely equal basis . . . or we will not participate at all." No one on either side believed, of course, that the U.S.-led alliance would give the Kremlin "equal" control over its antimissile system.[38]

In pursuing the one-way concessions implicit in "selective cooperation, " Obama, like Clinton and Bush before him, seemed unable or unwilling to connect the strategic dots of mutual security the way Reagan and Gorbachev had done in the late 1980s. In effect, Obama was asking Moscow to substantially reduce its long-range nuclear weapons while Russia was being surrounded by NATO bases with superior conventional forces and the potential to neutralize its reduced retaliatory capability. In that crucial respect, the new arms-reduction treaty was inherently unstable. If nothing else, Obama was undermining his hope of also negotiating a major reduction of Russia's enormous advantage in short-range tactical nuclear weapons, which Moscow increasingly considered vital for its national defense. Instead, as Medvedev also warned, unless the missile-defense conflict was resolved, there would be "another escalation of the arms race."[39]

The notion that Moscow would make unreciprocated concessions for the sake of a partnership with the United States, which arose after 1991, derived from the same false assumption: that post-Soviet Russia, diminished and enfeebled by having "lost the Cold War," could play the role of a great power only on American terms.[40] In reality, when Obama took office, Russia could obtain everything it supposedly needed from the United States, particularly in order to modernize, from other partners. Two of its bilateral relationships—with Beijing and Berlin, and increasingly with Paris—were already more fulsome and important to Moscow, politically, economically, and even militarily, than its barren relations, or "desert landscape," with a Washington that for two decades had seemed chronically unreliable, even duplicitous.[41]

Behind that perception lay a more fundamental weakness of the reset: conflicting American and Russian understandings of why it had been needed. Each side continued to blame the other for the deterioration of relations after 1991. Neither Obama nor the Clinton-era officials advising him conceded there had been any mistakes in U.S. policy toward post-Soviet Russia, and its architects still defended it with "special satisfaction."[42] Instead, virtually the entire U.S. political class persisted in blaming Russia and, in particular, Putin's "imperialist and anti-Western agenda," even though he had come to power only in 2000. In effect, this exculpatory history deleted the historic opportunities lost in Washington in the 1990s and later. It also meant that the success or failure of the reset was "up to the Russians" and that "Moscow's thinking must change," not Washington's.[43]

American policymakers may care little about history, but it is no arcane matter for their Russian counterparts.[44] For them, a reset was necessary because Washington rejected Gorbachev's proposals for "de-ideologizing inter-state relations" and a "new model of guaranteeing security" in favor of a "Pax Americana"; because there was a "new U.S. semi-cold war against Russia in 1991–2008"; because "the approach of the Clinton administration . . . was to wriggle all possible concessions from Moscow without giving Yeltsin anything in return"; because after September 11 "the Bush administration took Russia's support in

Afghanistan and Central Asia for granted"; and because Washington refused to "sacrifice its influence or policies in the post-Soviet space," including in Georgia.[45]

Putin and Medvedev personally were no less adamant about the prehistory of the reset and who was to blame. As I discuss in chapter 7, both Russian leaders earlier accused Washington of having "constantly deceived" Moscow. The acute sense of betrayal remained on their minds after the reset began. In 2010, Putin even admitted having been slow to understand the pattern of U.S. duplicity: "I was simply unable to comprehend its depth. . . . But in reality it is all very simple. . . . They told us one thing, and they did something completely different. They duped us, in the full sense of this word."[46]

Medvedev agreed: "Relations soured because of the previous U.S. administrations' plans." He even said what was widely believed but rarely spoken publicly by top Russian leaders, that Washington had not just armed and trained the Georgian military but had known in advance, perhaps encouraged, Saakashvili's surprise attack on South Ossetian civilians and Russian peacekeepers, which began the August 2008 war: "Personally," Medvedev complained, "I found it very surprising that it all began after the U.S. secretary of state paid a visit to Georgia. Before that . . . Mr. Saakashvili was planning to come see me in Sochi, but he did not come."[47]

Longtime adversaries whose understandings of their past relations are so starkly different are unlikely to create a durable partnership. Their memories and perspectives will constantly collide. Thus, the Russian leadership entered into the reset with expectations diametrically opposed to the unilateral concessions expected by the Obama administration: "America owes Russia, and it owes a lot, and it has to pay its debt." In 2010, the head of NATO was already assuring the international media that the reset would "bury the ghosts of the past." It was another example of how little the U.S.-led alliance understood or cared about history.[48]

The "ghost" barring a truly fundamental change in relations was, of course, the fifteen-year expansion of NATO to Russia's borders—the first and most fateful broken American promise.[49] Despite assurances of a "NATO-Russian friendship," the Obama administration did not disavow more NATO expansion and instead reaffirmed U.S. support for eventual membership for the former Soviet republics of Ukraine and

Georgia, Moscow's "red lines."[50] Again, no state that feels encircled and threatened by an encroaching military alliance, still more one committed to antimissile weapons designed to thwart retaliation—anxieties repeatedly expressed by Moscow—will ever feel itself an equal or secure partner of that alliance.

Indeed, expanding NATO eastward institutionalized an even larger, more profound geopolitical conflict with Russia. Moscow's protests and countersteps were indignantly denounced by American officials and commentators as "Russia's determination to reestablish a sphere of influence in neighboring countries that were once a part of the Soviet Union." Labeling this a "19th-century agenda," they insisted, "We do not recognize . . . any sphere of influence."[51] U.S. indignation grew when Medvedev responded by claiming for Russia a "sphere of strategic interests," or "privileged interests," in the former Soviet republics.

But what was NATO's eastward movement other than a vast expansion of America's sphere of influence—military, political, and economic—into what had previously been Russia's? No U.S. official or mainstream commentator would admit as much, but Saakashvili, the Georgian leader bent on joining the alliance, felt no such constraint. In 2010, he welcomed the growth of "NATO's presence in the region" because it enabled the United States and its allies to "expand their sphere of influence."[52] Of all the several double standards in U.S. policy making—"hypocrisy," Moscow charged—none did more to prevent an American-Russian partnership and to provoke a new cold war.

Nor will the "virtuous cycle of cooperation" called for by the U.S. official quoted in chapter 7 ever be possible while this profound geopolitical conflict exists. Is there any longer a way to resolve it, given that the new NATO states cannot now be deprived of membership? In chapter 7, I proposed that Washington end NATO expansion and the quest for military bases in the former Soviet republics, which Moscow considers its "near abroad," while the Kremlin reaffirms their political sovereignty. The fallacies and instability of Obama's attempted reset indicate the need for a more far-reaching solution.

The United States and its allies should honor retroactively their follow-up promise, also broken, that no military forces would be based in any new NATO country east of Germany—in effect, demilitarizing NATO's post-1994 expansion.[53] Without violating or diminishing the alliance's guarantee of collective security for all of its members, this grand accommodation would go far toward making possible an expansive partnership with post-Soviet Russia.

First, and crucially, it would redeem one of America's broken promises to Russia, thereby paying part of its "debt." Second, it would recognize that Moscow is entitled to at least one "privileged interest" in its former zone of Western security—the absence of a potential military threat. (Washington has long claimed this privilege for itself, defending it to the brink of nuclear war in Cuba in 1962.) Third, the demilitarization of NATO's expansion would alleviate Russia's historical fear of military encirclement while inspiring trust in Western partners. And fourth, this would reduce the Kremlin's concerns about missile defense sites in Eastern Europe, making it more willing to contribute Russia's considerable resources to the still unproven project.

Much else of essential importance both to America and Russia could then follow, from far greater reductions in all of their weapons of mass destruction to full cooperation against the looming dangers of nuclear proliferation and international terrorism. The result would be a second chance to regain the historic opportunity lost in the 1990s.

Twenty years after the Soviet breakup, Russia is again at a crossroads—and with it, inescapably, the United States. Moscow's choice between alternatives for modernizing the nation—authoritarian and thus menacing or at least partially democratic—will be decided inside Russia, not, as U.S. policymakers once thought, in Washington. But it will not be determined apart from Russia's relations with the outside world. Medvedev's call for "modernizing alliances" with the West represents one alternative. His opponents' retort that the West is neither worthy of emulation nor trustworthy expresses another.

American policy will be a crucial factor in the eventual choice. In the centuries-long struggle between reform and reaction in Russia, antiauthoritarian forces have had a political chance only when relations with the West were improving. Certainly, this was true in the twentieth century, when "Cold War tensions invariably worked to the advantage of hardliners within the Soviet Union."[54] In this regard, Washington still plays the leading Western role, for better or worse. Its decision to move NATO eastward, to take an especially lamentable example, continues to lend credence to neo-Stalinist assertions that the tyrant had been right in his iron-curtain vigilance against "hostile encirclement."

Yet America's national security depends on the outcome of the struggle in Moscow. All of the potential threats that unfolded in post-Soviet Russia after 1991, spelled out in chapter 7, continue to fester: the unprecedented "infrastructural nightmare" of a system laden with weapons of mass destruction; the inherent risks of nuclear proliferation and lethal accidents, even the launching of high-alert missiles because of misinformation; and the growth of ultranationalist and other extremist movements.

Russia's pro-Western modernizers hoped that Obama's proposed reset meant Washington finally understood these mutual perils and would at last pursue a policy of doing no harm. But they also remembered, as I pointed out, the reset's prehistory. In late 2010, Medvedev still worried that "alternatives await us" in U.S.-Russian relations. A leading pro-Western member of the Russian parliament was more explicit: "In Moscow and in Washington, people have been known to lose opportunities. . . . We have to hope that this time we won't lose the opportunity."[55]

That both Obama and Medvedev, who personified the reset, were under attack in their own countries for "traitorous" policies was an ominous sign. Nonetheless, the political prospects were better in Moscow in one important respect: a significant part of the Russian policy class clearly understood that the two countries had come not only to another turning point but possibly to the last chance for a post–Cold War relationship. Pro-Western Russians could no longer find comfort in their customary association of major policy alternatives with a successor generation of leaders; the youthful Obama and Medvedev were that generation.

No such urgency or even awareness was evident in the American establishment. Instead, the possibility of greater cooperation with Moscow accelerated the tendency to equate "the crimes and abuses of this Russian government" with those of Communist Russia. In the same vein, U.S. Cold War–era themes became more pronounced. Moscow's initiatives were again presented as "brazen Russian provocations." (Even Putin's historic apology to Warsaw for the Stalinist regime's massacre of Polish army officers at Katyn in 1940 was dismissed as a "trivial gesture" designed to "manipulate" foreign opinion.) Warnings that Moscow was trying "to play off . . . the European allies against the United States" re-appeared along with demands that Washington deploy military power to "roll back the Kremlin's growing regional influence." A Defense Department agent whose deception of Moscow caused a major breakdown in supplies for U.S. troops in Afghanistan was unrepentant: "I'm an old cold warrior, I'm proud of it."[56]

Obama's proposed reset also brought more extreme American views to the fore. Present-day Russia, a Washington expert warned, was even more dangerous than its Soviet predecessor: "This is not your father's Russia. . . . Today's Russian leadership is younger and tougher." Adding to this startling revelation was a *Wall Street Journal* editor's discovery that "Russia has become, in the precise sense of the word, a fascist state." Previously a fringe notion, by 2010 it had been taken up by an established American scholar in the journal of a leading university center of Russian studies.[57] (Readers may wonder if proponents of these ideas had any actual knowledge of the historical realities of Soviet Communism or Nazi Germany.)

Lost in this reckless (and uninformed) commentary were the multiple threats to America's national security lurking in Russia—as well as the flickering chance for cooperation with Moscow to avert them. Writing in influential American newspapers once valued for their informed analysis, veteran pundits assured readers that "nuclear war between Russia and America had become inconceivable"; that, indeed, despite the near miss in Georgia in August 2008, when the White House had considered American air strikes against Russian troops, the danger of any U.S.-Russian war was "minuscule"; and that "what was needed was not the chimera of arms control" but a "renewal of the arms race."[58]

Such myopia inspired an even more reckless view: the worse the situation inside Russia, the better for America. Thus, a *Washington Post* columnist, deriding the new nuclear-reductions treaty, reported with satisfaction on the "emaciated Russian bear." And a former Bush official, writing in the same newspaper, urged the Obama administration to "refuse to help Russian leaders with economic modernization," even though modernizing that country's infrastructures is essential for securing its devices of mass destruction. A university professor went further, hoping for "a destabilized Russia," deaf to warnings from Moscow that this would be "catastrophic."[59]

Political and media myopia, the familiar triumph of ideology over reality, abetted another unwise Washington decision. Despite the Kremlin's uncertain grip on its nuclear materials, indeed, despite alarm that uncontrolled wildfires in August 2010 might reach fallout from the 1986 Chernobyl reactor explosion, or even nuclear weapons facilities, the U.S. Senate voted, in December 2010, to ship massive quantities of spent fuel from American-built reactors to Russia for safekeeping and disposal. While Russian environmentalists protested this would turn their country into "an international radioactive waste dump," and a Moscow military expert warned that no Russian region was "truly safe,"[60] the Obama administration hailed the decision as a victory for its "reset."

None of these negative developments under President Obama was surprising. As I emphasized in chapter 7, a fundamental transformation of U.S.-Russian relations, essentially from a state of cold war to a strategic partnership, required bold, resolute leadership based on a full rethinking of the entire post-Soviet relationship, especially Washington's winner-take-all attitude. Given the citadels of vested institutional, professional, and personal interests in the failed policies since 1991, centered in Washington but with ample support throughout the nation's media and educational system, nothing less would result in a full "reset."

Several factors probably explain why Obama did not provide any of these essentials. One was his own irresolute nature, also displayed in his domestic policies. (To be fair, the first black U.S. president may have been reluctant to assault too many American citadels or orthodoxies, if any.) Nor did President Obama turn out to be a "thought leader."[61] Having surrounded himself with advisers tied to the failed Russia policies since 1991, there was no one in his inner circle to propose fundamentally different approaches, still less heretical ones, or even much rethinking.[62] As a result, Obama's reset was cast in the same fallacies that had made it necessary.

But the new president was not solely or even mainly to blame. The larger failure was that of the entire American policy establishment, including its legions of media opinion makers, think-tank experts, and academic intellectuals. Leaders who had previously enacted major improvements in U.S.-Russian relations, including Mikhail Gorbachev and Ronald Reagan, were influenced by unorthodox ideas advocated over time by dissenting thinkers inside or near the political establishment, however few in number and however much in disfavor they often were.[63]

No such nonconformist American thinking about Russia was in circulation before or after Obama took office, nor had it been for nearly twenty years. Reinforced by a cult of conventional "tough-minded" policymaking, which marginalized and invariably "proved wrong" even "eloquent skeptics" like George Kennan, the triumphalist orthodoxy still monopolized the political spectrum, from "progressives" to America's own ultranationalists, in effect unchallenged in the parties, media, policy institutes, and universities.[64] No revisionist lessons had been learned from, no alternative thinking inspired by, the failures of the past two decades.

In addition to the historical fallacies about the end of the Cold War and their policy implications, examined in chapters 6 and 7, three more recent tenets of neo-cold-war U.S. policy had become axiomatic. First, present-day Russia was as brutally antidemocratic as its Soviet predecessor. Evidence cited usually included the Kremlin's alleged radioactive poisoning of a KGB defector in London in 2006 and its persecution of the imprisoned oligarch Mikhail Khodorkovsky, on whom his U.S. advocates bestowed the mantle of the great Soviet-era dissenters Aleksandr Solzhenitsyn and Andrei Sakharov. Second, Russia's nature made it a growing threat abroad, especially to former Soviet republics, as demonstrated by its alleged "invasion and occupation of Georgia" in August 2008. And third, more NATO expansion was therefore necessary to protect both Georgia and Ukraine.[65]

All of these assertions were far from the full truth and in need of policy debate, though there was none. Moreover, one involved another Washington double standard. Moscow's military defense of Georgia's secessionist provinces, South Ossetia and Abkhazia, and recognition of their independent statehood were more justifiable, historically and politically, than was the U.S.-led NATO bombing of Russia's ally Serbia in 1999, which turned the Serbian province of Kosovo into an independent (and highly criminalized) state. If nothing else, Washington set the precedent for military intervention in conflicts in multiethnic states and for redrawing national boundaries.[66]

The Obama administration did nothing to discourage these or other anti-Russian axioms and too much to sustain them. By revising the reset to include democracy promotion, it reverted to a policy that had offended Moscow for many years while undermining democratic prospects in Russia, or at least doing nothing that actually nurtured them. (A second conviction of Khodorkhovsky over the administration's protests, in December 2010, was more evidence of that long-evident truth.) In addition, the intrusive policy again allied Washington with Yeltsin-era politicians who were closely associated with the creation of the hated oligarchical system and whose democratic credentials, based on their past record and contemptuous attitudes toward their own people, were highly suspect.[67]

Obama's re-endorsement of Saakashvili and the Georgian leader's NATO aspirations, which had already led to the proxy American-Russian war in 2008, also challenged Moscow's understanding of the reset.[68] And it was dangerous. The Kremlin had demonstrated that if provoked it would strike hard at a U.S.-client regime on the wrong side of its "red lines," especially in the North Caucasus region, where Islamic terrorism and social turbulence were threatening the Russian state. (In February 2011, Georgian state radio began potentially inflammatory broadcasts to the neighboring region.) Visiting Tbilisi in late 2010, even a mainstream American analyst found Saakashvili's "hotheaded" leadership "unpredictable and impulsive."[69] Nonetheless, the Obama administration continued training Saakashvili's military, which included joint NATO-Georgian exercises near the Russian border.

These recapitulations of failed U.S. policies, along with President Obama's newly declared intention of pursuing missile defense without constraints, seemed likely to severely limit his detente with Moscow and possibly destroy it. Certainly, they emboldened American enemies of the reset without causing any concerns in the policy establishment.[70] Leading experts continued to assure elite audiences that the United States, despite being embroiled in an unwinnable war and a corrosive economic crisis, could still "dominate world affairs"; that Moscow, despite having already regained crucial positions in its own neighborhood, notably in Ukraine, and established flourishing partnerships from China to Western Europe, was still too weak to resist a new U.S. cold war; and that "the road where Russia needs to go leads through Washington."[71]

Some readers may take heart from Hegel's bleak but ultimately affirmative maxim, "The Owl of Minerva spreads its wings only with the falling of dusk," even though night may be near. Of course, great turnabouts in international politics, as happened in the late 1980s, are always possible, and for this longtime observer of U.S.-Russian relations, hope still dies last. But other readers may find more compelling the instinctive response of Russians who, ever mindful of lost opportunities in their history, offer caution in such circumstances: "An optimist is an uninformed pessimist."

February 2011

ABOUT THE NOTES

IN composite notes, sources are given in the order they are cited in the text unless otherwise indicated. The notes themselves have been shortened in several ways. In most cases, subtitles of books are omitted and main titles abridged after the first citation in each chapter. The titles of most articles are also omitted, along with the traditional soft and hard signs in transliterations. And most newspapers, magazines, journals, and other periodicals are referred to throughout by initials or in shortened form, as follows:

AF	Argumenty i fakty
AHR	American Historical Review
APSR	American Political Science Review
BG	Boston Globe
CDPSP	Current Digest of the Post-Soviet Press
CDSP	Current Digest of the Soviet Press
Chronicle	Chronicle of Higher Education
CSM	Christian Science Monitor
EAS	Europe-Asia Studies
FA	Foreign Affairs
FBIS	Foreign Broadcast Information Service Daily Report: Soviet Union

ABOUT THE NOTES

FT	*Financial Times*
IA	*Istoricheskii arkhiv*
IHT	*International Herald Tribune*
JCWS	*Journal of Cold War Studies*
JMH	*Journal of Modern History*
JOD	*Journal of Democracy*
JRL	*Johnson's Russia List*
JRL Supplement	*Johnson's Russia List Research and Analytical Supplement*
KO	*Knizhnoe obozrenie*
KP	*Komsomolskaia pravda*
KZ	*Krasnaia zvezda*
LAT	*Los Angeles Times*
LG	*Literaturnaia gazeta*
LR	*Literaturnaia Rossiia*
MG	*Molodaia gvardiia*
MK	*Moskovskii komsomolets*
MN	*Moskovskie novosti*
MP	*Moskovskaia pravda*
MT	*Moscow Times*
NG	*Nezavisimaia gazeta*
NI	*Novye izvestiia*
NM	*Novyi mir*
NNI	*Novaia i noveishaia istoriia*
Novaia	*Novaia gazeta*
NR	*New Republic*
NS	*Nash sovremennik*
NT	*New Times*
NV	*Novoe vremia*
NY	*New Yorker*
NYRB	*New York Review of Books*
NYT	*New York Times*
OG	*Obshchaia gazeta*
OI	*Otechestvenaia istoriia*
ONS	*Obshchestvennye nauki i sovremennost*
PC	*Problems of Communism*
PG	*Parlamentskaia gazeta*
PK	*Politicheskii klass*
PPC	*Problems of Post-Communism*
PSA	*Post-Soviet Affairs*
PZH	*Politicheskii zhurnal*

Report	*Radio Liberty Report on the USSR*
RFE/RL	*Radio Free Europe/Radio Liberty Newsline*
RG	*Rossiiskaia gazeta*
RR	*Russian Review*
RT	*Rabochaia tribuna*
SEER	*Slavic and East European Review*
SI	*Sotsiologicheskie issledovaniia*
SK	*Sovetskaia kultura*
SM	*Svobodnaia mysl*
SR	*Sovetskaia Rossiia*
SS	*Soviet Studies*
VA	*Vestnik analitiki*
VE	*Voprosy ekonomiki*
VEK XX	*Vek XX i mir*
VF	*Voprosy filosofii*
VI KPSS	*Voprosy istorii KPSS*
VI	*Voprosy istorii*
VN	*Vremia novostei*
VRAN	*Vestnik rossiiskoi akademii nauk*
WP	*Washington Post*
WPJ	*World Policy Journal*
WS	*Weekly Standard*
WSJ	*Wall Street Journal*

NOTES

INTRODUCTION: ALTERNATIVES AND FATES

1. Shorter and somewhat different versions of chapters 1, 2, and 3 appeared, respectively, as an introduction to Nikolai Bukharin, *How It All Began: The Prison Novel* (Columbia University Press, 1998); a contribution to *Political Violence*, ed. Paul Hollander in honor of Robert Conquest (Palgrave Macmillan, 2008); and the introduction to *Inside Gorbachev's Kremlin: The Memoirs of Yegor Ligachev* (Pantheon Books, 1993). Chapter 4 was published as an article in *Slavic Review* (Fall 2004). A preliminary, skeletal version of chapter 7 appeared in *The Nation*, July 10, 2006. In each of these instances, I retained the right to use all or parts of the text for this book, which I already had in mind; I thank the publishers for that agreement. Chapters 5 and 6 have not been previously published in any form.

2. See Stephen F. Cohen, *Rethinking the Soviet Experience* (New York, 1985), chaps. 4–5; and several of the columns I wrote for a broader readership during those years, collected in Stephen F. Cohen, *Sovieticus: American Perceptions and Soviet Realities*, exp. ed. (New York, 1986). On the assumption that some of the same ideas circulated inside the Soviet political establishment, I also studied the uncensored writings of dissidents known as

samizdat, including those in a volume I edited, *An End to Silence: Uncensored Opinion in the Soviet Union* (New York, 1982).

3. For a similar formulation, see Martin Bunzel in *AHR* (June 2004): 845–58. For examples of what-if history, see Alexander Demandt, *History That Never Happened*, 3rd ed. (Jefferson, N.C., 1993); Robert Cowley, ed., *What Ifs? of American History* (New York, 2003); and Philip E. Tetlock, Richard Ned Lebow, and Geoffrey Parker, eds., *Unmaking the West: "What-If?" Scenarios That Rewrite World History* (Ann Arbor, Mich., 2006), which examines "imaginary people in an imaginary world" (3).

4. See Cohen, *Rethinking*, chaps. 1–2.

5. See my "revisionist" book, *Rethinking*, esp. chap. 1; and for a different personal experience and kind of revisionism, Sheila Fitzpatrick in *Slavic Review* (Fall 2008): 682–704.

6. Interview with Viktor Danilov in *Kritika* (Spring 2008): 370. Gorbachev was, of course, also an alternativist, as he reiterated in the words quoted at the top of this introduction, from an interview in *NG*, Nov. 6, 1997.

7. An often quoted line from the famous perestroika-era film *Pokaianie* (Repentance).

8. Donald J. Raleigh, *Experiencing Russia's Civil War* (Princeton, N.J., 2002), 418. "School of inevitability" is a Russian term, but it applies as well to the American case. See, e.g., Dmitrii Oleinikov in Karl Aimermakher and Gennadii Bordiugov, eds., *Istoriki chitaiut uchebniki istorii* (Moscow, 2002), 148.

9. For "the edge," see Aleksandr Tsipko in *VA*, no. 2 (2008): 14; and for the "knock," see the emigre Russian journalist and scholar Alexander Yanov in *International Journal of Sociology* (Summer–Fall 1976): 85.

10. Mikhail Shatrov in *Ogonek*, no. 4 (1987): 5. Some said more categorically, "a final chance" (Aleksandr Tsipko in *Megapolis-Express*, Jan. 3, 1991). For the officers, see Iu. V. Rubtsov in *OI*, no. 4 (2005): 187.

11. See, e.g., Ian Kershaw, *Fateful Choices* (New York, 2007); and Nelson D. Lankford, *Cry Havoc! The Crooked Road to Civil War, 1861* (New York, 2007).

12. This is what Yegor Yakovlev, quoted at the top of the introduction, had in mind in speaking of "the lessons of missed opportunities" (*MN*, Jan. 6, 1991). The tradition continues. A Russian prime minister of the 1990s, Viktor Chernomyrdin, famously explained, "We wanted things to be better, but they turned out as they always do."

13. Gorbachev told me about his favorable reaction to the book, which he read in a Russian translation published in the United States in 1980, and its influence on his ideological policy is recorded in the memoirs of his aide

Anatoly Chernyaev, *My Six Years With Gorbachev* (University Park, Penn., 2000), 138–39; and, similarly, in the remarks of another aide, Ivan Frolov, reported in Angus Roxburgh, *The Second Russian Revolution* (London, 1991), 68. Extravagant conclusions have been drawn from that small fact. The scholar Anthony D'Agostino (www.h-diplo@h-net.msu.edu, July 17, 2004) wrote, for example, that by misleading Gorbachev into believing there was a Bukharinist alternative to Stalinism, "Stephen Cohen's biography of Bukharin probably caused the fall of Soviet power in a more direct sense than any wire-pulling by Reagan or Bush" (www.h-diplo@h-net .msu.edu, July 17, 2004). Similarly, see the Russian historian Valerii Solovei in *PK*, no. 24 (Dec. 2006), Internet version, who remarks, "One can joke that Cohen bears a certain responsibility for perestroika." For our actual, more mundane relationship, see Gorbachev's foreword to a small book about me by Russian friends and colleagues, *Stiven Koen i Sovetskii Soiuz/ Rossiia* (Moscow, 2008), 9–12.

1. BUKHARIN'S FATE

1. Some sections of this essay borrow from my previous writings on Bukharin and his times: Stephen F. Cohen, *Bukharin and the Bolshevik Revolution: A Political Biography, 1888–1938* (New York, 1973 and 1980); *Rethinking the Soviet Experience* (New York, 1985), chap. 3; and my introduction to Anna Larina, *This I Cannot Forget: The Memoirs of Nikolai Bukharin's Widow* (New York, 1993), 11–33.

2. The letter to Feliks Dzerzhinsky, dated by archivists "not later than Dec. 24, 1924," was first published in *VI KPSS*, no. 11 (1988): 42–43.

3. Anonymous reviewer of George Katkov, *The Trial of Bukharin* (New York, 1969), in *TLS*, January 29, 1970; and, similarly, Tucker's introduction to Robert C. Tucker and Stephen F. Cohen, eds., *The Great Purge Trial* (New York, 1965), ix–xlviii. For different, less admiring interpretations of Bukharin's conduct during the trial, see *Rodina*, no. 8 (1995): 39–42; and Vesa Outtinen in *SM*, no. 8 (2007): 158–69.

4. See the surveys of Soviet public opinion on historical figures reported in *NYT*, May 27, 1988; *Moscow News*, no. 44 (1990); G. A. Bordiugov and V. A. Kozlov, *Istoriia i koniunktura* (Moscow, 1992), esp. chap. 2; and for Yeltsin, *SM*, no. 11 (1995): 62–63.

5. An important but relatively small part of the original transcript was published and analyzed by Yuri Murin, once a senior archivist at the Presidential Archive. See *NNI*, no. 1 (1995): 61–76; and *Istochnik*, no. 4 (1996): 78–92.

As I write, however, the full transcript, some 1,500 typed pages, remains inaccessible.

6. Vitaly Shentalinsky, *Arrested Voices* (New York, 1996), 285. The fate of Soviet writers and their manuscripts during the terror years, as revealed in archives, is the subject of this valuable book.

7. These instructions in Stalin's handwriting appear on documents I have seen. For the leader's voracious reading, see Robert C. Tucker, *Stalin in Power* (New York, 1990), 51–52. (With Tucker's first volume, *Stalin as Revolutionary*, this is the best biography of Stalin, including his role as architect of the terror.) Also see many documents in Katerina Clark and Evgeny Dobrenko, eds., *Soviet Culture and Power* (New Haven, Conn., 2007).

8. Larina, *This I Cannot Forget*, 336.

9. The only trace of the reels is a thirty-minute newsreel about the trial, *Verdict of the Court—Verdict of the People!* shown briefly in Moscow theaters in 1938 and preserved in an archive. It shows the defendants only fleetingly and only from behind. According to an unconfirmed report, the reels were destroyed on Stalin's orders. Several photographs alleged to be of Bukharin and other defendants at the trial have been published, but none is convincing and some are clearly miscaptioned. Scores of paintings done by Bukharin since childhood are also indicative. Only ten were recovered, from relatives and friends, when his surviving family was freed in the 1950s. Two more were found in 1996—one folded in old newspapers in a Moscow apartment; the other, having been anonymously held and sold, in the American state of Oregon.

10. Unless otherwise indicated, direct quotations from Bukharin in Lubyanka and my account of his prison circumstances are from his letters to Stalin itemized in note 11; his letter to his wife, which appears in Larina, *This I Cannot Forget*, 11–33; or a few other written communications by Bukharin and his jailers preserved in the NKVD and Presidential archives.

11. All four—dated April 15, September 29, November 14, and December 10—were found in the Presidential Archive described earlier. Copies are now in the Bukharin collection (F. 558) of the archive known as RGASPI in Moscow. One is twenty-two pages long, another barely two. Even before his arrest, Bukharin wrote many letters to Stalin, or "Koba" as he usually called him, partly as a precaution. As he explained to a childhood friend in 1936, the novelist and journalist Ilya Ehrenburg, "I have to write. Koba loves to receive letters" (quoted in Joshua Rubenstein, *Tangled Loyalties: The Life and Times of Ilya Ehrenburg* [New York, 1996], 153). It is almost certain that he wrote more than these four letters to Stalin from prison. In the early 1960s, a Party official investigating Stalin's crimes found "about ten" such

letters, several of which evidently have since disappeared. Olga Shatunov-skaia, *Ob ushedshem veke* (La Jolla, Calif., 2001), 298.

12. There are several bibliographies of Bukharin's writings. The most complete is Wladislaw Hedeler, *N. I. Bucharin: Bibliographie seiner Schriften und Korrespondenzen, 1912–1938* (Berlin, 2005).

13. The traces include the protocols of Bukharin's interrogations, a few Luby-anka internal documents written by Kogan, several notes and one letter to him from Bukharin, and the childhood memories and family possessions of Kogan's daughter, whom I located not far from Moscow in the early 1990s. When I brought Bukharin's widow and Kogan's daughter together in 1993, Anna Larina said of her husband and his Lubyanka interrogator, "They both were victims." On the other hand, Anna Larina, despite her years of suffering, was an exceedingly compassionate person. Nothing special can be read into Kogan's own fate. Almost all his NKVD colleagues also were shot.

14. After serialization in the mass-circulation journal *Znamia* in 1988, Anna Larina's memoirs were published in full as *Nezabyvaemoe* (Moscow, 1989). For the English-language edition, see this chapter, note 1. Only very re-cently have I felt free, with his permission, to name and publicly thank Gennady Burbulis.

15. See A. P. Ogurtsov's foreword to Nikolai Bukharin, *Tiuremnye rukopisi*, 2 vols. (Moscow, 1996), 2:5–28.

16. Thus, in the prison letter dated April 15, Bukharin begged Stalin to return the antifascist manuscript to him so he could make revisions and correc-tions and eliminate the repetitions "inevitable in such a method of writ-ing." It was not returned to him.

17. For a sample of his political caricatures, see A. Iu. Vatlin and L. N. Malash-enko, *Istoriia VKP(b) v portretakh i karikaturakh ee vozhdei* (Moscow, 2007); and a somewhat different version, Alexander Vatlin and Larisa Malashenko, eds. *Piggy Fox and the Sword of Revolution: Bolshevik Self-Portraits* (New Haven, Conn., 2006). For the doomed Mandelstam, see Bukharin's 1934 letter to Stalin in *Novaia*, Dec. 25, 2008.

18. On the eve of his arrest, Bukharin had his wife memorize a kind of last testament. Full of despair about the present, it was optimistic about the cleansing "filter of history" and "a future generation of Party leaders." See Larina, *This I Cannot Forget*, 343–44. Bukharin would have thought it fit-ting that it was finally published under Gorbachev.

19. Other telling polemics against Stalin included Bukharin's attribution of a variant of the slogan Stalin had used against him in 1928 and 1929, "There are no fortresses Bolsheviks cannot storm," to a tsarist military officer; and

a refutation of the charges that he had conspired to assassinate Soviet leaders by having his Leninist cousin reject terrorism on Marxist principle.

20. See Frezinsky's introduction in Nikolai Bukharin, *Vremena* (Moscow, 1994), 3–20.

21. As an example of why Bukharin's prison appeals, letters, and manuscripts must be read together for their meaning, a Western scholar, presumably unfamiliar with the novel, mistakenly concluded that when the doomed prisoner asked to be freed and "be called 'Petrov', Bukharin gave up on his very self" (Igal Halfin, *Terror in My Soul* [Cambridge, Mass., 2003], 281). Considering Bukharin's autobiography of "Petrov," the opposite was the case.

22. For that struggle from Stalin's death to the eve of Gorbachev's rise to power, see Cohen, *Rethinking*, chaps. 4–5.

23. See, respectively, A. B. Aristov's 1957 remarks quoted in *IA*, no. 4 (1993): 62; the Shvernik Commission's report in *Reabilitatsiia*, 3 vols. (Moscow, 2000–2004), 2:541–670; and Petr Pospelov in *Vsesoiuznoe soveshchanie o merakh uluchsheniia podgotovki nauchno-pedagogicheskikh kadrov po istoricheskim naukam* (Moscow, 1964), 298. For the students, see Evgenii Taranov in *SM*, no. 10 (1993): 102; and for the letter, D. T. Shepilov and V. P. Naumov in *VI KPSS*, no. 2 (1989): 51–52.

24. As he told several people I later knew in Moscow.

25. See the recollections of Andrei Kolesnikov in *Izvestiia*, Nov. 11, 2003; and Aleksandr Tsipko in *VA*, no. 3 (2005), Internet edition.

26. A. Fedosev in *Novyi zhurnal*, no. 151 (1983): 239. For an argument that their attachment to the NEP/Bukharinist model was a grave historical and theoretical mistake on the part of Communist reformers, see Oscar J. Bandelin, *Return to the NEP* (Westpoint, Conn., 2002).

27. *Khronika zashchity prav v SSSR* (New York), no. 27 (July–Sept. 1977): 16–17.

28. F. Janacek and J. Sladek, eds., *V revoluci a po revoluci* (Prague, 1967), 9, 281. A typescript review of my Bukharin biography by the Czech historian Hana Mejdrová made the same point.

29. As they told me before publishing my biography of Bukharin. For their writings, see, e.g., Zheng Yifan, "Reestimating Bukharin's Political Philosophy," *She Jie Li Shi* (World History), Feb. 2, 1981, 1–14.

30. Anatolii Chubais in *LG*, Nov. 18, 1992; and Boris Vishnevskii in *NG*, Feb. 14, 1988. I found Baburin's letter in the archive of the Communist Party Control Commission in an uncatalogued file related to Bukharin's trial, execution, and rehabilitation. For the Western study, see Moshe Lewin, *Political Undercurrents in Soviet Economic Debates* (Princeton, 1974), xiii.

31. *Dvadtsatyi vek* (London, 1976): 1:18.

32. David Anin in *Kontinent*, no. 2 (1975): 312–14; and Boris Shragin, Radio Liberty Seminar Broadcast, no. 38 012-R (1978).

33. See Mikhail Gorbachev, *Zhizn i reformy*, 2 vols. (Moscow, 1995), 1:365–69; his remarks in V. T. Loginov, ed., *A. I. Mikoian* (Moscow, 1996), 80; and, similarly, Aleksandr Tsipko in *Proryv k svobode* (Moscow, 2005), 338.

34. Anatolii Cherniaev, *Shest let s Gorbachevym* (Moscow, 1993), 183. The significance of the step was noted even by Jeanne J. Kirkpatrick, the conservative, anti-Soviet ambassador to the United Nations in the Reagan administration, who remarked that only Bukharin's rehabilitation finally convinced her "real changes were occurring" under Gorbachev. Interview in *Demokratizatsiya* (Summer 1994): 460.

35. Bordiugov and Kozlov, *Istoriia*, chap. 2; *Nedelia*, Feb. 5–11, 1990; and *VI KPSS*, no. 3 (1991): 151.

36. Anatolii Rybakov in *MN*, Nov. 27, 1988; L. Pavliuchik in *Pravda*, May 17, 1989.

37. G. Bordiugov and V. Kozlov in *Pravda*, Oct. 3, 1988.

38. See, respectively, Bukharin, *Tiuremnye rukopisi*; Bukharin, *Vremena*; *VRAN* 69, no. 7 (1999): 652–54; Vladimir Mamontov in *LG*, March 28–April 3, 2007; and *KO*, no. 27–28 (2008): 4. The prison manuscripts, except the full volume of poems, were reprinted as *Uznik Lubianki: tiuremnye rukopisi Nikolaia Bukharina* (Moscow, 2008). Commenting on the first edition, a veteran Soviet Marxist wrote: "Marxism in our country . . . was destroyed when Stalin shot Bukharin and his school": Leon Onikov in *NG*, Dec. 2, 1997. All four manuscripts have been published in English translations: *How It All Began* (New York, 1998); *Philosophical Arabesques* (New York, 2005); *Socialism and Its Culture* (Calcutta, 2006); and *The Prison Poems of Nikolai Bukharin* (Calcutta, 2009).

39. A. V. Fadin in *Kentavr* (Jan.–Feb. 1993): 92–97. Similarly, see Vadim Medvedev, *V komande Gorbacheva* (Moscow, 1994), 234, who speaks of a "noncatastrophic transformation."

40. V. Bushuev in *SM*, no. 12 (2005): 187; and V. Mau in *VE*, no. 11 (2000): 7, whose point about China is also made by Bushuev. Similarly, see E. G. Plimak, *Politika perekhodnoi epokhi* (Moscow, 2004).

41. Vadim Belotserkovskii in *SM*, no. 3 (2006): 170.

42. Beginning in the mid-1990s, the pro-Communist newspaper *Sovetskaia Rossiia* regularly published historical articles glorifying Stalin and denigrating Bukharin. For an attempt to salvage "Lenin's NEP" from Bukharin, see the Party's chief historian-ideologist, Iurii Belov, in the issues of Feb. 26, 1998, and April 21, 2007; Viktor Budarin in *Dialog*, no. 4–5 (2004): 27–40; and for "Bukharinization," Richard Kosolapov, *Polet sovy* (Moscow, 1994), 261. For examples of non-Communist opponents of the idea of a viable

Bukharinist or NEP alternative, see E. G. Gimpelson and I. B. Orlov in G. N. Sevostianov, ed., *Rossiia v XX veke*, 2 vols. (Moscow 2002), 2:52–60 and 101–16; and Mikhail Antonov in *LG*, April 9–15, 2008.

43. See Andrei Piontkovskii in *Novaia*, Feb. 3–5, 2003 and in *MT*, Nov. 10, 2003; Gleb Pavlovskii in *Izvestiia*, Sept. 9, 2003; Andrei Illarionov in *NG*, Nov. 14, 2005; Egor Gaidar, *Gibel imperii* (Moscow, 2006), 163, 428 and his comments in *JRL*, Aug. 24, 2006; and for Khodorkovsky, Aleksandr Minkin in *MK*, June 3, 2005, Grigory Yavlinsky quoted by Jeremy Page in *JRL*, Nov. 9, 2003, and Gleb Pavlovskii, gazeta.ru, April 1, 2004. According to a 1990 survey, the introduction of NEP was the most approved change in Soviet history, Matthew Wyman, *Public Opinion in Postcommunist Russia* (New York, 1997), 63. For Clinton, see the report by David Maraniss in *WP*, Sept. 13, 1998.

44. Knowing my longstanding interest in NEP, two of them emphasized this in discussions with me in Moscow in 2007. Similarly, see Vladimir Mau in *Kommersant*, Feb. 9, 2006.

45. For the revival of Stalinist-like modernization "projects," see the objections of Aleksandr Tsipko in *LG*, June 25–July 1, 2008. For examples of the pro-NEP response, see Aleksandr Iakovlev in *OG*, Feb. 3–9, 2000; Naum Korzhavin in *Novaia*, May 8–11, 2003; and I. V. Karatsuba, I. V. Kurukin, and N. P. Sokolov, *Vybiraia svoiu istoriiu* (Moscow, 2005), 554. In conversations with me and others in 2003, the self-described "alternativist" Viktor Danilov "urgently" called for a public forum on the "relevance of the Bukharinist alternative" because pro-Stalinist historians were again gaining the upper hand in Academy of Sciences institutes.

46. A. A. Igolkin in *VI*, no. 6 (2001): 151.

2. THE VICTIMS RETURN: GULAG SURVIVORS SINCE STALIN

1. For their story and my book, see chapter 1, n. 1.
2. In the fortieth anniversary edition of Robert Conquest's *The Great Terror* (New York, 2007), he remarked (xiii) that new materials on the terror are still "enough for generations of archaeologists." Having discussed this and other subjects with my friend Bob Conquest over the years, I owe him a significant debt of gratitude.
3. For a discussion, see Stephen F. Cohen, *Rethinking the Soviet Experience* (New York, 1985), esp. chaps. 1, 3–5.
4. For my first attempt, "The Friends and Foes of Change," see Stephen F. Cohen, Alexander Rabinowitch, and Robert Sharlet, ed., *The Soviet Union*

Since Stalin (Bloomington, Ind., 1980); and for subsequent ones, Cohen, *Rethinking.*

5. The best book was, of course, Conquest's *The Great Terror.* There was, however, a narrow but useful Ph.D. dissertation, Jane P. Shapiro, "Rehabilitation Policy and Political Conflict in the Soviet Union" (Columbia University, 1967); and, on a related subject, Mikhail Geller, *Kontsentratsionnyi mir i sovetskaia literatura* (London, 1974).

6. See Aleksandr Solzhenitsyn, *The Gulag Archipelago,* (New York, 1976), 3:445–68.

7. See Libushe Zorin, *Soviet Prisons and Concentration Camps: An Annotated Bibliography* (Newtonville, Mass., 1980). There were two important exceptions: Eugenia Ginzburg, *Within the Whirlwind* (New York, 1981); and Aleksandr I. Solzhenitsyn, *The Oak and the Calf* (New York, 1980).

8. Dariusz Tolczyk, *See No Evil* (New Haven, Conn., 1999), makes the same point but in an ideological way (pp. xix–xx, chaps. 4–5) that dismisses survivor-authors other than Solzhenitsyn. Similarly, see Leona Toker, *Return from the Archipelago* (Bloomington, Ind., 2000), 49–52, 73. Varlam Shalamov, perhaps the greatest Gulag writer, refused to be so dismissive of those lesser authors. See his letter to Solzhenitsyn in *NG,* April 9, 1998. For a contemporary Russian specialist who takes a position similar to mine, see Aleksei Simonov in "Pravda GULAGa," *Novaia,* Aug, 7–10, 2008.

9. They included *Sibirskie ogni, Baikal, Prostor, Angara, Ural, Poliarnaia zvezda, Sever, Na rubezhe,* and *Dalnii vostok.*

10. Radio Liberty in Munich maintained an ongoing catalogue, *Arkhiv samizdata.*

11. See Roy Medvedev and Giulietto Chiesa, *Time of Change* (New York, 1989), 99–100; and A. Antonov-Ovseenko, *Vragi naroda* (Moscow, 1996), 367. For my relationship with Medvedev, see our dialogue in *NNI,* no. 2 (2006): 94–101.

12. Baev felt free to tell his story only many years later. See A. D. Mirzabekov, ed., *Akademik Aleksandr Baev* (Moscow, 1997), chap. 1. In August 1968, the twenty-one-year-old Tanya Baeva participated in the famous "Demonstration of Seven on Red Square," protesting the Soviet invasion of Czechoslovakia. There were actually eight; the others were arrested and severely punished while Tanya avoided prosecution, though not subsequent persecution.

13. In addition to Bukharin's extended family, Antonov-Ovseyenko, and Roy Medvedev, my informants included, to list those whose names may be familiar to non-Russian readers, Yuri Aikhenvald, Lev Razgon, Igor Pyat-

nitsky, Lev Kopelev, Mikhail Baitalsky, Yuri Gaistev, Pavel Aksyonov, Yevgeny Gnedin, Kamil Ikramov, Natalya Rykova, and Leonid Petrovsky.

14. See Solzhenitsyn, *The Gulag Archipelago*; Medvedev, *Let History Judge* (New York, 1972); and Antonov-Ovseyenko, *The Time of Stalin* (New York, 1981), which appeared with my introduction.

15. Andrei Timofeev in *LG*, Aug. 23, 1995.

16. Several questionnaires were prepared after 1985. See *Gorizont*, no.7 (1989): 63–64; Nanci Adler, *The Gulag Survivor* (New Brunswick, N.J., 2002), 121; *Moskvichi v GULAGe* (Moscow, 1996), 51–52; and Orlando Figes, *The Whisperers* (New York, 2007), 662.

17. Figes, *The Whisperers*, is based on many more cases, and admirably so, but was researched when stealth was no longer necessary and with teams of assistants across Russia. See 657–65.

18. Stephen F. Cohen, ed., *An End to Silence* (New York, 1982); and Cohen, *Rethinking*.

19. Adler, *Gulag Survivor*.

20. As pointed out by Anne Applebaum in *Gulag* (New York, 2003), 515, their saga is "often ignored" even in histories of the Soviet Union.

21. For examples of memoirs, in addition to those cited in n. 7, see Anna Tumanova, *Shag vpravo, shag vlevo . . .* (Moscow, 1995); Aleksandr Milchakov, *Molodost svetlaia i tragicheskaia* (Moscow, 1988); Pavel Negretov, *Vse dorogi vedut na Vorkutu* (Benson, Vt., 1985); Anatolii Zhigulin, *Chernye kamni* (Moscow, 1989); Raisa Orlova and Lev Kopelev, *My zhili v Moskve* (Moscow, 1990); Mikhail Mindlin, *Anfas i profil* (Moscow, 1999); and Olga Shatunovskaia, *Ob ushedshem veke* (La Jolla, Calif., 2001). Most still focus, however, on life in the Gulag, as do, for example, those in Simeon Vilensky, ed., *Till My Tale Is Told* (Bloomington, Ind., 1999). For general Western studies, see n. 8; Adam Hochschild, *The Unquiet Ghost* (New York, 1994); Simon Sebag Montefiore, *Stalin* (London, 2003); Kathleen E. Smith, *Remembering Stalin's Victims* (Ithaca, N.Y., 1996); Catherine Merridale, *Nights of Stone* (New York, 2001); and Figes, *Whisperers*.

22. A point made when the Russian edition of Adler's book appeared in 2005. There are still few pages on the subject in Russian literature, as in Elena Zubkova, *Russia After the War* (Armonk, N.Y., 1998), chap. 16; and *Mir posle Gulaga* (St. Petersburg, 2004). The two main repositories, in Moscow, are the Memorial Society and Vozvrashchenie (Return). For archive volumes, see *Reabilitatsiia*, 3 vols. (Moscow, 2000–2004), and *Deti GULAGa* (Moscow, 2002), under the general editorship of A. N. Iakovlev. Bukharin's relatives are among the best documented returnee cases. See Anna Larin, *This I Cannot Forget: The Memoirs of Nikolai Bukharin's Widow* (New York, 1993); Mark Iunge, *Strakh pered proshlym* (Moscow, 2003); V. I. Bukharin,

Dni i gody (Moscow, 2003); A. S. Namazova, ed., *Rossiia i Evropa*, no.4 (2007): 190–296 (on Bukharin's daughter Svetlana Gurvich); and my introduction to Nikolai Bukharin, *How It All Began* (New York, 1998).

23. Vladlen Loginov, intro. to A. Antonov-Ovseenko, *Portret tirana* (Moscow, 1995), 3.

24. Aleksandr Proshkin in *SK*, June 30, 1988.

25. There is no agreed-upon figure for the number of people in the Gulag during that period, only a very large (and contradictory) Russian and Western literature on the subject. (Among the several problems involved are the percentages of criminal and political prisoners and how many inmates were there more than once.) I have used the figure given tentatively by the Memorial Society in recent years, possibly a conservative one. Though their figures are somewhat different, I am grateful for the expert advice of Stephen Wheatcroft and Alexander Babyonyshev (Maksudov).

26. See, e.g., Varlam Shalamov, *Kolymskie rasskazy* (London, 1978); Ginzburg, *Within*; Aleksandr I. Solzhenitsyn, *One Day in the Life of Ivan Denisovich* (New York, 1963); Boris Diakov, *Povest o perezhitom* (Moscow, 1966); and the exchange in *LG*, July 4–10, 2007.

27. On the eve of Stalin's death, according to archive sources, there were 2.7 million people in Gulag camps and colonies and 2.8 million in the "special settlements." A. B. Suslov in *VI*, no. 3 (2004): 125; *Istoriia stalinskogo GULAGa*, 7 vols. (Moscow, 2004–2005), 5:90. There are at least two uncertainties about this total figure of 5.5 million. The usual assumption that half of those in camps and colonies were criminals may be too high. And the number given for special settlements, which were mainly for specific deported groups and nationalities, may not include the many individuals released into exile after serving their camp sentences or those sentenced only to exile, some of whom I knew. See, e.g., the discussion in *Istoriia stalinskogo GULAGa*, 5:23–24, 90.

28. Emma Gerstein, *Moscow Memoirs* (New York, 2004), 456.

29. My files include dozens of such cases. In addition to those in *Deti GULAGa*, four must suffice here: Larina, *This I Cannot Forget*; Pyotr Yakir, *A Childhood in Prison* (New York, 1973); Kamil Ikramov, *Delo moego ottsa* (Moscow, 1991); and Inna Shikheeva-Gaister, *Semeinaia khronika vremen kulta lichnosti* (Moscow, 1998). For the record, Bukharin's son and others report that their orphanages were not the cruel, uncaring institutions usually depicted, as, e.g., by Vladislav Serikov and Irina Ovchinnikova in *Izvestiia*, May 1, 1988, and June 22, 1992; and Mikhail Nikolaev, *Detdom* (New York, 1985). For a study of orphanages during those years, see Catriona Kelly, *Children's World* (New Haven, Conn., 2007), 221–58.

30. "Spoilt biographies"—people "whose fates were ruined by political repression" (Aleksei Karpychev in *Rossiiskie vesti,* March 28, 1995)—run through Figes, *Whisperers.* Among the exceptions were the president of the Academy of Sciences Sergei Vavilov, the famous newspaper caricaturist Boris Yefimov, the actress Vera Maretskaya (all had brothers who were arrested and killed), the actress Olga Aroseva, whose father was shot, and the ballerina Maya Plisetskaya, whose father was executed and mother sent to a camp. See, respectively, Iu. N. Vavilov, *V dolgom poiske* (Moscow, 2004); Boris Efimov, *Desiat desiatiletii* (Moscow, 2000); the obituaries of Maretskaya in *Pravda,* Aug. 19, 1978, and *LG,* Aug. 30, 1978, which do not mention her brothers, and T. Iakovleva in *KP,* July 12, 1989, who does; Olga Aroseva and Vera Maksimova, *Bez grima* (Moscow, 2003); and *I, Maya Plisetskaya* (New Haven, Conn., 2001). Regarding benefits, see, e.g., the plight of Pyotr Petrovsky's widow, *Golosa istorii,* no. 22, book 1 (Moscow, 1990), p. 230.

31. *Istoriia stalinskogo GULAGa,* 3:38.

32. See, e.g., the correspondence between Gumilyov and Akhmatova in Gerstein, *Moscow Memoirs,* 448–70.

33. For Molotov's wife, see Viacheslav Nikonov in *KO,* no. 27–28 (2005): 3, and William Taubman, *Khrushchev* (New York, 2003), 246. For other relatives of leaders, see Roy Medvedev and Zhores Medvedev, *The Unknown Stalin* (New York, 2004), 107–8; for Communists, see Milchakov, *Molodost;* Shatunovskaia, *Ob ushedshem;* and Ivan Gronskii, *Iz proshlogo . . .* (Moscow, 1991), 192–96. For the doctors, Iakov Etinger in *NV,* no. 3 (2003): 38. For Fyodorova, Victoria Fyodorova and Haskel Frankel, *The Admiral's Daughter* (New York, 1979), 185. For the Starostins, *Moscow News,* Feb. 5–12, 1988. And for Rozner, Iurii Tseitlin in *Krokodil,* no. 7 (1989): 6.

34. *Reabilitatsiia,* 1:213. For the slow process, see the case of Vsevolod Meierkhold in B. Riazhskii, "Kak shla reabilitatsiia," *Teatralnaia zhizn,* no. 5 (1989): 8–11. For the period, see Adler, *Gulag Survivor,* chap. 3.

35. Meierkhold in B. Riazhskii, "Kak shla reabilitatsiia,", 89, 104. For the crowds, see Riazhskii, "Kak shla," 10. For the appeals, see Shatunovskaia, *Ob ushedshem,* 431; and Antonov-Ovseenko, *Portret,* 452.

36. Gerstein, *Moscow Memoirs,* 464.

37. *Reabilitatsiia,* 2:6, 9, and the documents in part 1. For examples of appeals, see Mikhail Rosliakov, *Ubiistvo Kirova* (Leningrad, 1991), 15–17; and Gerstein, *Moscow Memoirs,* 467. For the decision to read the speech publicly and reactions, see *Izvestiia TsK KPSS,* no. 3 (1989): 166, n. 1; and Medvedev and Medvedev, *Unknown Stalin,* 103–5. For examples of people who read or heard the speech, see also Anatolii Rybakov, *Roman-Vospominanie* (Moscow, 1997), 195; and Orlova and Kopelev, *My zhili,* 25.

38. My account of the commissions is based on two varying but generally compatible sources: *Reabilitatsiia*, 2:193, 792–93; and Shatunovskaia, *Ob ushedshem*, 274–77, 286–89. See also Adler, *Gulag Survivor*, 169–71; and Anastas Mikoian, *Tak bylo* (Moscow, 1999), 595. For "unloading parties," see Solzhenitsyn, *Gulag*, 3:489. Many of my returnees confirmed this account. Some estimates of people released by the commissions are considerably higher. See Medvedev and Medvedev, *Unknown Stalin*, 115.

39. V. N. Zemskov in *SI*, no. 7 (1991): 14.

40. Vladimir Lakshin in *LG*, Aug. 17, 1994; Vasilii Grossman, *Forever Flowing* (New York, 1972), chap. 1; Solzhenitsyn, *Gulag*, 3:506; E. Nosov in Iu. V. Aksiutin, ed., *Nikita Sergeevich Khrushchev* (Moscow, 1989), 98.

41. Antonov-Ovseenko, *Portret*, 451; Shatunovskaia, *Ob ushedshem*, 282.

42. Solzhenitsyn, *Gulag*, vol. 3:449.

43. For examples, see Negretov, *Vse dorogi*; Ginzburg, *Within*; Mikhail Vygon, *Lichnoe delo* (Moscow, 2005); *Mir posle Gulaga*, 36–40; and on Kazakhstan, Leonid Kapeliushnyi in *Izvestiia*, Dec. 17, 1992. Poetic expressions of such attachments appeared in the journals *Baikal* and *Prostor*. See also Adler, *Gulag Survivor*, 231–33.

44. Hochschild, *Unquiet Ghost*; Colin Thubron, *In Siberia* (New York, 1999), 38–48; and for skulls, Evgenii Evtushenko in *LG*, Nov. 2, 1988.

45. Cohen, ed., *An End*, 66–67.

46. Applebaum, *Gulag*, 512. For examples of freed prisoners too broken to go on, see the cases of Iulian Khrenov in *LG*, July 4–10, 2007; Boris Zbarskii in *Pravda*, April 5, 1989; and Daniil Andreev in *Grazhdanin Rossii*, no. 4 (1993). For those who survived, see the stories about Oleg Volkov in *Sobesednik*, no. 2 (1990); and Anna Nosova in *Ogonek*, no. 12 (1989). 5. A few—e.g., Olga Tarasova and Nikolai Glazov—lived to be one hundred or more. See *Nedelia*, no. 33 (1990); and *Eko*, no. 4 (1991): 197. All those I knew personally lived into their seventies or beyond. Bukharin's brother Vladimir died at eighty-eight.

47. Oleg Khlebnikov on Shalamov in *Novaia*, June 18–20, 2007; Gerstein, *Moscow Memoirs*, 423 (and, similarly, Mikhail Baitalsky, *Notebooks for the Grandchildren* [Atlantic Highlands, N.J., 1995], 420); and Lez Razgon, *True Stories* (Dana Point, Calif., 1997); Aleksei Snegov in *Vsesoiuznoe soveshchanie o merakh uluchshenii podgotovki nauchno-pedagogicheskikh kadrov po istoricheskim naukam, 18–21 dekabria 1962 g.* (Moscow, 1964), 270; the obituary of Valentin Zeka (Sokolov) in *Russkaia mysl*, Dec. 20, 1984; and Liudmila Saraskina, *Aleksandr Solzhenitsyn* (Moscow, 2008), 456. Regarding friendships, my Moscow acquaintances were good examples. Similarly, see Zhigulin, *Chernye kamni*, 265–71. For those who lived fearfully, see Adler, *Gulag Survivor*; and Figes, *Whisperers*. And for "prisoner's skin,"

see Janusz Bardach and Kathleen Gleeson, *Surviving Freedom* (Berkeley, Calif., 2003), 26.

48. For disparate examples, see Mirzabekov, ed., *Akademik Aleksandr Baev*, and Tumanova, *Shag*, 213–26.

49. See, respectively, V. Kargamov, *Rokossovskii* (Moscow, 1972), 147–48; Vladimir Lakshin, "Otkrytaia dver," *Ogonek*, no. 20 (1988): 22–24; N. Koroleva, *Otets*, vol. 2 (Moscow, 2002); editor's note in *LG*, Aug. 1–7, 2007; Mirzabekov, ed., *Akademik Aleksandr Baev*, *Moscow News*, Feb. 5–12, 1988; Tseitlin in *Krokodil*, no. 7 (1989): 6. Georgii Zhzhenov, *Prozhitoe* (Moscow, 2005); and Petr Veliaminov in *SR*, June 4, 1989.

50. For happy ends, in addition to ones listed earlier, see Mikhail Zaraev in *Ogonek*, no. 15 (1991): 15, where the term appears; Milchakov, *Molodost*; Mindlin, *Anfas and profil*; Tumanova, *Shag*; and Efim Shifrin in *AF*, no. 1 (1991). For unhappy ends, see Cohen, ed., *An End*, 101–2; and more generally, Adler, *Gulag Survivor*; and Figes, *Whisperers*. For the example of the homeless Wilhelm Draugel, see in *MN*, Dec. 31, 1989. For Shalamov, see Elena Zakharova in *Novaia*, Nov. 8–11, 2007; and for Berggolts, see Gerbert Kemoklidze in *LG*, Nov. 12–18, 2008.

51. See, e.g., Aleksei Savelev in *Molodoi kommunist*, no. 3 (1988): 57; and Natalya Rykova, on behalf of her mother, in *Reabilitatsiia*, 2:351. For a discussion, see Adler, *Gulag Survivor*, 29, 205–23; and for Levitin-Krasnov, his *Likhie gody* (Paris, 1977) and *V poiskakh novogo grada* (Tel-Aviv, 1980).

52. See, e.g., Shalamov's letters in *NG*, April 9, 1998, and in *KO*, no. 27–28 (1997); Mikhail Zolotonosov in *MN*, Sept. 10–17, 1995; similarly, Kim Parkhmenko in *NG*, Jan. 5, 1991; and on the dislike, Zinovy Zinik in *TLS*, Dec. 5, 2008, 6. For Kopelev and Ginzburg, see Iurii Kariakin, *Peremena ubezhdenii* (Moscow, 2007), 232; and Ginzburg, *Within*, 389–92.

53. The scientist and Svetlana Gurvich, a historian, were in politically sensitive professions.

54. See Antonov-Ovseenko, *Portret*, 469–77; and the pro-Memorial account in Smith, *Remembering*, 177–78.

55. See Karpov in *SR*, July 27, 2002, *Pravda*, April 26, 1995, and his *Generalissimus*, 2 vols. (Moscow, 2002); and Sviashchennik Dmitrii Dudko, *Posmertnye vstrechi so Stalinym* (Moscow, 1993).

56. See the 1962 document in *Rodina*, no. 5–6 (1993): 56–57.

57. See, e.g., *Izvestiia*, June 22, 1992; Ella Maksimova in *Izvestiia*, May 5, 1993; E. M. Maksimova, *Po sledam zagublennykh sudeb* (Moscow, 2007); and, similarly, *Deti GULAGa*, 12.

58. See, e.g., the accounts by Anthony Austin in *NYT Magazine*, Dec. 16, 1979, 26; by Adler, *Gulag Survivor*, 140–41; by Ginzburg in *Within*, 410–11; and for the brothers, see Vladimir Ryzhkov in *Novaia*, Feb. 21–27, 2008.

59. For the well-known example of Eugenia Ginzburg and Pavel Aksyonov, see Konstantin Smirnov, "Zhertva prinoshenie," *Ogonek*, no. 2 (1991): 18–21.

60. The wife and daughter of my friend Yevgeny Gnedin, e.g., remained utterly devoted to him. Similarly, see Milchakov, *Molodost*, 91–92; and Baitalsky, *Notebooks*, 389–91. For a contrary example, see Lakshin in *LG*, Aug. 17, 1994. More generally, see Adler, *Gulag Survivor*, 139–45.

61. See, e.g., Oleg Volkov, *Pogruzhenie vo tmu* (Moscow, 1992), 428–29. Solzhenitsyn and Aleksei Snegov had much younger post-Gulag wives. Among survivors who married other victims were Lev Razgon, Yuri Aikhenvald, and Antonov-Ovseyenko. Children included Irina Yakira and Yuli Kim, who married, and the famous novelist Yulian Semyonov, whose father spent many years in the Gulag and who married a victim's daughter. For freed men marrying younger women, see Olga Semenova, *Iulian Semenov* (Moscow, 2006). Similarly, see Figes, *Whisperers*, 566, 650.

62. For a discussion, see Adler, *Gulag Survivor*, 114–18; for a specific case, M. Korol on the discarded wife of Marshal Budyonny in *AF*, no. 23 (1993); and for a tragic (and heroic) one, Iulii Kim on Pyotr Yakir in *OG*, Feb. 8–14, 1996. According to N. A. Morozov and M. B Rogachev. (*OI*, no. 2 [1995]: 187), effects of the "syndrome" lasted for decades. For survivor circles, see Ginzburg, *Within*, 157; and Adler, *Gulag Survivor*, 134. And for nostalgia, Ludmilla Alexeyeva and Paul Goldberg, *The Thaw Generation* (Boston, 1990), 88; Bulat Okudzhava in *Novaia*, May 5–11, 2005; and even Solzhenitsyn, *Gulag*, 3:462.

63. For statutes and property compensation, see *Reabilitatsiia*, 2:181–83, 194–97, 333–34; and Adler, *Gulag Survivor*, 186–90. I heard of very few instances of possessions being returned, not even photographs, except ones saved by relatives and friends, but I learned of numerous instances of such items being held or sold by descendants of secret policemen. Similarly, see Liudmila Saveleva in *Izvestiia*, May 5, 1992; and Aleksandr Kokurin and Iurii Morukov, "Gulag," *SM*, no. 2 (2002): 109. For Vyshinsky, see Vera Chelishcheva in "Pravda GULAGa," *Novaia*, July 7–9, 2008.

64. E. Efimov in *Sotsialisticheskaia zakonnost*, no. 9 (1964): 42–45; and Lev Zaverin in *Soiuz*, no. 51 (1990): 9.

65. See Adler, *Gulag Survivor*, chap. 5 (for the quotes, 103, 161); similarly, *Golosa istorii*, 225; and various documents in *Reabilitatsiia*, vols. 1 and 2.

66. *Golosa istorii*, 185–86, 214–33; *Reabilitatsiia*, 2:370–71, 456–62, 474–75; Joshua Rubenstein, *Tangled Loyalties* (New York, 1996), 287–91, 303; Orlova and Kopelev, *My zhili*, 25.

67. Adler, *Gulag Survivor*, 171, 177; Ivan Zemlianushin in *Trud*, Dec. 24, 1992. The figures are probably compatible because the first refers to 1954 through 1961 and the second apparently to 1954 through 1964.

68. Adler, *Gulag Survivor*, 179, and passim for official opposition, which included Molotov (*Golosa istorii*, 214). For examples of the other obstructions, see Semen Vilenskii, ed., *Dognes tiagoteet* (Moscow, 1989), 1:5; G. Anokhin in *Izvestiia*, March 23, 1988; N. Zarubin in *Izvestiia*, March 31, 1995; and employers in Briansk described in *Lesnaia promyshlennost*, May 1, 1989. For the quotes about official attitudes, see Saraskina, *Aleksandr Solzhenitsyn*, 456.

69. See Zaraev in *Ogonek*, no. 15 (1991): 15; Adler, *Gulag Survivor*, 186; for the poem, Vladimir Kornilov in *MK*, July 13, 1966 (and, similarly, the tributes in Evgenii Gnedin, *Vykhod iz labirinta* [Moscow, 1994]); and for Gnedin's life, Stephen F. Cohen, *Sovieticus*, exp. ed. (New York, 1986), 104–7.

70. On the amnesty, see Miriam Dobson in Polly Jones, ed., *The Dilemmas of De-Stalinization* (London, 2006), 21–40; and Solzhenitsyn, *Gulag*, 3:452. A well-known Soviet film about the amnesty, *The Cold Summer of 1953*, was released in 1988.

71. Snegov in *Vsesoiuznoe soveshchanie*, 270; and, similarly, Vladimir Amlinskii in *Iunost*, no. 3 (1988): 53. The official newspaper *Izvestiia* later admitted that "false denunciation frequently became a ladder by which to climb to the top" (*CDSP*, Aug. 5, 1964, 20). The moral corruption of the living was a theme of the novels of Yuri Trifonov, a victim's son. See *NYT*, Dec. 16, 1979.

72. Relatives naturally appealed on behalf of their loved ones, and professionals sometimes on behalf of their colleagues. See, e.g., V. A. Goncharov, *Prosim osvobodit iz tiuremnogo zakliucheniia* (Moscow, 1998); N. S. Cherushev, ed. *"Dorogoi nash tovarishch Stalin!"* (Moscow, 2001); and "Akademiki v zashchitu repressirovannykh kolleg," *VRAN*, no. 6 (2002): 530–36. Friends and unrelated individuals sometimes tried to help, as, e.g., related by Razgon, *True Stories*, 81–86; Evgeniia Taratuta in *SK*, June 4, 1988; and Marina Khodorkovskaia in *Novaia*, May 16–18, 2005. In *Rasprava: prokurorskie sudby* (Moscow, 1990), some prosecutors are reported to have resisted. For reports of NKVD officers resisting or helping people, see Zhigulin, *Chernye kamni*, 262–64; I. Kon in *AF*, no. 18 (1988); V. Chertkov in *Pravda*, May 1, 1989; and Galina Vinogradova in *LG*, Nov. 12, 1997. For a few "good bosses" in the camps, see E. Boldyreva in *SK*, Sept. 14, 1989.

73. Lidiia Chukovskaia, *Zapiski ob Anne Akhmatovoi* (Paris, 1980), 2:115, 137 (and, similarly, Lev Razgon in *LG*, Dec. 13, 1995); and Applebaum, *Gulag*, 516–17. For a different perspective, see Miriam Dobson, "Contesting the Paradigms of De-Stalinization," *Slavic Review* (Fall 2005): 580–600.

74. See Cohen, ed., *An End*, chap. 2. For Monte Christo, Igor Zolotusskii and Kamil Ikramov in *MN*, June 18, 1989. And for revenge more generally, Lev Razgon in *Ogonek*, no. 51 (1995): 48; and Adler, *Gulag Survivor*, 123–24.

75. Antonov-Ovseenko, *Vragi*, 16. For the no-guilt view, see Aleksandr Shitov on Yuri Trifonov in *Novaia*, Aug. 29–31, 2005; for the opposing view, Vladimir Sapozhnikov in *LG*, Aug. 24, 1988; for Yuri Tomsky and Svetlana Stalin, Boris Rubin, *Moe okruzhenie* (Moscow, 1995), 187; for the guards, Figes, *Whisperers*, 631.

76. I was told the first episode. For the others, see, respectively, Zhigulin, *Chernye kamni*, 263; Valentin Kuznetsov in *KO*, no. 49 (1990): 3; Efim Etkind, *Notes of A Non-Conspirator* (New York, 1978), 113–14, 118, 204; and Aleksandr Borshchagovskii in *LG*, June 10, 1992. For similar episodes, see V. Volgin, "Dokumenty rasskazyvaiut," *Voprosy literatury*, no. 1 (1992): 257–83; Cohen, ed., *An End*, chap. 2; and N.N., "Donoschiki i predateli sredi sovetskikh pisatelei i uchenykh," *Sotsialisticheskii vestnik* (May–June 1963): 74–76.

77. See, e.g., Bronia Ben-Iakov, *Slovar argo Gulaga* (Frankfurt, 1982); Vladimir Kozlovskii, *Sobranie russkikh vorovskikh slovarei*, 4 vols. (New York, 1983); and, in the Soviet Union itself, K. Kostsinskii (Kirill Uspenskii), "Sushchestvuet li problema zhargona?" *Voprosy literatury*, no. 5 (1968): 181–91. For objections, see those cited by Elvira Goriukhina in the weekly supplement of *Novaia*, Sept. 14, 2007.

78. Quoted by Tseitlin in *Krokodil*, no.7 (1989): 6. Yevtushenko said at the time, "The intelligentsia is singing criminal songs." Quoted by Mikhail Roshchin in *Ogonek*, no. 41 (1990): 9. For a study written as early as 1979, see Iurii Karabchievskii, "I vokhrovtsy i zeki," *Neva*, no. 1 (1991): 170–76.

79. See the accounts of Iurii Panov in *Izvestiia*, Aug. 10, 1990; and Viktor Bokarev in *LG*, March 29, 1989.

80. See, e.g., *SK*, May 6, 1989; *Gorizont*, no. 6 (1989); *Ogonek*, no. 39 (1990): 8–11; *Tvorchestvo v lagerakh i ssylkakh* (Moscow, 1990); *Tvorchestvo i byt GULAGa* (Moscow, 1998); and Nikolai Getman, *The Gulag Collection* (Washington, D.C., 2001). For the sketches, see *Literator*, no. 35 (1989).

81. For "catacomb," see Paola Volkova in *NG*, May 30, 2001.

82. Konstantin Simonov in *Izvestiia*, Nov. 18, 1962. For examples of earlier works, see K. Simonov, *Zhivye i mertvye* (Moscow, 1959); V. Kaverin, *Otkrytaia kniga*, part 3 (Moscow, 1956); V. Panova, *Sentimentalnyi roman* (Moscow, 1958); N. Ivanter, "Snova avgusta," *NM*, nos. 8 and 9 (1959); and A. Valtseva, "Kvartira No. 13," *Moskva*, no. 1 (1957). For a few example from the early 1960s, see V. Nekrasov, "Kira Georgievna," *NM*, no. 6, 1961; Iu. Dombrovskii, "Khranitel drevnostei," *NM*, nos. 6 and 7 (1964); A. Vasiliev, "Voprosov bolshe net," *Moskva*, no. 6 (1964); A. Aldan-Semenov, "Barelef na skale," *NM*, no. 7 (1964); V. Aksenov, "Dikoi," *Iunost*, no. 12 (1964); Iu. Semenov, "Pri ispolnenii sluzhebnykh obiazannostei," *Iunost*, nos. 1 and 2 (1962); K. Ikramov and V. Tendriakov, "Belyi flag," *MG*, no. 12 (1962);

B. Polevoi, "Vosvrashchenie," *Ogonek*, no. 31 (1962); I. Stadniuk, "Liudi ne angely," *Neva*, no. 12 (1962); and I. Lazutin, "Chernye lebedi," *Baikal*, nos. 2–6 (1964) and no. 1 (1966).

83. For the imagery and quote, see Alexander Yanov, *The Russian New Right* (Berkeley, 1978), 15; and Solzhenitsyn, *Oak*, 16.

84. See, e.g., the complaints by Ivan Isaev in *IA*, no. 2 (2001): 123–24; and V. Ivanov-Paimen in *IA*, no.4 (2003): 23–24. For returning to Party work, see, e.g., Milchakov, *Molodost*, pp. 92–99; Rosliakov, *Ubiistvo*, p. 16; and D. Poliakova and V. Khorunzhii on Valentina Pikina in *KP*, March 17, 1988.

85. For Burkovsky, see Saraskina, *Aleksandr Solzhenitsyn*, 523. For Suchkov and Kheiman, see Emily Tall in *Slavic Review* (Summer 1990): 184; and V. Loginov and N. Glovatskaia in *VE*, no. 1 (2007): 154–56.

86. I frequently heard this derision. In addition to ones mentioned in the text, zeks in positions of power included Pyotr Yakir, whose family was close to Larina and Baeva, and Aleksandr Milchakov, whose son I knew in the 1980s. For Pikina, see Poliakova and Khorunzhii in *KP*, March 17, 1988; Shatunovskaia, *Ob ushedshem*, 273, 296; Grigorii Pomerants, *Sledstvie vedet katorzhanka* (Moscow, 2004), 7, 28, 37; and *Reabilitatsiia*, 1:168, 447, and 2:267, 299, 378, 453, 456, 482, 493, 793, 877. For Shatunovskaia and Snegov, see this chapter, n. 87.

87. For Shirvindt, who died in 1958, see Aleksandr Kokurin and Nikita Petrov, "MVD," *SM*, no. 4 (1998): 115–16. For Todorsky, see N. Cherushev, *1937 god* (Moscow, 2003), 407–35; *Reabilitatsiia*, 1:214, 460, and 2:376, 693–95, 793, 896; A. I. Todorskii, *Marshal Tukhachevskii* (Moscow, 1963); and V. Sokolovskii, "Boets i voennyi pisatel," *Voenno-istoricheskii zhurnal*, no. 9 (1964): 53–60. I was told a great deal about Shatunovskaia and Snegov long before printed sources on their roles became available. For the former, see Shatunovskaia, *Ob ushedshem*; and Grigorii Pomerants, "Pamiati odinokoi teni," *Znamia*, no. 7 (2006): 165–69 and his *Sledstvie*. For both, see Sergei Khrushchev, *Khrushchev on Khrushchev* (Boston, 1990), chap. 1; S. A. Mikoian, "Aleksei Snegov v borbe za 'destalinizatsiiu,'" *VI*, no. 4 (2006): 69–83; Mikoian, *Tak bylo*, chap. 48; and the name indexes in *Reabilitatsiia*, vols. 1–3, and in K. Aimermakher, ed., *Doklad N.S. Khrushcheva o kulte lichnosti Stalina na XX sezde KPSS* (Moscow, 2002).

88. Pomerants, "Pamiati," 165.

89. For the congress, exiles, and camps, see the sources on Shatunovskaya and Snegov in n. 87. For the quotes, see, respectively, Mikoian, *Tak bylo*, 589; Pomertants, "Pamiati," 166; Khrushchev, *Khrushchev on Khrushchev*, 13; and, similarly, Mikoian, "Aleksei Snegov." Pomerants calls Shatunovskaya Khrushchev's "gray Bishop" (*serym preosviashchenstvom*).

90. Mikoyan, who headed the first commission on rehabilitations, personally received and helped a remarkable number of returnees, as I was told and as is now well documented. For his own account, see Mikoian, *Tak bylo*, 589–90; and, in addition, *A. I. Mikoian* (Moscow, 1996). For Bukharin, see *Mikoian*, 79; and Dmitrii Pushken in *MN*, May 28–June 3, 1995. A well-informed historian thinks Mikoyan was "the most distraught by his conscience" (Miklós Kun, *Stalin* [Budapest, 2003], 290). For disagreements about his role under and after Stalin, see Sergo A. Mikoyan and Michael Ellman in *Slavic Review* (Winter 2001): 917–21.

91. Quoted in Roy Medvedev, *Khrushchev* (Garden City, N.Y., 1983), 89–91; and, similarly, Fedor Burlatsky, *Khrushchev and the First Russian Spring* (New York, 1988), 61–62. For the memorial, see *XXII sezd kommununisticheskoi partii Sovetskogo Soiuza, 17–31 oktiabria 1961 goda*, 3 vols. (Moscow, 1962), 2:587; and for *Ivan Denisovich*, see Saraskina, *Aleksandr Solzhenitsyn*, pp. 480–98. It should be added that "only" Khrushchev's own daughter-in-law, as he put it, was in the Gulag, from 1943 to 1954. See Tatiana Rybakova, *"Schastlivaia ty, Tania!"* (Moscow, 2005), 261–63.

92. For the Beria trial, see *Lavrentii Beria 1953* (Moscow, 1999). Among the witnesses were Pikina, Snegov, and Suren Gazarian, who wrote a memoir account. See *SSSR: Vnutrennie protivorechiia* (New York), no. 6 (1982): 109–46. For the congress, see S. I. Chuprinin, ed., *Ottepel 1953–1956* (Moscow, 1989), 461; for the showdown, *Molotov, Malenkov, Kaganovich 1957* (Moscow, 1998); and for Lazurkina, *XXII sezd*, 3:121. Solzhenitsyn's novella appeared in *NM* in November 1962.

93. Iurii Trifonov, *Otblesk kostra* (Moscow, 1966), 86; and, similarly, Cohen, ed., *An End*, 29–30.

94. *Memoirs of Nikita Khrushchev*, 3 vols. (University Park, Penn., 2004–2007), 2:209; Georgii Ostroumov in *Proryv k svobode* (Moscow, 2005), 288, and, similarly, Evgenii Evtushenko in *Novaia*, Jan. 26–28, 2004.

95. Suren Gazarian, "Eto ne dolzhno povtoritsa" (samizdat manuscript, 1966); Eugenia Ginzburg, *Journey Into the Whirlwind* (New York, 1967), and *Within*; Kopelev, *To Be Preserved Forever* (New York, 1977), *The Education of a True Believer* (New York, 1980), and *Ease My Sorrows* (New York, 1983); Razgon, *True Stories*; Gnedin, *Katastrofa i vtoroe rozhdenie* (Amsterdam, 1977); Baitalsky, *Notebooks*.

96. See Shatunovskaia, *Ob ushedshem*, esp. 296–361, and the 1963 Shvernik Commission report, to which she was a major contributor, in *Reabilitatsiia*, 2:541–670. On Snegov, Khrushchev, *Khrushchev*, 9–10; and Mikoian, "Aleksei Snegov," 81–82. On Todorsky, see this chapter, n. 87; and Milchakov, *Molodost.*

97. Oleg Litskevich in *SM*, no. 6 (2008): 135–44. For lower-ranking examples, see Anatolii Rybakov, *Roman-vospominanie* (Moscow, 1997), 84

98. Trifonov, *Otblesk*; L. P. Petrovskii, *Petr Petrovskii* (Alma-Ata, Kazakhstan, 1974); Yakir, *Childhood*; and Ikramov, *Delo*. Under a pseudonym, Antonov-Ovseyenko published a censored biography of his father in 1975 and much later an uncensored edition: A. V. Rakitin, *V. A. Antonov-Ovseenko* (Leningrad, 1989). Yuri Gastev, a returnee whom I knew well, prepared a documented biography of his father in order to facilitate the latter's posthumous rehabilitation. He did so at the suggestion of the procurator's office. (For an interesting personal account of Gastev at about that time, see Valerii Rodos, *Ia—syn palacha* [Moscow, 2008], 534–61.) A number of published books and articles began that way. Several children of prominent victims were given prized slots for graduate study at history institutes, including Yakir and Petrovsky. For the generals' children, see Iurii Primakov in *Gorbachevskie chteniia*, no. 5 (Moscow, 2007), 191–92.

99. A recurring charge at the 1957 Central Committee meeting. See *Molotov, Malenkov, Kaganovich.*

100. See, e.g., Efimov in *Sotsialisticheskaia zakonnost*, no. 9 (1964): 42–45; and Lev Zaverin in *Soiuz*, no. 51 (1990): 9.

101. Quoted in Medvedev, *Khrushchev*, 84; for "fashion," see Vladimir Lakshin in *LG*, Aug. 17, 1994. Shatunovskaya, in her capacity as an official Party investigator, had personally interrogated Kaganovich, Malenkov, and Molotov about past crimes. Pomerants, *Sledstvie*, 12.

102. See Nikita Petrov, *Pervyi predsedatel KGB Ivan Serov* (Moscow, 2005); Shatunovskaia, *Ob ushedshem*, 285–91; also on Suslov, see Mikoian, "Aleksei Snegov"; and, similarly on Molotov, see *Golosa istorii*, 214. For the lists, see *Reabilitatsiia*, 3:144.

103. Among them, e.g., Konstantin Simonov, Tvardovsky, and Ehrenburg.

104. For those developments, see Efimov in *Sotsialisticheskaia zakonnost*, no. 9 (1964): 42–45; and Lev Zaverin in *Soiuz*, no. 51 (1990): 9; Aimermakher, ed., *Doklad*; *Reabilitatsiia*, vol. 2, section 3; and *Molotov, Malenkov, Kaganovich.* Many documents existed—and still exist today—incriminating Khrushchev and Mikoyan. See *Reabilitatsiia*, 3:146–47; V. P. Naumov in *VI*, no. 4 (1997): 19–35; and Anatolii Ponomarov in *Rodina*, no. 10 (1994): 82–88. For Khrushchev's enemies circulating them, see *Neizvestnaia Rossiia* (Moscow, 1992), 1:294–95. For the role of archive documents more generally at that time, see Medvedev and Medvedev, *Unknown Stalin*, chap. 3. For Khrushchev's own role in the terror, see Taubman, *Khrushchev*, chaps. 5–6. And for a recent anti-Khrushchev account, E. Prudnikova, *Khrushchev: Tvortsy terrora* (Moscow, 2007).

105. N. Barsukov, "Proval 'antipartiinoi gruppy,'" *Kommunist*, no. 8 (1990): 99.

106. See N. Barsukov, "Oborotnaia storona 'ottepeli,'" *Kentavr*, no. 4 (1993): 129–43; Evgenii Taranov, "'Raskachaem leninskie gory!'" *SM*, no. 10 (1993): 94–103; and *Reabilitatsiia*, 2:7. For the quotation, see Nikita Petrov in *NV*, no. 23 (2000): 33; and, similarly, Gazarian in *SSSR*.

107. *Molotov, Malenkov, Kaganovich.*

108. Ibid., 137.

109. The latter number is from V. P. Pirozhkov in *Nedelia*, no. 26 (1989), who also reports that 1,342 were tried. Nikita Petrov, whom I follow in this regard, effectively debunks the number tried, in N. G. Okhotin and A. B. Roginskii, eds., *Zvenia*, (Moscow, 1991), 1:430–36. For the number executed, see Iu. S. Novopashin in *VI*, no. 5 (2007): 54–55; and for one executed hangman and the fate of his family, Rodos, *Ia—syn palacha*. For examples of the various punishments, see Kokurin and Petrov, "MVD," 114–18; and Robert Conquest, *Inside Stalin's Secret Police* (Stanford, Calif., 1985), 155–57.

110. Kokurin and Petrov, "MVD"; Aleksandr Kokurin, "GULAG," *SM*, no. 2 (2002): 98; *Aleksandr Fadeev* (Moscow, 2001) (and, similarly, Burlatsky, *Khrushchev*, 18); and Medvedev and Medvedev, *Unknown Stalin*, 116–17.

111. Khrushchev, cited in Medvedev, *Khrushchev*, 99 (and, similarly in Shatunovskaia, *Ob ushedshem*, 286); Gorbachev in *V politbiuro TsK KPSS: Po zapisiam Anatoliia Cherniaeva, Vadima Medvedeva, Georgiia Shakhnazarova (1985–1991)* (Moscow, 2006), 323–24; and Khrushchev, quoted by Mikhail Shatrov in *SM*, no. 10 (1994)_: 22. For his vulnerable position, see Khrushchev, *Khrushchev on Khrushchev*, 14.

112. Saraskina, *Aleksandr Solzhenitsyn*, 478. All quotes are from the proceedings, *XXII sezd*, vol. 3.

113. Shatunovskaia, *Ob ushedshem*, 297–300. For the final report, see *Reabilitatsiia*, 2:541–670.

114. I borrow the phrase from Vladimir Lakshin, "Ivan Denisovich, ego druzia i nedrugi," *NM*, no. 1 (1964).

115. *Den poezii 1962* (Moscow, 1962), 45. I remain grateful to the late Professor Vera Dunham, who located and translated the poem. For a list of other examples, see Cohen, *Rethinking*, 199n. 65; and the sources in this chapter, n. 82.

116. *Politicheskii dnevnik*, (Amsterdam, 1975), 2:123; and, similarly, Medvedev and Medvedev, *Unknown Stalin*, 116–17. For the cases, see N.N., "Donoschiki"; Cohen, ed., *An End*, 124–32, and generally, chap. 2. When Yudin died in 1968, official obituaries noted only his "long and glorious career" (*CDSP*, May 1, 1968, 39).

117. Read comparatively, e.g., the reviews of *Ivan Denisovich*, Iurii Bondarev; "Tishina," *NM*, nos. 3–5 (1962); and Diakov's memoirs, *Povest*, which began appearing in 1963. See also Lakshin, "Ivan Denisovich."

118. See the exchange between Ehrenburg and Viktor Ermilov in *Izvestiia*, Jan. 30 and Feb. 6, 1963; for Khrushchev, Taubman, *Khrushchev*, 596; and the anonymous letter from a Russian writer in *Encounter* (June 1964): 88–98.

119. See, e.g., E. Genri, "Chuma na ekrane," *Iunost*, no. 6 (1966), and his comments on a related Soviet film, *Ordinary Fascism*, in *NM*, no. 12 (1965); Fedor Burlatskii in *Pravda*, Feb. 14, 1966; Evgenii Gnedin, "Biurokratiia dvadtsatogo veka," *NM*, no. 3 (1966), and his "Mekhanizm fashistskoi diktatury," *NM*, no. 8 (1968); *Politicheskii dnevnik*, 2:109–22; and, similarly, Adler, *Gulag Survivor*, 194.

120. *Politicheskii dnevnik*, 2:123.

121. As I frequently heard from Russians who knew or studied them.

122. Translated by George Reavey, *The Poetry of Yevgeny Yevtushenko, 1953 to 1965* (London, 1966), 161–65. The poem appeared in *Pravda*, Oct. 21, 1962. On the same point, see Z. L. Serebriakova in *Gorbachevskie chteniia*, no. 4 (Moscow, 2006), 96.

123. For Snegov, Shatunovskaya, and the report, see *Reabilitatsiia*, 2:524; and Shatunovskaia, *Ob ushedshem*, 291. For the editorial and constitution, see Burlatsky, *Khrushchev*, 200–201, 215; and G. L. Smirnov's memoir in *Neizvestnaia Rossiia*, (Moscow, 1993), 3:377–81.

124. For the overthrow, and a somewhat different interpretation, see Taubman, *Khrushchev*, chap. 1; for the shift, Cohen, *Rethinking*, chap. 5; and for Solzhenitsyn, Saraskina, *Aleksandr Solzhenitsyn*, 525. A Russian scholar thinks the people behind Khrushchev's ouster "didn't mention the real reason." See Serebriakova, cited this chapter, n. 122.

125. Quoted in Taubman, *Khrushchev*, 14. For Suslov, see *Istochnik*, no. 2 (1996): 115; and for the proceedings, *Nikita Khrushchev 1964: stenogrammy plenuma TSK KPSS i drugie dokumenty* (Moscow, 2007).

126. Medvedev, *Khrushchev*, 98, gives a somewhat different version and dates it later than did my informants. Similarly, Party bosses were now heard to say: "Far too many were rehabilitated" (Solzhenitsyn, *Gulag*, 3:451). For neo-Stalinism after 1964, see Cohen, *Rethinking*, chap. 4; for Beria's men, O. Volin in *Sovershenno sekretno*, no. 6 (1989): 18; and for Solzhenitsyn, Saraskina, *Aleksandr Solzhenitsyn*, 535.

127. *Reabilitatsiia*, 2:5; Applebaum, *Gulag*, 557.

128. For the two episodes, see *Kremlevskii samosud* (Moscow, 1994), 209, 361; and *Reabilitatsiia*, 2:538–40. In 1966, Suslov labeled Snegov a "blackmailer" (*shantazhist*), which suggests Snegov may have had documents incriminating Suslov. See *Reabilitatsiia*, 2:510, and for the subsequent persecution of Snegov, 2:521–25.

129. Adler, *Gulag Survivor*, 196–97. For several "hangmen," see Antonov-Ovseenko, *Portret*; N. V. Petrov and K. V. Skorkin, *Kto rukovodil NKVD* (Moscow, 1999); and *Molotov, Malenkov, Kaganovich*. 137. For Sheinin, whose role in the terror is clear from documents I read in the Lubyanka archive and is recounted in Arkady Vaksberg, *Stalin's Prosecutor: The Life of Andrei Vyshinsky* (New York, 1991), see his *Zapisky sledovatelia* (Moscow, 1980) and his obituary in *Izvestiia*, May 31, 1967, both of which omit his Stalinist past. For one such former Gulag region, see *Pechorskii ugolnyi bassein* (Syktyvkar, 1957). According to Antonov-Ovseyenko, who was a zek in the region's Kolyma camp, most of the volume's editors and contributors had been camp bosses.

130. Antonov-Ovseyenko, *Time of Stalin*, xviii; Rodos, *Ia—syn palacha*, 344.

131. For Trifonov, whose *House on the Embankment* (1976) and *The Old Man* (1978) were especially important, see *NYT*, Dec. 16, 1979; and for Shatrov, the interview in *Figury i litsa*, no. 7, supplement in *NG*, April 13, 2000, and *Shatrov: tvorchestvo, zhizn, dokumenty*, 5 vols. (Moscow, 2006–2007).

132. Elena Bonner's father was executed and her mother, Ruth Bonner, freed under Khrushchev.

133. For Nuremberg, see, e.g., Vitalii Shentalinskii in *KP*, Oct. 17, 1990; and G. Z. Ioffe, looking back, in *OI*, no. 4 (2002): 164. For the "trial of Stalin," A. Samsonov in *Nedelia*, no. 52 (1988); the special issue of *MN*, Nov. 27, 1988; and Iurii Solomonov in *SK*, Sept. 9, 1989. And for the Memorial Society, Nanci Adler, *Victims of Stalin's Terror* (Westport, Conn., 1993).

134. For Aleksandr Milchakov's investigative articles, which appeared regularly in the press, see the interviews in *Izvestiia*, Nov. 11, 1988, and in *Vecherniaia Moskva*, April 14, 1990. For "hangmen on pension," see the stories in *Moscow News*, nos. 19, 28, 42 (1988), and nos. 10, 37 (1990); and *KP*, Dec. 8, 1989. For "martyrology," *Istoriia SSSR*, no. 3 (1988): 52.

135. As I heard repeatedly. Similarly, see, e.g., Iurii Orlik in *Izvestiia*, March 3, 1989; Shatunovskaia, *Ob ushedshem*, 430; and even Akhmatova, quoted by N. B. Ivanova in *Gorbachevskie chteniia*, no. 4, 81.

136. *Reabilitatsiia*, 3:507, 521–22. For the quote, see Orlik in *Izvestiia*, March 3, 1989.

137. Mikhail Gorbachev, *Zhizn i reformy* (Moscow, 1995), 1:38–42. Others in the leadership included Yegor Ligachev and Eduard Shevardnadze, whose wives' fathers had perished. For the charge, see the letter in *Izvestiia*, May 7, 1992; and, similarly, Vladimir Karpov's complaint about "rehabilitation euphoria," quoted by Zhanna Kasianenko in *SR*, July 27, 2002.

138. *Reabilitatsiia*, 3:7–8. For the SOS, see *KP*, Sept. 26, 1990; and for the dacha, Chelishcheva in "Pravda GULAGa."

139. *Reabilitatsiia*, 3:600–606; Adler, *Gulag Survivor*, 33. For the post-Soviet period generally, see Adler, *Gulag Survivor*, chap. 7; and Nanci Adler, "The Future of the Soviet Past Remains Unpredictable," *EAS* (Dec. 2005): 1093–119.

140. B.S. in *NG*, Sept. 21, 1993. More generally, see *Mir posle Gulaga*. A returnee who headed a Moscow city commission on rehabilitations in the early 1990s recalled that benefits were a "huge problem." A. Feldman, *Riadovoe delo* (Moscow, 1993), 58–60.

141. See, respectively, *Reabilitatsiia*, 3:507, 521–22; Leonid Goldenmauer in *KO*, no. 40 (2003): 7; A. T. Rybin, *Stalin v oktiabre 1941 g.* (Moscow, 1995), 5. And, similarly, see Evgenii Strigin, *Predavshie SSSR* (Moscow, 2005), 181–85; and Sigizmund Mironin, *Stalinskii poriadok* (Moscow, 2007).

142. Three examples of such volumes: *Reabilitatsiia*, vols. 1–3; *Deti GULAGa; 1937–1938 gg.: Operatsii NKVD* (Tomsk-Moscow, 2006). For an overview of Gulag-related monuments, museums, and other remembrances, see Arsenii Roginskii in *Novaia*, Dec. 11, 2008. In 2006, a former head of the KGB/FSB presented a literary award to a former zek, the poet Naum Korzhavin, and invited him to speak at its headquarters (*KO*, no. 48 [2006]: 4).

143. See, respectively, kremlin.ru, June 21, 2007, and Peter Finn in *WP*, July 20, 2007; Reuters dispatch, Nov. 2, 2000; *Der Spiegel* interview with Solzhenitsyn in *JRL*, July 24, 2007, which includes his favorable opinion of Putin; and kremlin.ru, Oct. 20, 2007, along with Itar-Tass dispatch the same day. The textbook was A. V. Filippov, *Noveishaia istoriia Rossii, 1945–2006 gg.* (Moscow, 2007), 81–94.

144. See, e.g., the special supplement in *Novaia*, Feb. 21–27, 2008; *55-i godovshchine so dnia smerti I.V. Stalina posviashchaetsia* (Moscow, 2008), 136; and Fillipov, *Noveishaia istoriia*, 93.

145. In 2006, an editor emphasized that the conflict between "two Russias," described by Akhmatova in 1956 and quoted earlier in this chapter, "has not been settled to this day" (*Gorbachevskie chteniia*, no. 4, 81). And in 1993, Memorial Society editors wrote: "The past, which left its traces on the lives of a majority of us . . . has not ended" (*Memorial-Aspekt* [June 1993]). For the open letter, see "Pravda GULAGa," *Novaia*, Dec. 4–7, 2008.

146. As a credential for this prediction, I take the immodest liberty of pointing out that I reached the same analytical conclusion before Gorbachev came to power. See Cohen, ed., *An End*, 22–50; and Cohen, *Rethinking*, chaps. 4–5.

147. Cited by Paul Goble in *JRL*, Feb. 24, 2006. For examples of grandchildren, in addition to Gorbachev, see V. V. Obolenskii's letter in *Ogonek*, no. 24 (1987): 6; Efim Fattakhov in *Sobesednik*, no. 21 (1989); and I. Shcherbakova, ed., *Kak nashikh dedov zabirali* (Moscow, 2007).

3. THE TRAGEDY OF SOVIET CONSERVATISM

1. After Gorbachev, Ligachev probably was the most written about political figure of the perestroika years, at least until the rise of Yeltsin. The standard version of his role appeared in most of the journalistic accounts. For scholarly studies, see Jonathan Harris, *Ligachev on Glasnost and Perestroika*, University of Pittsburgh Center for Russian and East European Studies, No. 706 (Pittsburgh, 1989); Baruch A. Hazan, *Gorbachev and His Enemies* (Boulder, Colo., 1990); and Jeffrey Surovell, "Ligachev and Soviet Politics," *SS*, no. 2 (1991): 335–74. The last goes to the other extreme, presenting a Ligachev without any real political or ideological differences with Gorbachev.

2. E. K. Ligachev, *Zagadka Gorbacheva* (Novosibirsk, 1992); Yegor Ligachev, *Inside Gorbachev's Kremlin* (New York, 1993).

3. On *Repentance* and Afghanistan, see Eduard Shevardnadze, *The Future Belongs to Freedom* (New York, 1991), 173; and the interview with Shevardnadze in *NG*, Nov. 21, 1991. For Eastern Europe, see the account of Ligachev's trip to Hungary in *WP*, April 26, 1987.

4. See, e.g., Nursultan Nazarbaev, *Bez pravykh i levykh* (Moscow, 1991), 165–66; Vadim Bakatin in *Sovershenno sekretno*, no. 10 (1991); Shevardnadze in *NG*, Nov. 21, 1991; and the interview with Abel Aganbegyan in *New Perspectives Quarterly* (Winter 1988–89): 28. On the other hand, for two leaders with nothing good to say about Ligachev, see Boris Yeltsin, *Against the Grain* (New York, 1990); and Anatoly Sobchak, *For a New Russia* (New York, 1992), though Sobchak says Ligachev "was sincerely convinced that he was in the right" (47). For a highly critical but in some ways empathetic portrait by a Soviet liberal journalist, see Vitalii Tretiakov, *Gorbachev, Ligachev, Yeltsin* (Moscow, 1990), 31–41.

5. See the accounts cited in the preceding note.

6. David Remnick in *WP*, October 15, 1990. For a different, negative impression, see Svetlana Allilueva in *Dialog*, no. 8 (1991): 109–10.

7. Before Ligachev, only two former Soviet leaders had published memoirs, but both did so abroad. Leon Trotsky's *My Life*, which he published in exile in 1930, said very little about actual leadership politics. And Khrushchev's memoirs, dictated in retirement to family members, first appeared in the United States in 1970 and in full in Russia only in 1999. For the full English-language edition, see *Memoirs of Nikita Khrushchev*, 3 vols. (University Park, Penn., 2004–2007). Ligachev completed his book before the Soviet Union ended in December 1991, and sections began to appear in the Soviet press in 1990. Nikolai Ryzhkov, also a member of the Gorbachev's top leadership, published his memoirs (*Perestroika: istoriia predatelstva*) in Mos-

cow later in 1992; and Gorbachev's appeared in Moscow in 1995, in two volumes, as *Zhizn i reformy.*

8. Andrei Gromyko, *Memoirs* (New York, 1990); Shevardnadze, *The Future*; and Yeltsin, *Against the Grain.* The Russian-language title of Yeltsin's book was *Confessions on an Assigned Subject.*

9. Aleksandr Bovin, who commented similarly in Stephen F. Cohen and Katrina vanden Heuvel, *Voices of Glasnost: Interviews with Gorbachev's Reformers* (New York, 1989), 225.

10. See interview with Abel Aganbegyan in *New Perspectives Quarterly* (Winter 1988–89): 28.

11. The pioneering study in this regard was Jerry F. Hough, *The Soviet Prefects* (Cambridge, Mass., 1969).

12. *XIX vsesoiuznaia konferentsiia kommunisticheskoi partii Sovetskogo Soiuza: stenograficheskii otchet* (Moscow, 1988), 2:84–85.

13. In Iurii Afanasev, ed., *Inogo ne dano* (Moscow, 1988), 125.

14. I heard such murmurings in Moscow in 1988. They were in print regularly by 1990. A former Ligachev aide later extended the argument back to 1985, though Ligachev never publicly embraced it. See the series of articles by Valerii Legostaev in *Den*, nos. 13–16 (1991).

15. For a fuller analysis, see Stephen F. Cohen, *Rethinking the Soviet Experience: Politics and History Since 1917* (New York, 1985), chap. 5.

16. *Pravda*, Feb. 14, 1988, and May 8 and Dec. 31, 1989. For "multiparty-ness," see, e.g., Kirill Gusev in *Nedelia*, no. 15 (1988); and L. Shevtsova in *Izvestiia*, Feb. 27, 1990. These and many other subsequent Soviet statements confirmed an analysis I first presented in 1978, which was frequently dismissed by other Western Sovietologists. See Stephen F. Cohen, Alexander Rabinowitch, and Robert Sharlet, eds., *The Soviet Union Since Stalin* (Bloomington, Ind., 1980), 16.

17. Aleksandr Galkin, "Blizok li kriticheskii chas?" *Poisk*, Dec. 28, 1989.

18. For English translations of Gorbachev's increasingly explicit "humane democratic socialism," see Mikhail Gorbachev, *The Socialist Idea and Revolutionary Perestroika* (Moscow, 1990), which first appeared in 1989; *Towards a Humane and Democratic Socialist Society: Report by Mikhail Gorbachev* (Moscow, 1990); and the materials published in *CDSP*, nos. 30–31 (1991). The best scholarly works on this subject are Archie Brown, *The Gorbachev Factor* (New York, 1996) and his *Seven Years That Changed the World* (New York, 2007).

19. *Materialy plenuma tsentralnogo komiteta KPSS: 25 aprelia 1989 goda* (Moscow, 1989), 71.

20. Quoted in Angus Roxburgh, *The Second Russian Revolution* (London, 1991), 80.

21. Ivan Polozkov in *SR*, March 7, 1991; and, similarly, in *LR*, June 29 1990, where he remarks that "no civilized country can manage without conservatives."

22. For the congress, see *XXVIII sezd kommunisticheskoi partii Sovetskogo Soiuza: stenograficheskii otchet*, 2 vols. (Moscow, 1991). Only 776 of the 4,035 delegates voted for him. Talking with delegates during the congress, and later reading their speeches, I had a strong sense that the majority preferred Ligachev's views to Gorbachev's. Why they nonetheless supported Gorbachev's candidate is a separate and complicated story, part of it being that they still feared political life without him.

23. I persuaded him to change the title for the English-language edition to *Inside Gorbachev's Kremlin*. See this chapter, n. 2; and for the second Russian edition, E. K. Ligachev, *Predosterezhenie* (Moscow, 1998).

24. A popular documentary film about the conference, titled *Pluralism*, clearly conveyed the point. Soon after the conference, Moscow's flea markets began featuring political buttons that proclaimed, "Tell Them—Boris!" and "Yegor—You're Wrong!"

25. See, for example, John Gooding, "Gorbachev and Democracy," *SS*, no. 2 (1990): 195–231; and Brown, *The Gorbachev Factor*.

26. Valerii Legostaev in *Zavtra*, no. 52 (Dec. 2000).

27. Based on a memoir account published in 1991 and private remarks by Aleksandr Yakovlev, David Remnick later concluded that Ligachev had in fact been behind the publication of Andreyeva's article and had "lied like a thief" about it (*NYRB*, March 25, 1993, 34–38). Possibly, but such accounts in 1991 usually had the purpose of discrediting Communist Party officials like Ligachev, and the charge did not appear in a posthumous volume of Yakovlev's unpublished remarks, letters, and memorandums. See Aleksandr Iakovlev, *Perestroika: 1985–1991* (Moscow, 2008). Nor is there conclusive evidence in the private notes made by Gorbachev's aides on Politburo disputes, though Ligachev is recorded as having said he liked the article and saw it before it was published. See *V Politburo TsK KPSS . . .* (Moscow, 2006), and for Ligachev, 307–8.

28. *Izvestiia*, Oct. 23, 1991.

29. For his report on his work in the Duma, see Egor Ligachev, *Otchet deputata* (Tomsk, 2003).

30. See e.g., his articles in *SR*, Dec. 18, 1997; Dec 27, 2003; Nov. 26, 2005; April 30, 2008; and his *Nasha tsel—sozidanie* (Tomsk, 2002).

31. Legostaev in *Zavtra*, no. 52.

32. Ibid.

33. Quoted by Remnick in *WP*, Oct. 15, 1990.

4. WAS THE SOVIET SYSTEM REFORMABLE?

1. Richard Sakwa, *Gorbachev and His Reforms, 1985–1990* (Englewood Cliffs, N.J., 1991), 357; and Ed A. Hewett in Alexander Dallin and Gail W. Lapidus eds., *The Soviet System*, rev. ed. (Boulder, Colo., 1995), 320. For examples of other works that assumed the system's reformability at the time, see R. V. Daniels, *Is Russia Reformable?* (Boulder, Colo., 1988); Barrington Moore Jr., *Liberal Prospects Under Soviet Socialism* (New York, 1989); George W. Breslauer, ed., *Can Gorbachev's Reforms Succeed?* (Berkeley, 1990); Stephen White, *Gorbachev in Power* (New York, 1990); Robert T. Huber and Donald R. Kelley, eds., *Perestroika-Era Politics* (Armonk, N.Y., 1991); Eugene Huskey, ed., *Executive Power and Soviet Politics* (Armonk, N.Y., 1992); Michael E. Urban, *More Power to the Soviets* (Brookfield, Vt., 1990); Jerry F. Hough, *Russia and the West*, 2nd ed. (New York, 1990); Graham Allison and Gregory Yavlinsky, *Window of Opportunity* (New York, 1991), esp. chaps. 1–2; and the authors cited in Jan Hallenberg, *The Demise of the Soviet Union* (Burlington, Vt., 2002), 177–86, 195, and by David Rowley in *Kritika* (Spring 2001): 414n. 9. For the U.S. government, see Michael R. Beschloss and Strobe Talbott, *At the Highest Levels* (Boston, 1993), chaps. 16–21; and Jack F. Matlock Jr., *Reagan and Gorbachev* (New York, 2004).

2. See, respectively, Anders Åslund, *How Russia Became a Market Economy* (Washington, D.C., 1995), 31 and chap. 2; M. Steven Fish, *Democracy from Scratch* (Princeton, N.J., 1995), 3; Michael Dobbs in *WP*, Dec. 15 1991; Beryl Williams in *RR* (Jan. 1997): 143; and David Saunders in *EAS* (July 1996): 868. Similarly, see Martin Malia, *The Soviet Tragedy* (New York, 1994); Fred Coleman, *The Decline and Fall of the Soviet Empire* (New York, 1996), xii, xv, xvi; Alec Nove, *The Soviet System in Retrospect* (New York, 1993), 7; Richard Pipes, *Communism* (London, 1994), 39; Wisła Suraska, *How the Soviet Union Disappeared* (Durham, N.C., 1998); Valerie Bunce, *Subversive Institutions* (New York, 1999), 37; Fritz W. Ermarth in *National Interest* (Spring 1999): 5; Stephen Kotkin, *Armageddon Averted* (New York, 2001), 181; Mark R. Beissinger, *Nationalist Mobilization and the Collapse of the Soviet State* (New York, 2002), 390; Katerina Clark and Evgeny Dobrenko, *Soviet Culture and Power* (New Haven, Conn., 2007), x; and Adam Ulam in *TLS*, Nov. 6, 1992. For notable exceptions, see Dallin in Dallin and Lapidus, eds., *The Soviet System*, chap. 58; David M. Kotz and Fred Weir, *Revolution from Above* (New York, 1997); Ronald Grigor Suny, *The Revenge of the Past* (Stanford, Calif., 1993); Archie Brown, *The Gorbachev Factor* (New York, 1997); Jerry F. Hough, *Democratization and Revolution in the USSR* (Washington, D.C., 1997); and Peter Reddaway and Dmitri Glinski, *The Tragedy of Russia's Reforms* (Washington, D.C., 2001). For an early but different

approach to this issue, see Alexander Dallin in Robert O. Crummey, ed., *Reform in Russia and the USSR* (Urbana, Ill., 1989), 243–56. And for an interesting treatment of the question from inside the political culture of Communist systems, see Zdeněk Mlynář, *Can Gorbachev Change the Soviet Union?* (Boulder, Colo., 1990).

3. Martin Malia in *Daedalus* (Spring 1992): 60; Alain Besançon in G. R. Urban, ed., *Can the Soviet System Survive Reform?* (London, 1989), 202; and A. M. Rosenthal in *NYT*, May 21, 1991.

4. Malia, *Soviet Tragedy*, 3, 5; Malia in Stéphane Courtoise et. al., *The Black Book of Communism* (Cambridge, Mass., 1999), xx; Malia in *Bulletin of the American Academy of Arts and Sciences* (November 1990): 8; Malia in Dallin and Lapidus, eds., *Soviet System*, 667; and Tony Barber in *FT*, Jan. 27, 2007, citing Malia. Similarly, see David Satter, *The Age of Delirium* (New York, 1996); Terry McNeill in Michael Cox, ed., *Rethinking the Soviet Collapse* (New York, 1998), 68; Daniel Chirot on "utter moral rot," as quoted in Philip G. Roeder, *Red Sunset* (Princeton, N.J., 1993), 15; the related examples cited by Rowley in *Kritika* (Spring 2001): 400n. 11; and Vladimir Brovkin's rendering of the views of Richard Pipes in *JCWS* (Winter 2006): 127–32. Even an admirer of Malia is troubled by his reliance on "an original sin of biblical proportions." Yanni Kotsonis in *RR* (Jan. 1999): 126. For a systematic critique of Malia's "essentialist" explanation, see Dallin in Dallin and Lapidus, eds., *The Soviet System*, chap. 58.

5. For these facts, see David Brion Davis in *NYT*, August 26, 2001; and Brent Staples in *NYT*, January 9, 2000. For these opinions, see, respectively, George W. Bush, who cites Adams, quoted by Richard W. Stevenson in *NYT* July 9, 2003; and the historian Steven Mintz, "A Slave-Narrative Documentary Is Limited, but Compelling," *Chronicle*, Feb. 7, 2003, B16. For "accursed thing," see the discussion by Stephen Hahn in *NR*, April 23, 2008, 51. For Reagan, see Raymond L. Garthoff, *The Great Transition* (Washington, D.C., 1994), 352.

6. The quotes are from Michael Dobbs in *WP Magazine*, June 9, 1996, 29; and Dusko Doder in *WP Book World*, March 22, 1998. Similarly, see Malia, *Soviet Tragedy*, 492; Michael McFaul in Andrew C. Kuchins, ed., *Russia After the Fall* (Washington, D.C., 2002), 27; Stephen White in *Slavic Review* (Summer 2002): 421; Beissinger, *Nationalist Mobilization*, 4, 341; Jack F. Matlock Jr., *Autopsy on an Empire* (New York, 1995), 293; Peter Kenez in *Kritika* (Spring 2003): 369. A critic of this kind of history writing, Reinhard Bendix, cited in the next note, calls it "hindsight bias." Historical opinion about the tsarist reforms of the nineteenth century and the fate of that system is an instructive analogy: "The collapse of the Tsarist autocracy in 1917 is no longer seen as proof incontestable of the ultimate or inevitable failure

of these reforms" (Ben Ekloff in Ekloff et al., eds., *Russia's Great Reforms, 1855–1881* [Bloomington, Ind., 1994], x).

7. For the fallacy and bias, see Reinhard Bendix quoted by Dallin in Dallin and Lapidus, eds., *The Soviet System*, 688. Mark Almond makes the first point in Niall Ferguson, ed., *Virtual History* (London, 1997), 392. There is also the truly silly triumphalism inspiring a well-known writer to tell us in 2008 that while he was there in 1982, as an "ignorant, neophyte" correspondent, he "did notice that the Soviet Union was on the verge of economic and social collapse" (P. J. O'Rourke in *WS*, Dec. 31, 2007/Jan. 7, 2008, 34).

8. For some exceptions, see George W. Breslauer, *Gorbachev and Yeltsin as Leaders* (New York, 2002), 266–70; Henry E. Hale, "Ethnofederalism and Theories of Secession" (unpublished manuscript, June 2001); Mark. R. Beissinger in *Slavic Review* (Summer 2006): 301; and especially, Hough, *Democratization*, which examines a number of the questions raised here. For other fields, see, e.g., Philip E. Tetlock and Aaron Belkin, eds., *Counterfactual Thought Experiments in World Politics* (Princeton, N.J., 1996); Ferguson, ed., *Virtual History*; Robert Crowley, ed., *What If?* (New York, 1999); and Andrew Roberts, ed., *What Might Have Been* (London, 2004). And for a vigorous defense of counterfactual reasoning in general, see Martin Bunzl in *AHR* (June 2004): 845–58.

9. For the quotes, see, respectively, Carolyn McGiffert Ekedakl and Melvin A. Goodman, *The Wars of Eduard Shevardnadze* (University Park, Penn., 1997), 50; Giulietto Chiesa, *Transition to Democracy* (Hanover, N.H., 1993), 203; and Peter Rutland in Cox, ed., *Rethinking the Soviet Collapse*, 43. For different versions of the institutional thesis, see Roeder, *Red Sunset*; Bunce, *Subversive Institutions*; and Richard Sakwa in Stephen White et al., eds., *Developments in Russian Politics 4* (Durham, N.C., 1997), 16, who writes: "The polity itself was incapable of reform." On the other hand, one scholar of the Soviet breakup concludes that it happened not because of the "rigidity" of the institutions but because they were "too flexible" (Steven L. Solnick, *Stealing the Soviet State* [Cambridge, Mass., 1998], 223).

10. R. Karklin quoted approvingly in John Keep, *Last of the Empires* (New York, 1995), 416. Similarly, see Robert Conquest quoted in Brown, *Gorbachev*, 252; Kotkin, *Armageddon*, 71–73; and Anthony D'Agostino, *Gorbachev's Revolution* (New York, 1998), 172. The argument is explicit or implicit in many books. See, e.g., Fish, *Democracy*; Nicolai N. Petro, *The Rebirth of Russian Democracy* (Cambridge, 1995); Michael Urban, *The Rebirth of Politics in Russia* (New York, 1997); Malia, *Soviet Tragedy*; Coleman, *The Decline and Fall*; John B. Dunlop, *The Rise of Russia and the Fall of the Soviet Empire* (Princeton, N.J., 1993); and Michael McFaul, *Russia's Unfinished Revolution* (Ithaca, N.Y., 2001). There is also the different but related view

that democratization was incompatible not only with the Soviet system but Russia's general traditions of governance. See, e.g., Theodore H. von Laue in Joseph L. Wieczynski, ed., *The Gorbachev Reader* (Salt Lake City, 1993), 149–51; and Walter M. Pinter in Crummey, ed., *Reform*, 243–56.

11. See, respectively, R. Karklins quoted in Kotz and Weir, *Revolution from Above*, 239n. 9; Michael Wines in *NYT*, Jan. 9, 2000; Fish, *Democracy*, 3, 51; Stephen Kotkin in *RR* (Jan. 2002): 50; and George Kennan quoted by Thomas L. Friedman in *NYT*, May 2, 1998. Similarly, see Joel C. Moses in *SS*, no. 3 (1992): 479; Malia in *Daedalus* (Spring 1992): 57–75; Thomas F. Remington in Robert V. Daniels, ed., *Soviet Communism from Reform to Collapse* (Lexington, Mass., 1995), 330–39; Leslie Holmes, *Post-Communism* (Durham, N.C., 1997), 57, 130–31; D' Agostino, *Gorbachev's Revolution*, 5; Michael McFaul in *San Francisco Chronicle*, June 13, 2004; Graham Allison in *BG*, Dec. 26, 2005; Leon Aron in *Demokratizatsiya* (Summer 2005): 435–59; the authors discussed by Rowley in *Kritika* (Spring 2001): 403–6; and the single-authored books cited in the preceding note. Looking back at that period, President Vladimir Putin of Russia gave a different interpretation of events: "Let's proceed from reality. Democracy in Russia was in fact issued from above" (*Izvestiia,* July 14, 2000). For an alleged defection from Soviet socialism, see also Åslund, *How Russia*, 51–52; and Michael McFaul in *WP*, Sept. 22, 2001. Few Russian historians think that democratization killed the system. See, e.g., T. E. Vorozheikina in *ONS*, no. 5 (2005): 21–22. For several who do, see V. Sogrin, *Politicheskaia istoriia sovremennoi Rossii, 1985–1994* (Moscow, 1994), 107, and in *OI*, no. 3 (2005): 8–9; R. G. Pikhoia in G. N. Sevostianov, ed., *Rossiia v XX veke*, 2 vols. (Moscow, 2002), 1:130, 143; and Aleksandr Tsipko in *VA*, no. 3 (2006): 209. For Western scholars who dissent from the notion of a revolution from below, see Kotz and Weir, *Revolution*; Hough, *Democratization*; Reddaway and Glinski, *Tragedy*, chaps. 3–4; Judith Devlin, *The Rise of the Russian Democrats* (Brookfield, Vt., 1995); Peter Rutland in *Transitions* (Feb. 1998): 16–17; Gordon M. Hahn, *Russia's Revolution from Above* (New Brunswick, N.J., 2002); and Walter D. Connor in *JCWS* (Fall 2003): 75.

12. A. S. Barsenkov, *Vvedenie v sovremennuiu rossiiskuiu istoriiu* (Moscow, 2002), 326; and Interfax report in *JRL*, April 20, 2007. A British specialist reached the same conclusion: "Russians, it seemed, wanted a 'socialism that worked'" (Stephen White, *Communism and Its Collapse* [New York, 2001], 75). In an opinion poll taken in late 1990, two-thirds of those surveyed still favored socialism (*Izvestiia TsK KPSS*, no. 2 [1991]: 51). Similarly, see M. K. Gorshkov in *Sociological Research* (Nov.–Dec. 2005): 72. For opinion on economic-social features of the system, see Matthew Wyman, *Public Opinion in Postcommunist Russia* (New York, 1997), chap. 7; the sur-

vey data collected in Iu. A. Levada, ed., *Est mnenie!* (Moscow, 1990), and his *Sovetskii prostoi chelovek* (Moscow, 1993); and even the data presented by a colleague of the anti-Soviet "shock-therapy" team that subsequently came to power, Tatiana Koval, in Yegor Gaidar, ed., *The Economics of Transition* (Cambridge, Mass., 2003), chap. 25. A number of Western scholars have also used detailed polling data to make similar and related points. See, e.g., Kotz and Weir, *Revolution*, 137–39; Hough, *Democratization*, 471; James R. Millar in Millar and Sharon L. Wolchik, eds., *The Social Legacy of Communism* (Washington, D.C., 1994), 5–7; Vladimir Shlapentokh, *A Normal Totalitarian Society* (Armonk, N.Y., 2001), 125, 208, 281n. 1; and Reddaway and Glinski, *Tragedy*, 92–94, 154. For an opposing view that only 10 to 20 percent of Soviet citizens "still supported the 'socialist choice,'" but without any evidence, see Leon Aron in *WP*, Dec. 24, 2006.

13. Wyman, *Public Opinion*, chap. 6; *RFE/RL*, March 16, 2001; I. V. Zadorin in *Gorbachevskie chteniia*, no. 3 (Moscow, 2005), 39. Less than a year after the breakup, two-thirds of those surveyed regretted it even in pro-Yeltsin Moscow (*Izvestiia*, Oct. 6, 1992). Alexei Yurchak, *Everything Was Forever, Until It Was No More* (Princeton, N.J., 2006) argues otherwise, but based on little empirical evidence, only personal experience and a few theoretical and literary models. For Yeltsin, see the pro-Soviet first edition of his autobiographical book, *Ispoved na zadannuiu temu* (Sverdlovsk, 1990); his presidential campaign speech in *FBIS*, June 3, 1991, 71–79; Mikhail Chelnokov, *Rossiia bez soiuza, Rossiia bez Rossii* (Moscow, 1994), 30–32; and Hough, *Democratization*, 279, 308, 333–34. Similarly, a member of the most radical prodemocracy group at the 1989 Congress, which included Yeltsin, later recalled that its struggle was "not against the USSR" (Iurii Boldyrev in *LG*, Jan 17–25, 2007).

14. Alexander Lebed, *My Life and My Country* (Washington, D.C., 1997), 321; Rodric Braithwaite, *Across the Moscow River* (New Haven, Conn., 2002), 242; Elem Klimov in *OG*, Aug. 23–29, 2001. Similarly, see Oleg Poptsov, *Khronika vremen "Tsaria Borisa"* (Moscow, 1995), 261; G. E. Burbulis in *Izvestiia*, Oct. 26, 1991; Aleksandr Tsipko in *LG* Dec. 20, 2006; Jonathan Steele, *Eternal Russia* (Cambridge, 1994), chap. 4; and Mark Kramer in *JCWS* (Fall 2003): 9. For a few of the many claims of an "August Revolution," see Peter Kenez in *The New Leader*, Sept. 9–23, 1991, 15–18; Martin Malia in *NYRB*, Sept. 26, 1991, 22–28, and in *PC* (Jan.–April 1992): 93; Anatole Shub in *PC* (Nov.–Dec. 1991): 20; John Gooding, *Rulers and Subjects* (London, 1996), 337–39; Leon Aron, *Yeltsin* (New York, 2000), chap. 10; Michael McFaul in Kuchins, ed., *Russia*, 27; and Urban, *Rebirth*, 252, who sees a "national resistance." For an exhaustive but unconvincing argument on behalf of such a revolution, see Harley Balzer in *Demokratizatsiya* (Spring 2005): 193–218.

Proponents of the "August Revolution" interpretation see Yeltsin as its leader or personification, but he himself later took pride in having been "able to save Russia from revolution" (quoted in Reddaway and Glinski, *Tragedy*, 226).

15. For the American revolution, see Michael Kammen, *A Season of Youth* (New York, 1978); for presidents and slave labor, Davis in *NYT*, Aug. 26, 2001, and Mintz in *Chronicle*, Feb. 7, 2003, B16; and for textbooks, James T. Campbell in *WP Book World*, Dec. 12, 2004, 3, and Robert William Fogel, *The Slavery Debates, 1952–1990* (Baton Rouge, La., 2006). Indeed, a historian of my own Southern state was still "comfortable" in 2005 with the role of the Confederacy's president and the "South's past" generally when viewed "in the context of their times" (Bill Ellis in *Kentucky Monthly* [June 2005]: 54). A leading American historian says of the founding fathers, "At least they provided some ideas that . . . could inspire later opponents of slavery" (George M. Fredrickson in *NYRB*, July 14, 2005, 42.) The same could be said of Lenin and Bukharin, e.g., in connection with post-Stalin reformers.

16. For a similar point, see John Miller, *Mikhail Gorbachev and the End of Soviet Power* (New York, 1993), 201. The equation is so widespread that it is used by scholars on opposite sides of the political spectrum. See Malia, *Soviet Tragedy*; Chiesa, *Transition to Democracy*, 202; and, similarly, Jeremy Smith, *The Fall of Soviet Communism* (New York, 2005). For the case, such as it is, for retaining "Communist" and "Communism" as analytical labels, see Andrew Roberts in *Slavic Review* (Summer 2004): 349–66; and for a thoughtful Russian study of the problem of conceptualizing and labeling the Soviet system, see D. V. Maslov, *Istoriograficheskie i metodologicheskie osnovy issledovaniia sostoianiia sovetskoi sistemy* (Sergiev Posad, 2004).

17. BBC interview with Gorbachev, March 8, 2002, in *JRL*, March 20, 2002. A Gorbachev aide later said their goal had been "a USSR that had broken with Communism" (Aleksandr Tsipko in *LG*, May 23, 2001). The former aide later argued that the Soviet Union's "Communist legitimacy" could have been replaced by the concept of "a special Eurasian civilization" (Tsipko in *LG*, Dec. 20, 2006). Even a pro-Yeltsin history concedes that "the majority of critics of the regime came out not against the soviets but the domination of the Communist Party" (Iu. M. Baturin et. al., eds., *Epokha Eltsina* [Moscow, 2001], 170). Russians expressed their agreement in two ways. First, by protesting against Communist Party rule while supporting the Soviet system in the late 1980s and early 1990s and later by regretting the end of the Soviet Union and expressing nostalgia for the Soviet era but without voting the Communist Party back into power. Similarly, see the survey results reported by Paul Goble in *JRL*, Jan. 2, 2006. For a similar point about Gor-

bachev's 1990 meaning of "Communism," see Andrzej Walicki, *Marxism and the Leap to the Kingdom of Freedom* (Stanford, Calif., 1995), 554–55, 617n. 177.

18. See, e.g., Urban, ed., *Can the Soviet System*, xiii; Remington in Daniels, ed., *Soviet Communism*, 331; and, similarly, Beissinger, *Nationalist Mobilization*, 401. As for the Party, one scholar writes: "the CPSU leadership (i.e., the Soviet system)" (Troy McGrath in *The Harriman Review* [Dec. 2002]: 15). More generally, as a Russian politician remarked in a related discussion, the question "depends on what we mean by the Soviet Union" (Aleksei Arbatov in *NG*, Jan. 16, 1997).

19. The new conception of the Soviet system was expressed in many perestroika-era publications, but for a striking example see Elena Bonner—Andrei Sakharov's widow and hardly a Soviet devotee—on power and property in *MN*, July 15, 1990.

20. For the "evolution," see this chapter, n. 63. Just how heretical the new tenets were may be judged by the growing opposition of Gorbachev's own former aide for ideology, himself a reformer. See G. L. Smirnov, *Uroki minuvshego* (Moscow, 1997). The new ideology was elaborated by Gorbachev in late 1989, reframed as the draft of a new Party program in early 1990, and debated and in effect adopted at the Twenty-eighth Party Congress in July. See, respectively, *Pravda*, Nov. 26, 1989; *Materialy plenuma tsentalnogo komiteta KPSS: 5–7 fevralia 1990 goda* (Moscow, 1990), 511–40; and *XXVIII sezd kommunisticheskoi partii Sovetskogo Soiuza: stenograficheskii otchet*, 2 vols. (Moscow, 1991), 1:55–101, and 2:255–68, 276–94. Gorbachev's aides continued to make the draft program increasingly liberal-democratic. See the draft and debates in *Pravda*, Aug. 8, 1991; and *SR*, July 27–30, 1991. For anti-Communist views inside the Party apparatus itself, see Aleksandr Tsipko in *VA*, no. 3 (2005): 213–37; and for the larger process, Archie Brown, ed. *The Demise of Marxism-Leninism in Russia* (New York, 2004), esp. 9–11, chaps. 2–4.

21. Thus a Gorbachev aide responsible for spelling out the new ideology argued at the same time that its role in Soviet life should be greatly diminished. See Georgii Shakhnazarov in *Kommunist*, no. 4 (1990): 46–59, and in *LG*, April 18, 1990.

22. As Gorbachev and his supporters fully understood. See V. A. Medvedev, *Prozrenie, mif ili predatelstvo?* (Moscow, 1997), 4–5, and earlier in *Pravda*, June 29, 1990.

23. See, e.g., Sakwa, *Gorbachev*, 192; John Gooding in *RR* (Jan. 1992): 36–57; and Chiesa, *Transition*, 3. There is also the opposite view, reflexive rather than considered, that the "CPSU remained the ruling Party" until August 1991 (Mark R. Beissinger in James Millar, ed., *Cracks in the Monolith* [Ar-

monk, N.Y., 1992], 213). In fact, as we are told by a member of the Central Committee at that time, "The Party had ceased to be a ruling political organization, and officials of the Central Committee apparat understood this better than anyone else" (Roy Medvedev, *Sovetskii Soiuz: poslednii god zhizni* [Moscow, 2003], 76). Similarly, see Vera Tolz, *The USSR's Emerging Multiparty System* (Washington, D.C., 1990).

24. Brown, *Gorbachev*, 310.

25. Gorbachev in *XXVIII sezd*, 2:201–2; and *Pravda*, April 13, 1990. On the latter claim, see also L. Shevtsova in *Izvestiia*, Feb. 27, 1990, who wrote: "We have much more political diversity than any other country in the world."

26. V. N. Kudriatsev in *Trud*, Nov. 11, 1988. For the constitutional aspects of Gorbachev's reforms, see Robert B. Ahdieh, *Russia's Constitutional Revolution* (University Park, Penn., 1997).

27. Elizabeth Teague in *Report*, Oct. 19, 1990, 9–10. For "checks and balances," see M. S. Gorbachev, *Izbrannye rechi i stati*, 7 vols. (Moscow, 1987–90), 7:161.

28. For the growing power of state ministries vis-à-vis the Party apparatus, see Stephen Whitefield, *Industrial Power and the Soviet State* (New York, 1993); David Lane and Cameron Ross in *Communist and Post-Communist Studies* 27, no. 1 (1994): 18–38; and Alexander Yakovlev, *The Fate of Marxism in Russia* (New Haven, Conn., 1993), 109–11. One Western historian even argues that by the 1980s the Party had lost its power to the state bureaucracies. Moshe Lewin, *The Soviet Century* (London, 2005), 348–51. On scholarly neglect of the Soviet state and its government, see Huskey, ed., *Executive Power*, pp. xii–xiii.

29. The figures are from Leon Onikov, *KPSS* (Moscow, 1996), 75, whose insistence that the apparat's control over the party remained intact does not square with actual developments or other accounts. See, e.g., Yegor Ligachev, *Inside Gorbachev's Kremlin* (New York, 1993), 109–11 and passim; and this chapter, note 30.

30. "Kadrovoe popolnenie perestroiki," *Pravda*, June 25, 1989; and the editorial, *Pravda*, June 14, 1989. For Gorbachev's remark, see A. S. Cherniaev, *Shest let s Gorbachevym* (Moscow, 1993), 356.

31. Graeme Gill, *The Collapse of a Single-Party System* (New York, 1995), 174–75; Mikhail Gorbachev, *Zhizn i reformy*, 2 vols. (Moscow, 1995), 2:575; and Boris Kagarlitsky, *Square Wheels* (New York, 1994), 142; and for an insider's testimony, Andrei Chuzhakin in *PZH*, no. 29 (2004): 76–77. Indeed, the coup leader told party officials to stand aside: "This is a purely state affair" (Iurii Prokofev, *Do i posle zapreta KPSS* [Moscow, 2005], 243). For examples of such Western accounts, see Beissinger in Millar, ed., *Cracks*, 213; and Michael Dobbs, *Down with Big Brother* (New York, 1997), whose treat-

ment of August 1991 is entitled "The Revolt of the Party." For attempts to substantiate that view, see G. A. Belousova and V. A. Lebedev, *Partokratiia i putch* (Moscow, 1992); and Hahn, *Russia's Revolution*, pp. 420–27.

32. Interpretation aside, the best summary discussion of the bureaucratic or nomenklatura class is Hough, *Democratization*, 51–57.

33. It was true even of Party apparatus bureaucrats. See Onikov, *KPSS*, 56; B. Iu. Berzin and L. N. Kogan in *SI*, no. 3 (1989): 21–22; and "Apparat protiv apparata?" *SK*, March 31, 1990. For a sample of nomenklatura political and economic views by mid-1990, see the survey of delegates to the Twenty-eighth Party Congress in *SI*, no. 11 (1990): 99–104.

34. I will return to this subject in the next chapter, but for two studies of the phenomenon, see Olga Kryshtanovskaia in *ONS*, no. 1 (1995): 51–65; and Viola Egikova in *MP*, May 26, 1994.

35. M. S. Gorbachev, *Razmyshleniia ob oktiabrskoi revoliutsii* (Moscow, 1997), 35; Dawn Mann in *Report*, Feb. 23, 1990, 1–6; and, for rank-and-file support from the beginning, Viktor Gushchin in *NG*, Sept. 9, 2000. For the "silent majority," see Liudmila Saveleva in *Izvestiia*, Sept. 3, 1988.

36. For the Party as "part of the state machine," see Lev Burtsev, *Izvestiia*, July 15, 1990; and, similarly, A. Zevelev in *Izvestiia*, Nov. 3, 1988.

37. Gorbachev, *Razmyshleniia ob oktiabrskoi revoliutsii*, 35; in *Materialy plenuma*, Feb. 5–7, 1990, 11–12; and, similarly, in *XXVIII sezd*, 2:201–2.

38. Tatiana Samolis in *Pravda*, July 1, 1991.

39. The episode was known as the Nina Andreyeva affair. See *SR*, March 3, 1988; and *Pravda*, April 5, 1988.

40. Brown, *Gorbachev*, 191. For the Central Committee, see Onikov, *KPSS*, 90–91. At the conference, Ligachev denied the obvious—"There are no factions, no reformers and conservatives, among us"—while Gorbachev emphasized the point about the factional 1920s (*XIX vsesoiuznaia konferentsiia kommunisticheskoi partii Sovetskogo Soiuza: stenograficheskii otchet*, 2 vols. [Moscow, 1988], 2:88, 175).

41. *Uchreditelnyi sezd kommunisticheskoi partii RSFSR: stenograficheskii otchet*, 2 vols. (Moscow, 1991); Gorbachev, *Zhizn*, 1:530–39; and the report by Elizabeth Tucker in *WSJ*, July 11, 1991.

42. Aleksandr Iakovlev in *Izvestiia*, July 2, 1991; and I. Maliarov in *Pravda*, Sept. 26, 1990. Or as a Soviet political scientist put it, "The CPSU is itself already a multiparty system in miniature" (L. Shevtsova in *Izvestiia*, Feb. 27, 1990).

43. See chap. 3, note 16. Years later, Gorbachev thought there would have been "at least three political parties"—social-democratic, Communist, and liberal. Mikhail Gorbachev, *Poniat perestroiku . . .* (Moscow, 2006), 369–70.

44. The words regularly used included "*razmezhevanie*" (dividing up), "*rasstavanie*" (parting of the ways), and even "*razvod*" (divorce).

45. For the conservatives, see the report by E. Savishev in *KP*, June 15, 1991; Oleg Shenin, *Rodinu ne prodaval i menia obvinili v izmene* (Moscow, 1994), 44; and Prokofev, *Do i posle*, 232–36, who mentions the presidency. For Gorbachev, see *Pravda*, July 3 and 26, 1991; his *Zhizn*, 2:547, 548; his interview in *NG*, Nov. 11, 1992; quoted in Andrei Grachev, *Gorbachev* (Moscow, 2001), 228; and Vasilii Lipitskii in *NG*, Aug. 3, 1991. For his aides and supporters, see Georgii Shakhnazarov, *Tsena svobody* (Moscow, 1993), 151; Vadim Medvedev, *V komande Gorbacheva* (Moscow, 1994), 130–31, 185–86, 207; and Sergei Alekseev, Fedor Burlatskii, and Stanislav Shatalin in *LG*, Jan. 30, 1991. For an insider's view of these developments, see Otto Latsis, *Tshchatelno splanirovannoe samoubiistvo* (Moscow, 2001), 349–70.

46. Aleksandr Iakovlev, *Omyt pamiati*, 2 vols. (Moscow, 2001), 1:505. For a similar argument from a different political perspective, see Liudmila Vartazarova in *Zavtra*, no. 31 (Aug. 1995).

47. Hahn, *Russia's Revolution*, p. 375; Mikhail Gorbachev and Zdeněk Mlynář, *Conversations with Gorbachev* (New York, 2002), 121; Gorbachev, *Poniat*, 373–74, where he adds that "a majority of the members" would have followed him because of Party discipline; and, similarly, Gorbachev, *Zhizn*, 2:578. One top aide thought that a formal split would not favor Gorbachev (Medvedev, *V komande*, 131), but several supporters and well-informed observers believed that a majority of Party members, at least 9 million, would follow him. See, e.g., Fedor Burlatskii, *Glotok svobody*, 2 vols. (Moscow, 1997), 2:189–90; Latsis, *Tshchatelno*, 345; German Diligenskii in *SK*, July 7, 1990; and Boris Pugaev in *Rossiia*, Aug. 3–9, 1991. It seems unlikely, however, that either wing of the CPSU would have had that many supporters in the event of a formal split; many Communists probably would have joined other breakaway parties or quit altogether. But even a million or so registered members would have been ample.

48. S. Sheboldaev in *Pravda*, Sept. 26, 1990; and White, *Gorbachev and After*, 256.

49. In early 1990, it was estimated that in a free election the Communist Party would have gotten 20 percent of the vote, nationalist and patriotic parties about 30 percent, and a social democratic one 50 percent (Sakwa, *Gorbachev*, 189). Had the CPSU split into two parties, it is reasonable to assume that the conservative wing would have gained much of the nationalist vote and the Gorbachev wing most of the social democratic vote. On the latter, see also White in *SEER* (Oct. 1994): 663. For an argument against the possibility of such a social-democratic party, see Vladlen Sorotkin in *Nedelia*, no. 9 (1991). Significantly, Aleksandr Yakovlev also did not believe in the "social-democratization" project. See Aleksandr Tsipko in *VA*, no. 2, 2006, Web site version (isoa.ru).

50. For similar arguments, see Miller, *Mikhail Gorbachev*, 147–48; and Brown, *Gorbachev*, 205–7, 272.

51. See, e.g., the interview with Yeltsin in *MN*, Jan. 14, 1990. For a somewhat different but not conflicting argument, see Atsushi Ogushi in *EAS* (July 2007): 731–32.

52. For similar arguments, see Miller, *Mikhail Gorbachev*, 146; and Kelley in Huber and Kelley, eds., *Perestroika-Era Politics*, 93.

53. As the leader of the post-Soviet Communist Party later said, it has become a "party of patriots" (Gennadii Ziuganov in *SR*, Oct. 24, 1995). Similarly, see Ivan Polozkov in *SR*, Feb. 28, 1991; E. Volodin in *SR*, Sept. 28, 1991; and Aleksandr Prokhanov in *KP*, Sept. 3, 1991.

54. Their first reaction was to declare that "in such circumstances they will not run in these elections because there is a hundred percent certainty they will not be elected." To which Gorbachev replied: "Really?! It turns out that the party should refuse to participate in leadership and in elections?" (*Materialy plenuma tsentralnogo komiteta KPSS: 25 aprelia 1989 goda* [Moscow, 1989], 91). Evidently, they soon figured out that if one in five first secretaries had lost, four others had won, one way or another. See V. Boikov and Zh. Toshchenko in *Pravda*, Oct. 16, 1989.

55. For the post-1991 party, see Joan Barth Urban and Valerii D. Solovei, *Russia's Communists at the Crossroads* (Boulder, Colo., 1997); and Luke March, *The Communist Party in Post-Soviet Russia* (New York, 2002). For the observer, see Vitalii Tretiakov in *RG*, April 24, 2003.

56. Joseph R. Blasi et. al., *Kremlin Capitalism* (Ithaca, N.Y., 1997), 21. Similarly, see William Moskoff, *Hard Times* (Armonk, N.Y., 1993), 6; Geoffrey Hosking, *The First Socialist Society*, 2nd ed. (Cambridge, Mass., 1993), 488; Miller, *Mikhail Gorbachev*, 205; Robert Strayer, *Why Did the Soviet Union Collapse?* (Armonk, N.Y., 1998), 115, 133; and Tony Barber in *FT*, Jan. 27, 2007, who summarized the prevailing opinion: "Gorbachev was . . . a flop as an economic reformer."

57. And they continued to do so to the end. See, e.g., Marshall I. Goldman, *What Went Wrong With Perestroika* (New York, 1992), esp. 210–11; and Jeffrey Sachs quoted in Lynn D. Nelson and Irina Y. Kuzes, *Radical Reform in Yeltsin's Russia* (Armonk, N.Y., 1995), 22–23. The same was true of many Soviet economists who later became "radical reformers." See, e.g., V. A. Naishul in F. M. Borodkin et. al., eds, *Postizhenie* (Moscow, 1989), 441–48. For explicit statements of the economy's reformability, see, e.g., Kotz and Weir, *Revolution*, esp. chap. 5; and Michael Ellman and Vladimir Kontorovich, eds., *The Destruction of the Soviet Economic System* (Armonk, N.Y., 1998), esp. chap. 2.

58. See, e.g., Aslund, *How Russia*, 28; and Gorbachev's critical remarks about foreign advisers in *FBIS*, Feb. 27, 1991, 81.

59. See, e.g., Gorbachev in *Pravda*, Sept. 18, 1990; and for radical reformers, S. S. Shatalin and N. Ia. Petrakov in *Pravda*, April 26, 1990. Put another way, "For many Soviet economists, the ideal still remained the policies of NEP" or "socialism with a human face" (Baturin et. al., eds., *Epokha Eltsina*, 170).

60. Aslund, *How Russia*, 28; Robert Service, *A History of Twentieth-Century Russia* (Cambridge, 1997), 492. For Gorbachev's comment on Yeltsin's remark, see *Zhizn*, 1:576; and for a sympathetic treatment of Gorbachev's proposal, Brown, *Gorbachev*, 137–40.

61. Padmai Desai, *Perestroika in Perspective* (Princeton, N.J., 1990), 106. Similarly, see Vasilii Leontev's letter in *MN*, Jan. 14, 1990; Ed A. Hewett's op-ed in *NYT*, March 25, 1990; and Richard Parker in *Atlantic Monthly* (June 1990): 68–80.

62. See, e.g., the laws on land, ownership, and enterprises in *Izvestiia*, March 7, 1990; *Pravda*, March 10, 1990; and *SR*, June 12, 1990. Until 1991, the laws were still somewhat euphemistic about private property and related matters, but even one of Gorbachev's harshest economic critics acknowledges their importance (Aslund, *How Russia*, 30).

63. Gorbachev, *Izbrannye*, 7:573. For the candidate, see Albert Makashov in *SR*, June 8, 1991. Similarly, see Iurii Prokofev in *Kommunist*, no. 13 (1990): 7; the now liberal Vadim Bakatin's account of his "metamorphosis" in *KP*, May 31, 1991; A. D. Nekipelov on his "rethinking theoretical views" and his "ideological evolution" in *ONS*, no. 4 (2005): 10–11, and *Proryv k svobode: o perestroike dvadtsat let spustia* (Moscow, 2005), 183–85; and the survey of delegates to the Twenty-eighth Party Congress in *SI*, no. 11 (1990): 99–100. This was the "evolution of views" later recalled by Ryzhkov in *Pravda*, Oct. 3, 1992.

64. David Remnick in *WP*, July 7, 8, 9, 1991; for a personal example and account, see Artem Tarasov, *Millioner* (Moscow, 2004), esp. chaps. 3–6. For the cooperatives, see Vladimir Tikhonov in *AF*, March 31–April 6, 1990, and in *LG*, Aug. 8, 1990; and Andrei Borodenkov in *MN*, July 1, 1990.

65. Mikhail Berger in *MT* (magazine ed.), March 12, 1995, 35. A post-Soviet finance minister and investment banker remarked, "It all began with Gorbachev" (Voice of America interview with Boris Fedorov, *JRL*, April 6, 2004). Similarly, see Iurii Burtin in *NV*, no. 20 (1994): 19; Egor Gaidar, *Gosudarstvo i evoliutsiia* (Moscow, 1995), 150; Roi Medvedev, *Zdorove i vlast v Rossii* (Moscow, 1997), 14–18; Aleksandr Golovkov in *NG*, Sept. 26, 1998; and R. Nureev and A. Runov in *VE*, no. 6 (2002): 21. For the view that

Gorbachev "lost his chance to introduce meaningful economic reforms," see Michael Dobbs in *WP*, Dec. 15, 1991.

66. See his public remarks in Lithuania, in January 1990, in *Nashi obshchie problemy vmeste i reshat* (Moscow, 1990).

67. For Gorbachev's struggle, see *Soiuz mozhno bylo sokhranit* (Moscow, 1995); and A. P. Nenarokov, ed., *Nesostoiavshiisia iubilei* (Moscow, 1992), 331–508. For his characterization of the old state, see Gorbachev, *Zhizn*, 1:495–96, and, similarly, 2:530. For Lincoln, see Gorbachev and Mlynář, *Conversations*, 129; and for the end of perestroika, Mikhail Gorbachev, *Dekiabr—91* (Moscow, 1992), and V. T. Loginov, ed., *Piat let posle Belovezhia* (Moscow, 1997).

68. Leon Onikov quoted in Smirnov, *Uroki*, 288.

69. For similar points about language, see Nelson and Kuzes, *Radical Reform*, 8; and Robert V. Daniels, *Russia's Transformation* (Lanham, Md., 1998), 212–13. Not surprisingly, a senior Sovietologist, having misformulated the issue, found "the sudden collapse difficult to explain even in retrospect. Why did the huge edifice collapse?" (Walter Laqueur, *The Dream That Failed* [New York, 1994], 71). To illustrate the crucial difference in formulation, compare Richard Lourie in *NYT Book Review*, April 5, 1998, 26 ("Soviet Russia . . . collapsed of its own weight") with the topic of a Russian roundtable discussion in *NG—Stsenarii*, Jan. 1, 1997: "Who Broke Up the Soviet Union: History, the West, Yeltsin, Gorbachev?"

70. See, respectively, Stephen Kotkin in *NR*, April 15, 2002, 27; Pipes, *Communism*, 41; and Alec Nove in Geir Lundestad, ed., *The Fall of Great Powers* (Oslo, 1994), 144. Similarly, see Hosking, *First*, 500; Vera Tolz and Iain Elliot, eds., *The Demise of the Soviet Union* (London, 1995), 21; Malia, *Soviet Tragedy*, 488; and Bunce, *Subversive Institutions*, 19, 36–37, and passim. To be fair, this is also the view of several serious Russian analysts. See, e.g., Vladimir Sogrin in *ONS*, no. 1 (1992): 147; Burlatskii, *Glotok*, 2:155–56; and Andranik Migranian in *NG*, June 14, 2000. But according to another Russian political scientist, "The defeat of the Communist system did not have to entail the breakup of the state" (Lilia Shevtsova in Anne de Tinguy, ed., *The Fall of the Soviet Empire* [Boulder, Colo., 1997], 76). For a similar Western dissenting opinion, see Richard Sakwa in *Demokratizatsiya* (Spring 2005): 266–67, who argues that apart from the party, the "broader political order . . . largely represented the aspirations of a majority of society" and had the "potential for significant evolution."

71. See this chapter, n. 28.

72. Shlapentokh, *Normal*, 164–66. Similarly, see S. V. Cheshko, *Raspad Sovetskogo Soiuza* (Moscow, 1996), 140–41; V. D. Solovei, *Russkaia istoriia* (Moscow, 2005), 154; and Brown, *Gorbachev*, 258–59.

73. Mark Kramer in *JCWS* (Fall 2003): 21. For the statistics, see Barsenkov, *Vvedenie*, 132; and Solovei, *Russkaia isoriia*, 159. More than a decade after the breakup, Russian language and Soviet education were still powerful forces in Central Asia. See the report by Zamira Eshanova in *RFE/RL*, Nov. 13, 2002. More generally, it was later reported that of the 142 million former Soviet citizens living outside Russia, at least 100 million knew the Russian language (Sergei Blagov in *Asia Times*, July 23, 2003).

74. Stephen Kotkin in *NR*, April 15, 2002, 27. In 1996, Gorbachev made a similar point about the former Soviet Union: "De facto the county still lives even though de jure it no longer exists" (*NG*, Dec. 25, 1996).

75. Suny, *Revenge*, 150. Even Russian anti-Communist critics of Gorbachev agree. See, e.g., Sergei Roy in *Moscow News*, Nov. 26–Dec. 2, 1998; and the group statement in *NG-Stsenarii*, May 23, 1996.

76. For the law, see *Pravda*, April 7, 1990; and for Gorbachev on the "process of 'divorce,'" *Zhizn*, 1:520–21. Some historians think that if an acceptable union treaty had been offered in early 1989, even the Baltic republics would have remained. See R. Kh. Simonian in *VI*, no. 12 (2002): 34–37; and, similarly, Feodor Burlatsky in Metta Spencer, ed., *Separatism* (Lanham, Md., 1998), 141.

77. Stanislav Shushkevich in *FBIS*, Sept. 30, 1991, 70; and Solzhenitsyn in *LG*, Sept. 18, 1990. Similarly, in November 1991, Yeltsin assured listeners: "It is hard to say how many states will enter the Union, but I have a firm conviction that there will be a Union" (quoted in Medvedev, *Sovetskii Soiuz*, 203). One Russian specialist believes it did not matter how many republics initially signed the treaty because others would have joined later (S. V. Cheshko in G. N. Sevostianov, ed., *Tragediia velikoi derzhavy* [Moscow, 2005], 465). That is, there is no reason to think, as one American specialist does, that a new Union would have had to include "all fifteen union republics" (Edward W. Walker, *Dissolution* [Lanham, Md., 2003], 186).

78. For the treaty, see *Izvestiia*, Aug. 15, 1991; and for strong pro-Union statements by Yeltsin and Kravchuk at the negotiations, *Natsionalnye interesy*, no. 2–3 (2001): 80, 88. It is often argued that Ukraine would not have actually signed the treaty—see this chapter, n. 80—but Gorbachev thought otherwise, as do several Russian specialists and at least one American. See Barsenkov, *Vvedenie*, 198; Iakov Pliais in *NG*, March 3, 1994. And, similarly, Cheshko in Sevostianov, ed., *Tragediia*; and Hale, "Ethnofederalism."

79. Mikhail Gorbachev, *On My County and the World* (New York, 2000), 132; Gorbachev in *Novaia*, Aug. 14–16, 2006; and Gorbachev in *Gorbachevskie chteniia*, no. 3, 69. For the seating, see also Gorbachev's press conference of Aug. 16, 2001 in *JRL*, Aug. 20, 2001.

80. For this interpretation, see Hahn, *Russia's Revolution*, chap. 8. And, similarly, Henry E. Hale, "The Strange Death of the Soviet Union," Harvard University Davis Center, Ponars Series No. 12, March 1999; and Burlatsky in Spencer, ed., *Separatism*, 146. Several Western scholars argue, on the other hand, that the treaty would have not worked. See, e.g., Miller, *Mikhail Gorbachev*, 198; Beissinger, *Nationalist Mobilization*, 390, 422–25; and, less emphatically, Hough, *Democratization*, 424–28. And some Russians agree, including Dmitrii Furman in *Proryv*, 329–30; and Viktor Sheinis in *SM*, no. 10 (2005): 105.

81. Anatoly Sobchak quoted in Brown, *Gorbachev*, 293. Similarly, see Sobchak in *MN*, Aug. 18–25, 1996; and Vladimir Lukin quoted in Hough, *Democratization*, 393.

82. To take a contingency considered earlier, according to a widely respected Russian economist, if the G7 had not sent Gorbachev home from London in July 1991 "with empty hands," without the financial assistance he desperately needed, the plotters would not have moved against him; the refusal even "urged" them on (Nikolai Shmelev in *SM*, no. 7 [1996]: 62, and no. 2 [1999]: 77, and in *Proryv*, 207). Similarly, see Viktor Sheinis in *SM*, no. 11–12 (2006): 178. Indeed, the plotters took steps in June and July to undermine his requests for Western aid. See Hahn, *Russia's Revolution*, 406; and Mark Kramer in *JCWS* (Winter 2005): 62. For the G7's rejection and the "big humiliation" it inflicted on Gorbachev, see Reddaway and Glinski, *Tragedy*, 178–82; and for the contrary view that Western aid would not have prevented the Soviet breakup, see Celeste Wallander in *JCWS* (Fall 2003): 164.

83. See, e.g., the post-August statements by Sobchak, Shushkevich, and Aleksandr Yakovlev in *FBIS*, Sept. 13, 33, Sept. 30, 70, and Oct. 2, 33; Roy Medvedev's account of the Congress in *NNI*, no. 2 (2003): 167, and of his own expectations in *LR*, April 4, 2003; for the economic union, Walker, *Dissolution*, 144; and for Yeltsin, Dzhuletto Keza, *Proshai, Rossiia!* (Moscow, 1997), 110. Another soon-to-be coconspirator, Shushkevich, made a similar statement (*FBIS*, Nov. 15, 1991, 26). Indeed, after August, Yeltsin was still considering having himself made president of the Soviet Union. See Boris Yeltsin, *Zapiski prezidenta* (Moscow, 1994), 154–55. Gorbachev, of course, continued to insist that the Union could be saved. See his *Zhizn*, vol. 2, chap. 44. For a different but related conception of the Union alternative that still existed after August, see Reddaway and Glinski, *Tragedy*, 245–46.

84. For the text, see *Pravda*, Nov. 27, 1991.

85. Martin Malia in *NYT*, Sept. 3, 1998; and Stephen Kotkin in *NR*, March 31, 2003, 34. Elsewhere, Kotkin dismisses "Gorbachev's quest for a non-existent

reformed socialism" (*East European Constitutional Review* [Fall 1997]: 118). Similarly, see Jeffrey W. Hahn in *Slavic Review* (Winter 1993): 851. Some Western scholars have treated the Gorbachev years as a "transition." See, e.g., Huber and Kelley, eds., *Perestroika-Era Politics*, 3; Archie Brown in *JOD* (Oct. 2001): 35; and Hahn, *Russia's Revolution*, chap. 8. The word "transition" (*perekhod*) and concept were regularly applied to Gorbachev's reforms by Soviet writers at the time.

86. Strayer, *Why*, 113.
87. I borrow the term "counterweights" from John N. Hazard, *The Soviet System of Government*, 5th ed. (Chicago, 1980), chap. 13. Originally published in 1957, it was the first to develop this important insight. For a similar and earlier approach, but focusing on the official ideology, see Barrington Moore Jr., *Soviet Politics—the Dilemmas of Power* (New York, 1965), 28, 339, first published in 1950; and for yet another perception of the system's "dual structure," Mlynář, *Can Gorbachev*, 84–85.
88. See, respectively, Gorbachev, *Izbrannye*, 6:352; Gorbachev, *Zhizn*, 1:390; A. S. Cherniaev in *10 let bez SSSR* (Moscow 2002), 8; and Gorbachev, *Zhizn*, 1:423. Thus, one American Sovietologist commented at this time, with considerable surprise, on "the coming to life of institutions that most people regarded as dead, sham, a grotesque caricature of what they ought to be" (Donald W. Treadgold in Wieczynski, ed. *Gorbachev*, 43).

5. THE FATE OF THE SOVIET UNION: WHY DID IT END?

1. Leontii Byzoev in *Pravda*, Feb. 16, 1991.
2. For a demonstration of an estimated 250,000 pro-Communists, see *Commersant*, Feb. 25, 1991; and for the "rally mania," *Pravda*, March 26, 1990.
3. Archie Brown, *The Gorbachev Factor* (New York, 1997), 270–71; and Roi Medvedev in *OI*, no. 5 (2003): 122.
4. Marshal Sergei Akhromeev, Gorbachev's top military adviser, quoted in Roi Medvedev, *Sovetskii Soiuz: poslednii god zhizni* (Moscow, 2003), 152. Similarly, see S. F. Akhromeev and G. M. Kornienko, *Glazami marshala i diplomata* (Moscow, 1992); Vladimir Kriuchkov, *Lichnoe delo*, 2 vols. (Moscow, 1996); and Valentin Falin, *Bez skidok na obstoiatelstva* (Moscow, 1999), 380–461, and his *Konflikty v kremle* (Moscow, 2000).
5. See, e.g., Vladimir Sokolov in *LG*, Sept. 12, 1990; Ivan Sidelnikov in *KZ*, Oct. 4, 1990; and L. Shvetsova and Pavel Gutioniov in *Izvestiia*, Oct. 8 and Nov. 27, 1990. For 1941, see Ivan Polozkov quoted in Otto Latsis, *Tshchatelno splanirovannoe samoubiistvo* (Moscow, 2001), 336; and Valentin Ras-

putin in *SR*, Dec. 14, 1990. The preceding quote summarized the charges as conveyed to Gorbachev's chief aide (Anatolii Cherniaev, *1991 god* [Moscow, 1997], 47).

6. Nikolai Petrakov in *FT*, Jan 26, 1991. See, e.g., the openly mutinous "Address to the People," whose signers included two active-duty generals, in *SR*, July 23, 1991. Its insubordinate intent was later acknowledged by one of its organizers, Gennadii Ziuganov in *SR*, July 26, 2001; and by its author, Aleksandr Prokhanov, in *NG Ex Libris*, March 2, 2006.

7. Anatolii Gromyko, *Andrei Gromyko* (Moscow, 1997), 201; A. Krasnov and Iu. Nikolaev in *SR*, June 15, 1991; Marshal Viktor Kulikov in *Moscow News*, Sept. 15–21, 1999. Similarly, see the account of Gorbachev's meeting with a large group of hostile officers, in *KZ*, Nov. 15, 1990; and for a close study of those reactions, Mark Kramer in *JCWS* (Winter 2005): 3–66, which included charges of "betrayal" (8, 25).

8. For public opinion, see S. Shpilko and Tatiana Zaslavskaia in *Izvestiia*, Jan. 17 and 18, 1991, the latter quoted here.

9. Joseph Nogee and R. Judson Mitchell, *Russian Politics* (Boston, 1997), 86; David Remnick in *WP*, Nov. 19, 1990; Richard Sakwa in *Russia and the World*, no. 19 (1991): 12.

10. See his important speeches on the subject in *Pravda*, March 1 and 2, 1991; his memoir explanation in *Zhizn i reformy*, 2 vols. (Moscow, 1995), 2:520–25; and the comments of his close adviser Georgii Shakhnazarov, *Tsena svobody* (Moscow, 1993), 147, 184. For Gorbachev's promise, see *Pravda*, March 16, 1990, and *XXVIII sezd kommunisticheskoi partii Sovetskogo Soiuza: stenograficheskii otchet*, 2 vols. (Moscow, 1991), 2:203; and for being a democrat, David Remnick in *WP*, Sept. 26, 1990. Such "moderate conservatives" were still on the Central Committee, according to Medvedev, *Sovetskii Soiuz*, 78. Because of their subsequent roles in the August 1991 coup, the leading members of Gorbachev's new government became known as hard-line reactionaries, but that was not their reputation when he embraced them in 1990. Indeed, pro-Gorbachev figures spoke favorably of them, as professionals and men, before and even after the coup attempt. On Valentin Pavlov, the new prime minister, whose moderate reformist views on the economy were set out in *Pravda*, Feb. 21, 1991, see, e.g., Cherniaev, *1991*, 100, 156; Otto Latsis in *LG*, Jan. 23, 1991; Aleksandr Golovkov in *NG*, Sept. 26, 1998; G. Popov in *VE*, no. 8 (2005): 139–44; and in his own words, Valentin Pavlov, *Upushchen li shans?* (Moscow, 1995). On the KGB chief Vladimir Kryuchkov, Aleksandr Iakovlev in *Trud*, Feb. 23, 1993. And for Boris Pugo, minister of internal affairs, see Chernyaev cited in Rodric Braithwaite, *Across the Moscow River* (New Haven, Conn., 2003), 240; and Gorbachev himself, in *Zhizn*, 1:408, who calls Pugo "a decent man."

Typically, Gorbachev's new vice president, Gennady Yanaev, characterized himself as an economic reformer against "shock" policies (*Glasnost*, Jan. 3, 1991). For a similar analysis, see Jerry F. Hough, *Democratization and Revolution in the USSR*, (Washington, D.C., 1997), 400, 442.

11. Stanislav Shatalin quoted by Abraham Brumberg in *NYRB*, June 27, 1991, 55; Michael Ellman and Vladimir Kontorovich in *EAS*, no. 2 (1997): 275. For "tactical," see Georgi Arbatov, *The System* (New York, 1992), 339; and Dimitri Simes, *After the Collapse* (New York, 1999), 82. And for "eternal values," Gorbachev quoted by Serge Schmemann in *NYT*, Jan. 23, 1991. During this period, Gorbachev repeatedly declared that he would never "turn back." See, e.g., *FBIS*, Feb. 15, 1991, 27, and Feb. 27, 1991, 78–79; and *Pravda*, March 2, 1991.

12. This latter point was occasionally made at the time. See, e.g., Peter Rutland in *Arguments and Facts International* 1, no. 4 (1990): 1, and Sergei Iastrezhemskii in *MN*, Nov. 5, 1989. And, similarly, Rair Simonyan cited by Bill Keller in *NYT*, May 14, 1990; and Mary Buckley, *Redefining Russian Society and Polity* (Boulder, Colo., 1993), 250–53. For the political fashion, see Fedor Burlatskii in *LG*, May 2, 1990; and, similarly, Edvard Shevardnadze in *LG*, April 18, 1990, who remarked: "Today, optimism is not in fashion. On the contrary, many compete in their pessimism, advancing the most terrible prognoses." To give a contemporary and retrospective example, see Oleg Gusarevich in *Pravda*, Jan. 8, 1990, who thought that glasnost and democratization had led to a "civil war" in public discourse; and Mark R. Beissinger, *National Mobilization and the Collapse of the Soviet State* (New York, 2002), 88, 124, who thinks that the first mostly free parliamentary election, in 1989, "rocked the country" and left the "Soviet regime . . . tottering on the edge." But why should the normal unruly aspects of democratic political life be interpreted in such an exceptional way? Indeed, as late as June 1991, Gorbachev's most critical adviser reported that the "situation is relatively stable now" (Aleksandr Yakovlev in *FBIS*, June 7, 1991, 27). For similar critiques of Moscow intellectual and Western press "hysteria" at the time, see Hough, *Democratization*, 262–65; Moshe Lewin, *Russia/USSR/Russia* (New York, 1995), 301; and Alexander Dallin's related point that the system had survived worse crises, in Dallin and Gail W. Lapidus, eds., *The Soviet System*, rev. ed. (Boulder, Colo., 1995), 674.

13. Alexei Izyumov in *Moscow Magazine* (April 1991): 28–31. Similarly, see V. N. Kudriavtsev in *Izvestiia*, Feb. 5, 1990; E. Batalov in *Izvestiia*, Nov. 26, 1990; Burlatskii in *LG*, May 2, 1990; and, Shevardnadze in *LG*, April 18, 1990. For a different view, based on personal observation and memory, see Valerii Solovei's review of an earlier version of this chapter in *PK*, no. 24 (Dec. 2006), politklass.ru.

14. *NG-Stsenarii,* Jan. 16, 1997; Cherniaev, *1991,* 20; Andrei Grachev, *Gorbachev* (Moscow, 2001), 119. Similarly, see Gorbachev's remarks in *Pravda,* March 2, 1991; and *FBIS,* March 31, 1991, 63, May 18, 1991, 23, and July 22, 1991, 18. An American economist, Ed Hewett, made an analogous point about the economy (quoted in Ben Eklof, *Soviet Briefing* [Boulder, Colo., 1989], 99).

15. David Arbel and Ran Edelist, *Western Intelligence and the Collapse of the Soviet Union* (London, 2003). Even Western scholars who saw "an irreversible process of breakdown" did not foresee the end of the Soviet Union. See, e.g., Peter Reddaway in *Report,* Aug. 25, 1989, 1. Nor did those who later insisted that the end had been inevitable, see, e.g., Martin Malia in *NYRB,* March 29, 1990, 26–27. For an exception, see Vladimir Kvint, a Russian scholar living in the United States, in *Moscow Magazine* (April 1991): 45; and for a partial exception, Zbigniew Brzezinski, *The Grand Failure* (New York, 1989), 245, who, writing in August 1988, thought that of the five "alternative outcomes," the end of the Soviet Union was the "much more remote possibility."

16. Gromyko, *Anatolii Gromyko,* 103; Nikolai Popov in *NV,* no. 11 (2005): 21; D. Zykin, "Model krakha SSSR," Internet protiv teleekrana, Oct. 21, 2005; and Sergei Baburin in *Natsionalnye interesy,* no. 5–6 (2001): 3. Similarly, see Anatolii Utkin in *NG,* Dec. 31, 1997; Sergei Kara-Murza in *SR,* Oct. 8, 2002; and V. V. Alekseev and S. A. Nefedov in *ONS,* no. 6 (2002)_: 66.

17. Stefan Hedlund in *RR* (Jan. 2007): 163.

18. Peter Kenez in *Kritika* (Spring 2003): 369. The explanation given by another veteran specialist, also "in retrospect," is equally unhelpful: "it appears that the U.S.S.R. was never really a viable country" (Strobe Talbott, introduction to Arbatov, *The System,* ix).

19. For overviews of several but not all of the explanations, see S. V. Cheshko, *Raspad Sovetskogo Soiuza* (Moscow, 1996), 8–19; V. V. Alekseev and E. V. Alekseeva in *OI,* no. 5 (2003): 4–6; Anatolii Utkin in V. I. Tolstykh, ed., *Perestroika* (Moscow, 2005), 126–38; F. N. Klotsvog in *OI,* no. 3 (2005): 176–81; Medvedev, *Sovetskii Soiuz,* chap. 5; A. V. Buzgalin and A. I. Kolganov, *Stalin i raspad SSSR* (Moscow, 2003), chaps. 2–3; D. V. Maslov, *Istoriograficheskie i metodologicheskie osnovy issledovaniia sostoianiia sovetskoi sistemy* (Sergiev Posad, 2004), 183–90; Leslie Holmes, *Post-Communism* (Durham, N.C., 1997), chap. 2; Rutland in *Transitions* (Feb. 1998): 14–21; Rowley in *Kritika* (Spring 2001): 395–426; Jeremy Smith, *The Fall of Soviet Communism* (New York, 2005); and Kramer in *JCWS* (Winter 2003): 3–16.

20. Consider, e.g., the relevant sections of Stephen Kotkin, *Armageddon Averted* (New York, 2001); Hough, *Democratization;* Carol Barner-Barry and Cynthia A. Hody, *The Politics of Change* (New York, 1995), esp. 3, 5, 131–32; Nick Bisley, *The End of the Cold War and the Causes of Soviet Col-*

lapse (New York, 2004); V. V. Isakov, *Raschlenenka* (Moscow, 1998), esp. 170; R. G. Pikhoia in G. N. Sevostianov, ed., *Rossiia v XX veke*, 2 vols. (Moscow, 2002), 1:121–45; V. V. Alekseev and E. V. Alekseeva in *OI*, no. 5 (2003): 3–20; Dmitri Trenin, *The End of Eurasia* (Washington, D.C., 2002), esp. chap. 2; Vitalii Tretiakov in *PK*, no. 24 (Dec. 2006), politklass.ru; and Tsipko in *LG*, Dec. 20, 2006. For "its own weight," see Stephen R. Sestanovich in *JRL*, Oct. 25, 2007; and Donald W. Treadgold, *Twentieth Century Russia*, 8th edition (Boulder, Colo., 1995), 430. Similarly, see Steven Lee Myers in *NYT*, Oct. 9, 2005; and Margaret Paxon in *JRL*, Aug. 3, 2004. For the Russian scholar, see Anatolii Utkin in *NG*, Dec. 31, 1997. There are also utterly trivial explanations such as the suggestion that President Reagan's wife Nancy "precipitated the end of the Soviet Union" (Diana McLellan in *WP Book World*, June 15, 2003, 5).

21. See, e.g., Sergei Cheshko in *NG*, Jan. 16, 1997; and N. Bikkenin in *SM*, no. 10 (2000): 98. For a few of the many examples in the Western literature, see Richard Lourie, *Sakharov* (New York, 2002), 404; and this volume, chap. 4, nn. 4, 6.

22. Martha Brill Olcott in *Slavic Review* (Spring 1995): 207; Rutland in *Transitions* (Feb. 1998): 16; and Beissinger, *Nationalist Mobilization*, 3. For "postfacto," see R. Kh. Simonian in *NNI*, no. 2 (2003): 57. For a similar critique of "retrospective determinism," see Stathis N. Kalyvas in *Annual Review of Political Science* 2 (1999): 323–43.

23. John P. Maynard in William Barbour and Carol Wekesser, eds., *The Breakup of the Soviet Union* (San Diego, 1994), 27. Similarly, see Martin Malia, *The Soviet Tragedy* (New York, 1994); the treatment of "civilization" in Kotkin, *Armageddon*; de Tinguy in Anne de Tinguy, ed., *The Fall of the Soviet Empire* (Boulder, Colo., 1997), 55; and Richard Pipes, *Communism* (London, 1994), 147–48.

24. Felipe Fernández-Armesto in *TLS*, Oct. 12, 2007, 5. For the preceding quote, see Wisła Suraska, *How the Soviet Union Disappeared* (Durham, N.C., 1998), 1; and for other examples, Bohdan Nahaylo and Victor Swoboda, *Soviet Disunion* (New York, 1990); Ann Sheehy in Vera Toltz and Iain Elliot, eds., *The Demise of the USSR* (London, 1995), 3; Alexander J. Motyl, *Imperial Ends* (New York, 2001), 10; Leon Aron, *Yeltsin* (New York, 2000), 478–79; Ariel Cohen, *Russian Imperialism* (Westport, Conn., 1996); Susanne Michele Birgerson, *After the Breakup of a Multi-Ethnic Empire* (Westport, Conn., 2002); Raymond Pearson, *The Rise and Fall of the Soviet Empire* (New York, 1998); John L. H. Keep, *Last of the Empires* (New York, 1995); and this chapter, n. 34. For obvious reasons, the "doomed-empire" explanation was also popular among Yeltsin's men who had helped abolish the Union. See, e.g., Gennady Burbulis and Sergei Vasilev cited in Lynn D.

Nelson and Irina Y. Kuzes, *Radical Reform in Yeltsin's Russia* (Armonk, N.Y., 1995), 10; and later Yeltsin himself, quoted in RIA Novosti dispatch, Dec. 7, 2006, in *JRL*, Dec. 7, 2006.

25. For an extended argument that the end of the Soviet empire in Eastern Europe was a major factor in ending the Soviet Union, see Kramer in *JCWS* (Fall 2003): 178–256; (Fall 2004): 3–64; and (Winter 2005): 3–96. A Soviet insider at the time reports, however, that "no one at the Central Committee or in the country's leadership noticed the departure of East Europe in 1989" because they were focused on dramatic events inside the country (Aleksandr Tsipko in *VA*, no. 2 [2005]: 225). For a scholarly attempt to relate the two, but which conflates and thus confuses them, see Beissinger in *Slavic Review* (Summer 2006): 294–303; and in *AAASS NewsNet*, Jan. 2008, 5.

26. As pointed out by Rowley in *Kritika* (Spring 2001): 418–19; and Beissinger, *Nationalist Mobilization*, 5–6, though he suggests otherwise in *AAASS NewsNet*, Jan. 2008, 1. For varying and shifting scholarly positions on this issue since 1991, see Beissinger in *Slavic Review* (Summer 2006): 294–303; and for the "imperial turn" in Western Russian studies more generally since 1991, the editors' comment in *Kritika* (Fall 2006): 705–12. The quote is from Anne Applebaum in *NYRB*, Feb. 12, 2004, 11. To take a telling example, few, if any, Western scholars despised the Soviet Union more than did Martin Malia, but even he denied it was an empire, "at least not in any usual sense of the word" (*Daedalus* [Spring 1992]: 66). One Western scholar who used the empire model presented a scenario of its doom, a clash with the Muslim world, that turned out to be fundamentally wrong (Hélène Carrère d'Encausse, *Decline of an Empire* [New York, 1981], esp. 277–84). For sharp criticism of her work by Russian scholars, see S. M. Iskhakov and V. A. Tishkov in G. N. Sevostianov, ed., *Tragediia velikoi derzhavy* (Moscow, 2005), 486, 502–3, 594.

27. Robert Kagan in *Foreign Policy* (Summer 1998), foreignpolicy.com. For opinions on this, see, e.g., Andrew J. Bacevich, *American Empire* (Cambridge, Mass., 2002); James B. Rule in *Dissent* (Fall 2002): 46; Max Boot in *WS*, Nov. 4, 2002, 26–29; Ivo H. Daalder and James M. Lindsay in *NYT*, May 10, 2003; the articles in *National Interest* (Spring 2003); Rich Lowry in *New York Post*, July 19, 2003; Niall Ferguson in *WSJ*, June 6, 2003; Kal Raustiala in *IHT*, July 2, 2003; G. John Ikenberry in *FA* (March/April 2004): 144–54; Corey Robin in *WP*, May 2, 2004; John Lewis Gaddis and Paul Kennedy in *NYT Book Review*, July 25, 2004, 23; Ronald Steel in *The Nation*, Sept. 20, 2004, 29–35; and David C. Henrickson in *WPJ* (Summer 2005): 1–22. For Russian commentaries on America's "road to Empire," see V. O. Pechatnov in *NNI*, no. 2 (2006): 85–88; and Sergei Samuilov in *SM*, no. 3 (2006): 34–44.

28. See, respectively, Ronald Grigor Suny, *Revenge of the Past* (Stanford, Calif., 1993), 157–60; Ben Fowkes, *The Disintegration of the Soviet Union* (London, 1997), vii; Dominic Lieven, *Empire* (New Haven, Conn., 2001), xii; Terry Martin, *The Affirmative Action Empire* (Ithaca, N.Y., 2001), 19; and Hough, *Democratization*, 216. For Russians, in addition, of course, to Gorbachev, see, e.g., R. Kh. Simonian in *VI*, no. 12 (2002): 27–39; Cheshko, *Raspad*; Boris Kagarlitskii in *NG*, Jan. 16, 1997; Sergei Roy in *Moscow News*, Sept. 8–14, 1999; and V. D. Solovei, *Russkaia istoriia* (Moscow, 2005), 138–39, 155–56, 158. Some Russians do argue that it was an empire. See, e.g., V. V. Sogrin in *ONS*, no. 4 (2002): 98; Egor Gaidar, *Gibel imperii* (Moscow, 2006); Alexei Arbatov in *Russia in Global Affairs* (Jan.–March 2006): 23–34; and the discussion in *OI*, no. 2 (2005): 211–16, and in Sevostianov, ed., *Tragediia*, esp. section 3. For the quote, see Motyl, *Imperial Ends*, 10; and, similarly, Suraska, *How the Soviet Union*, 1.

29. Holmes, *Post-Communism*, 34; and Trenin, *End*, 80. Similarly, see Nahaylo and Swoboda, *Soviet Disunion*, xii; Robert Strayer, *Why Did the Soviet Union Collapse?* (Armonk, N.Y.. 1998), 78; Richard Sakwa, *Gorbachev and His Reforms* (Englewood Cliff, N.J., 1991), 259; Martin, *Affirmative*, 18–19; and Maslov, *Istoriograficheskie*, 185, where the same point is made about Russian scholars. One American scholar tries to reconcile the anomalies by positing the Soviet Union's "resemblance" to an empire, but this could be true of many multiethnic states (Beissinger in *Slavic Review* [Summer 2006]: 294–303).

30. See Vladimir Shlapentokh, *A Normal Totalitarian Society* (Armonk, N.Y., 2001), 163–66; Solovei, *Russkaia istoriia*, 138–39, 158; and the remarks of the president of Kirgiziia, who was "grateful to the Soviet period" for his former republic's industrial and technological advances, in *SM*, no. 4 (2002): 52. Similarly, see Valerii Sidorov on Soviet Lithuania, in *VA*, no. 3 (2007): 52–55. Indeed, some Russian intellectuals and politicians insisted that their resource-rich republic was the real economic victim of the Union. For a discussion, see Hough, *Democratization*, 241–45; Fowkes, *Disintegration*, 152–56; and on this issue more broadly, Geoffrey Hosking, *Rulers and Victims* (Cambridge, Mass., 2006).

31. Lieven, *Empire*, xii. Similarly, see Suny, *Revenge*; Fowkes, *Disintegration*; and Astrid S. Tuminez in *JCWS* (Fall 2003): 135.

32. Cheshko, *Raspad*, 6; and, similarly, in Sevostianov, ed., *Tragediia*, 445. For the first quote, see Malia in *Daedalus* (Spring 1992): 66.

33. For this argument, see, e.g., Buckley, *Redefining*; Caroline Ibos in de Tinguy, ed., *Fall*, 134–53; and Leon Aron, *Russia's Revolution* (Washington, D.C., 2007), esp. chaps. 1–3. Similarly, see Holmes, *Post-Communism*, 57; David Lane in Michael Cox, ed., *Rethinking the Soviet Collapse* (New York,

1998), 159; and Lieven, *Empire*, 335. Matthew Wyman, *Public Opinion in Post-Communist Russia* (New York, 1997), 86, also argues that there was a "legitimacy crisis," but his own data seem not to confirm it.

34. See, respectively, Strobe Talbott in *JRL*, June 8, 2002; Hélène Carrère d'Encausse, *The End of the Soviet Empire* (New York, 1993), 219, 230, 270; Beissinger, *Nationalist Mobilization*, 8, 37; and Bernard Gwertzman in Gwertzman and Michael T. Kaufman, eds., *The Decline and Fall of the Soviet Empire* (New York, 1992), x. Similarly, see Strayer, *Why*, 132, 149; Keep, *Last*, 3, 333; Dina Zisserman-Brodsky, *Constructing Ethnopolitics in the Soviet Union* (New York, 2003); and several items cited this chapter, n. 24.

35. R. G. Pikhoia, *Sovetskii Soiuz* (Moscow, 1998), 674–75; and, similarly, Solovei, *Russkaia istoriia*, 147. For Central Asia and Azerbaijan, see, respectively, Fowkes, *Disintegration*, 190–91; and Geidar Aliev in *OG*, Aug. 16–22, 2001. Not even three of the purportedly most independent republic leaders—Zviad Gamsakhurdia of Georgia, Kravchuk of Ukraine, and Nursultan Nazarbaev of Kazakhstan—openly resisted. See, respectively, Gennadii Ianaev in *OG*, Aug. 15–21, 1996, who comments also on Kravchuk; and Oleg Poptsov, *Khronika vremen "Tsaria Borisa"* (Moscow, 1995), 259–60. For Kravchuk and Nazarbaev, see also Anatolii Butenko in *Pravda*, Sept. 18, 1991; and on the former, Andrew Wilson, *The Ukrainians* (New Haven, Conn., 2000), 166–68; and George Bush and Brent Scowcroft, *A World Transformed* (New York, 1998), 554.

36. Gordon M. Hahn, *Russia's Revolution from Above* (New Brunswick, N.J., 2002), 3–4; Boris Kagarlitskii in *NG*, Jan. 16, 1997; and *NG-Stsenarii*, May 23, 1996. Similarly, see Astrid S. Tuminez in *JCWS* (Fall 2003): 115–16; and Edward W. Walker, *Dissolution* (Lanham, Md., 2003), 2, 15n. 9. On the latter point, see Aleksandr Tsipko's early warning in *Izvestiia*, Oct. 1, 1991. For a fairly typical republic, see Martha Brill Olcott, *Kazakhstan* (Washington, D.C., 2002), 16, 35.

37. Beissinger's *Nationalist Mobilization* is a prime example of where, as Stephen Kotkin observed, "everything seems to be coded as nationalist" (*Kritika* [Summer 2007]: 530n. 127).

38. Cheshko in Sevostianov, ed., *Tragediia*, 451; and Boris Kagarlitskii in *NG*, Jan. 16, 1997. And, similarly, Boris Pankin, *The Last Hundred Days of the Soviet Union* (New York, 1996), 266–67; and Valery Tiskov, *Ethnicity, Nationalism, and Conflict in and After the Soviet Union* (London, 1997), 44–46.

39. *Pravda*, March 16, 1990. For a study, see Walker, *Dissolution*.

40. Oleg Rumyantsev in *MT*, June 17, 1995. Similarly, see Viktor Bondarev in *Rodina*, no. 7 (1995): 27; Nikolai Ryzhkov in *NS*, no. 2 (2006): 164; and even Sergei Shakrai, a drafter of the Union abolition documents, in *NG*,

May 16, 2000. One leading Russian democrat thought it did not mean "any more genuine sovereignty than [have U.S.] states" (Sergei Stankevich in *Demokratizatsiya* [Spring 1994]: 319). And though Gorbachev would later blame the resolution for undermining the Union, he is reported to have said at the time: "I don't see anything terrible. . . . It doesn't threaten the Union" (F. D. Bobkov, *KGB i vlast* [Moscow, 1995], 365).

41. For the confusion, see Wilson, *The Ukrainians*, 165; Pankin, *Last*, 264; Hough, *Democratization*, 479–80; and for the more widespread confusion, Walker, *Dissolution*, 6, 13. From the beginning, some Politburo members worried about possible interpretations of "sovereignty" (V. I. Vorotnikov, *A bylo eto tak . . .* [Moscow, 1995], 282). For the elite, see Joan DeBardeleben, *Russian Politics in Transition*, 2nd ed. (Boston, 1997), 129–30; Roman Laba in *Transition*, Jan. 12, 1996, 13; Henry E. Hale, "The Strange Death of the Soviet Union," Harvard University Davis Center, Ponars Series, No. 12, March 1999), 19–27; and this chapter, n. 44.

42. Hale, "Strange Death," 24–25. Similarly, see Walker, *Dissolution*, 15n. 9, 153–54; Brown, *Gorbachev*, 303; and for a Russian expert, Viacheslav Mikhailov in *NG*, April 12, 2001. For Gorbachev, see Hough, *Democratization*, 479–80; and, similarly, Andrei Grachev, *Dalshe bez menia . . .* (Moscow, 1994), 184–85. Another top Soviet leader, Anatolii Lukianov, later made the same point. *SR*, July 30, 1998.

43. U.S. State Department analysis in *JRL Supplement*, June 15, 2002; and Roman Solchanyk, citing a 2003 survey done in Kyiv, in *JRL*, Oct. 18, 2004. Similar survey results were reported by Interfax, Jan. 10, 2006, in *JRL*, Jan. 11, 2006.

44. Hale, "Strange Death," 19, 24. Similarly, see Fedor Burlatskii, *Glotok svobody*, 2 vols. (Moscow, 1997), 2:24, who calls the Ukrainian elite the "main battering ram" of the Union's destruction; and DeBardeleben, *Russian Politics*, 129–30, who notes the "definition of reality constructed by the elites."

45. Aleksandr Umnov in *NG*, Jan. 19, 2000; Stephen White, *Communism and Its Collapse* (New York, 2001), 77. Similarly, see Roi Medvedev, who adds Western Ukraine, in *OI*, no. 4 (2003): 113; Rutland in *Transitions* (Feb. 1998): 17; and Peter Reddaway and Dmitri Glinski, *The Tragedy of Russia's Reforms* (Washington, D.C., 2001), 245.

46. See, respectively, Phillip J. Bryson in *Slavic Review* (Winter 2005): 920; Barner-Barry and Hody, *Politics*, 3; Åslund, *How*, 52; and M. Steven Fish in *PSA* (Oct.–Dec. 2001): 355. Similarly, see Malia, *Soviet Tragedy*, 464, 473, 492–93; Aron, *Yeltsin*, 481–83; William Moskoff, *Hard Times* (Armonk, N.Y., 1993), 6–7, 233–35; and Orlando Figes in *NYT Book Review*, March 19, 1995.

47. See, e.g., the fervently anti-Marxist scholars in Lee Edwards, ed., *The Collapse of Communism* (Stanford, Calif., 1999); and the Marxist Hillel H. Ticktin in Cox, ed., *Rethinking*, chap. 4; and, similarly, Boris Kagarlitskii, *Marksizm ne rekomendovano dlia obucheniia* (Moscow, 2005), 302. For a Marxist objection to this explanation, see David M. Kotz and Fred Weir, *Revolution from Above* (New York, 1997), chap. 5 and page 226.

48. See, e.g., Egor Gaidar, *Dni porazhenii i pobed* (Moscow, 1996), chap. 5; Gaidar, *Gibel imperii*, esp. chaps. 7–8; and, similarly, Otto Latsis in *Izvestiia*, June 28, 1996. For similar criticisms of their claims, see Oleg Davydov in *NG*, Jan. 27, 2000; Renald Simonian in *SM*, no. 7–8 (2006): 20–21; Karen Shakhnazarov in *LG*, Jan. 24–30, 2007; and Valerii Bushuev in *SM*, no. 1 (2007): 196–97. According to a once-imprisoned dissident, it was only in 1992, after the onset of Gaidar's "reforms," that "for the first time, hungry people were visible" (Andrei Sinyavsky, *The Russian Intelligentsia* [New York, 1997], 29–30). And by the end of the decade, according to a leading American authority, there was "the specter of a hungry Russia, immersed in poverty" (Stephen K. Wegren in *PPC* [Jan./Feb. 2000]: 38.

49. For similar arguments, see White, *Communism*, 79; Kotz and Weir, *Revolution*, 74; Vladimir Tikhomirov in *EAS* (March 2000): 227; Valentin Pavlov in *LG*, July 18, 2001; and V. Shliapentokh in *VE*, no. 10 (2005): 153.

50. For similar points, see Robert V. Daniels in Cox, ed., *Rethinking*, 122; Moskoff, *Hard Times*, 234; Kotz and Weir, *Revolution*, 74–75; Nekipelov in *ONS*, no. 4 (2005): 9; and Shliapentokh in *VE*, no. 10 (2005): 153. For a debate on the subject, see Vladimir G. Treml and Michael Ellman in *RFE/RL*, June 4, 1993, 53–58.

51. For the economist, see James Millar quoted by Robert D. English in *International Security* (Spring 2002): 90n. 69. And for similarly revisionist analyses of earlier periods in Soviet economic history, G. I. Khanin in *EAS* (Dec. 2003): 1187–212; and Robert C. Allen, *Farm to Factory* (Princeton, N.J., 2003). For accounts warning against exaggerating the crisis at the time, see Richard Parker in *Atlantic Monthly* (June 1990): 68–80; and Peter Passell in *NYT*, April 7, 1991. And for some bright spots, see Lynn Turgeon in *JRL*, April 2, 1997; and V. S. Pavlov in *Izvestiia*, June 15, 1991, and later in *LG*, July 18, 2001.

52. For such warehouses, see Stephen Handelman, *Comrade Criminal* (New Haven, Conn., 1995), 67–68; and Alexandra George, *Escape from "Ward Six"* (New York, 1998), 584. The leadership understood that official price policy was the main cause of the problem. See, e.g., Anatolii Lukianov in *KP*, March 13, 1991; and Gorbachev cited in *Novaia zhizn*, Oct. 25, 2002. The same kind of "artificially created" shortages had occurred in 1928 and

1929, contributing to the end of NEP, a point made by Anatoly Sobchak in *FBIS*, Sept. 24, 1991, 68.

53. For the general hysteria, see Hough, *Democratization*, 262–65; Lewin, *Russia/USSR/Russia*, 301; and Dallin in Dallin and Lapidus, eds., *The Soviet System*, 674. The dire predictions were fueled both by Gorbachev's enemies and by his own representatives, who were trying to frighten the West into granting major financial aid lest a destabilized Soviet Union lose "control over one of the world's largest nuclear potentials." See, e.g., the letter by Grigory Yavlinsky and Yevgeny Primakov to the G7 in *NYT*, May 30, 1991; and Michael R. Beschloss and Strobe Talbott, *At the Highest Levels* (Boston, 1993), 384. For the "salt frenzy" of 2006, see *Moscow News*, Feb. 17–March 2, 2006.

54. Shakhnazarov in *LG*, Jan, 24–30, 2007. I ate in such cafeterias many times from the 1970s to the early 1990s. Similarly, see Braithwaite, *Across*, 296–97; and Renfrey Clarke in *JRL*, July 6, 1998. For personal testimony that the food situation was actually better before the abolition of the Soviet Union, not after, see Sinyavsky, *Russian Intelligentsia*, 29–30 and 47–48.

55. Michael Ellman and Vladimir Kontorovich, eds., *The Destruction of the Soviet Economic System* (Armonk, N.Y., 1998), 26 and passim; and, similarly, Kotz and Weir, *Revolution*; and Nelson and Kuzes, *Radical Reform*, chap. 1. Several political scientists and historians also agree. See, e.g., Hahn, *Russia's Revolution*, 217, 228–29; Hough, *Democratization*, chaps. 4, 11, 14; and Barsenkov, *Vvedenie*, 182.

56. A. N. Iakovlev in *Trud*, Sept. 27, 1991; and for Gorbachev, see Cherniaev, *1991*, 23. Similarly, see Gorbachev in *FBIS*, April 11, 1991, 15; and quoted in Robert G. Kaiser, *Why Gorbachev Happened*, exp. ed. (New York, 1992), 372.

57. For these developments, see this chapter, note 55. For railways, see Kramer in *JCWS* (Winter 2005): 44. For political sabotage, see A. N. Iakovlev, *Gorkaia chasha* (Yaroslav, 1994), 253, and quoted in Hough, *Democratization*, 353–54; Michael McFaul, *Russia's Unfinished Revolution* (Ithaca, N.Y., 2001), 97, 141; Reddaway and Glinski, *Tragedy*, 242, 277–78; and A. A. Sazonov, *Predateliami ne rozhdaiutsia* (Moscow, 2006), 11–14.

58. For an approving account of Yeltsin's actions, see John B. Dunlop, *The Rise of Russia and the Fall of the Soviet Empire* (Princeton, N.J., 1993), 266–69.

59. Gorbachev, *Zhizn*, 1:583.

60. *Na perepute (Novye vekhi)* (Moscow, 1999), 3. Similarly, see Natan Eidelman, *"Revoliutsiia sverkhu" v Rossii* (Moscow, 1989); Vladislav Surkov in *Ekspert*, no. 20 (2006): 105; Aleksandr Ianov, *Ten groznogo tsaria* (Moscow, 1997), esp. chap. 6; and for a somewhat different view, Solovei, *Russkaia istoriia*, chap. 5. See also Reddaway and Glinski, *Tragedy*, chap. 1.

61. Anatolii Cherniaev in *SM*, no. 4 (2005): 126. For the tragedy, see Ianov, *Ten*; this chapter, nn. 60 and 62; and for a similar thesis, Tim McDaniel, *The Agony of the Russian Idea* (Princeton, N.J., 1966).

62. For Gorbachev's place in this tradition, see, e.g., Aleksandr Tsipko in *KP*, March 16, 1991; Fedor Burlatskii on the "fate of reformers" in *LG*, June 27, 1990; M. F. Shatrov on the same subject in *SM*, no. 10 (1994): 23; V. Medvedev in *Proryv k svobode: o perestroike dvadtsat let spustia* (Moscow, 2005), 9; and Gorbachev's own famous lament, "I don't know any happy reformers." Elsewhere, commenting on the history I summarize in this paragraph, he explained, "The fates of Russian reformers are tragic" (M. S. Gorbachev, *Gody trudnykh reshenii* [Moscow, 1993], 25; in *KP*, Aug. 19, 1993); and, similarly, in Tolstykh, ed., *Perestroika*, 213. His wife put it more bluntly: "The thing about innovations is that sooner or later they turn around and destroy the innovators." Quoted in Beschloss and Talbott, *Highest Levels*, p. 230. For Lenin as a "tragic figure," see Iurii Burtin in *Krasnye Kholmy Almanakh* (Moscow, 1999), p. 462. For a critique of this "deterministic" interpretation of Russian reform, see A. B. Kamenskii in *VF*, No. 6, 2006, esp. pp. 25–26.

63. This is also the standard Western view. See, e.g., Tibor Szamuely, *The Russian Tradition* (London, 1974), chap. 10; Richard Pipes, *Russia Under the Old Regime* (New York, 1974), chap. 10; and Timo Vikavainen, *The Inner Adversary* (Washington, D.C., 2006). For a more differentiating account, Aileen M. Kelly, *Toward Another Shore* (New Haven, Conn., 1998); and for a Russian view, Aleksei Kiva in *SM*, no. 4 (2005): 170–80.

64. Aleksandr Tsipko, in *NG*, April 13, 1993; and, similarly, E. L. Petrenko in *OI*, no. 4 (2002): 200. For Western studies, see, e.g., Jonathan Steele, *Eternal Russia* (Cambridge, 1994), 58, 269–73; Hough, *Democratization*, 491–93; Lewin, *Russia*, 3–4, 301–3; McDaniel, *Agony*, 3–21, 147–48; and Yale Richmond, *Cultural Exchange and the Cold War* (University Park, Penn., 2003), which argues rather differently (esp. xiii–xiv) that a benign Russian intelligentsia, influenced by decades of official exchange programs with the United States, played a decisive role in the "collapse of Communism."

65. Iurii Poliakov in *SM*, no. 2 (1996): 23; Vladimir Iordanskii in *SM*, no. 8 (1997): 88; and Svetlana Shipunova in *SR*, May 16, 1995. According to another scholar—Iurii Oleshchuk in *SM*, no. 10 (2002): 27–34—it was not the real intelligentsia but a debased "semi-intelligentsia." For other academic examples, see A. A. Galkin in *"Perestroika" v transformatsionnom kontekste* (Moscow, 2005), 72–74; *Na perepute*; O. T. Bogomolov, *Moia letopis perekhodnogo vremeni* (Moscow, 2000), 163–66; and S. I. Romanovskii, *Neterpenie mysli, ili istoricheskii portret radikalnoi russkoi intelligentsii* (St. Petersburg, 2000). And for other Russian writers, Aleksandr Tsipko in

NG, April 9 and 13, 1993, *NG*, April 6, 1995, and *LG*, Nov. 21, 2001, and April 25–May 3, 2007; Andrei Siniavskii in *LG*, March 16, 1995; Andranik Migranian in *NG-Stsenarii*, no. 7 (1999); S. Kara-Mirza, *Anti-sovetskii proekt* (Moscow, 2002); several contributors to *Proryv*, 83, 237, 309–13, 326–29, 336–42; Naum Korzhavin in *Novaia*, Oct. 10–13, 2005; and Mikhail Antonov in *LG*, Feb. 21–27, 2007.

66. V. Ginzburg in *Izvestiia*, May 17, 1990; Aleksei Kiva in *KP*, April 15, 1991, *Izvestiia*, Feb. 26, 1991, and Dec. 10, 1990; Aleksandr Protsenko in *Izvestiia*, May 3, 1990; Kiva in *Izvestiia*, Jan. 24, 1991; and Nikolai Stoliarov in *Pravda*, April 2, 1991. Similarly, see Andranik Migranian in *LG*, Dec. 27, 1989; Fedor Burlatskii in *LG*, June 27, 1990; Leonid Ionin in *NV*, no. 27 (1990): 4–7; Gleb Pavlovskii in *Vek XX*, no. 4 (1991): 54–63; and on the evolutionary alternative, Kiva in *Izvestiia*, Feb. 26, 1991; and Leonid Abalkin in *Izvestiia*, March 14, 1991.

67. Aleksandr Tsipko in *KP*, March 16, 1991; G. Bordiugov and V. Kozlov in *Pravda*, Oct. 3, 1988. On NEP, see also Andrei Nuikin in *NM*, no. 1 (1988): 208–9; Tsipko in *SK*, May 26, 1990; Vladimir Volzhskii in *Nedelia*, July 23–29, 1990; A. N. Sakharov in *Kommunist*, no. 5 (1991): 60–71; and Aleksei Klimenko in *Pravda*, June 25, 1991. For the leadership, see Gorbachev's comments in *Pravda*, April 25 and July 26, 1991; and Aleksandr Iakovlev's analogy with the fate of the pro-NEP Bukharin group in the Politburo in 1929, in *Izvestiia*, July 26, 1991, and *LG*, Aug. 28, 1991.

68. See, respectively, N. Ia. Petrakov, *Russkaia ruletka* (Moscow, 1998), 93; V. Anfilov on Iurii Afanasev in *Pravda*, Feb. 22, 1991; and Nikita Bogoslavskii on himself in *Ogonek*, no. 45 (1990): 27. For similar comments on past conformity and penance, see Petrakov, *Russkaia ruletka*, 131, 279–81; Aleksandr Tsipko in *SK*, May 26, 1990; Aleksei Kiva in *NM*, no. 8 (1993); Judith Devlin, *The Rise of the Russian Democrats* (Brookfield, Vt., 1995), 16. Gorbachev is quoted by Tsipko in *Proryv*, 336. For a different explanation of their ideological conversion, see Kotz and Weir, *Revolution*, 65–66, 69–70; and for a critical interpretation of the intelligentsia in Soviet and post-Soviet times, Boris Kagarlitsky, *Russia Under Yeltsin and Putin* (London, 2002), chap. 2; and Sinyavsky, *Russian Intelligentsia*. For contrasting examples of leading *intelligenty* who changed radically and those who did not, see, respectively, Iurii Kariakin, *Peremena ubezhdenii* (Moscow, 2007); and Anatolii Rybakov *Roman-vospominanie* (Moscow, 1997).

69. For the plan, see *500 Days (Transition to the Market)* (New York, 1991); and for the IMF, Reddaway and Glinski, *Tragedy*, 176. Influential Western specialists insist that Gorbachev's rejection of the plan exposed him as a pseudoreformer or was a "fateful error." See, e.g., Malia, *Soviet Tragedy*, 479–80; Jack, F. Matlock, *Autopsy on an Empire* (New York, 1995), 419.

And, similarly, Kaiser, *Why Gorbachev*, 363; and George Soros in *Moscow News*, Oct. 30–Nov. 5, 1997. But even supporters of shock therapy under Yeltsin later admitted the 1990 plan was a "fairy tale," "utopianism," and "not realistic." See Gaidar, *Dni*, 68; V. V. Sogrin in *NNI*, no. 1 (1999): 86; and McFaul, *Russia's*, 100. Indeed, Yeltsin himself, who had supported the plan in 1990 and 1991, later called it a "child-like" example of "maximalism" (*MN*, Oct. 21, 2003).

70. D. Furman, *Nasha strannaia revolutsiia* (Moscow, 1998), 5. Another moderate called them a "party of fools" (Petrakov, *Russkaia ruletka*, 278–86). For a detailed account of intelligentsia politics, see Devlin, *Rise*.

71. See, e.g., Tatiana Zaslavskaia in *Sociological Research* (Jan.–Feb. 1993): 62, and in *OG*, March 8–14, 2001; Stanislav Govorukhin cited in *NG*, July 22, 1994; Liliia Shevtsova in *10 let bez SSSR* (Moscow, 2002), 28–29, in *Proryv*, 350, and in *MN*, March 3–9, 2006; L. I. Saraskina in *Gorbachevskie chtenii*, no. 1 (Moscow, 2003), 99–102; and Tatyana Tolstaya, *Pushkin's Children* (Boston, 2001), comparing her views on pp. 27–48 with those on pp. 182–83, and who is quoted here (59). For a harsh criticism of their earlier behavior, see Sinyavsky, *Russian Intelligentsia*.

72. See *MN*, Nov. 18–25, 1990; and for January 1991, the accounts in A. S. Cherniaev, *Shest let s Gorbachevym* (Moscow, 1993), 405–15, and *1991 god*, 56–57, 86.

73. Pankin, *Last*, 269. Similarly, see this chapter, n. 124.

74. John B. Dunlop in *JCWS* (Winter 2003): 124. Similarly, see Malia, *Soviet Tragedy*; Holmes, *Post-Communism*, 58; and V. V. Sogrin in *OI*, no. 2 (1995): 9–10. The most insistent Russian "objectivists" are those who played leading roles in the abolition of the Union or in the post-Soviet government that emerged from it but who denied their personal—that is, subjective—responsibility, as was noted even at the time (Sergei Markov in *Trud*, Dec. 15, 1991). See, e.g., Yeltsin's interview with Moscow Russian Television, on March 14, 1996, where he insisted that "the collapse" was "an objective process" and therefore "inevitable" (in *FBIS*, March 15, 1996, 18), and, similarly, Boris Eltsin, *Zapiski prezidenta* (Moscow, 1994), 152; Vladimir Mau and Irina Starodubrovskaya, *The Challenge of Revolution* (New York, 2001); Gaidar, *Dni*, 148–51; Vladimir Lukin in *LG*, Jan. 24–30, 2007; and Stanislav Shushkevich and the Russians cited in this chapter, n. 98.

75. Valerii Solovei in *SM*, no. 7 (2001): 95; and Dallin in Dallin and Lapidus, eds., *Soviet System*, 686. Similarly, see George W. Breslauer, *Gorbachev and Yeltsin as Leaders* (New York, 2002); Joel M. Ostrow in *EAS* (Dec. 2002): 1340; Reddaway and Glinski, *Tragedy*, 228; Robert V. Daniels in *The Nation*, Jan. 3, 2000, 25; the evidence presented in Brown, *Gorbachev*; and the sources cited in this chapter, nn. 76 and 77.

76. Roi Medvedev in *OI*, no. 4 (2003): 112. Similarly, see I. P. Osadchii, ed., *Ot katastrofy k vozrozhdeniiu* (Moscow, 1999); Cheshko in Sevostianov, ed., *Tragediia*, 466; Zigmund Stankevich, *Istoriia krusheniia SSSR* (Moscow, 2001), 439–41; Barsenkov, *Vvedenie*, 356–57; R. Kh. Simonian in *NNI*, no. 2 (2003): 57–58; and Tsipko in *LG*, Dec. 20, 2006. For public opinion, see Shlapentokh, *Normal*, 262n. 1; and a VTsION survey done on July 17–21, 2003, reported at wcion.ru.

77. William E. Odom, *The Collapse of the Soviet Military* (New Haven, Conn., 1998), 393; Joel C. Moses in Wieczynski, ed., *Gorbachev*, 141; and, almost identically, Shakhnazarov, *Tsena*, 133. Even authors who think other factors were primarily or powerfully responsible nonetheless strongly emphasize Gorbachev's role. In addition to Odom cited here (393, 397), see, e.g., Kotkin, *Armageddon*; Strayer, *Why*; Hough, *Democratization*; Fowkes, *Disintegration*, 196; and Treadgold, *Twentieth-Century Russia*, 430.

78. For the first view, see, respectively, Matlock, *Autopsy*, 663; Eduard Samoilov in *NG*, Oct. 13, 1992; Olga Chaikovskaia in *LG*, Oct. 21, 1992. And, similarly, Aleksandr Tsipko cited by John Lloyd in *FT*, April 24, 1995; and Vitalii Tretiakov in Tolstykh, ed., *Perestroika*, 9. For the second, see Joel M. Ostrow in *EAS* (Dec. 1997): 1537, and (Dec. 2002): 1340. Similarly, see Michael Mandelbaum in Wilham Barbour and Carol Wekesser, eds., *The Breakup of the Soviet Union* (San Diego, 1994), 44–50; Leonid Smoliakov in *NG*, Jan. 16, 1997; the section entitled "Katastroika" in Aleksandr Zinoviev, *Smuta* (Moscow, 1994), 5–183; Aslanbek Shogenov in *SR*, March 2, 2006; and the criticisms of Gorbachev's economic policies in Ellman and Kontorovich, eds., *Destruction*. And for "*konspirologiia*" (*Zavtra*, no. 26 [2003]), see, e.g., Aleksandr Zinoviev, *Gibel russkogo kommunizma* (Moscow, 2001), 80–87; V. Chertishchev quoted by F. Sizyi in *KP*, April 26, 1991; A. P. Sheviakin, *Razgrom sovetskoi derzhavy* (Moscow, 2005); Osadchii, ed., *Ot katastrofy*, 18; and S. G. Kara-Murza, *Vtoroe preduprezhdenie* (Moscow, 2005).

79. For Russian examples, see the preceding note. For fulsome examples on the U.S. side, see Peter Schweizer, *Victory* (New York, 1994) and *Reagan's War* (New York, 2000). For a very different view of Reagan's intent, see Jack F. Matlock Jr., *Reagan and Gorbachev* (New York, 2004).

80. Breslauer, *Gorbachev and Yeltsin*, 269; Vladimir M. Zubok in William C. Wohlforth, ed., *Cold War Endgame* (University Park, Penn., 2003), 216; and Zubok, *A Failed Empire* (Chapel Hill, N.C., 2007), chap. 10. Similarly, see Brown, *Gorbachev*.

81. Aleksandr Iakovlev in *MN*, March 11, 2005.

82. For accounts, see Dunlop, *Rise*, 267–69; Hahn, *Russia's Revolution*, 214–20; Stankevich, *Istoriia*, chap. 6; and A. S. Barsenkov and A. I. Vdovin, *Istoriia Rossii, 1938–2002* (Moscow, 2003), 386–89. Even an admirer, Dunlop,

describes these acts as Yeltsin's "autumn putsch" (267). Similarly, see Raymond L. Garthoff, *The Great Transition* (Washington, D.C., 1994), 479.

83. Nursultan Nazarbaev quoted by V. A. Popovich in *SR*, Oct. 5, 2002

84. Simes, *After*, 55; Brown, *Gorbachev*, 303. For the Belorussian leader, Shushkevich, who had been Lee Harvey Oswald's Russian tutor in Minsk (Steven Lee Myers in *NYT*, May 30, 2003), see his evasive remarks to Gorbachev on November 25, 1991, quoted by Iurii Baturin in *Novaia*, Dec. 11–13, 2006; his odd, contradictory account in *Ogonek*, no. 49 (1996): 10–14; and Gaidar, *Dni*, 150. An informed Russian reports that Yeltsin and Kravchuk had been conniving against the Union since September 1991, with Yeltsin encouraging the latter's separatist impulses (Sazonov, *Predateliami*, 123, 128). Similarly, see Nikolai Ryzhkov in *NS*, no. 10 (2006): 194–98; and Bush and Scowcroft, *A World*, 556.

85. Yeltsin quoted in *FBIS*, March 15, 1996, 18.

86. Yeltsin quoted in Medvedev, *Sovetskii Soiuz*, 20; and G. E. Burbulis cited by Boris Slavin in *Pravda*, Dec. 28, 1995. Similarly, see this book, chap. 4, n. 83; and for the polls, Gorbachev, *Poniat*, 338.

87. For a similar argument, see Brown, *Gorbachev*, 307. Gorbachev always believed that Ukraine would return to a union, and some Western specialists agree. See Gorbachev, *On My Country and the World* (New York, 2000), 151, and in V. T. Loginov, ed. *Piat let posle Belovezhia* (Moscow, 1997), 5–10, 104–5; and, e.g., Simes, *After*, 65–66. For Yeltsin's decision, see Hough, *Democratization*, 469. And, similarly, Gorbachev, *My Country*, 147; Aleksandr Tsipko in *Izvestiia*, Oct. 1, 1991; and this chapter, n. 84.

88. Aleksandr Gelman in *MN*, Feb. 25–March 3, 1996; and V. A. Nikonov in *10 let*, 36. On Gorbachev's "will," see also his comment in *NG*, Jan. 16, 1997; and Dmitrii Volkogonov, *Sem vozhdei*, 2 vols. (Moscow, 1995), 2:323. For Gorbachev's own comment on the purpose of power, see Mikhail Gorbachev and Zdeněk Mlynář, *Conversations with Gorbachev* (New York, 2002), 210; and, similarly, Brown, *Gorbachev*. Regarding the end of the Soviet empire in Eastern Europe, U.S. officials at the time had no doubt that Gorbachev's will was the decisive factor. See Don Oberdorfer, *The Turn* (New York, 1991), 361; and Beschloss and Talbott, *Highest Levels*, 92. Similarly, see Jacques Lévesque, *The Enigma of 1989* (Berkeley, 1997). Gorbachev's enemies did not disagree about who ended the Cold War: "This village idiot Misha Gorbachev vanquished Russia" (Rustem Vakhitov in *SR*, July 30, 2002).

89. For an opposing interpretation of Gorbachev's motivations, arguing that most of these developments resulted primarily from his struggle for power against Politburo opponents, see Anthony D'Agostino, *Gorbachev's Revolution* (New York, 1998). For Gorbachev's remark, see Cherniaev, *1991*, 324.

90. Gorbachev in *LG*, Dec. 4, 1991. Similarly, see *Pravda*, April 12, 1990; *Izvestiia*, Dec. 1, 1990; *FBIS*, Jan. 24, 1991, and Oct. 15, 1991, 30; *MN*, Nov. 3, 1991; and Gorbachev, *Gody*, 288. For the same point, see Dmitrii Furman in *NG*, March 3, 2006, and in *Proryv*, 333. One Gorbachev supporter later saw this as a grievous mistake in Russia (Tsipko in *LG*, Jan. 19, 2005).

91. For the quotes, see Zubok in Wolhforth, ed., *Cold War*, 229–32, which includes a discussion; and Alexandr Iakovlev, *Omyt pamiati*, 2 vols. (Moscow, 2001), 2:84. For being uniquely without blood on his hands, see also Ales Adamovich in *FBIS*, Dec. 24, 1990, 61; Gorbachev's assertion to Vitalii Korotich, "There's no blood on these hands, not a drop," in *Stolitsa*, no. 15 (1992): 7; and, similarly, Sergei Chuprinin in *Znamia*, no. 12 (1994): 163. For the uniqueness of his non-violence in the history of Russian leadership, see also *Proryv*, 105–6, 208–9, 283, 333; and Shevtsova in *MN*, March 3–9, 2006. For arguments that Gorbachev should have used more force, see, e.g., Grigory Pomerants and Vladimir Lukin in *Demokratizatsiya* (Winter 1996): 14–15, 24–25; Sergei Roy in *Moscow News*, Nov. 13–19, 1997; Andranik Migranyan quoted by John Lloyd in *FT*, April 24, 1995; and Pavel Iurev in *SM*, no. 2 (2007): 208–11.

92. For the quotes, beginning with "revolution," see, respectively, *FBIS*, Oct. 1, 1987; Gorbachev in *NG*, Jan. 16, 1997; Zubok in Wohlforth, ed., *Cold War*, 232; Gorbachev quoted in *Kak "delalas" politika perestroiki, 1985–1991* (Moscow, 2004), 9; Liliia Shevtsova in Valentin Tolstykh, ed., *Mnogaia leta . . . Mikhailu Gorbachevu—70* (Moscow, 2001), 455; and Fedor Burlatskii in *NG*, June 7, 1994. For similar remarks by Gorbachev, see his *Gody*, 10; and Cherniaev, *Shest let*, 279, 380. For similar arguments that his nonviolence was ultimately "fatal" for the Soviet state, see Grachev, *Gorbachev*, 443; and Hough, *Democratization*, 250, 332, 488–89, 498. Gorbachev's refusal to arrest Yeltsin and his co-conspirators against the Union in December 1991—"I cannot do that"—is often misinterpreted as a lack of "political will" when it was actually his will to adhere to his credo. See, e.g., Sazonov, *Predateliami*, 135–36.

93. Gorbachev in *Novaia zhizn*, Oct. 25, 2002; and interviewed by NTV, Moscow, March 7, 2004, in *JRL*, March 8, 2004. On Yeltsin as a "tsar," see also Gorbachev quoted in Dzhuzeppe Boffa, *Ot SSSR k Rossii* (Moscow, 1996), 226. For the critic, see Otto Latsis in *Izvestiia*, Aug. 22, 1991.

94. See, respectively, Donald Murray, *A Democracy of Despots* (Boulder, Colo., 1995), 5; John Lloyd quoted in Hough, *Democratization*, 328; Yeltsin, *Zapiski*, 269; Vitalii Tretiakov in *PK* (April 2006), politklass.ru; and Vyacheslav Kostikov quoted by Jean Mackenzie in *Russia Review*, Feb. 26, 1996, 14. Similarly, see Sergei Markov quoted in Murray, *Democracy*, 222; Sergei Roy in *Moscow News*, March 3–9, 1999; Roy Medvedev interviewed

by Giulietto Chiesa in *FBIS*, Aug. 15, 1989, 61; Andranik Migranian in *KP*, Jan. 23, 1991; and Konrad Lyubarsky and Andrei Pionkovsky quoted by Richard Sakwa in *Demokratizatsiya* (Spring 2005): 261.

95. See, e.g., his memoirs: Eltsin, *Zapiski*, and Yeltsin, *Midnight Diaries* (New York, 2000); Aron, *Yeltsin*; Herbert J. Ellison, *Boris Yeltsin and Russia's Democratic Transformation* (Seattle, 2006); and Timothy J. Colton, *Yeltsin* (New York, 2008).

96. Ivan Laptev quoted by Egor Iakovlev, two men who knew Yeltsin well, in *OG*, Feb. 14–20, 2002. As is clear from Yeltsin's memoirs (*Zapiski* and *Midnight Diaries*), the hatred grew first from an envy of Gorbachev's top position, then from resentment over having been appointed a candidate rather than a full Politburo member by the leader, and later from humiliation over the way Gorbachev ousted him. (Their relationship is treated by Marc Zlotnik in *JCWS* [Winter 2003]: 128–64.) Once Yeltsin had the power, he humiliated Gorbachev in various large and petty ways. Years later, Yeltsin continued to make it clear that "I dislike him" (ORT interview, Oct. 7, 2000, in *JRL*, Oct. 12, 2000).

97. For the quotes, see, respectively, Yeltsin cited by Sergei Belyayev in *FBIS*, June 20, 1991, 57 (and, similarly, his radio address in *FBIS*, June 3, 1991, 74–75, and quoted by Boris Slavin in *Proryv*, 151); Riina Kionka in *Report*, Feb. 1, 1991, 15; Robert V. Daniels in *Dissent* (Fall 1993): 493; Matlock, *Autopsy*, 403; and Furman in *Proryv*, 329. To take an important example, it was reported that "Yeltsin had not read the Five Hundred Days Plan which he was backing so enthusiastically," while Gorbachev, who opposed it, "had read every word twice" (Braithwaite, *Across*, 293). Similarly, see Matlock, *Autopsy*, 418. For examples of Yeltsin's other conflicting positions, see, on perestroika, *FBIS*, Jan. 18, 1990, 131; June 3, 1991, 72; and Cherniaev, *1991*, 39. And on shock therapy, *KP*, Aug. 8, 1990; and *Izvestiia*, Dec. 4, 1991. In one such instance, Gorbachev remarked: "I didn't understand whether or not this was one and the same person" (*Pravda*, April 16, 1991), and, similarly, *Poniat*, 358, where Gorbachev reports Yeltsin was still sending him Leninist greetings on holidays right up to 1991. Yeltsin's enemies later itemized his shifting positions. See, e.g., Mikhail Chelnokov, *Rossiia bez soiuza, Rossiia bez Rossii* (Moscow, 1994), 30–33; and Viktor Trushkov in *Pravda*, March 16, 1996. Similarly, see Hough, *Democratization*, 279, 308, 333–34, 339–40. Yeltsin later seemed to acknowledge the validity of the charge, at least in part. See Eltsin, *Zapiski*, 32. For a similar interpretation of Yeltsin's political nature, see Kagarlitsky, *Russia Under*, 77–83.

98. Stanislav Shushkevich in Logionv, ed., *Piat let*, 156. Similarly, see Gennadii Burbulis in *Rodina*, no. 9 (1995): 74; Sergei Shakhrai in *NG*, Dec. 10, 1996; Iu. M. Baturin et al., eds., *Epokha Eltsina* (Moscow, 2001), 181–82;

Pikhoia, *Sovetskii Soiuz*, 688, 718; Egor Gaidar in *NI*, June 1, 2006; and Yeltsin himself and the other Russian writers cited this chapter, n. 74. Many Western scholars agree. See, e.g., Beissinger, *Nationalist Mobilization*, 438; and Aron, *Yeltsin*, 472–79. For accounts (and assertions) of Gorbachev's growing possibilities, see Yuriy Afanasyev in *FBIS*, Sept. 20, 1991, 20–21; Grachev, *Dalshe*, 184, who is quoted here; Boris Slavin in *Gorbachevskie chteniia*, no. 3 (Moscow, 2005), 111; Cheshko, *Raspad*, 278, and in Sevostianov, ed., *Tragediia*, 266; and Gorbachev, *Poniat*, 351–55.

99. *FBIS*, Dec. 10, 1991, 16. Diverse authors have made this point. See, e.g., Burlatskii, *Glotok*, 2:201–2; Anatolii Karpychev in *Pravda*, Jan. 25, 1992; and Simes, *After*, 65–66. The leader of Soviet Kazakhstan, for example, refused to sign the Belovezh documents on the grounds that "without the agreement of my parliament and government, I can't sign anything!" (N. A. Nazarbaev in Loginov, ed., *Piat let*, 157).

100. Braithwaite, *Across*, 266; Iakovlev, *Omyt*, 2:82. For other independent Russians, see, e.g., the journalist Vitalii Tretiakov in *NG*, Dec. 19, 1991, and again in *RG*, Aug. 19, 2004; the democratic deputy Nikolai Engver quoted by Fred Hiatt in *WP*, Feb. 5, 1992; the poet Naum Korzhavin in *OG*, Jan. 11–17, 2001; Cheshko in Sevostianov, ed., *Tragediia*, 466; and Aleksandr Solzhenitsyn in *MN*, April 28, 2006. Until they contrived a legal fig leaf, Yeltsin's aides knew the act was illegal. See A. V. Kozyrev in Loginov, ed., *Piat let*, 161–62; and the discussion of this issue in Stankevich, *Istoriia*, 299–312, and in Walker, *Dissolution*, 169. In 1998, the Belovezh act was the main article of impeachment brought against Yeltsin by the Communist-led parliament. See *SR*, Aug. 6, 1998. On fearing arrest, see Viacheslav Kebich quoted by Grigorii Iavlinskii in *MN*, Feb. 11–18, 1996, Grachev, *Gorbachev*, 409, Barsenkov, *Vvedenie*, 351, Hough, *Democratization*, 482–83; and for the military chief, Gaidar, *Dni*, 150. For "super-secrecy," see Eltsin, *Zapiski*, 150. Kravchuk later remarked that Belovezh "was not for people with weak nerves" (quoted in Wilson, *The Ukrainians*, 169). Many Western specialists have justified or glossed over Yeltsin's coup as a "democratic coup d'etat" or Gorbachev having "been voted out of office" (Hosking, *First*, 498; and Strobe Talbott in *NYT*, Feb. 24, 2005).

101. See, e.g., Brown, *Gorbachev*, 287; Hough, *Democratization*, 459, 481; Brent Scowcroft, VOA interview, in *JRL*, Dec. 3, 1999; Iurii Afanasev in *LG*, Sept. 15, 1993; V. A. Nikonov in *10 let*, 38 (who contrasts them as follows: "Mikhail Sergeevich liberated East Europe in order to continue reforms . . . Yeltsin let go the other Soviet republics in order to be done with Gorbachev's government"); Boris Kagarlitsky, *Square Wheels* (New York, 1994), 174, Burlatskii, *Glotok*, 2:201; Ivan Laptev quoted by Egor Iakovlev in *OG*, Feb. 14–20, 2002; Cheshko, *Raspad*, 278; Grachev, *Gorbachev*, 257; Sergei

Parkhomenko and Sergei Stankevich quoted by David Remnick in *NY*, March 11, 1996, 78, 79; Tatyana Tolstaya in *NYRB*, June 23, 1994, 3–7; Sazonov, *Predateliami*, 134; Ilia Milshtein in *NV*, no. 4 (2006): 13; and even one of Yeltsin's collaborators at Belovezh, Stanislav Shushkevich in *Ogonek*, no. 49 (1996): 13. This was, of course, always Gorbachev's opinion. When asked by Gorbachev what he would tell the people after Belovezh, Yeltsin replied: "I will say I am taking your place" (quoted by N. A. Nazarbaev, who was present, in Loginov, ed., *Piat let*, 158).

102. Leonid Shebarshin, a former high KGB official, quoted in Milt Bearden and James Risen, *The Main Enemy* (New York, 2003), 497. Similarly, Iurii Afanasev in *SM*, no. 1 (2005): 48; and Shakhnazarov, *Tsena*, 261. Two of the plotters later bitterly blamed the others for this lack. See Oleg Shenin in *Trud*, Aug. 19, 2004; and Valentin Varennikov in *Zavtra*, no. 38 (Sept. 20, 2006). For reflections on the importance of a "will to power" (*volia k vlasti*) at this time, see L. Shevtsova in *Izvestiia*, May 15, 1991; and for Yeltsin's need for the Kremlin, Vitalii Tretiakov in *PK* (July 2006), politklass.ru.

103. Burlatskii, *Glotok*, 2:186; George F. Kennan in *NYRB*, Nov. 16, 1995, 8. On the 1917 analogy, see also K. L. Maidanik in *"Perestroika" v transformatsionnom*, 76; and Vadim Mezhuev in *Proryv*, 313.

104. See, e.g., Z. L. Serebriakova in Loginov, ed., *Piat let*, 111; Osadchii, ed., *Ot katastrofy*, 24; Grachev, *Final Hours*, 150; and Aleksandr Afanasev in *LG*, July 11, 2001. A few authors insist, on the other hand, that "overwhelming majorities . . . *voted* to abolish" the Soviet Union, but there is no record of any such voting (M. Steven Fish in *PSA* [Oct.–Dec. 2001]: 356). Similarly, see V. V. Sogrin in *VF*, no. 1 (1998): 9; and Ariel Cohen in *Washington Times*, Aug. 21, 2001. On the contrary, as a Russian with impeccable political credentials put it, Belovezh was "a seizure of power 'behind the back' of the people" (Dmitrii Furman in *Novaia*, June 7–9, 2004). Another Russian scholar thinks "Russians had lost . . . even the will to struggle—to struggle for the preservation of the country" (Solovei, *Russkaia istoriia*, 182).

105. Similarly, see Barsenkov, *Vvedenie*, 353–54. For a different explanation, see Alexei Yurchak, *Everything Was Forever, Until It Was No More* (Princeton, N.J., 2006), which argues without empirical evidence and unconvincingly that the Soviet people were inwardly, though unknowingly, ready for the end of their state and country.

106. Barsenkov, *Vvedenie*, 351, 353, where Barsenkov notes that even Gorbachev initially thought this was the case; and Vladimir Kuznechevskii in *RG*, Dec. 26, 1991. Similarly, see B. Kagarlitskii in *SM*, no. 1 (2002): 122; Sergei Karaganov cited in *RFE/RL*, Oct. 7, 2002; and Valerii Bushuev in *SM*, no. 2 (2005): 121. Even the astute Soviet journalist Otto Latsis termed it "a new version of the union treaty" (quoted in Ellison, *Boris Yeltsin*, 62).

Certainly, that was the impression given by Kravchuk and Shushkevich immediately after Belovezh. See their remarks in A. P. Nenarokov, ed., *Nesostoiavshiisia iubilei* (Moscow, 1992), 490–91; and, similarly, Yeltsin's in Isakov, *Raschlenenka*, 295–301 and those of his foreign minister Andrei Kozyrev, quoted by Fred Hiatt in *WP*, Dec. 13, 1991. Initial Russian polls favorable to the announced Commonwealth reflected this misperception, not anti-Soviet sentiment, as Beissinger concludes in *Nationalist Mobilization*, 387.

107. Sergei Markov in *Trud*, Dec. 15, 2001; and, similarly, Kagarlitskii in *SM*, no. 1 (2002): 122. Yeltsin and Kravchuk are reported to have worried that "if we go to the people and announce that there is no Union and propose nothing in its place—there will be an inevitable explosion" (Wilson, *The Ukranians*, 169–70). Yeltsin's defenders later insisted that "Kravchuk's separatist interests shattered" the aspiration (Mikhail Leontev in *Segodnia*, March 1, 1996). Whatever the case, the divergences, or "betrayals," were immediately apparent. See, e.g., Fred Hiatt in *WP*, Dec. 13, 1991; and John Lloyd in *NR*, Jan. 6 and 13, 1992, 18–20. For the drinking, see Remnick in *NY*, March 11, 1996, 78–79; and Sazonov, *Predateliami*, 135; and for Shushkevich feeling "deceived," *Ogonek*, no. 49 (1996): 10–14. Reports of the influence of alcohol persisted. See, e.g., Yelena Lankina in *Moscow News*, Dec. 8, 2006; and Alyaksandr Lukashenko cited in *RFE/RL*, Dec. 8, 2006.

108. The proceedings are reprinted in Isakov, *Raschlenenka*, 294–364.

109. Vitalii Tretiakov in *NG*, June 14, 2000; Gorbachev in *Pravda*, Aug. 16, 1995; and, similarly, in *Novaia zhizn*, Oct. 25, 2002.

110. V. I. Sevastianov in Isakov, *Raschlenenka*, 325. Similarly, see Evgenii Shaposhnikov, *Vybor*, 2nd ed. (Moscow, 1995), 139. For having "rubber-stamped," see Markov in *Trud*, Dec. 15, 2001.

111. Vadim Pechenev, *"Smutnoe vremia" v noveishei istorii Rossii* (Moscow, 2004), 88. Similarly, see Markov in *Trud*, Dec. 15, 2001; Gorbachev, *On My Country*, 158–59; and Barsenkov, *Vvedenie*, 353–56. One deputy who voted against ratification, Sergei Baburin, opposed this misconception at the session (*Natsionalnye interesy*, no. 5–6 [2001]: 3). For Yeltsin, see Isakov, *Raschlenenka*, 295–301; and, similarly, his remarks soon after that the Commonwealth was "capable of preserving the many-centuries-old common political, legal, and economic space, which we almost lost," as quoted by Fred Hiatt in *WP*, Dec. 13, 1991.

112. For the quotes, see, respectively, Gennadii Ziuganov in *SR*, June 26, 2004; Kagarlitsky, *Square Wheels*, 161; R. A. Medvedev in *NNI*, no. 2 (2003): 167–69; and Vartazarova in *Zavtra*, no. 31 (Aug. 1995). Similarly, on the fears of a "witch hunt" and even a repetition of 1937 and the general mood of Communists, see Prokofev, *Do i posle*, 266–68; Markov in *Trud*, Dec. 15,

2001; Baturin, ed., *Epokha*, 177; Aleksandr Bessemetnykh in *KP*, Aug. 31, 1991; Valentin Falin in *NYT*, Aug. 31, 1991; and Vitaly Ganyushkin in *NT*, no. 43 (1991): 12–13. For Vice President Aleksandr Rutskoi, see Vasilii Lipitskii in *NG*, Aug. 12, 1993.

113. For the military and KGB, see, respectively, Brian D. Taylor and John B Dunlop in *JCWS* (Winter 2003): 17–66, 94–127; and for the military, also, Hough, *Democratization*, 483–89. For a bitter lament over the army's compliance, see Aleksandr Tsipko in *Proryv*, 343.

114. Vladislav M. Zubok in Geir Lundestad, ed., *The Fall of the Great Powers* (Oslo, 1994), 169; and, similarly, Matlock, *Autopsy*, 400.

115. For examples of the former, see Furman, *Nasha*, 47–54; Zubok in Lundestad, ed., *Fall*, 161–66; Buzgalin and Kolganov, *Stalin*, 51–56, 67–68; Zykin, "Model"; Vadim Belotserkovskii in *SM*, no. 10 (2005): 94; and Evan Mawdsley and Stephen White, *The Soviet Elite from Lenin to Gorbachev* (New York, 2000), 256–74. For the latter, see Egor Gaidar, *Gosudarstvo i evolutsiia* (Moscow, 1995), 135; Gennadii Lisichkin in *LG*, Aug. 8, 2001; Olga Kryshtanovskaia, *Anatomiia rossiiskoi elity* (Moscow, 2005), 318; and Stephen L. Solnick, *Stealing the Soviet State* (Cambridge, Mass., 1998); and, on East Europe, Kramer in *JCWS* (Fall 2004): 60–63. Long before, several formerly pro-Soviet Marxists had worried about this possibility, notably Leon Trotsky in *The Revolution Betrayed*, first published in 1937; and Milovan Djilas in *The New Class* (New York, 1957).

116. For the former, see, e.g., Gaidar, *Gosudarstvo*, chaps. 4–5; A. B. Chubais in Chubais, ed., *Privatizatsiia po-rossiiski* (Moscow, 1999), 287–88; Kotz and Weir, *Revolution*, part 2; and Hough, *Democratization*, 1–3. For the latter, see Sergei Kara-Murza in *SR*, Nov. 30, 1995; Iurii Burtin in *Oktiabr*, no. 8 (1997): 161–76; V. I. Zhukov, *Reformy v Rossii 1985–1995 gody* (Moscow, 1997), 26; and A. Kolev, *Miatezh nomenklatury* (Moscow, 1995).

117. For good overviews of the process, see Kryshtanovskaia, *Anatomiia*, 195–201, 291–318; A. D. Radygin, *Reforma sobstvennosti v Rossii* (Moscow, 1994), 48–57; R. Nureev and A. Runov in *VE*, no. 6 (2000): 18–31; Andrew Barnes, *Owning Russia* (Ithaca, N.Y., 2006), chap. 3; and, in Moscow, Kagarlitsky, *Square Wheels*. For an insider view of the process in the oil industry, see Lev Tchurilov, *Lifeblood of Empire* (New York, 1996), chap. 17.

118. See Barnes, *Owning*, chap. 3; for the Communist Party youth organization, Solnick, *Stealing*; for a partial inventory of the Party's property, *KP*, June 4, 1998; and for the military, Col. A. Kandalovskii in *KP*, Nov. 27, 1991. The best-known example and trend-setter was Viktor Chernomyrdin, Soviet minister for gas and oil, who became head and billionaire shareholder of the privatized gas giant Gazprom. See Marshall I. Goldman, *The Piratization of Russia* (London, 2003), chap. 6.

119. Kagarlitsky, *Square Wheels*, 155.
120. A number of scholars have emphasized this point. See, e.g., Valerie Bunce, *Subversive Institutions* (New York, 1999); and Robert V. Daniels, *The Rise and Fall of Communism in Russia* (New Haven, Conn., 2007), chap. 32. For republic leaders who wanted to be presidents like Gorbachev, see Vorotnikov, *A bylo*, 366–67; and Grachev, *Gorbachev*, 323.
121. As Fedor Burlatskii pointed out early on, in *Izvestiia*, Feb. 10, 1990. Similarly, see Sazonov, *Predateliami*, 43, 72.
122. As many scholars and observers concluded. See, e.g., Jeff Hahn in *PSA* (Jan.–March 2000): 64–68; Tuminez in *JCWS* (Fall 2003): 82, 126, 133; S. Barzilov and A. Chernyshov in *SM*, no. 4 (2002): 44–45; Roi Medvedev in *OI*, no. 4 (2003): 114; and Cheshko, *Raspad*, 238, 263, for a similar point. In *Nationalist Mobilization* (36–37), Beissinger argues, to the contrary, that elites did not create but followed popular "tidal forces" of nationalism, though he appears to contradict himself on 428–29.
123. Beissinger, *Nationalist Mobilization*, 428–29; and, similarly, Pankin, *Last*, 266–67. In this connection, Shevardnadze warned the Bush administration against trusting Kravchuk (Bush and Scowcroft, *A World*, 554).
124. Aleksei Kiva in *PG*, April 4, 2003; Iurii Afanasev, ed., *Sovetskoe obshchestvo*, (Moscow, 1997), 2:595; Medvedev in *OI*, no. 4 (2003): 112. Similarly, see Pankin, *Last*, 269, who speaks of "imposed dissolution"; Cheshko, *Raspad*, 282, who calls it "abolition" (*otmena*); Josef Joffe in *NYT*, Feb. 10, 2003, who terms it "suicide by self-destruction"; and Samuilov in *SM*, no. 3 (2006): 42, who prefers "self-liquidation" (*samolikvidatsii*).
125. John Higley and György Lengyel, eds., *Elites After State Socialism* (Boulder, Colo., 2000), 237; and Solnick, *Stealing*, 7. Similarly, see Kotz and Weir, *Revolution*; Fritz W. Ermarth in *National Interest* (Spring 1999): 6; Furman, *Nasha*, 53–54; Nureev and Runov in *VE*, no. 6 (2000): 18–31; and Gaidar, *Gosudarstvo*, chap. 4. For other arguments that property was not the primary cause of the Soviet breakup, see Beissinger, *Nationalist Mobilization*, 8; Ellman and Kontorovich, eds., *Destruction*, 3, 27; David Lockwood, *The Destruction of the Soviet Union* (New York, 2000), 130–32; and Latsis, *Tshchatelno*, 461–62. Many overviews of various factors do not even include property. See, e.g., Holmes *Post-Communism*, chap. 2; Smith, *Fall*; Leon Aron on the "mystery" of the Soviet breakup in *JOD* (April 2006): 21–35; and the sources in this chapter, n. 19.
126. For the argument, see Bunce, *Subversive Institutions*; and Daniels, *Rise and Fall*, chap. 32.
127. Private communication from a former Kremlin staffer. That is, "they were not all prepared to fight for their independence" (Cheshko, *Raspad*, 275). Also, see this chapter, n. 122.

128. For the argument that the outcome was a post-Soviet system based on "nomenklatura capitalism," see Iurii Burtin, *Ispoved shestidesiatnika* (Moscow, 2003), 330–71; and, similarly, Boris Kagarlitskii, *Restavratsiia v Rossii* (Moscow, 2000); Stanislav Menshikov, *Anatomiia rossiiskogo kapitalizma* (Moscow, 2004), 21–34; Andrei Bunich, *Osen oligarkhov* (Moscow, 2005); Aleksandr Lebed in *MN*, May 12–19, 1996; and Kotz and Weir, *Revolution*.

129. An Estonian independence activist quoted by R. Kh. Simonian in *VI*, no. 12 (2002): 37.

130. A point emphasized by Hahn, in a somewhat different context, in *PSA* (Jan.–March 2000): 60; and by a Russian writer who remarked, "Yeltsin threw the match" (Lisichkin in *LG*, Aug. 8, 2001). For Gorbachev, see *Novaia*, Feb. 21–23, 2005.

131. For the quotes, see Nikolai Nikolaev in *Novaia*, Aug. 15–17, 2005; and Leonid Zamiatin in *NV*, no. 16 (1997): 17. For a survey of the economic and political preferences of the Moscow elite in mid-1991, see Judith S. Kullberg in *EAS* 46, no. 6 (1994): 929–53.

132. For Gorbachev, see, respectively, *Pravda*, June 1 and 17, 1991; *FBIS*, May 16, 1991, 34, and Sept. 19, 1991, 20. For perestroika, see Tsipko in *LG*, Jan. 19, 2005; and, similarly, N. Bikkenin in *SM*, no. 11 (2000): 102; A. V. Riabov in *"Perestroika" v transformatsionnom*, 56–60; Vladlen Loginov in *Gorbachevskie chteniia*, no. 3, 159; and Gorbachev himself in *Poniat*, 375. In the end, in order to negotiate a new Union treaty, Gorbachev had to increasingly cede property on their territories to the republics. See Barsenkov, *Vvedenie*, 117; and Cheshko, *Raspad*, 268, 272.

133. For similar interpretations, see Furman, *Nasha*, 50–54; and Kotz and Weir, *Revolution*, chaps. 7–8. The personal values of Gorbachev, for whom "the pursuit of property was not a motivating force," were also important; while in power, he did not even own a dacha. See Archie Brown and Oksana Gaman-Golutvina in Brown, ed., *Contemporary Russian Politics* (New York, 2001), 290–91, 307; Aleksandr Iakovlev and Gorbachev in *MN*, March 11, 2005 (and, similarly, Tsipko in *Proryv*, 344); and Sazonov, *Predateliami*, 170. Elsewhere, Tsipko points out Yakovlev's refusal even to "privatize his state dacha," though it was a commonplace practice after 1991 (*VA*, no. 2 [2006]: 217). For an opposing view insisting that Gorbachev, too, had abandoned socialism, see Stanislav Menshikov in *Monthly Review* (Oct. 1997): 51–52; and Boris Kagarlitsky in *In These Times*, April 14, 1997.

134. Reddaway and Glinski, *Tragedy*, 34, 89, 171–72, 253.

135. For somewhat different versions of Yeltsin's exhortation, see Hahn in *PSA* (Jan.–March 2000): 64; and Stankevich, *Istoriia*, 257. For the reformer, see Fedor Burlatsky in *WP*, Nov. 10, 1991. Gorbachev later remarked that Yeltsin had "solved this problem of the nomenklatura simply: he gave it every-

thing" (*Gorbachevskie chteniia*, no. 1 [Moscow, 2003], 163); and, similarly, in *PK*, no. 2 (2005): 57. And indeed observers quickly noticed that republic officials were in "a rush to seize all-union property and to declare 'sovereignty' over local resources" (Serge Schmemann in *NYT*, Oct. 8, 1991).

136. For example, he gave Moscow's mayor some of the city's valuable real estate; gave Kravchuk traditional Russian territories and valuable holdings in Ukraine; and, it seems, gave generals their state-owned dachas (David K. Shipler in *NY*, Nov. 11, 1991, 50; Liudmila Butuzova in *MN*, Aug. 19, 2005; Nikolai Ryzhkov in *NS*, no. 10 [2006]: 198; and Hough *Democratization*, 487–88). For Yeltsin's confiscations, see this chapter, note 82. For the elites, see Pankin, *Last*, 257; Grachev, *Gorbachev*, 287; and, similarly, Hahn in *PSA* (Jan.–March 2000): 60, 76.

137. Pavel Voshchanov quoted by Vladimir Isakov in *SR*, Dec. 7, 1996.

6. GORBACHEV'S LOST LEGACIES

1. Or as his leading interpreter has written: "the country Gorbachev bequeathed to his successors was freer than at any time in Russian history" Archie Brown, *Seven Years That Changed the World* [New York, 2007], 330). On Gorbachev as democratizer, see also Brown, *The Gorbachev Factor* (New York, 1997); and his contributions to Archie Brown and Lilia Shevtsova, eds., *Gorbachev, Yeltsin, Putin* (Washington, D.C., 2001).

2. See, e.g., Mikhail Gorbachev, *Perestroika* (New York, 1987), 57; M. S. Gorbachev, *Izbrannye rechi i stati*, 7 vols. (Moscow, 1987–1990), 4:316; and in *Izvestiia*, April 17, 1991.

3. Charles Krauthammer in *WP*, April 27, 2007; *NYT* editorial, May 9, 2000; David Remnick in *NY*, May 21, 2001, 37. Similarly, see Margaret Shapiro in *WP*, Dec. 9, 1993; Michael Wines in *NYT*, June 5, 2000; and Trudy Rubin in *Philadelphia Inquirer*, Dec. 13, 2003. For an early example of this revisionism, see *NR* editorial, Sept. 9, 1991, 7–9. President Bill Clinton led the way. See the exchange on "democracy" and "reform" in his joint press conference with Yeltsin, in *WP*, April 5, 1993. Even later, Clinton's national security adviser insisted that Yeltsin "should be remembered as the father of Russian democracy" (Samuel R. Berger in *WP*, Nov. 15, 2001).

4. Timothy J. Colton and Michael McFaul in *PPC* (July/Aug. 2003): 12. Similarly, see Michael McFaul, Nikolai Petrov, and Andrei Ryabov, *Between Dictatorship and Democracy* (Washington, D.C., 2004), esp. 2; and McFaul in *The Wilson Quarterly* (Spring 2000): 42. It is a central theme of three American biographies of Yeltsin, though more balanced in the latter one: Leon Aron, *Yeltsin* (New York, 2000); Herbert J. Ellison, *Boris Yeltsin and*

Russia's Democratic Transformation (Seattle, 2006); and Timothy J. Colton, *Yeltsin* (New York, 2008). In contrast, see this chapter, n. 1; Peter Reddaway and Dmitri Glinski, *The Tragedy of Russia's Reforms* (Washington, D.C., 2001); Robert V. Daniels in *The Nation*, Oct. 20, 2008, 30–36; and Russia's leading political scientist, Lilia Shevtsova, *Yeltsin's Russia* (Washington, D.C., 1999) and her *Russia—Lost in Transition* (Washington, D.C., 2007).

5. See, e.g., Iu. M. Baturin et al., eds., *Epokha Eltsina* (Moscow, 2001); Oleg Moroz, *Khronika liberalnoi revoliutsii* (Moscow, 2005); and Marsha Lipman cited by David Hoffman in *WP*, May 8, 1999, who is quoted here.

6. Eduard Samoilov in *NG*, Oct. 13, 1992. Similarly, see Vladimir Motyl in *Izvestiia*, Sept. 7, 1991; and Olga Chaikovskaia in *LG*, Oct. 21, 1992.

7. See, respectively, Michael Wines in *NYT*, June 14, 2001; Liesl Schillinger in *NYT Book Review*, July 2, 2006; Fareed Zakaria in *Newsweek*, June 16, 2003, 33; and Nicholas D. Kristof in *NYT*, Dec. 15, 2004.

8. See, respectively, Martin Malia, *The Soviet Tragedy* (New York, 1994), 499; Stephen Kotkin in *JMH* (June 1998): 406; Adam Ulam in *TLS*, Nov. 6, 1992, 23; Edward W. Walker, *Dissolution* (Lanham, Md., 2003), 170; Rajan Menon in *The Harriman Forum* (Spring 1997): 13; and Mark R. Beissinger, *Nationalist Mobilization and the Collapse of the Soviet State* (New York, 2002), 441. Similarly, see M. Steven Fish in *Demokratizatsiya* (Spring 2005): 241–53; this book, chap. 4, n. 85; the critical comments on part of this chapter by Karen Dawisha and Stephen E. Hansen in *Slavic Review* (Fall 2004): 527–52; Glennys Young on "triumphalist belief" among historians, in *RR* (Jan. 2007): 100, 117; and, on the "mythical" alternatives NEP and perestroika, Anthony D'Agostino, *Gorbachev's Revolution* (New York, 1998), 172; and Martin Malia in *Daedalus* (Spring 1992): 74. For dissenters from the revived no-alternative orthodoxy, see Reddaway and Glinski, *Tragedy*, esp. 5, 9, 16, 252–55, 636–41; Nelson and Kuzes, *Radical Reform*; Jerry F. Hough, *Democratization and Revolution in the USSR* (Washington, D.C., 1997); Brown, *Gorbachev*, chaps. 5–9; Robert V. Daniels, *The Rise and Fall of Communism in Russia* (New Haven, Conn., 2007), part 4; and Moshe Lewin, *The Soviet Century* (New York, 2005), chap. 27.

9. Richard E. Ericson in *Journal of Economic Perspectives* (Fall 1991): 25; and Eugene Huskey in *APSR* (Dec. 1998): 968. Similarly, see Michael McFaul in *FA* (Jan.–Feb. 1995): 89; Malia in *Daedalus* (Spring 1992): 69; Richard Pipes in *Commentary* (March 1992): 30–31; and, for more examples and a discussion, Stephen F. Cohen, *Failed Crusade*, updated ed. (New York, 2001), 40–42, 293n. 69.

10. See, respectively, Vitalii Tretiakov in *MN*, Nov. 26, 1989; Robert G. Kaiser, *Why Gorbachev Happened* (New York, 1991), 171; and James Billington in *NYT Book Review*, June 17, 1990.

11. A. S. Cherniaev, *Shest let s Gorbachevym* (Moscow, 1993), 345; Gorbachev quoted on "heresy" by Valerii Badov in *RT*, Aug. 30, 1990; and by Anatolii Strelianyi in *Literaturnoe obozrenie*, no. 12 (1990): 12; Gorbachev in *Izvestiia*, March 25, 1991; William E. Odom, *The Collapse of the Soviet Military* (New Haven, Conn., 1998), 94; and David Price-Jones, *The Strange Death of the Soviet Empire* (New York, 1995), 5. See also Dusko Doder and Louise Branson, *Gorbachev* (New York, 1990), who reported early on that fundamentalists feared the "Soviet government had been hijacked by a heretic" (176).

12. Michael McFaul in *WP*, Sept. 30, 2000. See also this chapter, n. 4; and, similarly, Padmai Desai, *Conversations on Russia* (New York, 2006), vii–viii, 3.

13. For such "modernization," see A. V. Fadin in *Kentavr* (Jan.–Feb. 1993): 92–97; and for the tradition, Reddaway and Glinski, *Tragedy*.

14. For the quotes, see, respectively, *LG*, Dec. 4, 1991; *Materialy obedinennogo plenuma tsentralnogo komiteta i tsentralnoi kontrolnoi kommissii KPSS* (Moscow, 1991), 8; M. S. Gorbachev, *Gody trudnykh reshenii* (Moscow, 1993), 10; Gorbachev, *Izbrannye*, 4:327, 360; and *Pravda*, July 26, 1991. A top Gorbachev aide characterized their goal as a "non-catastrophic" transformation (Vadim Medvedev, *V komande Gorbacheva* [Moscow, 1994], 234).

15. The first quote is from Tatiana Vorozheikina in *ONS*, no. 5 (2005): 17–22. See also this chapter, n. 28. The strongest proponents of perestroika as a "lost alternative" and the Soviet breakup as a "tragic mistake" were, of course, Gorbachev partisans. See, e.g., four publications on the occasion of the twentieth anniversary of his rise to power: *Proryv k svobode* (Moscow, 2005); *"Perestroika" v transformatsionnom kontekste* (Moscow, 2005); V. I. Tolstykh, ed., *Perestroika* (Moscow, 2005); and *Gorbachevskie chteniia*, no. 3 (Moscow, 2005). For Gorbachev himself, see, e.g., his *Poniat perestroiku . . .* (Moscow, 2006), esp. 365–79; M. S. Gorbachev and B. F. Slavin, *Neokonchennaia istoria*, 2nd ed. (Moscow, 2005); and, of course, his memoirs, Gorbachev, *Zhizn i reformy*, 2 vols. (Moscow, 1995).

16. Colton and McFaul in *PPC* (July/Aug. 2003): 20

17. Vitalii Tretiakov in *RG*, Nov. 19, 2003; and, similarly, A. V. Buzgalin in *JRL*, Feb. 2, 2002.

18. Ann Cooper, executive director of the Committee to Protect Journalists, in *MT*, July 7, 2005. Similarly, see Yevgenia Albats quoted by Oksana Yabloka in *MT*, June 7, 2006. Gorbachev's own daughter lamented, "Journalism now is a dangerous business" (quoted by Gregory L. White in *WSJ*, Dec. 1–2, 2007).

19. Russians involved in the 1989 and 1990 campaigns later made this point. See, e.g., Alla Iaroshinskaia and Boris Vishnevskii in *Novaia*, March 25–28, 2004, and March 21–23, 2005.

20. See Valerii Vyzhutovich in *Izvestiia*, May 4, 1994; Konrad Liubarskii and Aleksandr Sobianin in *NV*, no. 15 (1995): 6–12; and Shevtsova, *Yeltsin's Russia*, 96–97.

21. M. Steven Fish in *Demokratizatsiya* (Spring 2005): 248; and Aleksandr Kolesnichenko in *NI*, Nov. 13, 2006. Similarly, see Boris Kagarlitsky, *Square Wheels* (New York, 1994), 5, 16; Grigorii Iavlinskii in *Itogi*, March 20, 2004; and Dmitrii Furman in *NG*, March 3, 2008.

22. For Gorbachev's reluctance, see Jonathan Steele, *Eternal Russia* (Cambridge, Mass., 1994), 261. Oddly, Steele nevertheless concludes that Gorbachev merely "paid lip-service to the notion of parliament" (256). Reading the published proceedings of the Soviet legislatures of 1989 through 1991 is a vivid reminder of a singular political moment in Russia to date.

23. Olga Kryshtanovskaya and Stephen White in *PSA* (Oct.–Dec. 2003): 289–306; and Kryshtanovskaya quoted by Arkady Ostovsky in *FT*, Feb. 24, 2003. For a full study, see Olga Kryshtanovskaia, *Anatomiia rossiiskoi elity* (Moscow, 2005).

24. Yakovlev in *NV*, no. 32 (2004): 21. For a more measured analysis of civil society during and after perestroika, see *Gorbachevskie chteniia*, no. 5 (Moscow, 2007).

25. Jonathan Weiler, *Human Rights in Russia* (Boulder, Colo., 2004), 2. In 2005, the leading civil rights activist, Sergei Kovalev, said that the "human rights situation in Russia is simply catastrophic" (Radio Ekho Moskvy, Sept. 22, 2005). The early stage of this development after Gorbachev is discussed by several contributors to Carol R. Saivetz and Anthony Jones, eds., *In Search of Pluralism* (Boulder, Colo., 1994).

26. L. Piiasheva in *Pravda*, April 21, 1995; Liliia Shevtsova in Valentin Tolstykh, ed., *Mnogaia leta: Mikhailu Gorbachevu—70* (Moscow, 2001), 453; Gavriil Popov, *Snova v oppozitsii* (Moscow, 1994), 81.

27. Mikhail Khodorkovskii quoted by Anastasia Kornia in *NG*, Sept. 12, 2005. The adage continues: "And anyone who thinks it can be reconstructed has no head." There are harsher variations: "Everyone except perhaps liberals and other members of the 'fifth column' regret the breakup of the USSR. Sensible people can't conduct themselves otherwise" (L. G. Ivashov in *SR*, Dec. 7, 2006).

28. Aleksandr Galkin in *Proryv*, 86. For examples of non-Gorbachevists, see Dmitrii Furman in *SM*, no. 11 (2003): 9–30 and his *Nasha strannaia revoluitsiia* (Moscow, 1998), part 1; Fedor Burlatskii in *NG*, March 2, 2001; Shevtsova, *Yeltsin's Russia*, 14–15; Boris Kagarlitskii in *SM*, no. 1 (2002): 122; and Aleksandr Buzgalin in *JRL*, Jan. 21, 2000. On the other hand, Russians directly involved in the abolition of the Soviet state or the ensuing Yeltsin

regime were politically constrained from rethinking what had happened. See, e.g., Baturin et al., eds., *Epokha Eltsina*, and the latter two authors of Joel M. Ostrow, Georgiy A. Saratov, and Irina M. Khakamada, *The Consolidation of Dictatorship in Russia*, (Westport, Conn., 2007). It was also true of non-Russian citizens, as, e.g., Andrei Shleifer, *A Normal Country* (Cambridge, Mass., 2005). Of course, there were also Russian intellectuals who thought there had been no perestroika alternative. See, e.g., V. V. Sogrin in *ONS*, no. 4 (2002): 95–100; and a number of contributors to Baturin et al., eds., *Epokha Eltsina*.

29. See, respectively, Mortimer B. Zuckerman in *US News and World Report*, Feb. 26, 2007; Stephen Sestanovich in *WP*, March 3, 2005; *WP* editorial, Dec. 11, 2007; *NYT* editorial, Sept. 14, 2004; and Michael McFaul in *WS*, Nov. 17, 2003. Indeed, the *New York Times* initiated a series of articles devoted to "Putin's Counterrevolution" (see nytimes.com/world). Similarly, see *WP* editorial, Nov. 16, 2003, and Feb. 8, 2007; Fred Hiatt in *WP*, Sept. 20, 2004; Amy Knight in *TLS*, May 28, 2004, 7; McFaul in *WP Book World*, Feb. 6, 2005, 8; Peter Baker and Susan Glasser, *Kremlin Rising* (New York, 2005); Colton and McFaul in *PPC* (July/Aug. 2003): 12; McFaul, Petrov, and Ryabov, *Between Dictatorship*, esp. 2; McFaul in *The Wilson Quarterly* (Spring 2000): 42; Aron, *Yeltsin*; Ellison, *Boris Yeltsin*; and Colton, *Yeltsin*.

30. See, e.g., Fiona Hill in *JRL*, Nov. 28, 2003; this chapter, n. 1; Reddaway and Glinski, *Tragedy*; Daniels in *The Nation*, Oct. 20, 2008, 30–36; and Shevtsova, *Yeltsin's Russia*. For "rollback," see, among many others, Philip P. Pan in *WP*, Sept. 21, 2008.

31. Anders Aslund, *How Russia Became a Market Economy* (Washington, D.C., 1995), 2. The very few include Reddaway and Glinski, *Tragedy*; Brown, *Seven Years*; Daniels, *Rise and Fall*, part 4; Lynn D. Nelson and Irina Y. Kuzes, *Property to the People* (Armonk, N.Y., 1994), esp. 31–32; and, perhaps alone among mainstream American journalists, William Pfaff in *IHT*, Sept. 24, 1999. As Reddaway and Glinski remind us (2), most Western commentators "exulted" over the Soviet breakup. Indeed, an American political scientist warned against anyone ready to "forgive a communist leader who thought [democratization] might be possible" (Karen Dawisha in *APSR* [June 1999]: 476).

32. See, e.g., Robert Service, *Russia* (Cambridge, Mass., 2003), 4–5 and chap. 22.

33. See, e.g., Valerie Bunce in *PSA* (Oct.–Dec. 1998): 324–25, 348; Gordon M. Hahn and Walter D. Connor in *Demokratizatsiya* (Spring 2005): 166, 189; and David M. Kotz and Fred Weir, *Revolution from Above* (New York, 1997), 6–7. For Russian objections to the "myth," see Karen Brutents in

SM, no. 1 (2005): 174; Viktor Kuvaldin in Olga Zdravomyslova, ed., *10 let bez SSSR* (Moscow, 2002), 110; Dmitriy Ryurikov, *Russia Survives* (Washington, D.C., 1999), 15–18; and Ignat Pavlov in *SM*, no. 7–8 (2006): 223.

34. The nineteenth-century conservative thinker M. N. Katkov quoted by Kirill Aleksandrov in *NV*, no. 27 (2005): 8; and, similarly, Anatolii Karpychev in *Pravda*, Jan. 25, 1992.

35. Even one of Yeltsin's former press secretaries could still write nearly fifteen years later, "We can in no way understand what the disintegration of the USSR meant for us" (Viacheslav Kostikov in *AF*, Nov. 9, 2005).

36. A. S. Barsenkov and A. I. Vdovin, *Istoriia Rossii, 1938–2002* (Moscow, 2003), 382–93. For the correspondent, see John Lloyd in *NR*, Jan. 6 and 13, 1992, 18.

37. See, e.g., Lilia Shevtsova in Anne de Tinguy, ed., *The Fall of the Soviet Empire* (Boulder, Colo., 1997), 86; A. V. Buzgalin in *JRL*, Feb. 2, 2002; Dmitrii Furman in *SM*, no. 11 (2003): 9–30; Ryurikov, *Russia*, 15–20; Aleksandr Panarin in *LG*, Feb. 20, 2002; and, similarly, Vladimir Putin, kremlin.ru (Sept. 2, 2005). For similar formulations of "revolution from above" in 1991, but without the historical reference to Stalin's, see Kotz and Weir, *Revolution*; and Gordon M. Hahn, *Russia's Revolution from Above* (New Brunswick, N.J., 2002); and for one with the analogy, V. P. Danilov in T. I. Zaslavskaia and L. A. Arutiunian, eds., *Kuda idet Rossiia?* vol. 1 (Moscow, 1994), 125–26.

38. See this volume, chap. 5, n. 100; and, similarly, Julia Wishnevsky in *Report*, Nov. 13, 1992, 22.

39. See, e.g., Aleksandr Tsipko, in *KP*, Nov. 7, 1991, and in *VA*, no. 3 (2008): 29; Burlatsky in *WP*, Nov. 10, 1991; Anatolii Sobchak in *LG*, Jan. 15, 1992; Viktor Petrovskii in *NG*, Feb. 26, 1993; Furman, *Nasha*, 73–74; S. V. Cheshko in G. N. Sevostianov, ed., *Tragediia velikoi derzhavy* (Moscow, 2005), 466; Reddaway and Glinski, *Tragedy*, whose subtitle is *Market Bolshevism Against Democracy*; and, similarly, Nelson and Kuzes, *Radical Reform*, 12–16. In Russia, we are told, "there is almost general agreement" that the ideology of post-Soviet Yeltsinism was "Soviet Communist ideology turned inside out" (Boris Kagarlitsky, *Russia Under Yeltsin and Putin* [London, 2002], 55).

40. For a similar point, see Joel Hellman in Andrew C. Kuchins, ed., *Russia After the Fall* (Washington, D.C., 2002), 96; and, early on, Vasilii Lipitskii in *NG*, Aug. 12, 1993.

41. Dmitrii Furman in *SM*, no. 11 (2003): 12. Even a democratic reformer known for her moderation called Belovezh "simply high treason" (Tatyana I. Zaslavskaya in *Demokratizatsiya* [Spring 2005]: 299).

42. Nikolai Shmelev in *Trud*, April 13, 2005. The extent of poverty was disputed. Following official Russian statistics, many Western commentators
thought it affected less than 20 percent of the people. Shmelev, a highly
respected economist of moderate views, put the figure at "70 to 80 percent," which was almost certainly correct. For production, see Ryurikov,
Russia, 19.

43. Iurii Afanasev in *SM*, no. 11 (2004): 3. Similarly, see Nikolai Petrakov, *Eko-
nomicheskaia "Santa-Barbara"* (Moscow, 2000), 223; and Vitalii Tretiakov
in *NG*, Dec. 18, 1999, and in *Novaia*, Sept. 8–10, 2005.

44. For the first episode, see K. V. Kharchenko, *Vlast-imushchestvo-chelovek*
(Moscow, 2000); for the second, V. Danilov et al., eds., *Tragediia sovetskoi
derevni*, 5 vols. (Moscow, 1999–).

45. Aleksandr Tsipko in *LG*, May 23, 2001.

46. Aleksandr Libman in *SM*, no. 9 (2005): 54. Similarly, see Aleksandr Panarin
in *LG*, Feb. 20, 2002; Garri Kasparov in *Novaia*, Dec. 15, 2008; and Hellman
in Kuchins, ed., *Russia*, 106. For the nomenklatura's "top-down" wishes,
see Reddaway and Glinski, *Tragedy*, 34, 268, 319.

47. For a fuller account of these developments, see Cohen, *Failed Crusade*,
135–41, 158–77; and Boris Yeltsin, *Midnight Diaries* (New York, 2000),
232–34.

48. For a fuller account, see Cohen, *Failed Crusade*, part 2.

49. Tatyana I. Zaslavskaya in *Demokratizatsiya* (Spring 2005): 312, uses a more
decorous translation. For the "off-shore" elite, see V. Iu. Surkov, *Osnovnye
tendentsii i perspektivy razvitiia sovremennoi Rossii* (Moscow, 2007), 32.
Surkov, the Kremlin ideologist, used the expression for his own purposes
but not entirely unfairly, adding that the elite does not "see its future or the
future of its children in Russia." For the survey, see *VN*, Aug. 24, 2005; and,
similarly, *NG*, Aug. 16, 2005.

50. Aleksandr Tsipko in *LG*, Dec. 20, 2006.

51. See, e.g., James H. Billington, *Russia Transformed* (New York, 1992); and
Malia, *Soviet Tragedy*. For a discussion of their persistence and the policy
implications, see Cohen, *Failed Crusade*.

52. Aleksandr Zinoviev in *Zavtra*, no. 2 (1993). For "exulting," see Reddaway
and Glinski, *Tragedy*, 2.

53. See Thomas L. Friedman in *NYT*, Aug. 2, 2006; Malia, *Soviet Tragedy*, 485,
487, and in *PC* (Jan.–April 1992): 93; Hélène Carrère d'Encausse, *The End
of the Soviet Empire* (New York, 1993), 219, 230 (and, similarly, Billington,
Russia); Bukovsky in *NR*, Jan. 6 and 13, 1992, 44; Leon Aron in *Commentary* (December 2006): 20; Service, *Russia*, 338; and Marshall T. Poe, *The
Russian Moment in World History* (Princeton, N.J., 2003), 89. Gordon M.

Hahn is similarly critical of this myth, in *Demokratizatsiya* (Spring 2005): 167, as are Reddaway and Glinski, *Tragedy*. An equally large myth saw the breakup freeing "reformers in the republics" from "reactionaries in the center" (Roman Szporluk in *NYT*, Jan. 23, 1991). In reality, freed from a reforming Soviet Moscow, reactionaries took control of property and power in many republics.

54. For this development, see Reddaway and Glinski, *Tragedy*, chaps. 5–6; and, similarly, Judith Delvin, *The Rise of the Russian Democrats* (Brookfield, Vt., 1995), chap. 8. For the quote, see Egor Gaidar, *Gosudarstvo i evolutsiia* (Moscow, 1995), 135.

55. *Vek XX*, no. 6 (1990): 15–19. Dated March 30, 1990, this little-known document was drafted by a group headed by Chubais, later Yeltsin's leading practitioner of shock-therapy privatization (see V. Ia. Gelman in *ONS*, no. 4 [1997]: 66–67; and Boris Vishnevskii in *NG*, Feb. 14, 1998). It grew out of a larger debate, begun in 1989, over the need for an "iron-hand" regime in the Soviet transition. It may be that these anti-Marxist intellectuals initially "favored the free market more than democracy" (Reddaway and Glinski, *Tragedy*, 59), but once in power they did not practice either.

56. Stanislav Shatalin in *FBIS*, March 27, 1991, 29. Similarly, see Ales Adamovich in *FBIS*, Nov. 27, 1992; and Svetlana Klishina in *Izvestiia*, April 17, 1992. For the preceding quote, see Valentin Tolstykh, ed., *O strategii rossiiskogo razvitiia* (Moscow, 2003), 198; and, similarly, Gelman on their views, in *ONS*, no. 4 (1997): 66–67. For early alarm over the fate of elected soviets, see German Diligensky in *NT*, no. 51 (1991): 16–17; and Tatiana Vorozheikina in *Vek XX*, no. 1 (1992): 25–30. A property-driven campaign against the Moscow Soviet was already under way. See Kagarlitsky, *Square Wheels*. For Russia and the "Pinochet Option" in international context, see Naomi Klein, *The Shock Doctrine* (New York, 2007), chaps. 11–12.

57. Natalia Borova in *LG*, July 11–17, 2007; and, similarly though less harshly, Devlin, *The Rise*, 258.

58. For continued "dreaming of a Russian Pinochet," see Nikolai Rabotiazev in *NG*, Sept. 23, 2000. Similarly, see Vitalii Naishul in *LG*, Nov. 30–Dec. 6, 1995; Boris Vishnevskii on Alfred Kokh in *Novaia*, Feb. 28–March 3, 2002; Andrei Riabov on Gaidar in *Novaia*, Feb. 16–19, 2006; Oleg Liakhovich's apologia for Pinochet in *Moscow News*, Dec. 15–21, 2006; and Irina Khakamada quoted by Michael Spector in *NYT Magazine*, Jan. 29, 2007, 57. For similar Russian criticisms of the role of "liberals" in de-democratization, see note 39. Even some of Chubais's admirers admit he was uninterested in democracy. See, e.g., Leonid Radzikhovskii in *RG*, May 31, 2005; and M. Berger and O. Proskurina, *Krest Chubaisa* (Moscow, 2008). A few of Yeltsin's intellectual supporters later regretted the antidemocratic conse-

quences of his measures. See, e.g., Evgenii Iasin in *MN*, Nov, 11, 2003; and Evgenii Kiselev in *Novaia*, Oct. 6–8, 2008. For a "lighthearted" and distasteful self-justification of the role played by Chubais's team, see Alfred Kokh and Igor Svinarenko, *A Crate of Vodka* (New York, 2009).

59. For this sad episode, see Cohen, *Failed Crusade*.

60. Following "liberals," see, respectively, Natalia Gevorkian in *Liberaly o narode* (Moscow, 2006), 43; Yuri Karyakin quoted in Andrei Sinyavsky, *The Russian Intelligentsia* (New York, 1997), 20; Dmitrii Furman in *OG*, July 12–18, 2001; Viktor Erofeyev in *NYT*, Feb. 29, 2008; and Alfred Kokh quoted by Vladimir Shlapentokh in *EAS* (Nov. 1999): 1168. Similarly, see Galina Starovoitova in *NG*, July 30, 1991; the letter to Putin signed by intellectuals in *Izvestiia*, Dec. 5, 2000; Kokh quoted in *SR*, Feb. 2, 2002; Kokh and Svinarenko, *Crate*; Artemii Troitskii in *Novaia*, Nov. 24–26, 2003; Vladimir Gryaznevich in *St. Petersburg Times*, Feb. 7, 2006; and Sergei Kovalev in *NYRB*, Nov. 22, 2007. *Liberaly o narode* is a malicious but representative sampler of such statements, and Sinyavsky, *Russian Intelligentsia*, a protest against them, esp. 16, 20–21, 31.

61. S. A. Korobov in *SR*, Aug. 19, 2006. For the argument that there were post-Soviet alternatives to shock therapy in 1992, see, e.g., Aleksei Kiva in *SM*, no. 2 (2007): 64–65; and Vadim Belotserkovski in *SM* no. 12 (2007): 54–55.

62. Shevtsova in Tolstykh, ed., *Mnogaia*, 453.

63. Gorbachev's speech on receiving the American National Constitution Center's 2008 Liberty Award (Sept. 19, 2008), on the Center's Web site. More fully, see Gorbachev, *Zhizn i reformy*, vol. 2. For historians and participants, see this chapter, n. 75.

64. Dan Bilefsky and Michael Schwirtz in *NYT*, Sept. 8, 2008. Similarly, see the survey of Russians reported in *Novaia*, Aug. 11–13, 2008; the Ossetian quoted by Andrew Kramer and Ellen Barry in *NYT*, Sept. 11, 2008; the Russians by Michael Schwirtz in *NYT*, Sept. 30, 2008; the Georgian by Ellen Barry in *NYT*, Oct. 10, 2008; and V. Trifimov in *SR*, Sept. 20, 2008, who wrote: "America fought Russia . . . in South Ossetia." Henry Kissinger and George Schultz worried that the war "will be treated as a metaphor for a larger conflict" (*WP*, Oct. 8, 2008). And rightly so. See, e.g., Aleksei Bogaturov and Aleksei Fenenko in *SM*, no. 11 (2008), who, from a Russian perspective, see the war as a watershed moment in U.S.-Russia relations. For the background and an analysis, see George Friedman in *NYRB*, Sept. 25, 2008, 24–26.

65. For the surprise, see, e.g., the report of the Central Asia–Caucasus Institute in *JRL*, Aug. 31, 2008; and a U.S. military officer responsible for Georgian affairs quoted by Helene Cooper and Thorn Shanker in *NYT*, Aug. 13,

2008. Similarly, see the war having been a "shock" that "jolted" the Bush administration, as remarked by Stephen Sestanovish in *FA* (Nov./Dec. 2008): 12, and reported by Stephen Lee Myers and Thom Shanker in *NYT*, Aug. 15, 2008.

66. Rice in *JRL*, Jan. 24, 2008; and David Ignatius in *WP*, Sept. 4, 2008. Similarly, see Michael McFaul's congressional testimony in *JRL*, Sept. 9, 2008; Ambassador William J. Burns in *JRL*, Nov. 12, 2007; John R. Bolton in *WP*, Oct. 20, 2008; Ronald D. Asmus and Richard Holbrooke in *WP*, Aug. 11, 2008; U.S. Secretary of Defense Robert Gates in *JRL*, Oct. 24, 2007; *WS* editorial, Aug, 25, 2008, 7; and Robert Kagan in *NR*, April 23, 2008, 44.

67. On the latter point, see, e.g., U.S. Deputy Secretary of State Matthew Bryza in *JRL*, Sept. 24, 2008; on ideology, see Tom Nichols, National Review Online, Dec. 8, 2008; and for all of the reasons, see Pavel K. Baev in *AAASS Newsnet*, Oct. 2007, 1. The points appear regularly in official and media statements, but for a sophisticated defense of the argument see Brown, *Seven Years*, 240–41.

68. Robert Kagan in *WP*, May 2, 2008, is supported by Stephen Kotkin in *NYT*, July 6, 2008. In 2003, the U.S. ambassador to Moscow complained that a "values gap" was the main obstacle in the relationship (quoted by Stephen Sestanovich in *FA* [Nov./Dec. 2008]: 12, though here I am quoting Ronald D. Asmus in *WP*, Dec. 13, 2008). For ideologues on the American side, see, e.g., Robert Kagan, *The Return of History and the End of Dreams* (New York, 2008); Sestanovich in *FA* (Nov./Dec. 2008): 12–28; McFaul's congressional testimony in *JRL*, Sept. 9, 2008; Council of Foreign Relations, *Russia's Wrong Direction*, Task Force Report No. 57 (New York, 2006); most of the Russia-related events of the American Enterprise Institute, as, e.g., the one reported in *JRL*, Oct. 15, 2008; and for an Anglo-American example, Edward Lucas, *The New Cold War* (New York, 2008). On charges that Putin's Russia is "fascist" or analogous to Nazi Germany, see, e.g., Leon Wieseltier in *NR*, Feb. 27, 2008, 48; Richard Pipes's letter in *FT*, July 22, 2008; Zbigniew Brzezinski interviewed at huffingtonpost.com, Aug. 8, 2008; and *WP* editorial, Sept. 2, 2008.

69. See Friedman in *NYRB*, Sept. 25, 2008, 24–26.

70. Steven Lee Myers in *NYT*, Aug. 16, 2008; and for the preceding quote, *NYT* editorial, Aug. 27, 2008.

71. Almost immediately in 1985, for example, Gorbachev privately nullified the "Brezhnev Doctrine," which gave the Kremlin the right to decide the domestic and foreign policies of Eastern Europe's Communist states, and made clear his intention to end the Soviet occupation of Afghanistan. See Brown, *Seven Years*, 242–43.

72. For the history of "New Thinking," see Robert D. English, *Russia and the Idea of the West* (New York, 2000); for its application, Brown, *Seven Years*, chap. 9; and for insider accounts of the new policies, Anatoly Chernyaev, *My Six Years with Gorbachev* (University Park, PA, 2000), Andrei Grachev, *Gorbachev's Gamble* (Malden, Mass., 2008), and Jack F. Matlock Jr., *Reagan and Gorbachev* (New York, 2004).

73. Quoted in Norman A. Graebner, Richard Dean Burns, and Joseph M. Siracusa, *Reagan, Bush, Gorbachev* (Westport, Conn., 2008), 142. Similarly, see Matlock, *Reagan and Gorbachev*, xiv, and for "another era," 302.

74. Bush quoted in Graebner et al., *Reagan*, 130. On Malta "symbolically representing the end of the . . . Cold War world," see Raymond L. Garthoff, *The Great Transition* (Washington, D.C., 1994), 404–8.

75. See, e.g., Graebner, et. al., *Reagan*; Matlock, *Reagan and Gorbachev*; Grachev, *Gorbachev's Gamble*; Brown, *Seven Years*, chap. 9; Kiron K. Skinner, ed., *Turning Points in Ending the Cold War* (Stanford, Calif., 2008); William C. Wohlforth, ed., *Witnesses to the End of the Cold War* (Baltimore, Md., 1996); and Dick Combs, *Inside the Soviet Alternate Universe* (University Park, Penn., 2008), chaps. 9–10.

76. George Bush and Brent Scowcroft, *A World Transformed* (New York, 1998), xiv; Philip Zelikow and Condoleezza Rice, *Germany United and Europe Transformed* (Cambridge, Mass., 1995), 363. Reagan agreed: "I think both sides won" (quoted by Jack Matlock Jr. in Desai, *Conversations on Russia*, 331). The secretary general of NATO concurred: "There are no losers, only winners," as quoted by Flora Lewis in *NYT*, July 21, 1990.

77. At the Republican National Convention later that year, Patrick J. Buchanan, one of Bush's rivals for the nomination, gave primarily Reagan and secondarily Bush credit for "the policies that won the Cold War." The party's 2008 nominee, Senator John McCain, was no less certain: "Ronald Reagan won the Cold War" (quoted by Michael Cooper in *NYT*, Feb. 24, 2008). Bush adumbrated this revised view in December 1991, claiming that the end of the Soviet Union was "a victory for the moral force of our values" (transcript of his speech on Dec. 25, *NYT*, Dec. 26, 1991). For the reaction in Moscow, see, e.g., Viacheslav Stepin in Tolstykh, ed., *Perestroika*, 69.

78. *NYT*, Oct. 28, 2002.

79. Michael McFaul in Skinner, ed., *Turning Points*, chap. 7; and James M. Goldgeier and Michael McFaul, *Power and Purpose* (Washington, D.C., 2003), where it is said that Yeltsin's abolition of the Soviet Union had the effect of "erasing the cold war in an instant" (1). For a more sophisticated but equally triumphalist account, see John Lewis Gaddis, *The Cold War: A New History* (New York, 2005). Upon reading it, a reviewer wrote: "The

Soviet Union was no more. The cold war was over" (William Grimes in
NYT, Dec. 18, 2005).

80. Tony Judt, reviewing Gaddis, *The Cold War*, and quoting David Caute, in
NYRB, March 23, 2006, 11–12, 15.

7. WHO LOST THE POST-SOVIET PEACE?

1. Clinton administration official cited by Daniel Williams in *WP*, March 13,
1993; Steven Erlanger in *NYT*, July 28, 1993. The crusade is the subject of
my book *Failed Crusade: America and the Tragedy of Post-Communist Russia*, updated ed. (New York, 2001). It was not the first U.S. crusade in Russia. For previous ones, see David S. Foglesong, *The American Mission and
the "Evil Empire"* (New York, 2007).

2. Years later, for example, a leading foreign-affairs columnist was still insisting, "Who lost Russia is an unfair and idiotic question" (Jim Hoagland in
WP, Oct. 28, 2007). By then, the prevailing opinion was that Putin's Kremlin had "lost the West" (Stephen Blank in *JRL*, Nov. 30, 2007). That same
year, on the other hand, it was formulated more correctly in Dmitry K.
Simes, "Losing Russia," *FA* (Nov.–Dec. 2007): 36–52.

3. *NYT* editorial, March 13, 2006; Andrew C. Kuchins in *JRL*, May 14, 2002.

4. Retired Gen. William Odom, paraphrased and quoted by Lars-Erik Nelson
in *Daily News* (New York), Jan. 2, 2000; Thomas E. Graham Jr. in *JRL*,
June 21, 1999. Similarly, see Odom in Nikolas K. Gvosdev, ed., *Russia in the
National Interest* (New Brunswick, N.J., 2004), chap. 17. For more on this
notion, see Cohen, *Failed Crusade*, 208–9.

5. Mark Katz in *MT*, Jan. 26, 2004. Similarly, see Lionel Beehner, "Why Russia Matters Less Than We Think," huffingtonpost.com, Jan. 2, 2008; Rajon
Menon and Alexander J. Motyl, "The Myth of Russian Resurgence," *The
American Interest* (March–April 2007); Nina Khrushcheva in *MT*, May 17,
2006, who assures readers there will not be another cold war because "Russia is not important enough;" and Deputy Assistant Secretary of State Matthew Bryza of the United States, who says it is because Russia is too weak
(cited in Interfax dispatch, *JRL*, Sept. 24, 2008).

6. Iurii Afanasev in *SM*, no. 1–2 (2006): 3. For the "demographic disaster,"
see Nicholas Eberstadt in *NYT*, Oct. 25, 2008; and, similarly, Murray Fesh-
bach in *WP*, Oct. 5, 2008. For an equally if not more grim report, see Nade-
zhda Popova in *Argumenty nedeli*, translated in *JRL*, Oct. 9, 2008.

7. *JRL*, Feb. 9, 2006. An independent Russian analyst characterized Putin as
the "cement" of the political system (Mikhail Rostovskii in *MK*, Aug. 14,
2006).

8. Peter Reddaway in *Newsweek International*, March 14, 2005. As a result of the 2008 financial crisis, according to a Russian publication, "All talk of Russia as an island of stability has dried up" (Roland Oliphant in *JRL*, Oct. 28, 2008). For the anomalous political system, economy, and property rights more generally, see Stefan Hedlund in *PPC* (July/Aug. 2008): 29–41.

9. See, respectively, the reports by Thom Shanker in *NYT*, Oct. 22, 2008; by AP in *WP*, May 9, 2008; two resolutions by the U.S. House of Representatives in *JRL*, April 2, 2008; the 2008 film *Indiana Jones and the Kingdom of the Crystal Skull*; the subtitle of Steve LeVine, *Putin's Labyrinth: Spies, Murder, and the Dark Heart of the New Russia* (New York, 2008) (similarly, Edward Lucas, *The New Cold War: Putin's Russia and the Threat to the West* [New York, 2008]); views cited in OSC report in *JRL*, May 8, 2008; Masha Gessen in *Vanity Fair* (Oct. 2008): 336–38, 380–86; and Alan Cowell in *IHT*, Aug. 1, 2008. For Churchill's aphorism, see also Cohen, *Failed Crusade*, 76–77. There was a torrent of such examples on the Russian side, one being the 2008 film *Strangers*. See Ezekiel Pfeifer in *St. Petersburg Times*, Nov. 18, 2008.

10. See, respectively, *WSJ* editorial, June 2, 2008; Jim Hoagland in *WP*, Dec. 2, 2004; *WP*, editorials, March 21, 2006, and Dec. 22, 2004; *WP*, editorials, March 21, 2006, and Dec. 2, 2004; Eric Lipton in *NYT*, Aug. 20, 2008, congressional testimony of Strobe Talbott in *JRL*, Nov. 1, 2007; and *NYT* editorial, Dec. 30. 2007. Similarly, see Council on Foreign Relations, *Russia's Wrong Direction* (New York, 2006); Fred Hiatt in *WP*, Aug, 18, 2008; Cathy Young in *WS*, Sept. 1, 2008; Steven Lee Myers and Thom Shanker in *NYT*, Aug. 15, 2008; Ronald D. Asmus and Richard Holbrooke in *WP*, Aug. 11, 2008; Stephen Sestanovich in *FA* (Nov./Dec. 2008): 12–28; Alexander Vershbow in *JRL*, Oct. 28, 2008; Leon Aron, "Putin's Cold War," *WSJ*, Dec. 26, 2007; Jackson Diehl in *WP*, June 19, 2006; William Kristol in *NYT*, Aug. 11, 2008; LeVine, *Putin's Labyrinth*; Lucas, *The New Cold War*; and Michael McFaul and Kathryn Stoner-Weiss in *FA* (Jan./Feb. 2008): 68–84.

11. See, e.g., Simon Sebag Montefiore in *NYT*, Aug. 24, 2008; Leon Aron in *USA Today*, Aug. 12, 2008; Stephen Kotkin on "a Soviet hangover" in *FT*, March 6, 2004; and Secretary of Defense Robert M. Gates quoted by Thom Shanker in *NYT*, Sept. 20, 2008.

12. Rice, address at the German Marshall Fund, Sept. 18, 2008, Dept. of State Web site. Another senior Bush administration official also emphasized, "It's been their responsibility, not ours" (quoted by Paul Richter in *LAT*, Jan. 29, 2008). Similarly, see Stephen Blank in *JRL*, Nov. 30, 2007; and sources in this chapter, nn. 10 and 51.

13. James Traub in *NYT*, Aug. 10, 2008; and Anatol Lieven in *LAT*, March 19, 2006. (Similarly, see Michael O'Hanlon in *Washington Times*, Dec. 2, 2008,

who while critical of U.S. policy concludes that "cynical and ruthless Russian politicians are the primary problem.") Traub excluded two people from the right-minded consensus as "naive," me and Henry Kissinger. For other Americans who do not adhere to it, at least not fully, see Anthony T. Salvia in *JRL*; Nov. 30, 2007, and March 31, 2008; Jack F. Matlock Jr., *Reagan and Gorbachev* (New York, 2004); Dmitry K. Simes in *FA* (Nov.–Dec. 2007): 36–52; Ronald Steel in *NYT*, Aug. 24, 2008; David Bromwich, huffingtonpost.com, Sept. 24, 2008; Gordon M. Hahn in *JRL*, Aug. 25, 2008; Ted Galen Carpenter in *JRL*, July 30, 2008; Robert V. Daniels in *JRL*, June 24, 2008; *BG* editorial, July 20, 2008; and Patrick Buchanan, worldnetdaily.com, Feb. 4, 2004, Dec. 29, 2004, Nov. 30, 2005, and May 9, 2006; Buchanan, creators.com, Nov. 30, 2007; and Buchanan in *American Conservative*, June 4, 2007.

14. See, e.g., the sections on Russia and Yeltsin in Bill Clinton, *My Life* (New York, 2004); Strobe Talbott, *The Russia Hand* (New York, 2002), and his congressional testimony in *JRL*, Nov. 1, 2007; Derek Challet and James Goldgeier, *America Between the Wars* (New York, 2008), and Goldgeier's interview with Bernard Gwertzman in *JRL*, July 9, 2006; Robert D. Asmus in *NR*, Aug. 12, 2008, and in *WP*, Dec. 13, 2008, and with Holbrooke in *WP*, Aug. 11, 2008; Vershbow in *JRL*, Oct. 28, 2008; Derek Shearer, huffingtonpost.com, Aug. 20, 2008; Jeremy D. Rossner's letter in *NYT*, Aug. 24, 2008; and Madeleine Albright in *JRL*, Dec. 15, 2008. For a somewhat different but equally critical analysis of the Clinton Russia policy, see Michael Mandelbaum, "America, Russia, and Europe," in *JRL*, Oct. 24, 2008.

15. Sen. Joseph Lieberman quoted in AP dispatch, *JRL*, Aug. 21, 2008; *NYT* editorial, Aug. 12, 2008; and, similarly, *WP* editorial, March 8, 2008.

16. Quoted by Peter Finn in *WP*, July 16, 2008; and by Ellen Barry in *NYT*, Sept. 20, 2008. Similarly, see Medvedev's remarks at the Valdai meeting, kremlin.ru, Sept. 12, 2008.

17. Secretary of Defense Gates, speech in England, Sept. 19, 2008, DOD Web site. And, similarly, Secretary of State Rice, address at the German Marshall Fund, Sept. 18, 2008, Dept. of State Web site; and in *JRL*, May 4, 2006.

18. Holbrooke in *WP*, Dec. 14, 2004; and, similarly, *NYT* editorial, March 8, 2008. Holbrooke soon claimed Georgia, too, as a vital U.S. interest (*WP*, Nov. 27, 2006).

19. Anders Aslund in *WS*, Jan. 17, 2005, 17–18; and, similarly, the lessons suggested by Michael McFaul in the concluding chapter of Asland and McFaul, eds., *Revolution in Orange* (Washington, D.C., 2006). For the name-calling, see, respectively, Jackson Diehl in *WP*, Jan. 31, 2005; George F. Will in *WP*, Dec. 14, 2003; and Homan W. Jenkins Jr. in *WSJ*, Jan. 5, 2005. See also sources in this chapter, n. 50.

20. Council on Foreign Relations, *Russia's Wrong Direction*. Similarly, the Washington Russia specialist Celeste Wallander declared that the Russian political system as a whole "lacks any legitimacy" (*JRL*, Dec. 3, 2006).

21. Vice President Dick Cheney quoted by AP in *WP*, Sept. 7, 2008.

22. For examples, see Cohen, *Failed Crusade*, part 1 and pp. 124–35.

23. See the *AP* report by Desmond Butler in *Moscow News*, Oct. 5–11, 2007; and Joseph Cirincione, theglobalist.com, Oct. 24, 2007.

24. See the exchange between Clinton and Yeltsin at a joint press conference, in *WP*, April 5, 1993; and Samuel R. Berger in *WP*, Nov. 15, 2001. For more on Yeltsin as the "personification of Russian reform," see Cohen, *Failed Crusade*, especially part 1. Perceptive Russians understood that the Clinton administration had "a strategy of indirect actions" (Viacheslav Dashichev in *SM*, no. 1 [2008]: 152).

25. See the following note. Pending access to archive documents, at least three factors seem to have played a role: Yeltsin's psychological need for Western, particularly American approval (and perhaps protection) in the face of growing Russian resentment over his abolition of the Soviet state and subsequent policies; the Kremlin's need for Western loans, largely controlled by Washington; and Yeltsin's abiding desire to replace Gorbachev in the West's esteem. (Later, some Russian analysts believed that the financial corruption of people around Yeltsin, and their accounts abroad, played an even larger role.)

26. Talbott, *The Russia Hand*, 201, 363, and other similarly revealing passages in the book; and Richard Holbrooke quoted by William Finnegan in *NY*, Oct. 15, 2007, online. Even a Yeltsin insider and beneficiary of U.S. policy understood that the Russian president was "perceived as a puppet of the West, his policies dictated by the U.S." (Alfred Kokh in *CSM*, Oct. 15, 2008).

27. James M. Goldgeier and Michael McFaul, *Power and Purpose* (Washington, D.C., 2003), 4 and, similarly, 59–60. For the administration's Caspian oil pursuit, see Michael T. Klare, tomdispatch.com, Sept. 2, 2008. Years later, Clinton's secretary of state, Madeleine Albright, reiterated the administration's operational view in the 1990s: "We won the Cold War. They lost the Cold War" (*JRL*, Dec. 15, 2008).

28. See Secretary of State James Baker's pledge to Gorbachev, quoted in Philip Zelikow and Condoleezza Rice, *Germany Unified and Europe Transformed* (Cambridge, Mass., 1995), 182; and, similarly, Stephen F. Szabo, *The Diplomacy of German Reunification* (New York, 1992), 61–65.

29. For the American denials, see, respectively, Michael Beschloss in *NYT Book Review*, Jan. 15, 2006, 9; Rice in *JRL*, Jan. 24, 2008; and both Stephen Kotkin in *NR*, May 29, 2006, 36, and Tom Nichols in *Toronto Star*, May 11,

2006. Similarly, see Rose Gottemoeller in *NYT*, May 4, 2007. For the Russian view, beginning with Putin, see nytimes.com, Oct. 6, 2003; Iulii Kvitskinskii in *SR*, Jan. 26, 2006; and *Izvestiia* headline, Jan. 10, 2006. On being deceived, see also the Duma debate quoted by Guy Faulconbridge, Reuters dispatch, Nov. 7, 2007; and Dmitrii Rogozin in *LG*, Aug. 27–Sept. 2, 2008. On Russian views of the new cold war, see also Sergei Karaganov in *RG*, Aug. 29, 2008; Sergei Rogov in *JRL*, Oct. 6, 2008; Aleksei Pushkov in *LG*, June 11–17, 2008; and Gen. Leonid Shebarshin in *LG*, March 28–April 3, 2007. For broken promises, see also President Dmitri Medvedev at the Valdai meeting, kremlin.ru, Sept. 12, 2008.

30. Anthony T. Salvia in *JRL*, March 26, 2006.
31. Speech in Sidney, March 16, 2006, State Dept. Web site.
32. Quoted by Steven Lee Myers in *NYT*, May 5, 2006.
33. Council on Foreign Relations, *Russia's Wrong Direction*.
34. Keir Lieber and Daryl Press in *FA* (March/April 2006): 43.
35. For a survey, see the Levada Center's findings in *JRL*, Sept. 25, 2008. A once exceedingly pro-American (and influential) policy intellectual remarked, "We don't trust anybody, especially the United States" (Sergei Karaganov quoted by Megan K. Stack in *LAT*, Aug. 25, 2008). Similarly, see Karaganov in *RG*, Aug. 29, 2008; Rogov in *JRL*, Oct. 6, 2008; and Masha Lipman in *WP*, Oct. 4, 2008, who reports: "The United States no longer has a sympathetic constituency in Russia." On the absence of anti-Americanism during the Cold War, see also Alexei Arbatov, quoted by Alan Cullison and Jeanne Whalen in *WSJ*, April 1, 2003.
36. See, e.g., V. Iu. Surkov, *Osnovnye tendentsii i perspektivy razvitiia sovremennoi Rossii* (Moscow, 2007).
37. *Kommersant*, May 5, 2006, quoted by Oliver Bullough, Reuters dispatch, May 5, 2006.
38. Evgenii Primakov in *AF*, Dec. 21, 2005; Surkov in *CDPSP*, Oct. 27, 2004, 2–3; Solzhenitsyn in *MN*, April 28, 2006. Similarly, see Aleksandr Dugin in *LG*, Dec. 5–11, 2007; Maksim Lavrentev in *LG*, March 12–18, 2008; and Generals Nikolai Makarov and Leonid Ivashov in *Izvestiia*, Dec. 17, 2008.
39. Even before the war, Russian generals, protesting overflights by NATO aircraft from neighboring bases, were warning: "If they violate our border, they should be shot down" (*RFE/RL*, March 30, 2004).
40. See Michael Wines and Celestine Bohlen in *NYT*, Feb. 20, April 2, and May 8, 2000; and Thomas M. Nichols in *WPJ* (Winter 2002/2003): 13–22. As late as 2004, Secretary of State Colin L. Powell commended Putin for having "moved in a democratic way" (*USA Today* interview, Oct. 18, 2004).
41. A point made by Stephen Kotkin in *Prospect Magazine*, reprinted in *JRL*, March 26, 2008; and, similarly, by Anna Matveeva in *The Guardian*, Dec. 13,

2008. On Putin, see Leon Aron in *NR*, Nov. 5, 2007, 42; and, similarly, William Grimes's review (*NYT*, July 1, 2005) of Peter Baker and Susan Glasser, *Kremlin Rising* (New York, 2005), which created the impression of a "fishy-eyed, simple-minded man . . . a thorough-going mediocrity."

42. See, respectively, Bruce P. Jackson and Jim Hoagland in *WP*, Oct. 28, 2003, and Dec. 22, 2004; Jackson Diehl in *WP*, Oct. 28, 2003; and Nicholas Kristof in *NYT*, Dec. 15, 2004. Similarly, see *Economist* editorial, Aug. 24–31, 2007, on how "the West tried to be a friend."

43. As reported by Radio Ekho Moskvy, in *JRL*, Dec. 16, 2002. For an itemization of perceived broken promises, see Viktor Baranets in *KP*, Feb. 15, 2007.

44. Putin speech at Munich and Medvedev's state of the nation address, kremlin.ru, Feb. 10, 2007, and *JRL*, Nov. 6, 2008. An *Izvestiia* headline on Oct. 9, 2008, described Medvedev's address as "his own 'Munich Speech.'" At a press conference following his speech, Putin himself foresaw the accusation of a "Second Cold War" (kremlin.ru, Feb. 10, 2007). For examples, see Brian Whitmore in *RFE/RL*, Dec. 26, 2007; and Anne Penketh in *The Independent* (UK), Aug. 26, 2007, who reports that the "new Cold War" had its "origins" in the speech. The Russian newspaper *Kommersant*, on the other hand, announced that "a second cold war" had begun with a speech by Vice President Cheney in Vilnius almost a year earlier (*CDPSP*, May 31 and June 7, 2006, 1). For Russia's "sovereignization of foreign policy," see Dmitrii Bulin in *PK*, no. 27 (2007), online.

45. Vagif Guseinov in *VA*, no. 3 (2007): 7. And, similarly, Sergei Karaganov in *RG*, March 24, 2006; and Vladimir Orlov in *JRL*, Dec. 11, 2008.

46. According to a report, Bush's National Security Council was contemptuous of arms control as "baggage from the Cold War" (Dafna Linzer in *WP*, March 12, 2006).

47. A leading example was the Washington-based American Committee on East-West Accord, whose members included top corporate executives, retired military officers and other government officials, prominent policy intellectuals such George F. Kennan and John Kenneth Galbraith, and independent scientists. (I, too, was a member.) Its purpose was to improve U.S.-Soviet relations by persuading political leaders, the media, and public opinion to support such policies. See, e.g., its publication *Détente or Debacle: Common Sense in U.S.-Soviet Relations* (New York, 1979).

48. Among the Reaganites were disparate figures such as Patrick J. Buchanan, Reagan's ambassador to Moscow Jack Matlock; his personal friend and advisor on Russia, Suzanne Massie; and a younger former appointee, Anthony Salvia. For Buchanan, see worldnetdaily.com, Feb. 4, 2004, Dec. 29, 2004, Nov. 30, 2005, and May 9, 2006; creators.com, Nov. 30, 2007; and

American Conservative, June 4, 2007; for Matlock, see *Reagan and Gorbachev;* for Massie, see *JRL,* Dec. 22, 2008; for Salvia, see *JRL,* Nov. 30, 2007; and for Gorbachev, *JRL,* June 4, 2006.

49. For the crusading media of the 1990s, see Cohen, *Failed Crusade,* esp. part 1; and for the post-2000 period, my articles "American Journalism and Russia's Tragedy" and "The Media's New Cold War" in *The Nation,* Oct. 2, 2000, and Jan. 31, 2005. For an example of the monopoly, see the writers used to comment on the fifteenth anniversary of the Soviet breakup (Peter Baker, Leon Aron, Michael McFaul, and Stephen Sestanovich) in *WP,* Dec. 24, 2006; and for a similar pattern on "public" radio, see the NPR broadcast featuring Yeltsin-era "reformers" in *JRL,* March 7 and 9, 2007. For the historian, see Robert V. Daniels, *Russia's Transformation* (Lanham, Md., 1998), 193.

50. Kristof in *NYT,* Dec. 15, 2004; Thomas Oliphant in *BG,* Dec. 21, 2004. On "fascist," see also Will in *WP,* Dec. 14, 2003; Leon Wieseltier in *NR,* Feb. 27, 2008, 48; Richard Pipes's letter in *FT,* July 22, 2008; and *WP,* editorial, Sept. 2, 2008; Cathy Young in *NR,* Feb. 27, 2008, 48; Zbigniew Brzezinski, huffingtonpost.com, Aug. 8, 2008; and Paul Johnson in *Forbes,* Oct. 13, 2008. Regarding deaths, I have in mind, of course, those of Anna Politkovskaya and Aleksandr Litvinenko.

51. See, respectively, Bret Stephens in *WSJ,* Nov. 28, 2006; Anne Applebaum in *WP,* Nov. 24, 2004; Ana Palacio and Daniel Twining in *WP,* March 11, 2006; and Elisabeth Bumiller in *NYT,* Dec.2, 2004. For later examples of blaming Russia alone for the Georgian War, even after it was clear Georgia had initiated the fighting, see Asmus and Holbrooke in *WP,* Aug. 11, 2008; Fred Hiatt in *WP,* Aug. 18, 2008; and in this chapter, note 128.

52. Daniel Johnson in *New York Sun,* March 21, 2006.

53. Allen C. Lynch in *Great Decisions* (New York: Foreign Policy Association, 2008), 51; and Putin cited by RIA Novosti, May 13, 2006.

54. Mark Almond in *The Guardian,* Jan. 21, 2006; and similarly Anatole Kaletsky, an associate editor, in *The Times* (UK), June 7, 2007, who concluded, "It is not Russia but America and Europe that have restarted the Cold War."

55. David Remnick on National Public Radio, in *JRL,* Oct. 4, 2007; and for a report that it is a "commonly held" opinion among U.S. diplomats and scholars, Andrew C. Kuchins in *JRL,* Nov. 21, 2006.

56. See, respectively, Stanislav Belkovskii in *Vedomosti,* June 26, 2006; Aleksandr Tsipko summarizing the charge by others, in *LG,* Jan. 24–30, 2007 (and, similarly, Aleksei Kiva in *LG,* Aug. 10, 2005); John Laughland in *The Spectator* (UK), Oct. 9, 2004, repeating the charge of "appeasement," which I, too, heard in Moscow; and Vitalii Tretiakov explaining accusations of

betrayal made by others, in *MN*, March 22, 2006. Similarly, see Iu. Kotov in *SR*, April 10, 2004; and most of the items cited in this chapter, n. 58. See also Aleksandr Droban's demand for a "policy breaking completely with the time of Gorbachev and its legacy" (*LG*, Dec. 5–11, 2007). A reliable observer reported that top Russian military officers "will never forgive" Putin for "placating Bush" by allowing U.S. bases in Central Asia (Boris Kagarlitsky in *The Progressive* [March 2005], reprinted in *JRL*, March 3, 2005). That hostility seemed to be reflected in Aleksei Pilko's article in the military paper *KZ*, June 14, 2006, and in Gen. Leonid Ivashov's remarks in *KP*, May 1, 2006.

57. See, e.g., Sergei Karaganov in *RG*, June 30, 2006; Evgenii Kiselev on Radio Ekho Moskvy, in *JRL*, Nov. 10, 2008; and Matthew Bunn cited by Hubert Wetzel in *FT*, March 9, 2005. In 2006, Putin's modernization campaign took the form of four funded "national projects"—in health care, education, housing, and agriculture. Medvedev was appointed to oversee them.

58. For "naive" and "illusions," see Alexander Pikayev quoted by Sharon FaFraniere in *WP*, March 7, 2003; and Gen. Leonid Ivashov, fednews.ru, March 23, 2006. For the quotes that follow, see, respectively, Valentin Falin in *JRL*, March 5, 2006 (and, similarly, Lavrentev in *LG*, March 12–18, 2008); Natalia Narochnitskaia in *Bolshaia politika*, no. 1–2 (2006): 53; and Aleksandr Dugin in *Izvestiia*, April 13, 2005. For permanent cold war against Russia, see also Aleksandr Zinoviev, *Gibel russkogo kommunizma* (Moscow, 2001); Shebarshin in *LG*, March 28–April 3, 2007; and Vladimir Savelev in *LG*, Dec. 26–31, 2007.

59. Dmitrii Rogozin in *LG*, Aug. 27–Sept. 2, 2008; and Dugin in *Izvestiia*, April 13, 2005. On "deceits," see also Baranets in *KP*, Feb. 15, 2007.

60. For "hard-line," see Pilko in *KZ*, June 14, 2006. For overviews of their thinking, see the analyses by Yury Fedorov and OSC in *JRL*, May 30, 2006, and May 8, 2008; and Andrei P. Tsygankov in *PPC* (March/April 2008): 49–52.

61. See, respectively, Anatolii Utkin in *Rodnaia gazeta*, July 20, 2006; Foreign Minister Sergei Lavrov on the Cold War in *RG*, no. 45 (March 2006); Ivashov, fednews.ru, March 23, 2006: Aleksei Pushkov in *Trud*, May 13, 2005; KGB/FSB officer quoted in *Economist*, Aug. 24–31, 2007; and Pikayev quoted by Sharon FaFraniere in *WP*, March 7, 2003. Similarly, see Kiva in *LG*, Aug. 10, 2005.

62. As noted by Aleksei Arbatov in *Gazeta*, April 12, 2007; and, similarly, by Karaganov in *RG*, March 24, 2006. Speaking of Cold War "inertia," Putin himself noted, "Both here and in the United states, there are still many people who are guided by outdated mentality" (interview with *NYT*, nytimes.com Oct. 6, 2003). The Russian ambassador to Washington em-

phasized the same point (Yuri Ushakov in *WP*, Oct. 8, 2003). Similarly, see President Bush quoted by Jim Ruttenberg and Andrew E. Kramer in *NYT*, July 16, 2006.

63. Vitalii Tretiakov in *Izvestiia*, Aug. 28, 2008 (and, similarly, Dmitri Trenin in *Newsweek*, Sept. 1, 2008); and Medvedev, kremlin.ru, Sept. 12, 2008. Elsewhere Medvedev explained, "Russia had no option" (*FT*, Dec. 16, 2008), and "this was the only course of action we could take" (kremlin.ru, Dec. 24, 2008).

64. See, respectively, the obviously official statement by Andrei Feyashin, RIA Novosti, in *JRL*, Nov. 10, 2008; Dmitri Rogozin quoted by Clifford J. Levy in *NYT*, Aug. 28, 2008; and kremlin.com, Feb. 8, 2008. Similarly, see Putin, "National security is not based on promises" (quoted by Helene Cooper in *NYT*, Aug. 18, 2008), and "We didn't start this" (quoted in *RFE/RL*, Feb. 13, 2008); Medvedev, "We are not the ones. . . . It's NATO" (quoted by Ellen Barry in *NYT*, Sept. 3, 2008), and "This was not our fault" (kremlin.ru, November 18, 2008); and Viktor Kremeniuk, "The West must be the first to make concessions" (*JRL*, Sept. 5, 2008). For Russia having "had enough" of U.S. behavior toward it, see also Andrei Stoliarov in *LG*, Nov. 19–25, 2008.

65. Alexei Arbatov in "Behind the Headlines" supplement to *WP*, Sept. 24, 2008. The expression "eye-for-an-eye" is attributed disapprovingly to Arbatov and others by Lilia Shevtsova, opendemocracy.net, Nov. 3, 2008, in *JRL*, Nov. 17, 2008.

66. Masha Lipman in *WP*, Oct. 4, 2008, who previously blamed bad relations on the "unpardonable consequences of Russia's geopolitical aspirations" (*WP*, Jan. 30, 2006). For a profoundly embittered Russian policy intellectual who had vested his career in such a partnership and whose feeling of having been betrayed by his American colleagues was evident, see Karaganov in *RG*, March 24, 2006.

67. See, e.g., Vladislav Surkov in *Ekspert*, Nov. 20, 2006, 108, and in *JRL*, June 28, 2006; Sergei Samuilov in *SM*, no. 3 (2006): 42–43; and Aleksandr Tsipko in Karl Aimermakher et al., eds., *Preodolenie proshlogo i novye orientiry ego pereosmysleniia* (Moscow, 2002), 90.

68. Goldgeier and McFaul, *Power and Purpose*, 59; Sarah E. Mendelson and Theodore P. Gerber in *FA* (Jan./Feb. 2006): 2–8; Katherine E. Graney in *JRL*, Dec. 12, 2008; and *WP* editorial, Feb. 27, 2008.

69. Putin interview with *Time* magazine, kremlin.ru, Dec. 19, 2007. Putin added, "This is the main problem in our relations," though by 2008 he would not have cited it as the "main" one.

70. Mark Katz in *MT*, Jan. 26, 2004; Anne Applebaum in *WP*, April 19, 2003; *WP* editorial, March 2, 2008.

71. Vladimir Socor in *WSJ*, Sept. 19, 2003; Catherine Belton in *MT*, May 19, 2006 (and, similarly, Michael McFaul in *San Francisco Chronicle*, July 21, 2005); and Jim Hoagland in *WP*, May 21, 2006. Similarly, see Stephen Sestanovich's congressional testimony in *JRL*, March 18, 2004; Richard Holbrooke in *WP*, Feb. 16, 2005; and Gregory Feifer on National Public Radio, in *JRL*, March 6, 2007.

72. Stephens in *WSJ*, Nov. 28, 2006; Sestanovich in *JRL*, March 18, 2004; and Council on Foreign Relations, *Russia's Wrong Direction.*

73. For the original, see the senior Bush official quoted by Thorn Shanker in *NYT*, Nov. 12, 2008, which is only one of dozens of examples.

74. Vladimir Socor in *WSJ*, Jan. 10, 2003; Charles Krauthammer in *WP*, Dec. 3, 2004; Mark Brzezinski and Mark Lenzi in *BG*, Sept. 14, 2003.

75. For an example of the widespread view that an actual "U.S.-Russian alliance" was in the making, see Robert Legvold in Gvosdev, ed., *Russia*, 63–76; and, similarly, Anatol Lieven in *International Affairs* (Moscow) (Oct. 2007): 24.

76. Stanislav Kondrashov in *VN*, Jan. 19, 2002; Medvedev, kremlin.ru, Oct. 8, 2008. Similarly, see Aleksei Pushkov in *NG*, March 21, 2003; Pavel Felgenhauer in *MT*, Sept. 11, 2003; Fyodor Lukyanov in *MT*, Sept. 12, 2006; and Kokh in *CSM*, Oct. 15, 2008. Still worse, some Washington insiders blamed the Kremlin for the disappointed expectations. See Angela E. Stent quoted by Peter Baker in *WP*, Oct. 5, 2007.

77. Katz in *MT*, Jan. 26, 2004. Similarly, see President Bush and a State Department official quoted on Russia's "isolation" by Steven Lee Myers in *NYT*, Aug. 16 and 19, 2008; Bush's assertion that Russia's actions in Georgia could exclude it from "the diplomatic, political, economic and security structures of the 21st century" (quoted by Myers in *NYT*, Aug. 14, 2008); and Stephen Kotkin's assertion, "The only true friend Russia has is U.S. foreign policy" (fpri.org, March 6, 2007).

78. As I argued nearly a decade ago in *Failed Crusade*, 217–18.

79. Dmitri Trenin in *FA* (July/Aug. 2006): 92; and Medvedev quoted by Michael Abramowitz in *WP*, Nov. 16, 2008.

80. For a similar argument, see George Friedman in *NYRB*, Sept. 25, 2008, 24–26.

81. Thomas L. Friedman in *NYT*, May 10, 2006.

82. *RFE/RL*, April 20, 2006. Similarly, see the negotiations between Russia and China reported by Andrew E. Kramer in *NYT*, Oct. 9, 2008.

83. Dmitry K. Simes, nationalinterest.org, Oct. 30, 2008.

84. George Friedman quoted in *Deutsche Welle*, Feb. 15, 2006.

85. Putin quoted by Jim Ruttenberg and Andrew E. Kramer in *NYT*, July 16, 2006. For a similar point, see Padma Desai in *WSJ*, Feb. 16, 2007. For Mos-

cow's complex interests in the Muslim world, see Jacques Lévesque in *Le Monde diplomatique* (Dec. 2008).

86. An Azeri quoted by Sabrina Tavernise in *NYT*, Oct. 23, 2008.

87. Garry Kasparov quoted by David Remnick in *NY*, Oct. 1, 2007, 77. Some journalists are so passionately anti-Kremlin they seem to hope the nuclear state "implodes" (Edward Lucas in *JRL*, May 8, 2006).

88. For the argument that inadequate U.S. support was the primary cause of democracy promotion's failures, see Goldgeier and McFaul, *Power and Purpose*, 347–54.

89. See, for example, the accounts of Vice President Cheney's attack in Lithuania on the Kremlin in 2006 and subsequent trip to Kazakhstan, and the Russian reaction, as reported by Steven Lee Myers, Ilan Greenburg, and Andrew E. Kramer in *NYT*, May 5 and May 6, 2006; and in *CDPSP*, May 31 and June 7, 2006, 1–4. Similarly, his appearance in Baku in 2008 with two Western oil executives, reported by Myers in *NYT*, Sept. 4, 2008.

90. Even if this is not the case, leading Western journalists and specialists still think Russian oligarchs are "the most progressive force with any remaining power" and "our best bet" for "Russia's eventual return to a more democratic path" (Chrystia Freeland in *FT*, Aug. 22, 2008); similarly, see Anders Aslund in *JRL*, May 12, 2008. For examples of the continuing Russian memory of the U.S. role in "privatization" and in the destruction of the parliament, see Denis Novikov in *SM*, no. 8 (2007): 23; Igor Mikhailov in Tolstykh, ed., *Perestroika*, 145; and Iurii Boldyrev in *LG*, Oct. 8–14, 2008.

91. Rodric Braithwaite in *FT*, March 12, 2008. If so, Americans are merely echoing the contempt many Russian liberals have for their own people, as I pointed out earlier.

92. See, respectively, David Satter in *WS*, Nov. 13, 2006, 8; *Economist*, May 6, 2006, 1; Thomas L. Friedman in *NYT*, May 10, 2006; DeVine, *Putin's Labyrinth*, 10; Allan Sloan in *WP*, May 2, 2006; and again DeVine, *Putin's Labyrinth*, 10, whose book is replete with such views. Similarly, see Olga Carlisle quoted by Michael T. Kaufman in *NYT*, Aug. 4, 2008; Lucas in *JRL*, May 8, 2006, who thinks post-Soviet "Russian imperialism has become a lot more sinister"; and Dinitia Smith in *NYT*, Dec. 18, 2008, who warns even more gravely that "Russian civilization is but a fragile surface beneath which brew shadows and ineluctable forces of history, ready to erupt at any moment and bring with them chaos."

93. For "de-sovereignization," nuclear weapons, and energy, see Vitalii Ivanov and Konstantin Simonov in *NG*, April 28, 2006 (and, similarly, Vladislav Surkov in *CDPSP*, Oct. 27, 2004, 1–3); Pilko in *KZ*, June 14, 2006; and Valentin Falin and Gennadii Evstafev in *MN*, Sept. 25, 2006. For energy, see also Andrei Lebedev in *JRL*, May 12, 2006; Dmtirii Orlov in *Izvestiia*, July 17,

2006; and Andrei Efremov in *LG*, June 20–26, 2007. For nuclear weapons, see also Dugin in *CDPSP*, May 18, 2005, 1–4; and FBIS analysis in *JRL*, June 22, 2005. For the Cold War, see Sergei Roy in *JRL*, April 21, 2006; and sources in this chapter, n. 58.

94. Interview with the *Dallas Morning News*, Nov. 9, 2007, in *JRL*, Nov. 12, 2007. For the quotations, see Francis Fukuyama in *The National Interest* (Summer 1989): 3; and John Lewis Gaddis, *The Cold War* (New York, 2008), xi.

95. Michael Gerson in *WP*, Sept. 19, 2008. For "declinism," see, e.g., Robert D. Kaplan in *WP*, Dec. 17, 2008.

96. George F. Kennan, *American Diplomacy* (New York, 1952), 112. The article quoted here first appeared in *FA* (April 1951). Though Kennan's advice was forgotten, as usual, it was recalled many years later by the former British ambassador to Moscow, Rodric Braithwaite, in *FT*, March 12, 2008. During my years teaching at Princeton, I sometimes discussed this issue with Kennan, usually in the company of Professor Robert C. Tucker, who had served with Kennan when he was ambassador to Moscow. Both men still adhered strongly to Kennan's principle.

97. Liliia Shevtsova in *Novaia*, Oct. 20–22, 2008. Shevtsova thinks this support is a reason for more intrusive U.S. democracy promotion (see opendemocracy.net, Nov. 3, 2008, in *JRL*, Nov. 17, 2008), but I think it is a reason not to discredit or otherwise burden would-be Russian democratizers with American interventions. Another Russia analyst disagrees with Shevtsova, arguing that if international conditions enable Russia to develop middle-class capitalism, it will evolve into a democratic system on its own. See Dmitri V. Trenin, *Getting Russia Right* (Washington, D.C., 2007). For an example of how cold-war tensions harm Russian democrats and abet their opponents, see Radio Ekho Moskvy in the aftermath of the Georgian War, reported by Philip P. Pan in *WP*, Sept. 15, 2008.

98. Tsipko in Aimermakher et al., eds., *Preodolenie proshlogo*.

99. Arbatov in *WP*, Sept. 24, 2008.

100. The U.S. press widely interpreted Medvedev as having demanded for Russia, on August 31, 2008, a "sphere of influence." In fact, he spoke of "regions in which Russia has privileged interests," and earlier, on August 29, a "sphere of strategic interests." On this important matter, see Peter Rutland in *MT*, Oct. 14, 2008.

101. Condoleezza Rice quoted by William Branigin in *WP*, Sept. 19, 2008; and Anatoly Utkin in *Profil*, no. 33 (2008), as translated in *JRL*. Utkin is the author of the best Russian biography of Franklin Delano Roosevelt.

102. Shevtsova (opendemocracy.net, Nov. 3, 2008, in *JRL*, Nov. 17, 2008) attributing the view disapprovingly to Moscow foreign-policy specialists.

103. William Safire in *NYT*, Feb. 9, 2004; and Socor in *WSJ*, Jan. 10, 2003.

104. *NYT*, Feb. 5, 1997. According to a leading American historian, "Kennan did not always get it right. . . . He warned of a new cold war [as a result of NATO expansion]. But his fears proved unfounded" (Douglas Brinkley in *NYT*, February 17, 2004).

105. Quoted by Peter Baker in *WP*, April 5, 2008.

106. Nikolai Patrushev, head of the FSB, in *Izvestiia*, Oct. 2, 2008; and Putin in *CDPSP*, March 4, 2008, 1. For assurances that NATO enlargement "expands peace and security," see Asmus in *WP*, Dec. 13, 2008; and Daniel Fried in *NYRB*, Oct. 23, 2008, 80.

107. Vitalii Tretiakov, an editor and policy intellectual with ties to the Kremlin, in *Izvestiia*, Sept. 11, 2008. Putin used the term "red lines," it seems, in a conversation with Bush about Georgia. See Helene Cooper in *NYT*, Aug. 18, 2008.

108. Sergei Karaganov quoted by Megan R. Stack in *LAT*, Aug. 25, 2008.

109. Natalia Narochnitskaya quoted by Peter Finn in WP, April 3, 2006. A U.S. nongovernmental research institution agrees: "Ukraine is critical to the long-term defense and survival of the Russian state" (Peter Zeihan, stratfor.com, Jan. 4, 2006).

110. Dmitri Trenin in *Newsweek*, Sept. 1. 2008; and also see the other sources cited in this chapter, n. 63.

111. *WP* editorial, March 26, 2006; Holbrooke in *WP*, Dec. 14, 2004; Krauthammer in *WP*, Dec. 3, 2004.

112. For the warning, see President Medvedev quoted in *Moscow News*, June 11–19, 2008. Similarly, see Vyacheslav Nikonov in *Der Spiegel*, Oct. 16, 2008; Liliia Shevtsova in *NG*, Dec. 16, 2005. In Moscow, sources close to high-level security officials told me that "some people would consider it a declaration of war." For an echo of those discussions, see Karaganov quoted by Stack in *LAT*, Aug. 25, 2008, who says "it will be seen as an act of belligerence."

113. A Russian close to the Kremlin said "a non-aligned Ukraine is preferable for us" (Nikonov in *Der Spiegel*, Oct. 16, 2008). The Finland model was proposed in *SM*, no. 9 (2008): 59. Robert V. Daniels recommends "Finlandization," though perhaps only for Georgia (*The New Leader* [Sept./Oct. 2008]: 11); and, also for Georgia, a British academic cites Austria's neutrality after World War II (Mark Almond in *JRL*, Nov. 17, 2008). In a survey in Moldova, another divided former Soviet republic, 55 percent favored neutrality, though about the same percent chose Russia as a "strategic partner" (*JRL*, Oct. 30, 2008, and. similarly, *JRL*, Dec. 19, 2008).

114. David Holley and Kim Murphy in *LAT*, June 3 and 8, 2006. Television footage of the protests is even more compelling.

115. See this volume, chap. 6, n. 73.

116. Condoleezza Rice interviewed in *NYT Magazine*, Nov. 16, 2008, 47; *NYT* editorial, Aug. 27, 2008. For similar Russian comments about the infrastructure even earlier, see Vladislav Surkov in *JRL*, March 12, 2006; and Oleg Liakhovich in *Moscow News*, March 31–April 6, 2006. Russia's early-warning system became impaired in the 1990s, and, according to Russian authorities themselves, this was still the case a decade later. See Cohen, *Failed Crusade*, 270–71; Gen. Yury Baluyevsky cited by Leon Aron in *WSJ*, Dec. 26, 2007; and Anatoliy Baranov in *JRL*, Jan. 29, 2008. Similarly, most reported cases of black-market nuclear materials in 2008 still involved components stolen from facilities in Russia and other former Soviet territories.

117. See, respectively, Roland Oliphant in *JRL*, Oct. 28, 2008; Stephen Kotkin's assertion about the middle class and society, fpri.org, March 6, 2007; and Putin quoted by Clifford J. Levy in *NYT*, Nov. 21, 2008. Two years earlier, Boris Kagarlitsky warned that "oil prosperity maintains the illusion of stability" (*JRL*, April 12, 2006).

118. Richard Lourie in *MT*, Nov. 24, 2008; and Boris Orlov in *Izvestiia*, May 25, 2006.

119. CIA director George Tenet quoted by Susan Ellis in a USIA release, *JRL*, Feb. 3, 2000. Similarly, see FBI director Louis J. Freeh quoted by Douglas Farah in *WP*, Oct. 2, 1997; and Robert E. Rubin's warning, "If Russia destabilizes, the costs to the United States are going to be vastly greater than anything we can possibly think of" (quoted in Reuters dispatch, *JRL*, March 19. 1999).

120. See Vagif Guseinov, cited this chapter, n. 45; and Sergei Lavrov quoted by Aleksandr Golts in *JRL*, June 27, 2008. For mistrust, see Sergei Karagonov in *RG*, Dec. 24, 2008.

121. See Secretary of Defense Gates, speech in England, Sept. 19, 2008, DOD Web site; and the Russian Foreign Ministry spokesperson quoted by Steven Lee Myers in *NYT*, Sept. 24, 2008. Similarly, see Medvedev on Washington's need to "make a choice," quoted in *WP* editorial, Nov. 6, 2008; and Foreign Minister Lavrov's warning, "The U.S. will have to choose between its virtual Georgia project and its much broader partnership with Russia" (*WSJ*, Aug. 20, 2008).

122. On "missile madness," Jane M. O. Sharp, theworldtoday.org, Dec. 2007; and on events having "turned even [U.S.] doves into hawks," see the Bush official quoted by Helene Cooper in *NYT*, Aug. 19, 2008.

123. Alexei Arbatov, opendemocracy.net, Oct. 15, 2008. Similarly, see Aleksei Bogaturov and Aleksei Fenenko in *SM*, no. 11 (2008): 8.

124. I plagiarize myself here, having cited Hegel in the same connection in *Failed Crusade*, 276–77.

125. See, respectively, Karl Schwarzenberg cited by Helene Cooper in *NYT*, Aug. 20, 2008; Dmitry Trenin in *JRL*, Oct. 6, 2008; and John R. Bolton in *WP*, Oct. 20, 2008. Similarly, and puzzlingly, see Dimitry K. Simes, nationalinterest.org, Oct. 30, 2008, who nonetheless warns of cold-war-like realities.

126. See, respectively, Alexander J. Motyl, a Rutgers University professor, in *Kyiv Post*, Jan. 17, 2008 (and, similarly, Lucas in *JRL*, May 8, 2006); Rice interviewed in *NYT Magazine*, Nov. 16, 2008 (and, similarly, Leon Aron's indifference to a possible Russian accidental nuclear attack in *WSJ*, Dec. 26, 2007); Judy Dempsey's report on Lithuania in *NYT*, June 19, 2008; and Jim Hoagland on Finland in *WP*, Sept. 14, 2008 (and similarly Asmus and Holbrooke in *WP*, Aug. 11, 2008).

127. Lee Hamilton in *Indianapolis Star*, June 19, 2006. For an exception, See Rep. Curt Weldon in *MT*, June 20, 2006, who lost his bid for reelection.

128. See Cathy Young on the *NYT* opinion page, Nov. 21, 2008; and Clifford J. Levy on the front page, Nov. 27, 2008. (Focusing on terror-era archives under Putin, Levy omitted the complexities I point out in chapter 2.) In a similar vein, see Svante E. Cornell in *NYT*, Aug. 12, 2008; and Fred Hiatt in *WP*, Aug. 18, 2008. Despite evidence to the contrary, the *Times* repeatedly accused the Kremlin of initiating the August 2008 war in Georgia. When the evidence could no longer be ignored, the paper finally published an article blaming Georgia's leaders (Nov. 7, 2008) but without expressly retracting its previous, influential coverage. For a fuller examination of the *Times*'s coverage, see Mark Ames, thenation.com, Dec. 19, 2008; and on similar "editorial malpractice" by the *Washington Post*, Ames in *The Nation*, Dec. 29, 2008, 8–9.

129. Robert H. Donaldson and Joseph L. Nogee in *Tulsa World*, Aug. 24, 2008. For television, see, e.g., Tom Brokaw's assertions on NBC's *Meet the Press*, Nov. 30, 2008. CNN essentially permitted President Mikheil Saakashvili of Georgia to tell the story of the war.

130. See, e.g., Traub in *NYT*, Sept. 7, 2008; Sestanovich in *FA* (Nov./Dec. 2008): 12–28; Leon Aron, aci.org, Jan. 16, 2008; the statement by former U.S. and Russian ambassadors in *IHT*, Sept. 24, 2007 (and similarly the joint statement in *JRL*, Sept. 29, 2008). For partial or more substantial exceptions, see Simes, "Losing Russia"; Mandelbaum in *JRL*, Oct. 24, 2008; Mortimer Zuckerman in *US News and World Report*, Dec. 6, 2007; Henry Kissinger and George P. Shultz in *WP*, Oct. 8, 2008; and Kissinger in *WP*, July 8, 2008.

131. Lieven in *International Affairs* (Moscow) (Oct. 2007): 27–28.

132. For the quotes in the order they appear, see George Packer in *NY*, Dec. 20/27, 2004; Jackson Diehl in *WP*, June 19, 2006; Mendelson and Ger-

ber in *FA* (Jan./Feb. 2006): 3; Lieven in *International Affairs* (Moscow) (Oct. 2007): 27–28; *WP* editorial, March 28, 2006; and Anne Applebaum in *WP*, Dec. l, 2004. (The latter charge was directed, I should acknowledge, at my wife, Katrina vanden Heuvel, editor of *The Nation*.) Similarly, see Michael McFaul in *WP*, Dec. 21, 2004; McFaul and Stoner-Weiss (on "Putin apologists") in *FA* (May/June 2008): 163; Cathy Young in *Reason Magazine*, Oct. 24, 2008; the reply by Glenn Greenwald, salon.com, Oct. 25, 2008; and the attack on Mary Dejeveky by Cathy Fitzpatrick, opendemocracy.net, March 12, 2008. The most shameful example, however, was Fredo Arias-King's suggestion that Strobe Talbott, a top Clinton adviser and appointee, may have made a "Faustian bargain" with the KGB (National Review Online, Dec. 8, 2008).

133. Traub in *NYT*, Aug. 10, 2008. Again, Traub included me among the "naive."

134. James Carroll in *BG*, Oct. 27, 2008.

135. Quoted in Talbott, *The Russia Hand*, 185. Yeltsin's heavy drinking and drunkenness appear frequently in this memoir.

136. Unnamed official quoted by Thom Shanker and Steven Lee Myers in *NYT*, Oct. 13, 2007.

137. For examples of this notion, see Council on Foreign Relations, *Russia's Wrong Direction*; and Sestanovich in *FA* (Nov./Dec. 2008): 12–18.

138. Two other examples: by 2009, no Americans were among the world's top heavyweight boxers, a division the Unites States once dominated; and by 2010, the United States, lacking its own spacecraft will be completely dependent on Russian shuttles for transporting astronauts and cargo to and from the international space station. There are other examples in Fareed Zakaria, *The Post-American World* (New York, 2008), even though he persists in thinking of the Unites States as "a global superpower."

139. The expression is that of Yuri V. Ushakov, a former Russian ambassador to Washington, in *WSJ*, Feb. 13, 2006.

140. Quoted by Andrew E. Kramer in *NYT*, Aug, 19, 2008.

141. Soltan Dzarasov in Tostykh, ed., *Perestroika*, 44.

142. Referring to her background in academic Soviet studies, Secretary of State Rice liked to say, when relations were growing worse, "I will tell you: Russia today is not the Soviet Union"; "It's not the Soviet Union and that's a good thing"; "This isn't the Soviet Union"; and "We've come a long, long way from when there was a hammer and sickle above the Kremlin." See *JRL*, Oct. 23, 2007, Feb. 3, 2005, May 10, 2006, and May 22, 2006. President Bush echoed her: "Nobody's going to give up on Russia. We know it's not the Soviet Union" (*JRL*, May 22, 2006). Historians and psychologists might reflect on the meaning of this refrain. Whatever the explanation, Rice often

seemed baffled by developments, having "a difficult time explaining," for example, Putin's landmark speech in Munich in 2007 or the emergence of "a different Russia than we expected." See *JRL*, Feb. 18, 2007; and *Fox News Sunday* (TV), Dec. 7, 2008. For the record, her counterpart in the Clinton administration, Madeleine Albright, also a reputed expert on Russia, was "very surprised" by Medvedev's threat to counter U.S. antimissile sites with deployment of Russian missiles (*JRL*, Nov. 17, 2008).

143. Anthony T. Salvia in *JRL*, April 28, 2006.

144. Senator Barack Obama's Web site, Nov. 1, 2005; Obama on *Meet the Press*, NBC TV, Dec. 7, 2007; and Obama's Web site, Oct. 2, 2007.

145. See John Edwards quoted in Bloomberg dispatch, March 8, 2006; Richard Holbrooke quoted by Steven R. Weisman in *NYT*, Sept. 12, 2004 (and, similarly, his article in *WP*, Feb. 16, 2005); and the pro-Democratic columnist E. J. Dione Jr. in *WP*, May 9, 2006.

146. Michael McFaul, a Stanford University professor, who is cited in that connection frequently in this chapter and in chapter 6. In particular, McFaul was a fervent democracy promoter during the Yeltsin years and a bitter critic of Putin for having, he thought, betrayed its achievements.

147. Biden reported and quoted by Stephanie Ho on Voice of America, Dec. 3, 2006; for his acceptance speech, see *NYT*, Aug. 27, 2008. Similarly, see his article in *WSJ*, March 24, 2008; and congressional statement in *JRL*, June 13, 2008.

148. There were only a few. Though to no good purpose, it seems, I was perhaps the earliest and most persistent. See my *Failed Crusade*, which includes my warnings published since the early 1990s. For warnings of Russian testing and intimidation, see, e.g., the U.S. State Department official John Rood quoted by Reuters in *NYT*, Dec. 18, 2008; *WP*, editorial, Dec. 6, 2008; and, for "kowtowing" and "capitulation," *WP*, editorials, Jan. 3 and March 4, 2009.

149. President Medvedev quoted by Michael Abramowitz in *WP*, Nov. 16, 2008.

EPILOGUE FOR THE PAPERBACK EDITION

1. David A. Andelman, review of *Soviet Fates and Lost Alternatives*, posted in *World Policy Institute* (blog), Sept. 14, 2009, http://www.worldpolicy .org/wordpress/2009/09/14/david-a-andelman-soviet-fates-and-lost-alternatives-by-stephen-f-cohen. For similarly favorable receptions, see William W. Finan Jr. in *Current History* (Oct. 2009): 341–42; Jochen Hellbeck in *The Nation*, Dec. 7, 2009, 39; and Jerry Hough in *Slavic Review* (Summer 2010): 453–55.

2. See this volume, chapter 3, page 65.

3. Michael Scammell, review of *Zhivago's Children*, by Vladislav Zubok, *NYRB*, Jan. 14, 2010, 53–55.

4. See, respectively, Steven Rosefielde and Stefan Hedlund, *Russia Since 1980* (Cambridge, 2009); Mary Dejevsky in *The Independent* (UK), March 16, 2010; Charles Krauthammer in *WP*, Dec. 18, 2009; Michael Beschloss in *NYT Book Review*, Oct. 4, 2009, 1; Fred Hiatt in *WP*, July 19, 2010; and Samuel Charap and Alexandros Petersen, foreignaffairs.com, Aug. 20, 2010. Many other examples could be cited. For recent exceptions, see Brown, *Seven Years That Changed the World* (New York, 2007), on the Gorbachev and other alternatives, and, to a lesser extent, Daniel Treisman, *The Return* (New York, 2011), chap. 1; Robert D. Kaplan on negative consequences of the Soviet breakup, in *WP*, Dec. 5, 2010; and Jack F. Matlock Jr., *Superpower Illusions* (New Haven, Conn., 2010), on U.S. Russia policy before and after 1991, and, also to a lesser extent, Andrei Shleifer and Daniel Treisman in *FA* (Jan./Feb. 2011): 122–38.

5. For chaps. 2, 4–5, and 6, see, respectively, Stiven Koen, *Dolgoe vozvrashchenie* (Moscow, 2009); Stiven Koen *"Vopros voprosov": Pochemu ne stalo Sovetskogo Soiuza?* (Moscow, 2007); and *Novaia*, Dec. 16, 2009 and March 1, 2010. For the disavowal of a "general line" or "single viewpoint" on history, see the Academy of Sciences historian Liubov Sidorova in *LG*, Dec. 8–14, 2010.

6. See, e.g., Sergei Baburin, Sergei Kara-Murza, and Aleksandr Shatilov in *LG*, May 19–25, 2010.

7. See, e.g., Gorbachev, "Perestroika Lost," *NYT*, March 14, 2010, and in *Novaia*, April 26, 2010; Ligachev, *Kto predal SSSR?* (Moscow, 2010); for NEP, Maksim Kantor in *Novaia*, Sept. 6, 2010, and Sergei Antonenko in *Rodina* no. 1 (2011), 4; and, for Stalin, this chapter, nn. 16–18.

8. Mikoyan, quoted by Kirill Iukhnevich in *Gorbachevskie chteniia*, no. 5 (Moscow, 2007), 213; for the journalist, see Tamara Eidelman in *Russian Life* (May/June 2009).

9. Interview with Pavlovsky, kreml.org, Dec. 28, 2009. For other examples of reopening discussion of past alternatives, see Iurii Luzhkov and Gavriil Popov in *MK*, Jan. 21, 2010; Pavel Gutionov in *Novaia*, April 19, 2010; and the interview with Ruslan Khasbulatov, pravda.ru, Oct. 6, 2010.

10. Dmitrii Fomin in *SM*, no. 2 (2010): 223. Similarly, on the other side of the political spectrum, see I. E. Diskin, *Proryv* (Moscow, 2008); and this chapter, nn. 12–15. According to President Medvedev, "over 60 percent of the public utilities infrastructure" was obsolete and unless modernized "there will be a disaster" (RIA Novosti dispatch in *JRL*, Nov. 23, 2010).

11. Dmitrii Andreev in *PK*, June 22, 2009.

12. For the first view, see Mikhail Delyagin, quoted by Sergei Mitrofanov, Politkom.ru, Jan. 3, 2010. And, similarly, see Aleksandr Prokhanov in *Zavtra*, March 4, 2009; the roundtable discussion, in *Zavtra*, Dec. 31, 2009; and Iurii Mukhin, *Stalin protiv krizisa* (Moscow, 2009). For the second view, see, e.g., Aleksandra Samarina in *NG*, Nov. 2, 2009; Aleksandr Budberg in *MK*, Dec. 28, 2009; Aleksandr Rubtsov in *Novaia*, July 12, 2010; Vladimir Ryzhkov in *MT*, Feb. 9, 2010; Andrei Kolesnikov in *Novaia*, November 29, 2010; and Igor Iurgens in *Novaia*, February 2, 2011. For "alternatives," "slaves," "soft," and "fateful choices," see, respectively, Sergei Dubinin in *SM*, no. 2 (2010): 5; O. V. Gaman-Golutvina, *Politicheskie elity Rossii* (Moscow, 2006), 413; Konstantin Grigorev in *NG*, Nov. 9, 2009; and Kirill Rogov in *Novaia*, Oct. 11, 2010. For a discussion of the alternatives at the level of professional economists, see the survey by Joachim Zweynert in *EAS* (June 2010): 547–69.

13. See, e.g., Stanislav Belkovskii in *MK*, July 26 and Aug. 3, 2010; Dmitrii Bykov in *Novaia*, Sept. 1, 2010; Vladislav Inozemtsev in *MT*, Oct. 15, 2010; and, similarly, Grigorii Iavlinskii in *SM*, no. 11 (2010): 165–68.

14. See, e.g., the editorial in *NG*, May 26, 2010; and, similarly, Vladimir Frolov in *MT*, Nov. 28, 2010.

15. Medvedev, on kremlin.ru, Sept. 10, 2010. A year before, Medvedev issued a manifesto, "Rossiia vpered!" (kremlin.ru, Sept. 10, 2009), widely interpreted as a call for democratic modernization, as was a program drafted by an institute associated with him (*JRL*, Feb. 19, 2010). For Medvedev as a would-be democratic or liberalizing leader, see Gordon M. Hahn in *Demokratizatsiya* (Summer 2010): 228–59. On the other hand, even a policy intellectual close to the Medvedev camp admitted: "All successful Russian modernizers were brutal despots. All modernizers who shunned repression were failures" (Frolov in *MT*, Nov. 29, 2010).

16. Mikhail Delyagin, quoted by Mitrofanov, Politkom.ru, Jan.3, 2010. For the economists, see Zweynert in *EAS* (June 2010): 547–69. Similarly, see the views of the historian Aleksandr Danilov discussed by Oleg Khlebnikov in *Novaia*, Dec. 13, 2010.

17. See Prokhanov, the roundtable discussion in *Zavtra*, Dec. 31, 2009; Mukhin, *Stalin protiv krizisa*; and Vladimir Smyk in *MG*, no. 9 (2010): 241, 254. These popular opinions about the 1990s are acknowledged even by anti-Stalinists. See, e.g., Aleksandr Tsipko in *NG*, Sept. 22, 2010.

18. See, respectively, the critical review by V. M. Lavrov and I. A. Kurliandskii of a textbook by A. S. Barsenkov and A. I. Vdovin in "Pravda GULAGa," *Novaia*, Sept. 15, 2010; the interview with Medvedev in *Novaia*, Feb. 2, 2009; and his blog, kremlin.ru, Oct. 30, 2009.

19. That this remains a widespread opinion, see, e.g., Iurii Afanasev, Aleksei Davydov, and Andrei Pelipenko in *Novaia*, Oct. 16, 2009; Sergei Baburin in *LG*, March 24–30, 2010; and Aleksandr Tsipko in *NG*, June 29, 2010.

20. For compelling accounts, see Andrei Bunich, *Osen oligarkhov* (Moscow, 2005); V. A. Lisichkin and L. A. Shelepin, *Rossiia pod vlastiu plutokratii* (Moscow, 2003), chaps. 4–10; and esp. Gaman-Golutvina, *Politicheskie elity*, chap. 6. And for Gorbachev, see *Novaia*, December 10, 2010.

21. See. e.g., Gaman-Golutvina, *Politicheskie elity*, 413–22; Inozemtsev in *MT*, Oct. 15, 2010; Baburin in *LG*, March 24–30, 2010; Ivan Rozirskii in *LG*, Sept. 22–28, 2010; Sergei Mitrokhin, Politkom.ru, June 15, 2010; and Gennadii Ziuganov in *Pravda*, Sept. 23, 2010.

22. Vladimir Shlapentokh in *Journal of Communist Studies and Transition Politics* (Dec. 2008): 523–24; Andrei Andreev in *Essays and Analyses*, vol. 12, (Moscow, 2007), 94–96. For the characterization of the "vertical," see Gaman-Golutvina, *Politicheskie elity*, 340, 353; and Alexei Navalny, quoted by Will Englund in *WP*, Nov. 13, 2010.

23. See, e.g., Grigorii Iavlinskii in *VE*, no. 9 (2007); Igor Makurin's call for a "reform of property," in *SM*, no. 11 (2010): 151–64; Gennadii Ziuganov, *Imia modernizatsii—sotsializm* (Moscow, 2010), 102; and Grigorii Khanin's discussion of Mikhail Kalashnikov in *SM*, no. 8 (2009): 159–68.

24. Igor Iurgens in *Kommersant*, Oct. 21, 2010. Similarly, see Iurgens's citing of three figures prominently associated with the oligarchichal system as exemplary modernizers, in *Novaia*, February 2, 2011.

25. For Kennan, see Andelman, review in *World Policy Institute* (blog), and Finan in *Current History* (Oct. 2009), both cited this chapter, n. 1. For the criticism, see Amy Knight in *NYRB*, Feb. 11, 2010; Archie Brown in *RR* (April 2010): 356; and Robert Legvold in *FA* (Nov./Dec. 2009): 166.

26. Several veteran Western observers instinctively termed Obama's reset a "new detente." See Paul Taylor, Reuters column, Feb. 2, 2009; Jim Hoagland and Jackson Diehl in *WP*, Feb. 22 and Feb. 23, 2009; Melvin A. Goodman in *JRL*, Feb. 26, 2009; and Walter Laqueur in *FA* (Nov./Dec. 2010): 155.

27. Thomas Graham, interviewed by RIA Novosti, in *JRL*, Dec. 28, 2010; Peter Baker in *NYT*, Nov. 7, 2010; Eugene Ivanov in *JRL*, Nov. 23, 2010; and, similarly, Nikolas K. Gvosdev, nationalinterest.org, Oct. 28, 2010; and Simon Tisdale in *The Guardian*, Nov. 16, 2010. In his State of the Union address in January 2011, President Obama declared, "We have reset our relationship with Russia" (*WP*, Jan. 26, 2011).

28. See, respectively, David J. Kramer and Jackson Diehl in *WP*, Sept. 18 and Feb. 23, 2009; John R. Bolton and John Yoo in *NYT*, Nov. 10, 2010; Ariel

Cohen in *WSJ Europe*, Aug. 11, 2010; and Ralph Peters in *NY Post*, Sept. 18, 2009. Similarly, see John Vinocur in *NYT*, June 16 and Oct. 25, 2009; editorials, Charles Krauthammer, and Robert Kagan in *WP*, Feb. 20, March 4, Oct. 16, 2009, and May 25, July 30, and Nov. 9, 2010; Irving M. Selzer in *WS*, Aug. 29, 2010; 12; Steve Levine, foreignpolicy.com, Nov. 11, 2010; and the open letter to Obama signed by thirty-nine prominent policy intellectuals, in *JRL*, July 2, 2009. A would-be Republican presidential candidate, Mitt Romney, termed the centerpiece of the reset, the New START treaty, Obama's "worst foreign policy mistake yet" (*WP*, July 6, 2010). More generally, see Andrei Tsygankov, *Russophobia* (New York, 2009).

29. Aleksandr Dugin, quoted by Andrei Kolesnikov in *Novaia*, Oct. 25, 2010; and Leonid Ivashov in *NG*, July 13, 2009. Similarly, see Dugin and Ivashov in *LG*, Oct. 27–Nov. 2 and Nov. 24–30, 2010; and Gennady Zyuganov in *JRL*, Nov. 12, 2010. China, Russia's new "strategic partner," also criticized Medvedev's "pandering to Western countries" (Tian Wenlin in *JRL*, Aug. 10, 2010).

30. See Liliia Shevtsova in *Novaia*, Dec. 1, 2010; testimony by Andrei Illarionov to the U.S. House Committee on Foreign Affairs, Feb. 25, 2009; and the survey reported by Susan Richards, opendemocracy.net, Feb. 25, 2009. For less extreme but similar liberal opposition, see Ludmila Alexeeva and Gregory Shvedov in *WP*, March 30, 2009; Lev Gudkov, Igor Klyamkin, Georgy Satarov, and Lilia Shevtsova in *WP*, June 9, 2009; Sergei Kovalyov in *JRL*, May 27, 2009; Evgenii Kiselev in *Novaia*, June 22, 2009; Vladimir Abarimov in *JRL*, July 30, 2009; and Mikhail Kasyanov, Vladimir Milov, Boris Nemstov, and Vladimir Ryzhkov in *WP*, Feb. 21, 2011.

31. See, e.g., Obama's speech at the United Nations, as reported by Scott Wilson in *WP*, Sept. 24, 2010; the report of remarks by Michael McFaul in *MT*, Sept. 10, 2010; Saakashvili's satisfaction with his meetings with Obama and Secretary of State Hillary Clinton's remarks on Georgia in *JRL*, Nov. 11 and Oct. 7, 2010; and approval of the "reset of the reset" by Robert Kagan in *WP*, Oct. 1, 2010, and by Brian Whitmore in *JRL*, Aug. 6, 2010.

32. For example, immediately following Obama's July 2009 summit meeting with Medvedev in Moscow, at which he assured the Russian president that his administration regarded Russia as an equal and downplayed the possibility of NATO expansion to Georgia and Ukraine, his own vice president, Joseph R. Biden Jr., publicly stated virtually opposite opinions (see Biden's interview in *WSJ*, July 24, 2009; and reports of his trips to Georgia and Ukraine by Ellen Barry in *NYT*, July 23 and 24, 2009). Meanwhile, a U.S. warship suddenly appeared in Georgia's territorial waters (AP dispatch, July 14, 2009). These developments led Medvedev to wonder, "Who is shaping the U.S. foreign policy, the president or respectable members of his team?" (quoted by Andrew E. Kramer in *NYT*, July 26, 2009). Simi-

larly incongruous events followed, including the arrest of ten Russian spies in the United States immediately following an Obama-Medvedev summit meeting in Washington in June 2010. Russian officials interpreted the arrests as a "plot . . . to reverse the warming relations" or as the result of a struggle inside the Obama administration (see Fred Weir in *CSM*, June 30, 2010; and Ilya Kramnik in *JRL*, Sept. 6, 2010). In perhaps a related example, the Georgian leader Mikheil Saakashvili, worried he might be downgraded by Obama, appealed to his "good contacts" in Washington, including Vice President Biden, Secretary of State Clinton, and one of her top aides, Richard Holbrooke, all known to be strong supporters of the U.S. Georgian project (interview in *Newsweek*, April 20, 2009). On the Russian side, the articles attacking Medvedev, cited this chapter, n. 29, clearly had high-level backing; and a Moscow analyst thought the arrest of a pro-U.S. democratic activist, Boris Nemtsov, in December 2010 was a calculated "strike against the reset" (Aleksei Makarkin, quoted by Kathy Lally in *WP*, January 12, 2011). It is important to remember that such mysterious events often occurred during the Cold War when previous detentes were unfolding; see Stephen F. Cohen, *Sovieticus*, exp. ed. (New York, 1986), 134–38.

33. See, respectively, Obama quoted by Peter Baker in *NYT*, July 3, 2009; and, before becoming secretary of state, Hillary Clinton by Ellen Wulfhorst, AP dispatch, Jan. 7, 2008. Obama's Russia adviser, Michael McFaul, it was said, "never tires" of denouncing Putin as the "principle obstacle" (Vladimir Golyshev in *JRL*, Nov. 1, 2010). In an unsuccessful and much resented attempt to downgrade Putin, the Obama administration proposed that he cochair a commission with Biden and was told, "Putin is not a vice president" (quoted by Peter Baker in *NYT*, July 14, 2009). For the wager on Medvedev, see Obama, quoted by Jackie Calmes and Peter Baker in *NYT*, Nov. 22, 2010; Biden, quoted by Christian Caryl, foreignpolicy.com, Nov. 24, 2010; and editorial in *WP*, Dec. 28, 2010.

34. Obama, quoted by Sheryl Gay Stolberg in *NYT*, Nov. 14, 2010. Putin's reaction was to warn Washington "not to interfere with the sovereign choice of the Russian people" (quoted by Ellen Barry in *NYT*, Dec. 2, 2010). Similarly, see a Kremlin aide quoted by David Ignatius in *WP*, July 5, 2009; and for the perception of Washington's support of Medvedev, see Aleksei Mukhin in *JRL*, December 30, 2010.

35. See, respectively, Dmitry Suslov in *JRL*, July 17, 2009; Liliia Shevtsova in *Novaia*, June 22, 2008; and Michael McFaul in *JRL*, July 2, 2009, who is quoted even more candidly by Michael A. Feltcher and Philip Pan in *WP*, July 5, 2009. A "progressive" American analyst agreed with the administration's conception of the reset, which was "to maximize the extent to which Russian policies complement our objectives" while being "prepared

to muster the diplomatic, military, and economic tools to respond when Russia's actions run counter to our interests" (Samuel Charap, american-progress.org, May 20, 2009).

36. *Kommersant*, Aug. 30, 2010. Similarly, see Aleksei Pushkov in *AF*, no. 1 (2011). Putin later charged, "We continue to be told, 'We don't want to take your interests into account; we are going to do whatever we want'" (interview with Larry King, *JRL*, Dec. 2, 2010). For Medvedev's weakened position, see the attacks on him cited this chapter, n. 29; implicitly by Suslov in *JRL*, July 15, 2009; and for the reset as "one of the main brands of Medvedev's government," Stanislav Belkovskii in *MK*, Jan 17, 2011. A Russian Medvedev supporter worried that "he risks being portrayed as a U.S. stooge" (Vladimir Frolov in *MT*, Feb. 14, 2011).

37. See Obama, quoted by Peter Baker in *NYT*, Dec. 19, 2010; the Senate resolution adopted on Dec. 22, 2010; Moscow's reaction reported by gazeta.ru, Dec. 19 and 24, 2010, RIA Novosti and the BBC Russian Service on Dec. 24, 2010, and ITAR-TASS on Dec. 27, 2010; and Medvedev, quoted by Ellen Barry in *NYT*, Dec. 25, 2010.

38. kremlin.ru, Nov. 20 and Dec. 12, 2010. For Putin, see this chapter, n. 36. Indeed, during this same period, the Obama administration and NATO were developing a secret military plan to defend the Baltic states and Poland against Russia, as later reported by Scott Shane in *NYT*, Dec. 7, 2010.

39. See n. 38. For the tactical weapons, see Walter Pincus in *WP*, Dec. 28, 2010; and for Moscow's reliance on them, Aleksei Fenenko in *NG*, Jan. 17, 2011, and Vladimir Isachenkov, AP dispatch, Jan 13, 2011.

40. "The road where Russia needs to go leads through Washington" (Clifford Kupchan, quoted in russiatoday.com, Sept. 8, 2010). Similarly, see Vice President Biden in *WSJ*, July 24, 2009; George Will in *WP*, April 19, 2009; and Jeffrey Mankoff in *JRL*, Aug. 25, 2010. Even if Russia "needs better relations with the West . . . to bolster its modernization campaign," as Mankoff argued, why equate "the West" solely with the United States?

41. For China and Germany, see, e.g., Vinogradov, *Kitaiskii model*; and Viacheslav Dashichev's advocacy of a Russian-German alliance without the United States, in *SM*, no. 10 (2009): 175–84. In December 2010, Medvedev and President Nicolas Sarkozy of France said that Russia's purchase of four French warships "illustrates the will and capacity in France and Russia to develop large-scale partnerships in all areas, including defense and security" (quoted by Edward Cody in *WP*, Dec. 25, 2010). For "desert landscape," see M. K. Bhadrakumar in *JRL*, Oct. 11, 2010.

42. Strobe Talbott in *JRL*, July 21, 2009; and, similarly, James M. Goldgeier in *JRL*, Sept. 15, 2009, and (somewhat earlier) Richard Holbrooke in *WP*, March 21, 2005.

43. See, respectively, editorial in *WP*, Jan. 8, 2009; Matthew Kaminski in *WSJ*, Feb. 13, 2009; and David J. Kramer in *WP*, March 6, 2009. Similarly, see Eugene Rumer and Angela Stent in *JRL*, April 13, 2009; Jeffrey Mankoff in *JRL*, May 7, 2009 and Sept. 7, 2010; Charap, americanprogress.org, May 20, 2009; and Charap and Petersen, foreignaffairs.com, Aug. 20, 2010. Kaminski summed up the prevailing view: "At every step of the way, Russia sought to undermine this great post–Cold War project." Similarly, see Ronald D. Asmus in *WP*, Dec. 26, 2009. As a former high-level CIA official replied, these opinions "ignore the anti-Russian policies of the Clinton and Bush administrations" (Melvin A. Goodman, pubrecord.org, Feb. 25, 2009). Blaming Putin over the years has produced an array of absurd statements such as this: "He has introduced an aggressive foreign policy that opposed Western countries on issues such as the war in Iraq and the expansion of NATO" (Gregory Feifer, on National Public Radio, March 5, 2007). But, as readers know, many people in the West also opposed the Iraq war and NATO expansion. There have been a few exceptions to this blame-Russia syndrome; see, e.g., Matlock, *Superpower Illusions*; Shleifer and Treisman in *FA* (Jan./Feb. 2011) 4; and Anatol Lieven in *The Nation*, Jan 12, 2009.

44. A common Russian criticism of U.S. foreign-policy making is its "lack of historical thinking." See, e.g., Sergei Samuilov in *SM*, no. 11 (2010): 82.

45. See, respectively, editorial in *SM*, no. 12 (2008): 109–10; Dashichev in *SM*, no. 10 (2009): 178; and Alexey Pushkov, nationalinterest.org, Sept. 3, 2010. Similarly, see Vasilii Voropaev, *Izvestiia*, Jan. 15, 2009; Dmitry Rogozin in *MT*, March 31, 2009; Ilya Kramnik in *JRL*, Sept. 6, 2010; and Putin, interview in *Kommersant*, Aug. 30, 2010.

46. Putin, interview in *Kommersant*, Aug. 30, 2010.

47. *WP*, March 31, 2009; and kremlin.ru, Sept. 10, 2010. Similarly, Medvedev complained, "We have been led around by the nose for a long time" (quoted by Peter Baker in *NYT*, June 23, 2010).

48. An adviser to Medvedev and Putin quoted by David Ignatius in *WP*, July 5, 2009; and Anders Fogh Rasmussen quoted by Tisdale in *The Guardian*, Nov. 16, 2010. The statement seemed especially vacuous since Fogh Rasmussen also said that NATO's "fundamentals . . . will not change because they make as much sense as they have done for the past sixty-one years," that is, since the height of the Cold War (RIA Novosti, in *JRL*, Oct. 8, 2010).

49. Though the issue is still disputed on the American side, Gorbachev and subsequent Russian leaders had good reason to believe that in 1990 the United States and its allies had promised not to expand NATO beyond a united Germany. See Mary Elise Sarotte in *Diplomatic History* (Jan. 2010): 119–40; and the *Der Spiegel* report in *JRL*, Nov. 26, 2008. Later, Yeltsin

thought he had assurances from Clinton that former Warsaw Pact countries would not be offered NATO membership, but they soon were (Goldgeier in *JRL*, Sept. 15, 2009).

50. See Secretary of State Clinton, quoted in ITAR-TASS, in *JRL*, Oct. 7, 2010; and NATO's secretary general Fogh Rasmussen, quoted by Steven Erlanger in *NYT*, Nov. 3, 2010.

51. See, respectively, John Vinocur in *NYT*, May 5, 2009; Nicholas Kulish in *NYT*, July 17, 2009; and Vice President Biden, quoted by Ellen Barry in *NYT*, July 22, 2009. Similarly, see Biden in *WSJ*, July 24, 2009; editorial in *WP*, July 14, 2009; Goldgeier in *JRL*, Sept. 15, 2009; Asmus in *WP*, Dec. 26, 2009; and Sharap and Petersen in *JRL*, Aug. 23, 2010.

52. Saakashvili, interview, echo.sk.ru, as in *JRL*, Aug. 30, 2010. Certainly, this is how Russian specialists viewed NATO expansion. See, e.g., Samuilov in *SM*, no. 11 (2010): 84. A compelling argument can be made that NATO expansion was also a new form of containment, the primary U.S. policy during the Cold War. For this view from Moscow, see Mikhail Troitsky in *JRL*, Dec. 29, 2010.

53. Military bases in the new NATO countries remain a major Moscow concern. See the report by Vladimir Solovev in *Kommersant*, Oct. 27, 2010, which includes demands that they not house "significant forces."

54. Archie Brown, *The Rise and Fall of Communism* (New York, 2009), 601.

55. Quoted by Peter Baker, in *NYT*, Dec. 1, 2010, and July 4, 2009, respectively.

56. See, respectively, Senator John McCain, quoted by Peter Baker in *NYT*, Dec. 17, 2010; Charles Krauthammer in *WP*, Feb. 20, 2009; John Vinocur in *NYT*, Oct. 25, 2010; Ariel Cohen in *WSJ*, Aug. 11, 2010; and Charles Squires, quoted by Andrew E. Kramer in *NYT*, Dec. 21, 2010. On the allies, similarly see Constanze Stelzenmiller in *FA* (March/April 2009): 89–100; and Gregory Feifer and Brian Whitmore in *NR*, Sept. 23, 2010, 22–25. For Putin, see Sam Schulman in *WS*, Jan. 3/ Jan. 10, 2011, 28.

57. See, respectively, Ariel Cohen in *CSM*, April 23, 2009; Bret Stephens in *WSJ*, July 17, 2007; and Alexander J. Motyl in *The Harriman Review* (Columbia University) (March 2010): 1–14.

58. See, respectively, Bruce Blair, Damon Bosetti, and Brian Weeden in *NYT*, Dec. 7, 2010; Jackson Diehl in *WP*, Nov. 22, 2010; George F. Will in *WP*, April 19, 2009; and for air strikes, Ben Smith in *Politico*, Feb. 3, 2010. Similarly, see the editorial and Jim Hoagland in *WP*, Nov. 20 and Dec. 12, 2010. On the contrary, a prominent Russian policy scholar believed, in the aftermath of the Georgian war, that "the possibility of a direct military clash between Russia and the United States cannot be ruled out" and indeed "has been increasing ever since 1991" (Nikolai Kosolapov, quoted by Troitsky in *JRL*, Dec. 29, 2010).

59. George F. Will in *WP*, Dec. 2, 2010; David J. Kramer in *WP*, Sept. 20, 2010; Motyl in *The Harriman Review* (March 2010): 14. Some of Russia's implacable "democratic" oppositionists also hoped for "the rubble of the regime" (Evgeniia Albats in *The New Times*, no. 1–2 [2009]), but other Russians, including the Communist leader Gennady Zyuganov, warned this could have "catastrophic consequences" in nuclear Russia (kprf.ru, Jan. 23, 2009). Similarly, see Sergei Roy in *JRL*, March 6, 2009.

60. See the reports by Michael Schwirtz in *NYT*, Aug. 11, 2010; and by Pavel Felgenhauer and Claire Bigg in *JRL*, Aug. 6 and Dec. 1, 2010.

61. Laurence H. Summers used the term to characterize his own role in the administration's economic policies, as quoted by Sheryl Gay Stolberg in *NYT*, Feb. 17, 2009.

62. Consider, for example, Michael McFaul, the leading academic proponent of democracy promotion in Russia since the 1990s and since 2009 Obama's Russia adviser on the National Security Council. McFaul's views, restated in a 2009 book, were so extreme that two of his former academic colleagues sharply criticized his "broad policy prescription" as involving "risky endeavors" and urged "much greater caution than McFaul allows" (Valerie Bunce and Sharon Wolchik in *Perspectives on Politics* (Sept. 2010): 923–25).

63. For the case of Gorbachev, see Robert D. English, *Russia and the Idea of the West* (New York, 2000).

64. See Richard Holbrooke's treatment of Kennan in *WP*, March 3, 1995; and for the cult, the many obituaries and other articles occasioned by Holbrooke's death in mid-December 2010. Holbrooke, who played a major role in NATO expansion and Russia policy generally since the 1990s, was personally close to Georgia's Saakashvili, who regarded him as "my teacher." See his interview in *Newsweek*, April 20, 2010; and this chapter, n. 32. For the conventional views of purported left-of-center critics of U.S. policy, see, e.g., Charap, americanprogress.com, May 30, 2009; Charap and Petersen in *JRL*, Aug. 23, 2010; and Wayne Merry in "Russia Now," supplement in *WP*, June 24, 2009, who nonetheless insisted that "the Cold War mentality is much stronger in Russia than in America."

65. For Khodorkovsky, see Joe Nocera in *NYT*, Nov. 6, 2010; and Jackson Diehl in *WP*, Nov. 18, 2010. A *WP* editorial (Dec. 6, 2010) even found Khodorkovsky's trial "shocking" by comparison with "the show trials of Soviet times," which were the centerpiece of Stalin's Great Terror. For examples of the Georgia axiom, see Svante E. Cornell and S. Frederick Starr, eds., *The Guns of August 2008* (Armonk, N.Y., 2009); and Ronald D. Asmus, *A Little War That Shook the World* (New York, 2010). While books such as these, along with countless other anti-Russian accounts and editori-

als, circulate widely in the United States, a detailed Moscow reply must be downloaded—*The Tanks of August* (cast.ru/eng/?id=386)—and remains virtually unknown. Independent European investigations, on the other hand, blame Saakashvili for starting the war, as some European Union officials privately do. See Rein Mülerson, opendemocracy.net, Aug. 17, 2010; and Paul Taylor in *JRL*, Jan. 14, 2009. Secret cables later released by Wiki-Leaks suggest that U.S. officials in Georgia at the time knew, or could have known, the truth but reported instead false statements by the Saakashvili government. See C. J. Chivers in *NYT*, Dec. 2, 2010. For calls for seemingly unlimited NATO expansion on these grounds, see Dennis Corboy, William Courtney, and Kenneth Yalowitz in *IHT*, Jan. 6, 2009; editorials in *WP*, March 30 and July 19, 2009; Anne Applebaum in *WP*, Nov. 23, 2010; and the two books cited earlier in this note.

66. As a number of non-American observers have pointed out. See, e.g., James Bissett in *The Globe and Mail* (Toronto), May 12, 2009; and Robert Copper's review of Asmus, *A Little War That Shook the World*, in *TLS*, May 28, 2010, 11–12. For Kosovo, see Chuck Sudetic in *WP*, Jan. 8, 2011.

67. The new U.S.-designated leader of the "Russian democratic movement" was Boris Nemtsov, a deputy prime minister under Yeltsin. (See, e.g., the open letter to Obama signed by thirty-seven American "experts," from info@foreignpolicy.org, Aug. 11, 2010.) Nemtsov, who had close ties to McFaul (see this chapter, n. 62), was given an audience with Obama in Moscow in July 2009; in December 2010, when Nemtsov was arrested for a demonstration, Obama issued a statement supporting "his work in promoting democratic development in Russia" (quoted by Michael Schwirtz in *NYT*, Jan. 4, 2011). Despite having played a direct role in the policies that undermined democracy and bred corruption in the 1990s, Nemtsov blamed only Putin for these developments (see, e.g., the BBC report in *JRL*, June 15, 2010; and *Kommersant*, Nov. 18, 2010). And while a sympathetic *Washington Post* correspondent characterized Nemtsov as "a luminous political star" of the 1990s (January 29, 2011), other Russians were quick to point out this hypocrisy (see, e.g., Sergei Roy in *JRL*, March 6, 2009; and Aleksandra Samarina in *NG*, Nov. 26, 2010). One Russian prodemocracy party refused to collaborate with Nemtsov and another former high-level Yeltsin official because "they are for democracy with the oligarchs" (report by Lyudmila Alexandrova in *JRL*, Sept. 20, 2010). Contemptuous remarks about ordinary Russians by professed democrats (noted in chapter 6), now including several close to Medvedev, continued to grow, as did objections by more nationalist, though scarcely less democratic, intellectuals. For the latter, see, e.g., Aleksandr Tsipko in *NG*, June 29, 2010; Stanislav Belkovskii

in *MK*, Aug. 26, 2010; and Vladimir Poliakov and Valerii Solovei in *LG*, Sept. 22–28, 2010.

68. See, e.g., Putin in *Kommersant*, Aug. 30, 2010. For Moscow's view that Obama's new emphasis on democracy promotion was "inappropriate" in the context of the "reset," see Mikhail Margelov, quoted in RIA Novosti dispatch, Jan. 6, 2011; and Aleksei Ostrovsky, quoted by Ellen Barry in *NYT*, Jan. 7, 2011.

69. Walter Russell Mead in *JRL*, Nov. 3, 2010. For the broadcasts, see Ellen Barry in *NYT*, February 13, 2011.

70. For enemies of the reset, see John McCain, David J. Kramer, Robert Kagan, and Charles Krauthammer in *WP*, Aug. 8, Sept. 20, Dec. 23, and Dec. 24, 2010, respectively; and Ariel Cohen in *WSJ*, Aug. 11, 2010.

71. See, respectively, Barry Blechman and Alex Bollfrass in *NYT*, June 27, 2010; Goldgeier in *JRL*, Sept. 15, 2009, and, similarly, Stephen Kotkin in *FA* (Sept./Oct. 2009): 137; and Clifford Kupchan, quoted in russiatoday.com, Sept. 8, 2010.

INDEX